Capitalism and Citizenship

We live in a world of unprecedented riches and poverty. The riches are those of material comfort and splendour; of easy access to things and places which in the past were granted only to a tiny minority of the world's population but which now are enjoyed by increasing numbers of so-called ordinary people. The poverty includes the obvious miseries of acute material need, sickness and ignorance, but also, and increasingly, a poverty of popular political engagement in the richest countries in the world. This book is about the latter form of poverty.

Capitalism and Citizenship argues that this poverty is the direct result of the system which has yielded our unprecedented riches, namely capitalism. As we have become materially rich, we have become socially poor, and this social poverty has undermined our willingness and ability to become politically engaged. By studying the work of political and social theorists, mainly Karl Marx, Sigmund Freud and Hannah Arendt, but including also Norbert Elias, Jürgen Habermas and Manuel Castells, the author provides a historical analysis of the different manifestations of capitalism which have brought us to our present situation of social and political poverty.

At the same time, the book offers an investigation of the potential for a new kind of citizenly sociability arising out of our societies of 'uncertainty' in which states and corporations are either denying the existence of uncertainty (as in the field of genetic engineering) or attempting to transfer it to individuals (as in public and private pensions provision). The text concludes by considering what form this new citizenly sociability might take.

Kathryn Dean teaches political and social theory in the Department of Political Studies at the School of Oriental and African Studies, University of London. Her research interests include historical materialism, psychoanalysis, citizenship theory and medium theory. She is presently working on a study of citizenship and communication which aims to synthesize political theory and medium theory within a historical materialist problematic.

Critical realism: interventions
Edited by Margaret Archer, Roy Bhaskar, Andrew Collier, Tony Lawson and Alan Norrie

Critical realism is one of the most influential new developments in the philosophy of science and in the social sciences, providing a powerful alternative to positivism and postmodernism. This series will explore the critical realist position in philosophy and across the social sciences.

Critical Realism
Essential readings
Edited by Margaret Archer, Roy Bhaskar, Andrew Collier, Tony Lawson and Alan Norrie

The Possibility of Naturalism, 3rd edition
A philosophical critique of the contemporary human sciences
Roy Bhaskar

Being & Worth
Andrew Collier

Quantum Theory and the Flight from Realism
Philosophical responses to quantum mechanics
Christopher Norris

From East to West
Odyssey of a soul
Roy Bhaskar

Realism and Racism
Concepts of race in sociological research
Bob Carter

Rational Choice Theory
Resisting colonisation
Edited by Margaret Archer and Jonathan Q. Tritter

Explaining Society
Critical realism in the social sciences
Berth Danermark, Mats Ekström, Jan Ch. Karlsson and Liselotte Jakobsen

Critical Realism and Marxism
Edited by Andrew Brown, Steve Fleetwood and John Michael Roberts

Critical Realism in Economics
Edited by Steve Fleetwood

Realist Perspectives on Management and Organisations
Edited by Stephen Ackroyd and Steve Fleetwood

After International Relations
Critical realism and the (re)construction of world politics
Heikki Patomaki

Capitalism and Citizenship
The impossible partnership
Kathryn Dean

Also published by Routledge

Routledge Studies in Critical Realism
Edited by Margaret Archer, Roy Bhaskar, Andrew Collier, Tony Lawson and Alan Norrie

Marxism and Realism
A materialistic application of realism in the social science
Sean Creaven

Beyond Relativism
Raymond Boudon, cognitive rationality and critical realism
Cynthia Lins Hamlin

Education Policy and Realist Social Theory
Primary teachers, child-centred philosophy and the new managerialism
Robert Wilmott

Hegemony
A realist analysis
Jonathan Joseph

Realism and Sociology
Anti-foundationalism, ontology and social research
Justin Cruickshank

Critical Realism
The difference it makes
Edited by Justin Cruickshank

Critical Realism and Composition Theory
Donald Judd

On Christian Belief
A defence of a cognitive conception of religious belief in a Christian context
Andrew Collier

In Defence of Objectivity and Other Essays
Andrew Collier

Capitalism and Citizenship
The impossible partnership

Kathryn Dean

Routledge
Taylor & Francis Group
LONDON AND NEW YORK

First published 2003
by Routledge
11 New Fetter Lane, London EC4P 4EE

Simultaneously published in the USA and Canada
by Routledge
29 West 35th Street, New York, NY 10001

Routledge is an imprint of the Taylor & Francis Group

© 2003 Kathryn Dean

Typeset in Garamond by Taylor & Francis Books Ltd
Printed and bound in Great Britain by MPG Books Ltd, Bodmin

All rights reserved. No part of this book may be reprinted or
reproduced or utilised in any form or by any electronic,
mechanical, or other means, now known or hereafter
invented, including photocopying and recording, or in any
information storage or retrieval system, without permission in
writing from the publishers.

British Library Cataloguing in Publication Data
A catalogue record for this book is available from the British Library

Library of Congress Cataloging in Publication Data
Capitalism and citizenship: the impossible partnership/ Kathryn
Dean.
 p. cm.
Includes bibliographical references and index.
1. Political participation. 2. Capitalism. I. Title.
JF799.D43 2003
306.3'42–dc21   2003046518

ISBN 0–415–27273–4 (hbk)
ISBN 0–415–27274–2 (pbk)

For Deirdre, my daughter
and in memory of
Margaret, my mother

Contents

Preface	x
Acknowledgements	xiii
Introduction: the problem	1

PART I
Theoretical foundations — 9

1. Human nature: indeterminate and indeterminable — 11
2. Capitalism: culture of worldlessness — 25

PART II
The bourgeois public sphere — 45

3. The worldly world of the bourgeois subject — 47
4. Parenting and the constitution of bourgeois *sensus communis* — 64

PART III
From place to space: the death of worldliness — 81

5. The institution of commodity fetishism — 83
6. Abstract labour and the network society — 103
7. Abstract consumption and the dissolution of the ego — 122
8. Abstract knowledge, or, disorganized capitalism and the vicissitudes of science — 142

Conclusion: citizenship and the recovery of worldliness — 162

Notes	182
Bibliography	200
Index	222

Preface

The exhaustion of political imagination has been a recurrent topic of social and political theory for some time now. In the early 1960s Daniel Bell published a book of essays called *The End of Ideology*, with the subtitle *The exhaustion of political ideas in the fifties*. Bell was pleased that ideology had come to an end since, as the scientized millenarianism of social engineering, it had turned its face away from the present for the sake of the future. Invoking the words of Thomas Jefferson, Bell reminded us that 'the present belongs to the living'. In the early 1990s, Francis Fukuyama echoed Bell's theme by proclaiming, in effect, that there is nothing but the present, since we have now come to the end of history. If ideology ended in the suffering and madness of depression and totalitarianism, history ended because humanity (or that part of it which inhabits the Anglo-American world) had arrived at a form of life so satisfying that to think of anything better would be impossible. For Bell, ideology had given political imagination a bad name; for Fukuyama, the western way of life had rendered it redundant. However, neither was whole-mindedly celebratory about this marginalizing of imagination. Bell stressed the need for utopia as a vision of human potential that fuses 'passion and intelligence'. Fukuyama mourned the replacement of greatness by the paltriness of our preoccupation with acquiring and spending.

If the end of history was marked by the battle of Jena, some of us took some time to accept this fact, which was brought home to us on the night the Berlin Wall came down. Now the world could face up to the inevitable and return to the path from which it had strayed in following the leadership of Soviet Russia. As we went through the 1990s we discovered that the end of history is a condition of unprecedented inequality and instability; a condition, moreover, which is globally visible through the mediations of the internet and television. In part because of these extraordinary means of visibility, which are also means of invisibility, a global power which has never been stronger and more intrusive has never been more illegitimate. Illegitimacy inheres in power's unresponsiveness to those whom it rules – in its blindness and deafness to the human sufferings and natural devastations that its rule incurs, an unresponsiveness that, in British domestic politics, is manifest in the draining of responsibility from parliament to executive and from executive to coteries of personal 'advisors' to the prime minister.

By the end of the 1990s, signs of resistance, or what Ricardo Blaug describes as 'outbreaks of democracy', were becoming evident; outbreaks which have been encouraged by the disorderliness and injustice of contemporary life and the manifest incompetence of our leaders. These outbreaks share little but their dissatisfaction with these leaders. They are refusals of the present which are sometimes expressed as demands for inclusion in the status quo, sometimes as demands for its transformation. The important point about these refusals is that they are expressed outside the remit of normal politics. They are expressions of political imagination in that they refuse the terms of existing political discourse by insisting upon taking democracy seriously. Democracy is here a challenge to power that insists that the powerless be heard. It is a democracy that either refuses representation or insists that representation be taken more literally than contemporary institutions of representation can bear.

This book is about public-spirited citizenship. Democracy is an important part of what public-spirited citizenship is about, but it is only a part. It is only a part because democracy need involve nothing more than an assertion of rights and an insistence that such rights be respected. In fact, modern citizenship has been overwhelmingly a matter of rights: rights to life, liberty and happiness; rights to privacy and property. Getting to the contemporary heart of these matters, a British government White Paper called *The Citizens Charter* (published in 1991) defined citizenship as 'people's rights to be informed and choose for themselves'. In this document, the essence of citizenship was taxpaying and consumption. Citizen as taxpayer was entitled to receive the information which would enable citizen as consumer to choose wisely from among the commodities and services on offer. True, this citizen was also required to be responsible, or to be committed to the national good. Responsibility was here a matter of cultivating the capacities for effective participation in a market society which would yield the private goods we all desire and provide the resource base for the public goods we all need. What responsibility was *not* was the responsibility to deliberate on what private and public good might or could mean.

It seems unlikely that the multitudinous outbreaks of democracy which are presently taking place will be coopted through the mode of inclusion that is promised in the charter just described. That promise is utopian in the sense that it assumes a possibility which contemporary conditions render impossible, i.e. equal access to the means of responsibility. More than this, it conceptualizes responsibility within the terms of a capitalist way of life. Increasingly, though, it is becoming difficult to sustain this narrow, even narcissistic conception of responsibility. Hanging over us all is the possibility that we are destroying our planet, or at least destroying sources of life for ourselves and other species with whom we share the planet. Whereas Bell felt it incumbent upon him to remind us that the world belongs to the present, we are now living as if the world belongs only to the present – or, more accurately, to that small, disproportionately powerful part of the present that enjoys the fruits of our capitalist way of life; that we have received nothing of significance from the past and that we owe nothing either to those who are presently excluded from our way of life, or to the future. This study is undertaken in the belief that we can and should recover a sense of indebtedness to past, future and 'other'; that we have potentials for responsibility which have been neglected in the course of becoming modern. The responsibility in question is what Hannah Arendt describes as care for the world; a responsibility that could be a satisfying task because it is one which must be carried out 'in concert' with others. Capitalism has always been incompatible with this necessary human task.

I said before that democracy is necessary but not sufficient for the practice of citizenship. It is necessary because citizens have interests (in their own self-reproduction) which need satisfying if they are to be citizens at all. However, citizens also need an independence of spirit and means which enables them to distance themselves from their own concerns so as to deliberate and decide in the general interest. Citizens need to have a sense of autonomy if they are to be disinterested in this way and they need to be disinterested in this way if they are to be the kinds of citizens the world needs now: citizens who take responsibility for world care. This conception of citizenship is utopian in the sense that contemporary culture provides few of the resources needed for its practice. To the contrary. Our duty to the 'community' involves duties to capitalism (duties to labour and to shop) whose fulfilment renders world care impossible.

Understanding how we got to the point at which labouring and shopping are the defining activities of our world is an important dimension of a theory of citizenship. Understanding our potentials for citizenship and the conditions needed for the actualisation of these potentials is another. This study attempts to enhance our understanding of these matters by tracing the historico-cultural trajectory which brought us to the point at which labouring and shopping are the defining activities of our world. Having sketched out the history of our commodified present and of the experiences which have forced us to forget our capacities for responsible autonomy, it looks to the present for sources of a post-labouring, post-shopping culture: a culture capable of nurturing a public-spirited, rather than merely formal-legal, mode of citizenship. In doing so it is engaging in a form of utopian thinking which, it is hoped, will contribute to the revitalization of our political imagination.

Acknowledgements

Those to whom I owe deep gratitude include Alan Norrie, a dedicated and enthusiastic editor from whose incisive reading of, and comments on, the manuscript I benefited enormously. Peter Dickens also read a completed draft and provided me with many thought-provoking suggestions. The advice of the anonymous reviewer also contributed much to the improvement of the original version of the book. Warm thanks are due to Richard Boyd, Catherine Guest, Nick Hostettler, Mark Laffey, Brita Pouget, Linda Taylor and Tom Young who provided me with advice and support over the years and to Angus Stewart who supervised the doctoral thesis in which the book originates. Parts of the book were presented as work in progress to the Department of Political Studies seminar at the School of Oriental and African Studies, University of London, and I benefitted from the comments of my colleagues on these occasions. Above all, I must thank Deirdre Dean for her sustained and stimulating intellectual companionship over the years. It is worth stating that no one mentioned here is responsible for the imperfections which remain in the final version.

Introduction
The problem

In recent years, political theory has become preoccupied with the question of public-spirited citizenship; a citizenship of responsibilities as well as of rights. Increasing theoretical interest in this form of citizenship has been aroused by a sense that, at its moment of apparent triumph, capitalist liberal democracy is wholly inadequate in the face of the 'dark times' in which we now live (Isaac 1998). A plethora of urgent problems requires a strong, visionary and extraordinarily knowledgeable leadership supported by either a docile, high tax-paying electorate or an active citizen body which will take on significant responsibility for their resolution. The most fundamental problem is the apparent unsustainability of our western way of life, which manifests itself in regular crises related to unpredicted and (in some cases) unpredictable political, moral, climatic and agricultural events and disintegrations (or events which are all of these simultaneously). These crises have been bringing to popular awareness the dark side of the extraordinary benefits that modern life has secured for peoples in the Euro-American parts of the world. The hidden costs are beginning to come to light (Soper 1999). Among these are the increasing disparities between rich and poor on both local and global levels, disparities which, being rendered visible to all through electronic media, have encouraged migrations to the prosperous world at a time when, while we have never been more prosperous, we have also, apparently, never been more anxious and therefore are in no mood to make the sacrifices that a hospitable welcome to these migrants would demand (Soysal 1994). Neither, apparently, are we in the mood to pay the costs of dealing with our own, emergent problems related to the increasing ratio of old to young and of poor to prosperous, as well as the costs of an environmentally unsustainable mode of life. States' capacities to carry out the bureaucratic actions needed to begin to deal with these problems have been seriously eroded by this apparent popular resistance to contributing to their costs. Electorates are perceived by politicians to be calculating, egoistic, nomadic voters, ready to switch from one party to another as self-interest dictates. This perception is evinced in a timid government orientation expressed in the pursuit of policy objectives through manipulative, rather than educative, means. Taxation is increased by 'stealth', and behaviour is shaped by financial penalties.

Commentators who see this governmental perception as accurate are divided between those who consider egoism to be an innate and ineradicable human disposition and those who blame capitalism for its explosive growth in the contemporary Euro-American world. Among the former are public choice theorists who prescribe a depoliticized world of free-market institutions which will activate the 'hidden hand' whereby 'private vices' become 'public benefits' (Buchanan 1991). That is to say, they prescribe the economization, or privatization, of the political, since they deem public-spiritedness to be contrary to human nature. Opposed to this position are theorists such as John Dryzek (1996) who consider self-interest or 'economic rationality' to be the product of capitalism, and one which, moreover, constitutes voters as the 'gravediggers' of democracy. Following Habermas (1979; 1989), Dryzek hopes for the cultivation of communicative rationality, a human potential whose existence is inferred from that of speech. He looks to the emergence of counter-capitalist discursive spaces (provided by some of the 'new social movements') as sources of communicative rationality. Out of such movements may emerge a better democracy than is possible through established political institutions: a democracy which is active participative and citizen-driven, rather than passive and voter-driven.

It is possible to agree with Dryzek that economic rationality is the historico-culturally specific attainment of capitalism, which is, moreover, antithetical to the needs of democracy (or, at least, to the needs of a democracy capable of rising to the challenge of our dark times), without proposing communicative rationality as its superior 'other'. The problem is that Dryzek shares with Habermas (and indeed with his economistic adversaries) a universalistic analytic problematic which is incapable of getting to theoretical grips with the issues at stake here. Thinking about capitalism and citizenship requires systematic attentiveness to the culturally specific modes of subjectivation which nurture dispositions towards economic rationality (Balibar 1994). It also requires the abandonment of dichotomous characterizations of rationality as either communicative or economic. As used by Dryzek, economic and communicative rationality are oppositions which fail to capture the sources, historicity and complexity of human needs and capacities and the different ways in which such needs and capacities are constituted. Habermas's work on communicative rationality, while it is undeniably theoretically sophisticated and comprehensive, shares some of the misleading universalizing and dichotomizing assumptions of all analytic theory, including that of public choice. It is marked by a rationalism which leaves us in the dark as to how public-spiritedness might emerge (Bernstein 1995). In effect, Habermas's theory of communicative action perpetrates what Derek Sayer (1987) describes as the 'violence of abstraction' on its object of study. For this reason, it is the wrong place to start if we want to understand public-spiritedness and its sources.

The argument

A more promising source of enlightenment is Habermas's work on the bourgeois public sphere (1992a) which, written in the spirit of the early Frankfurt School, transcends the misleading oppositions which haunt works written in an analytical register by engaging dialectically and phenomenologically with the historico-cultural. In doing so, it begins to approach an understanding of what exactly it was about late eighteenth-century western Europe that enabled the emergence of a novel form of collective action which was, in some notable respects, public-spirited. It was public-spirited in the sense that it manifested a politicized sociability not modelled on kinship. It is the particularity of that early work which shows us how we may go about understanding sources of public-spiritedness in the world today, not the retreat into universalism which Habermas's later work represents. What Habermas's analysis demonstrates is that the bourgeois public sphere was populated by subjects whose rationality had not yet been detached from its sociable moorings. It is worth noting that the purpose in examining the bourgeois world is not to present it as a problem-free 'model' of public-spiritedness but to enable the formulation of sensible judgements about the potential for a post-capitalist public-spiritedness having global, rather than merely class, scope.

In this study I shall use the concept of anaclisis to connote the fusion of the rational and the sociable, with the sociable here encompassing a sense of responsibility in the dual sense of 'commitment to obligations and responsiveness to relationships' (Gilligan 1986: 238). For public-spirited citizens, 'commitment to obligations' would include, necessarily, commitment to participation in decision-making on public matters. I adapt the concept of anaclisis from Freud, who uses it to make an argument about the nature of narcissistic relations (Freud 1984a). Whereas narcissistic relations are characterized by self-centredness, or psychic withdrawal from the world (which, for Freud, may be due to the experience of sickness, of mourning, or of other forms of pain or frustration), anaclitic relations are characterized by psychic attachment to the world. Elaborating on Freud's cryptic comments on anaclisis and narcissism, I shall consider the role of good parenting (both cultural and individual) in constituting individual dispositions towards anaclisis rather than narcissism. Good parenting provides emergent subjects with the experience of relatively benign dependence; an experience which promotes the enjoyment of that interdependence which is a necessity of all human life. Guided by Freud's usage, I conceptualize anaclitic rationality as a mode of rationality involving the fusion of 'economic' and 'communicative' rationality; a mode of rationality which is the bearer of Eros, or 'social love'.

Using a dialectical critical realist framework, and borrowing fairly freely from the work of, primarily, Marx, Arendt and Freud, the present study aims to understand public-spirited citizenship in terms of the constitution of, first, a relatively autonomous and, up to a point, public-spirited bourgeois subject and, second, the atomistic subject motivated by what Dryzek calls economic rationality. It does so by constructing a brief and schematic history of the emergence of economic rationality through the differentiations (instituted by different modes of capitalism) which effected the practical abstraction of rationality from sociability. The intention here is to show that what we take to be economic rationality is, in fact, part of a nexus of dispositions expressive of capitalism's failure to satisfy the human need for an intelligible and sociable world. A task for responsible citizenship would be to understand and attempt to satisfy this basic human need. Yet, responsible citizenship is most likely to be found where this need has been recognized and attended to. The brief and highly selective history of capitalist forms of subjectivity to be advanced here is intended as clarification of the issues involved in this bind, rather than as a solution to the problem. Clarification will be sought in relation to two questions. First, what are the capacities needed for the practice of public-spirited citizenship in a globalizing world? Second, in what ways does capitalism impede the development of these capacities?

In speaking of public-spirited citizenship I am speaking of a specific kind of radically democratic collective action. This is the collective action of strongly-individuated, self-consciously committed citizens. These are citizens who are relatively autonomous, therefore neither manipulated nor coerced, who are free of the different constraints of atomism and fusion. Atomism involves the illusion that individual human beings are self-sufficient; that they owe nothing to their culture for what they are (Marx 1994). Fusion involves 'oversocialization', or the absence of a sense of distinctive individuality (Wrong 1961). Citizenship in this sense constitutes a specific form of social strength which contrasts with that modelled on kinship, the tendency of which is to subordinate individuals to the group and to pitch the group against others in a kind of zero-sum game of interest politics. Where groups relate to one another on the principle of kinship, they relate narcissistically. The public-spirited citizen, unlike kin-members as traditionally conceived (or members of that modern extension of kin-relations – the nation), is a committed yet potentially critical group member who is motivated by feelings of responsibility for a world which is shared by many groups and in which well-being (or, more modestly, the basic means of livelihood) is very unevenly distributed. Where group membership has this character, groups relate to one another anaclitically rather than narcissistically. This is the kind of group membership (the membership of public-spirited citizens) which is needed in a world becoming steadily more global in character (Balibar 2001; Linklater 1998).

Given that many of the most intractable problems which we face have an ineradicably global dimension, and given, moreover, the new kinds of ethnic plurality which are being experienced in western European states, the character of the 'public' in public-spirited citizenship will be highly complex, incorporating both global and local dimensions. It will be a kind of 'civic cosmopolitanism' which has a basis in lived reality, or as Delanty puts it, a matter of the polis as well as the cosmos (Delanty 2000: 142, 140). We can only become cosmopolitan (conceive of membership in a community called 'humanity') on the basis of the everyday experience of community membership. Regarding the category of 'humanity', since the emergence of the atomic threat we have been coming to experience a 'global present' such that humanity is no longer merely a humanist concept and ideal, but is becoming a fact of life (Arendt 1968b: 84). Beyond this, we are today becoming 'globalized' in that we are being advised, first, that humanity itself is (or should be) at the disposal of capitalism and, second, that humanity itself is under threat, not from atomic obliteration, but from the possible effects of the western way of life and/or, more recently, from world 'terrorism' (Buck-Morss 2001). Simultaneously, some of the very processes which are 'humanizing' us in this sense are also generating movements of peoples such as to render previously 'national' populations more culturally heterogeneous and (re)distributions of activities and processes such as to render causal processes (which previously had been relatively transparent to the knowing gaze of scientific experts) progressively more opaque, not only to common sense, but also to science (Beck 1992). These new facts of life impose on us the burden of a citizenship willing to assume new kinds of global and local responsibilities if justice is to be served and if nature is to be respected.

It needs stressing that this burden cannot (or should not) be borne equally by all of the groups that inhabit the world. Given the great and growing inequalities between and within states, public-spirited citizenship as a lived condition of active responsibility (of rights and obligations) will be practised in various ways (Young 1996). In relation to the problem of global warming, for instance, the peoples of the Euro-American world bear a greater responsibility for the emergence of this problem (and are likely to suffer less from its effects) than those in poorer countries (McGibben 2001). If progress is to be made in solving this particular problem, those best off, and therefore those most strongly formed by capitalist social relations, will be required to make the greatest sacrifices. Or, the burden will fall most heavily on precisely those peoples among whom economic rationality is most highly developed. For this reason, if for no other, a systematic exploration of capitalist subjectivities in the context of the desirability of public-spirited citizenship is of great urgency in the present conjuncture.

My assumption is that a global form of public-spiritedness is a human potential whose development seems both necessary and impossible in the world today. It seems necessary because our present political institutions lack either the commitment or the authority and resources needed to care for the world in a manner compatible both with worldly and natural well-being, and it seems impossible because our lives are wholly dependent on a culture (capitalism) which needs to destroy in order to reproduce itself. This is the bind. Our world is now wholly dependent on a mode of production which is destroying us. Public-spirited citizenship is about taking responsibility for halting the process of destruction. Yet we have been formed to practise world destruction rather than world care, so if we are to become citizens we must go against our own natures as these are presently constituted.

In chapters one and two I elaborate on the major concepts which will bear my argument about the incompatibility of capitalism and citizenship and about the human characteristics which render us capable of public-spiritedness. The overarching theoretical framework is a Marxian dialectical critical realism, or a realism partly informed by the philosophy of science of Roy Bhaskar, which stresses the historico-cultural nature of both humans and capitalism. The incompatibilities of capitalism and citizenship are indicated through a discussion of Marxian, Arendtian and Freudian categories (of activity, worldliness and the reality principle) which will be combined to theorize, on the one hand, human powers (inhering in the potential for imaginative activity) and the needs which are associated with those powers (for a sociable and intelligible world), and, on the other, the powers (extraordinary capacity to 'produce' surpluses) and needs (world-mastery through subsumption under the law of value) of capitalism which, as presently actualized and satisfied, have constituted a world which is both unsociable and unintelligible. The focus in the first chapter is on humanity as a prematurely-born, indeterminate organism which is capable of indeterminable development and which, for this reason, needs a sociable, intelligible world, which is to say, cultural parenting, or, a reality principle. In chapter two, I provide a brief account, derived mainly from Karl Marx, as interpreted by Louis Althusser and Moise Postone, of capitalism's 'nature', which inheres in the imperative that the world be subsumed under the law of value. Once actualized, this imperative sets nature (including humanity) on a volatile journey characterized by a dialectical and contradictory rather than linear and evolutionary trajectory which has, to date, unfolded through four different capitalist modes.

Having laid out the theoretical underpinnings of the brief history of capitalism and its subjectivities which is the substance of the argument, I set out in chapters three and four my understanding of the novel form of cultural parenting (of the bourgeoisie) represented by the hybrid bourgeois mode of capitalism (that capitalism which subsumed labour 'formally' rather than 'really') and constitutive of a class-specific, theoretical form of common sense (*sensus communis*) which had some of the characteristics of public-spiritedness. Here concepts of the 'civilizing process' (Norbert Elias), of the bourgeois public sphere (Habermas) and of the 'psychologized' split psyche (Freud) will provide the resources for understanding the conditions of possibility (a new mode of differentiation which maintained a balance between personal and impersonal mediations) of this new sense. In chapter four I elaborate on the particular family form, the bourgeois oedipal family, through which emergent bourgeois subjects experienced this cultural parenting and cultivated the intellectual and emotional maturity required for the acquisition of *sensus communis*. The latter is theorized with the help of Freud's concepts of sublimation and secondary process functioning. The necessity of personally authoritative parenting to the cultivation of the dispositions and capacities needed for this functioning is theorized with the help of his (suitably historicized) account of the oedipal family.

Chapters five to eight elaborate on the progressively pure capitalism that emerged (the real subsumption of labour under capital) as the workshop was replaced by the industrialized factory. In chapter five, the effects of this 'deworlding' transition are understood as a manifestation of commodity fetishism, which, as industrialization proceeded, was instituted through abstract labour and money/capital, thereby rendering differentiations progressively abstract or impersonal. Commodity fetishism also penetrated the capitalist household so as to reconfigure the anaclitic rationality which hybrid bourgeois capitalism had sustained. This reconfiguration involved the splitting of rationality and sociability. The result was an oedipal family quite different from that of the hybrid bourgeois form; a family which nurtured narcissism rather than anaclisis. At this point, the conditions of possibility for both authoritative personal parenting and cultural parenting began to dissolve.

Having considered liberal industrial capitalism in terms of the concept of commodity fetishism, I turn in chapters six, seven and eight to analyse 'organized' and 'disorganized' capitalism. The former effected a temporary restoration of cultural parenting but this was at the expense of the authority of individual parents. In chapter six the key concept is abstract labour, whose different manifestations are explored by taking the factory and the network as the typical and contrasting organizational principles of capitalism's organized (the former) and disorganized (the latter) modes. Whereas organized capitalism tends towards a reified form of commodity fetishism, dereification becomes more consequential as the network principle becomes predominant. At this point cultural parenting comes to an end.[1] Dereification, whose significance in relation to the reality principle I begin to understand with the help of Arendt's analysis of capitalism's process character, is expressed in novel kinds of abstract labour whose nature is understood with the help of Manuel Castells's account of the 'network society'.

Moving beyond abstract labour, I turn in chapter seven to discuss the abrogation of cultural parenting involved in abstract consumption, which nurtures a peculiarly worldless form of imagining, namely, fantasizing, whose nature is understood with the help of Freud's analysis of daydreaming and whose psychic effects are elaborated by borrowing Lacan's concepts of the real, imaginary, symbolic and lack. These concepts enable the theorization of psychic dissolution consequent on the experience of a combination of harsh impersonal mediations and fantasized intimacy which make up a 'reality' principle which no longer provides cultural parenting. Hence my claim that it is a virtual reality principle. This is a reality principle which, while it has abrogated its parenting function, retains the performance principle which informs all modes of capitalism. In this case, performance dictates that subjects behave 'as if' they were autonomous while being simultaneously at the unquestioning disposal of value's law. This experienced contradiction is one possible source of public-spiritedness.

Another is the cognitive contradiction which, I argue in chapter eight, we are beginning to experience now as the 'regime of truth' (the peculiar kind of abstract knowing which is science) that became essential for capitalism during the nineteenth century becomes reconfigured in dereifying (as opposed to reifying) mode. Using Arendt's concept of determinant judgement as a point of departure, I elaborate on the overdetermined character of this contradiction (and on the worldless character of a science functioning at the dictates of value) as inhering in the changing nature of the world as capitalism reduces it to process, difficulties (of the kind discussed by Ulrich Beck) emergent from science's failure to theorize the necessarily relational nature of the world, and the exacerbation of these difficulties through the more intensive, extensive and speedy commodification of science now. The result is an emergent contradiction between what we need to know in order to reproduce ourselves and what we can know under contemporary de-differentiating conditions. What may render this contradiction one source of public-spiritedness is the fact that, as the riskiness of a world constituted by science becomes more manifest, subjects as individuals are being required to take charge of those matters which were previously the duty of the state. Simultaneously, the disorganization effected by contemporary capitalism is disabling economic rationality at the moment of its most urgent need. Out of this experience may emerge the motivational source of the quest for a better rationality than capitalism has afforded us so far.

In the conclusion, Arendt's account of citizenly rationality as the rationality of reflective judgement is used to elaborate on the nature of a *sensus communis* which would be adequate to the tasks of global citizenship, as understood from a Marxian point of view. As a world-oriented activity, the major task of reflective judgement would be to restore care of the world and of nature, or, to reinstitute cultural parenting. This reinstitution would involve the domestication of value's law to the needs of worldly creatures and the reconfiguration of science and the supervision of scientists' activities to ensure their compliance with worldliness.

The emergent cognitive contradiction is moving us beyond the reified, relatively predictable condition temporarily constituted by organized capitalism (a reified condition which drove critical theorists to despair) and may have moved us closer to the point at which we will become liberated from commodity fetishism. If this liberation is to be the basis of a more widespread and generous form of human flourishing than our great wealth has enabled up to now, we need to ensure not a return to the relatively secure *status quo ante* the dereification of everyday life effected by disorganized capitalism (a return which is impossible in any case) but a movement towards a post-capitalist worldly world, one which subsumes the advances enabled by capitalism itself. Clearly this is a long-term and highly demanding task with no guarantee of success.

Part I
Theoretical foundations

1 Human nature
Indeterminate and indeterminable

The question of autonomy remains alive in western social and political theory (Cooke 1999; Held 1989) following years of poststructuralist-induced disenchantment with the form of individuality with which the idea of autonomy is associated; a disenchantment which found a faint echo in the camp of critical theory through the displacement of the philosophy of consciousness by the problematic of intersubjectivity (Benjamin 1990: ch. 1; Habermas 1970). Both poststructuralism and critical theory assured us, although in very different ways, that talk of 'the subject' was ill-advised, and both directed our attention to the fact that subjects are 'constructed' (Butler 1993) or 'situated' (Benhabib 1992) rather than self-grounding or self-identical. These arguments demanded either the rejection or fundamental rethinking of Enlightenment's claim that human beings are creatures capable of self-direction; creatures who can autonomously think, judge and act responsibly as individuals in the absence of powerful others (human or supernatural) capable of doling out rewards or punishments (Best 1995: ch. 1; Cascardi 1992; Touraine 1995).[1] Nevertheless, the principle of individual autonomy hovers over our institutions in present-day Euro-American cultures. Moreover it does so ideologically, by which I mean that autonomy tends to be naturalized as a capacity whose only conditions of possibility are formal-legal. As such it facilitates oppressive cultural demands while encouraging hubristic individual hopes, hence the poststructuralist project to make us forget about 'the subject' (Foucault 1983: 216; Lacan 1980: 26–7).

Once we accept the claim that subjectivity, therefore autonomy, is 'made' rather than 'found', i.e. cultural rather than natural, the temptation is to abrogate the responsibilities which autonomy brings with it and, faced with the overwhelming problems which our modern world has thrown up, to opt (theoretically and/or practically) for nihilism and/or hedonism. Fortunately, not all have made this choice, as is evident in the ongoing theoretical interest in autonomy and in (possibly) practical manifestations of public-spiritedness which suggest that individuals continue to take autonomy (in the sense of responsibility for participation in public activity) seriously. It may be that the recent anti-capitalist demonstrations are expressions of what Hannah Arendt describes as world care.[2]

12 *Theoretical foundations*

An understanding of the nature and scope of these practical manifestations of a (possibly) responsible autonomy will be advanced by a return to earlier accounts of how and why Enlightenment's promise of autonomy was bound to become empty as capitalism made its way through the world. In arriving at this understanding we will also come to find evidence of our presently (largely) unactualized potentials for the kinds of world-engagement which autonomy presupposes and promises. By reminding ourselves of these potentials we may be less daunted by the responsibilities which face us now.

This first part of the study sets out in very general terms the theory which underpins my claim that, first, public-spiritedness is a feasible utopia and second, capitalism and public-spiritedness are incompatible. While the latter claim is not novel, it is hoped that the arguments offered in its support here will contribute to an understanding of the political implications of those extraordinary changes which have been taking place since the 1980s. Understanding these implications is, as Moise Postone has pointed out, a major task for political theory now (1992: 176). My contribution to this task begins in this chapter with a discussion of the theory of human nature which underpins my argument about capitalism and citizenship. This theory sets out to conceptualize the combination of necessity and freedom which characterizes human life with the help of aspects of Roy Bhaskar's critical realism, which is also used as a unifying perspective within which Marxian, Arendtian and Freudian components of the theory will be integrated.[3] Having elaborated on these three major strands of the theory, the chapter will conclude with a brief section on the possibilities of citizenship. Capitalism will be dealt with in chapter two.

I Humanity and its theorization

Dialectical critical realism: the possibility of human action

The perspective taken in this study is that of dialectical critical realism; a perspective which is in part informed by Roy Bhaskar's philosophy of science. This philosophy is an argument about the combination of lawfulness and intentionality which is involved in the successful practice of science (1989; 1997). It is in this respect an exemplar of the explanation needed to avoid both voluntarism and determinism in our explanation of human activity. In that explanation two distinctions are important: that between powers or potentials and their actualization, and that between open and closed systems. In open systems, powers are co-present with myriad others which may facilitate or negate their actualization or which may merely be indifferent to them. So, the concept of open system points to the possibility of non-actualization of powers and the impossibility of predictability or determinism. Indeed, the predictable actualization of powers may be the result of intentional human activity rather than of nature. Bhaskar enables us to understand the ways in which closed systems are the result of human action, rather than of natural determinations, for example, the closed systems manufactured in the laboratory (Bhaskar 1989: ch. 2). Using Bhaskar's concepts, we can think of human organisms as 'systems' which, for reasons to be explored below, are by nature 'open'. That is to say, we are not determined in our functioning. In fact, because of our peculiar causal powers, we are indeterminate in a particular way, or in a way which needs the completion of culture.[4] We can think of cultures as 'systems' which seek 'closure' (i.e. predictability and reproduction) but which are themselves more or less open to the environment. Expressed otherwise, culture is the imposition of lawfulness on a part of nature, a lawfulness which 'leans on', but is not determined by, nature itself.[5] (For reasons which will be discussed in chapter two, capitalism is a culture which, while it seeks closure as relentlessly as any so-called traditional culture, constantly and necessarily trips over its own feet in doing so.)

The prevalence of open over closed systems is one reason for rejecting determinism and, therefore, political fatalism. The second reason has already been implied, namely the specific human potential for imaginative action which 'transgresses' the natural. This is clear in Bhaskar, in whose account of science imagination in the shape of intentional human action is crucial. Science depends on the coexistence of real causal powers of non-human nature and on the specifically human causal power for imaginative activity. In relation to science, imaginative activity is oriented to acquiring knowledge of human or non-human natural powers for the purposes of their practical manipulation. Extrapolating from this domain-specific analysis of Bhaskar, this study sets out to show the particular conditions which may be conducive to the practice of a globally-oriented public-spirited citizenship.

The meaningful conceptualization of citizenship requires that we understand the natural as potential rather than as determination and that we take seriously the human potential for intentional activity. Or, in Bhaskarian terms, it is because 'causes' do not inevitably prevail that it is meaningful to speak of 'reasons' and it is because humans are particular kinds of creatures that 'reasons' can be 'causes' (1994: ch. 5). Humans are creatures who are capable of initiating novel projects; of bringing something new into the world, be it through action on non-human (or indeed, human) nature or through communicative interaction with other humans. It is because of the uniquely human potential for intentional activity (which includes the potential for self-conscious self-direction) that we can speak of autonomy without uttering nonsense. It is because of the need for cultural actualization of this potential that we utter nonsense where we speak only of autonomy.

Humanity: the cultural animal

The argument hinges on the centrality of 'cultural parenting' to creatures who are born 'incomplete', or, creatures who need a 'world' (i.e. a built habitat that is both shared, therefore sociable, and relatively durable, therefore knowable by its inhabitants) if we are to know how to go on, or, to reproduce ourselves as recognizable human creatures. Incompleteness, or 'prematurity', is a matter of the indeterminate character of human nature; an indeterminacy with which is associated our potential for 'indeterminable development' (Arendt 1989: 59). The faculty of imagination is profoundly implicated in this potential for indeterminable development, as will be seen. In this study, three manifestations of imagination will be important: *praxis*, used in the Marxian sense to connote making, or the imposition of form on nature; *natality*, used in a particular Arendtian sense to connote the political activity of acting 'in concert', or participating in dialogical speech with fellow-citizens; and *fantasy*, used in a Freudian sense to connote a world-avoiding use of imagination as compensation for feelings of frustration or loss.[6]

Humanity: the active animal, or, the Marxian viewpoint

Human indeterminacy is what compels, and human imagination is what allows, the 'work of culture' (Freud 1973a: 112), which, in the most general sense, is a work of imposing form on nature. In relation to the human animal, this imposition of form is a work of parenting. This work is understood by Marx as 'the forming of the five senses' which he conceives of as 'a labour of the entire history of the world down to the present' (Marx 1977: 96).[7] We will understand the work of culture as a practice which involves both the 'material' and the 'ideal'. Given that humanity is in question these are abstractions from a reality in which ideal and material are always fused in a manner which is constrained, but not determined, by the material in question. The historical materialism of *The German Ideology* (Marx and Engels 1976) is here understood as a materialism of practices (Althusser 1990b; Balibar 1996). Practices may be largely reproductive or largely transformative. In any case, they involve the more or less active and self-conscious use of human imagination.

It is important to note here that practices are simultaneously implicated in world- and subject-constitution. Or, practice is a dialectical activity involving the imposition of form on both human and non-human nature; an activity which produces, on the one hand, a world or built environment and, on the other hand, subjects who inhabit that world (Dickens 2001). This realist approach to understanding the world involves the necessary transcendence of the antinomies which have informed the liberal social sciences (Lukács 1971: 110–49). The world is the result of a never-ending dialectical interaction between human and non-human nature the results (cultures or worlds) of which provide the context within which form is imposed on individual human organisms.[8] For the purpose of this study, subjectivity will be thought of as the imposition of a culturally-specific 'form' on newborns. The question then arises as to the individual 'reception' of this form. This is a matter which may be understood as a dialectic of relatively passive absorption and active engagement. Expressed otherwise, the imposition of form on individual humans involves a dialectic of human and cultural powers and needs (on which more later).

The point is that humanity is an active (world-building, self-changing) species in that it possesses imagination and is compelled to put that imagination to use so as to reproduce itself. Imagination is here a 'power' (*Kraft* in Marxian terms) which is actualized in the first instance under the compulsion of a 'need' (*Bedurfnis*); the need to 'produce', rather than merely 'find', the necessities of life (Ollman 1976: ch. 7).[9] Marx understands these distinctively human powers and needs in terms of the potential for world-building or praxis, which, ideally, takes the form of individually consequential, imaginative activity engaged in with others for the purpose of producing useful and beautiful objects among and within which humans can live. This is what has been conceptualized as the 'activity drive' by the psychoanalyst Ernest Schachtel (1963: esp. ch. 5), this being the human drive towards engagement with the world as a source of interest and wonder. Schachtel attributes to this drive a non-instrumental or a-functional character which, for Marx, would be achieved only under communism (Marx 1977; Postone 1993; Rattansi 1982). Moreover, capitalism has 'instrumentalized' and commodified this drive in a way which orients it towards mastery of human and non-human nature, mastery being a particular, worldless manifestation of praxis (Lukács 1971; Sohn-Rethel 1978).[10]

For Marx, we might say, the essence of human nature is the potential for praxis (the potential for – sometimes intentional, sometimes unintentional – transformation rather than reproduction) of the world, therefore transformation also of ourselves. The actualization of this potential requires supportive social relations. Humanity is a '*zoon politikon*' or, 'an animal which can develop into an individual only in society' (Marx 1973: 84). The very idea of acting alone is meaningless. It is not only that acting is always acting *with* others. Beyond this, and more fundamentally, acting is always also acting *through* others, or, human potentials are only activated through culturally specific social relations (Marx 1976b; Sève 1978). Therefore, the ways in which and the degree to which the potential for praxis will be actualized depends on the environment or culture into which individual human organisms are born. Insofar as opportunities exist for the cultivation of human 'free conscious activity', a culture will be 'rich'; insofar as such opportunities are unavailable, a culture will be 'poor' (Marx 1977: 68). The more needs one has, the more richly human one becomes (Heller 1976; Fraser 1998). Capitalism is both progressive and regressive in this regard. While in this study capitalism's regressive character will be stressed, it is worth registering my recognition that, prior to capitalism, humanity's potential for praxis was actualized very unevenly. It is capitalism which creates the conditions for the universal individual enjoyment of this human power (Marx 1973: Introduction). However, as will be seen, while enhancing opportunities for the nurturing of imaginative activities, capitalism also subsumes

16 *Theoretical foundations*

humans under a totality, or an impersonal system of commodifying social relations (Althusser 1984a; Gorz 1989; Kosik 1976) thereby domesticating imagination to the needs of value and draining the world of both sociability and intelligibility. This loss of sociability and intelligibility involves the loss of worldliness.

Humanity: the worldly animal, or, the Arendtian viewpoint

In referring to the historical formation of the five human senses, Marx is directing our attention to the prematurity of the human animal; to the fact that we are born needing the completion of culture. The fact and implications of human prematurity or natural 'incompletion' are crucial to Arendt's political theory also in two senses. First, she associates this fact with the human capacity for 'indeterminable development', therefore for imagination and sociability (Arendt 1958: ch. 1; 1989: 59, 8–9). Second, from this fact she somehow derives the human need for a world, meaning a built environment of durable objects and relatively stable personal social relations. (The 'somehow' here implies a theoretical deficiency which can be made good with Freud's account of the reality principle, on which more below.[11])

Worldliness connotes the need of prematurely-born, incompletely natural creatures for a habitat which is sociable and intelligible at the everyday level, or at the level of bodily immersion in practices. Because we are embodied creatures we need to know through the body, or kinesthetically (Bourdieu 1992).[12] This point, which should be too obvious to need stating, needs stating because of the rationalism which has marred the Western philosophical tradition since Plato (Arendt 1978).[13] In this study I use the concept of sensuous presencing to elaborate on Arendt's account of worldliness and to understand the character of social relations needed for the 'cultivation of the five senses' in the mode of anaclitic rationality (Arendt 1958: 136–9; 1968a; 1973b: ch. 10). Presence can be worldly or worldless. Worldly presencing begins with a presencing that is experienced sensuously, that is, in a directly-experienced place inhabited in common with other directly-experienced individuals (Arendt 1978: ch.1; Curtis 1999). When in the midst of sensuous presencing we have a world at our fingertips; a world composed of humanly-made, durable, tangible things, as well as of durable, face-to-face social relations. The experience of a sensuously and intelligibly available world inhabited by sensuously-present speaking humans endows us with the stability, particularly important for emergent subjects, which our particular human kind of embodiment requires.

The shared sense which habitation as world has constituted for most of human history has had the character of common sense, which I understand as a kinesthetic, anaclitically rational sense of how to reproduce self and world. Commonness derives from the shared experience of the tangible durable objects which furnish the world; objects which are already there when we arrive and which will survive our passing. This shared experience is a matter of educating individuals' five senses so as to constitute an intra-individual coherent experience of the world and to ensure that this coherent experience coheres with that of other individuals who inhabit the same world. So, individuals are constituted through common sense as particular kinds of subjects having particular kinds of dispositions, abilities and skills specific to a particular time and place. Common sense is here a form of attachment to others and to the shared world, and its existence connotes a sociable and intelligible world, or, a world which is produced through the directly-experienced cooperation of its individual members, and without the necessity of scientific expertise. In short, common sense connotes a way of feeling as well as of knowing (Arendt 1989: 67–8; 1994).

Dialogical speech is a key constituent in the individual acquisition of common sense, therefore of anaclitic rationality. As a necessary bearer and constituent of common sense, speech is a kind of enabling constraint which injects an element of determinacy into creatures who essentially lack determination (Arendt 1994: 318). It is the bearer and constituent of a reality which is *ours* rather than *mine*. While the sense of what is 'ours' may be imaginatively constituted through print and, now, electronic media of communication (Anderson 1991; Rheingold 1993) it is crucial, for the purposes of this study, to understand the centrality of face-to-face speech (of sensuous presencing within a shared place) to the constitution of anaclitically rational subjects.[14] Such speech is necessary, but not sufficient, for the constitution of public-spirited citizenship now (Bickford 1996).

It is worth noting that through speech we develop a sense, not only of sameness, but of others' difference from and possible resistance to ourselves. Speech is not only a bearer of the experience of commonness, but it is a necessary bearer of commonness. The fact that it also expresses difference is what makes speech, for Arendt, the supremely political faculty. As bearer of difference, it expresses, not only different interests, but the imagination of individuals occupying different locations, therefore different perspectives on a world which is experienced as shared. In this way, dialogical speech is, or can be, the bearer of natality, a mode of imagination through which something new is disclosed. Natality connotes the capacity not only to imagine, but to act on imagination so as to begin something new. It manifests itself in a primary sense in the child's play activity, which is a fantasy grounded in the experienced world (Arendt 1977d; Moore 1987: 140). In this study my interest is in 'secondary', or 'political', natality which is expressed in action in concert in the public sphere. Action in concert here means speech in concert, or public deliberation through which may be disclosed (which has disclosed in the past) new forms of public life (Arendt 1958).[15] It is important to note here the difference between disclosure and imposition of the new.

Understood in this way, natality is contrasted with the concept of imaginative activity (making) connoted by the Marxian concept of praxis which involves the imposition of form on nature, as in the work of the architect (Marx 1976a: 284).[16] Arendt's objection to the 'making' characterization of action in concert (as in the 'making' of history) is that it involves the imposition of form (in the manner of a blueprint) on what exists, rather than looking for the emergence of something new out of the speaking communication of citizens.[17] For Arendt (and, following Arendt, Habermas) Marx's conception of human activity is unacceptably technological or instrumental (Arendt 1958: ch. 3; Habermas 1987: ch. 2). While not accepting this verdict on Marx's own theory, I do accept that Marx's theoretical silence on the question of citizenship has left dogmatic Marxists with a politically toxic mixture of scientism and making as their model of revolutionary action. Marx's understanding of the difference between 'making' and 'action' is manifested in his political sociology, but unfortunately is not theorized by him.[18] As read here, Arendt's conception of natality provides the theoretical space for elaborating on the nature of the political action of citizens (on which more in the conclusion).[19]

Humanity: the premature animal, or, the Freudian viewpoint

Arendt's account of human nature is underdeveloped but remarkably prescient in relation to our contemporary condition. I shall elaborate on that account with the help of Freudian and (in chapter seven) Lacanian psychoanalysis, using the concepts of world and reality principle as markers for my theoretical bridge-building.[20] Where Arendt says world, Freud says reality principle (Freud 1984c). What both connote is indeterminacy or prematurity, which bears as heavy a theoretical burden in Freudian as it does in Marxian and Arendtian theory (Chasseguet-Smirgel and Grunberger 1986; Lacan 1980: 1–7). If we keep in mind the fact that, as Julia Flower MacCannell (1991: 68) puts it, Freud 'makes culture a parent' while never losing sight of the centrality of human embodiment, we will read psychoanalytic categories as concepts which transcend the distinction between nature and culture (Flax 1990: ch. 3). We will be happy to agree with Ricoeur (1970) that psychoanalysis is an 'energetic-hermeneutics'. As such, and as Wolfenstein argues (1993: ch. 1), it is dialectical, critical and realist.[21]

It is because of the real nature of humans that a 'science' of human nature must embrace both biology and culture, and it is because of the real nature of humans that Freud insists upon the distinction between instinct and drive (Freud 1984b; Cavell 1993: ch. 2; Lacan 1979: ch. 13; Whitebook 1995: 164).[22] The point of this distinction, as read here, is to insist on the 'mixed' nature of humanity as both biological and cultural; as cultural because instinctually incomplete. Considered in this way, the drive is a concept which enables us to develop a theoretical language capable of transcending the misleading dichotomies of biology and culture. It enables us to understand biology as the 'without which not' of culture, and culture as the 'without which not' of humanity (Carrithers 1992). As noted before, culture is that which fills the 'gap' in imperfectly natural creatures who need completion if they are to know how to go on in the world. Here the 'without which not' connotes a necessity which is not determining in its effects. The phrase connotes the necessity of conditions of possibility rather than of determination. The drive is the 'interface' between the potentially human, which is the peculiarly incomplete biology of the unformed human organism and the realized humanity of that organism once it has been culturally formed. As a theory of the cultural formation of indeterminate creatures, Freud's theory is not, and cannot be, a 'biological determinism'.[23] The drive is an impulse to action coming from within the organism and is indeterminate in its effects because its effects will be a matter, in significant part, of cultural shaping. Some cultures have greater determining power than others and, as will be seen in later chapters, contemporary capitalism shapes 'indeterminately'. Beyond this, though, humanity is a species which has the potential for praxis (transforming rather than merely reproducing a world) and for natality (acting in concert with others so as to disclose something revelatory about the world). This potential for transformation is implicit in Freud's notion of the cure and in his concept of sublimation (on which more later).

Culture fulfils its parenting task by providing subjects with a reality principle. This is encountered by the emergent subject in the form of 'representatives' which shape drives (Freud 1984b). This understanding enables us to make sense of, and develop, Arendtian and Marxian claims relating both to humanity's potential for citizenship and to capitalism's potential for dehumanization through 'deworlding'. What will be argued is that the shaping of drives is a fundamental need of organisms marked by indeterminacy, or, indeterminacy brings with it the need for relative determinacy. Representatives are doing the work of culture in that through the shaping of drives a sense of (a culturally-specific) reality is acquired by the emergent subject who learns what the culture requires and allows and therefore learns to think and act in a particular way. It is in this sense that the Freudian reality principle is theorized here and it is from this point of view that the reality principle of contemporary capitalism is criticized.[24]

The imposition of form on the bundle of potentials and needs that is the raw human organism involves an interactive relationship between representatives and emergent subjects. Representatives are ideas or groups of ideas embedded in practices and borne in the first instance by parental figures, with whom emergent subjects come to relate via investment or cathexis (Freud 1985b:152). As read here, the concept of cathexis connotes a dialectical activity implicating culture and organism. It involves culture's 'occupation' of the biological by way of the emergent subject's more or less active response to an 'invitation' to attend to a part of the world in a particular manner (Brennan 1992: 67, n. 40).[25] Or cathexis involves the animation of emergent or fully-formed subjects in relation to a particular part of the world (already culturally constituted) to which their culture has drawn their attention. It is what renders the representative meaningful for subjects in the sense that, in cathecting an object, subjects are being made aware of that part of the world in relation to an experienced need or

20 *Theoretical foundations*

interest.[26] At the same time, where cathexis takes place, representatives constitute bodily needs in particular ways. They are the form which individual consciousness of bodily needs takes, both 'parties' to the constituting activity (representatives, on the one hand, human organisms on the other) being constrained, but not determined in their functioning.

What of the impulses or potentials of which the drives are manifestations? As we know, Freud is largely concerned with two classes of drives: ego drives concerned with individual self-preservation; and sex drives concerned with cultural reproduction. In this study, the sex drives will be understood in terms of the human orientation to others, or, the sex drive as a matter of Eros (Freud 1984e: ch. 4). While Freud posits a fundamental antagonism between sex and ego drives (or a contradiction between tendencies towards fusion – sex drive – and atomism – ego drive) he provides the resources for understanding the benefits to both subject and culture of maintaining these drives in balance.[27] In fact, this balance is what the concept of anaclisis implies, and relations which are marked by anaclisis are relations which enable subjects to live relatively satisfying lives. The quality of anaclitic relationship is captured by Freud in terms of the combination of a mother's love and a father's protection (1984a: 84). Where relations with parents are marked by this combination emergent subjects will become capable of social love. Or, through the experience of benign dependence on the earliest objects responsible for emergent subjects' care mature subjects will come to enjoy the fact of human interdependence. However, if the sense of dependence is to be compatible with relatively autonomous subjectivity it must be counterbalanced by individuating practices which nurture an ego-governed psyche. An ego-governed psyche is the psyche of a subject with a strong, but not atomizing, sense of self and the capacity for self-direction.

It is worth noting that, as Schachtel (1963: ch. 1) points out, Freud conceptualizes drive as need rather than potential. I take this to be due to the harshness of the capitalist culture whose debilitating effects Freud was attempting to cure.[28] Since, as indeterminate creatures we need culture, we need not assume, as Freud does, that this involves a necessary clash of interests between organism and culture, unless we assume, as he did, that the human condition is necessarily, rather than contingently, contradictory or tragic and, perhaps, in the absence of convincing evidence to the contrary we should assume this for now. We should be clear, though, that the cultural shaping of subjects requires different degrees and kinds of discipline or deprivation.[29] While the early Freud is largely concerned with sexual deprivation, this is in part because he considers the effects of this form of deprivation to be most clearly observable, but also, and perhaps more important, because this form of deprivation had become extreme in late nineteenth-century capitalist families (Freud 1985d; Poster 1978: ch. 1). However, he also acknowledges at times the 'mythical' and indefinite character of the drives and the incompleteness of his drive theory (Brennan 1992: 148).[30] Moreover, in *Three Essays on Sexuality* (1977a) he provides a list of seven component drives, among which are included the drives for mastery and knowledge.

Whatever Freud's doubts and reservations about his own theory of the drives, there is evidence that openness to the world (curiosity and sociability, in other words) is present in the infant from very early days. Jessica Benjamin (1990) insists upon the infant's need to recognize and be recognized by its mother as a drive independent of both sex and ego. Schachtel identifies a 'positive tension feeling of eagerness and ... enjoyment' in activity (1963: 25). While Freud does not rule out this openness (indeed, and as will be seen, he believes it essential for human health) he considers this to be (in drive terms) the costly result of a painful process of subjectivation. Or, expressed otherwise, he believes that openness is 'secondary' rather than 'primary'; that rather than being an innate human potential, it emerges out of the individual's necessary encounter with culture or 'civilization'.[31] However, if we read Freud in an historico-cultural context, we can understand this painfulness as a capitalist, rather than human biological, requirement, as noted before. In reminding ourselves of this we will be more disposed to accept the evidence of those who argue for the independence of the drive towards world-openness as an openness not necessarily expressed in the drive to mastery.

In historicizing Freud's account of the drives and their vicissitudes, we can understand the 'drive' to mastery as a specific historico-cultural shaping of the activity drive; a shaping which, during the time of Freud's writing, required a major sacrifice of the sex drives and later (today) of the ego drive. It is this 'surplus repression' (Freud 1985d; Marcuse 1987: 35) which renders subject-formation such a conflict-riven, frustrating experience for the individual, who suffers much along the rocky road to maturity (a destination which may remain out of reach for many). If we bear this in mind, we will understand Freud's argument about the best possible resolution of the Oedipal complex as one which nurtures the abilities to engage with the world in a loving and active manner (through sublimation), not as the fragile and momentary triumph of culture over obdurate human biology, but rather as the outcome of a mode of relative determinacy which nurtures innate (rather than culturally engendered) human potentials. In any case, Freud is quite clear that the cultivation of the ability to form attachments is essential for human well-being and he understands that well-being also in terms of the sublimation rather than repression of the drives. Sublimation is one of Freud's underdeveloped, but potentially most fruitful, concepts (Ricoeur 1970: ch. 2; Whitebook 1995: ch. 5), and will be discussed in greater detail in chapter four. As used in this study, it connotes an adaptation of organism to culture which actualizes potentials for sociability, praxis and natality. This usage is compatible with Freud's understanding that, if not innate potentials, these are powers that may become constituted in the course of child development, and that the enjoyment of these powers is a source of profound satisfaction for creatures who can never be wholly happy (Freud 1973a: 423–4; 1984c: 41–2).[32]

II Indeterminacy, autonomy and public-spiritedness

Understanding the fact and significance of human prematurity advances our understanding of the conditions of possibility for the practice of public-spirited citizenship. Citizenship is understood here in terms of the individual dispositions and competencies which its practice requires. At the highest level of generality these dispositions and competencies are understandable as a combination of autonomy and public-spiritedness or 'civic virtue' as Dagger (1997: ch. 1) puts it.[33] Autonomy is a manifestation of praxis (Marx's concept) and natality (Arendt's concept). Both concepts refer to the active and irrepressible character of human imagination, and to the necessity of sociability for its actualization. The sociability of humans relates to our need for cultural completion, or, to the fact that we can only realize our potentials through and with other humans. Public-spiritedness or civic virtue involves the recognition that this is the case. The civic virtue required for a global public-spiritedness is a virtue which requires the intellectual and emotional competencies associated with the concept of *sensus communis* (Arendt 1989: 70–2), which I interpret as a theoretical form of common sense. As a manifestation of common sense, *sensus communis* is a matter of anaclitic, rather than economic or communicative, rationality, though it necessarily encompasses the concerns entailed in the concept of economic rationality (the satisfaction of 'interests') and the intersubjective disposition entailed in the concept of communicative rationality (Benhabib 1992; Bickford 1996: ch. 3). As noted previously, anaclitic rationality is a multidimensional form of rationality; one which refuses the faculties (rationality, sociability, imagination) which were separated through capitalist industrialization. This re-fusion is a matter of reconfiguring human faculties, capacities and dispositions in a world- rather than capitalist-oriented way.

An acceptance of the reality of human potentials for natality, praxis and sociability is needed if we are to take public-spiritedness to be a feasible utopia. Recognizing that our abilities and gratifications are the result not only of personal effort but of the resources with which our culture has provided us, constitutes the motivational resources for public-spiritedness. In this study the argument will be made, on the basis largely of Habermas's account of the bourgeois public sphere, that hybrid bourgeois capitalism instituted a class-specific mode of cultural parenting which enabled those who experienced it to actualize their potentials for relative autonomy and a class-specific form of public-spiritedness. While recognizing that this actualization was at the expense of myriad excluded others, both within and without Europe, I want to argue that, in spite of these exclusions, the class-specific experience of hybrid bourgeois (male) subjects remains of theoretical and political interest insofar as it constituted a politicized sociability which transcended the limitations of kinship and which had some of the attributes of public-spiritedness. In understanding the conditions of possibility of this bourgeois mode of group membership, we will begin to grasp also the conditions of possibility of a global form of public-spirited citizenship, one which is inclusive rather than exclusive and marked by cultural plurality rather than homogeneity. An examination of conditions of possibility will begin in chapters three and four.

Summary and conclusion

To summarize this chapter before moving on to discuss capitalism, I begin with a dialectical critical realist understanding of humans as creatures whose particular causal powers (our 'hybrid' biological-cultural, or incompletely natural, nature) enable us (indeed *require* us) to act upon nature so as to reproduce ourselves. This hybridity is understood here in terms of our 'indeterminacy', incompletion or prematurity. As incomplete, indeterminate or prematurely-born creatures we need the completion of culture. Indeterminacy, though, is a matter of powers as well as needs: the powers to act imaginatively on and in the world, thereby developing ourselves and the world in 'indeterminable' ways. So, acting on nature functions in a dialectical rather than linear way. Yes, we must act, but the specific nature of neither action nor outcomes is determined. I am drawing on the work of Marx and Arendt to understand our active, imaginative capacities, and on Arendt and Freud to elaborate on Marx's claim about the historico-cultural forming of the five senses, or, as I am expressing it, our need for cultural completion. Marx's conceptualization of activity as praxis (in the sense of making, or, the imposition of form on nature) is inadequate to a theorization of citizen activity (an activity which is described approvingly by him in his writings on the Paris Commune). Arendt's concept of natality paves the way for such theorization, focusing as it does on the specifically political activity of acting communicatively or 'in concert'. Regarding our need for cultural completion, Arendt discusses this in terms of our need for a world (a bounded, directly-experienced built place inhabited in common with others). I am using the concept of sensuous presencing to connote the character of experience and social relations, expressed in and borne by face-to-face dialogical speech, which worldliness in this sense necessarily encompasses, and stressing the necessity (although, now, insufficiency) of such sensuous presencing if natality is to be nurtured. To complete Arendt's sketchy account of our incompleteness I turn to Freud as theorist of the energetic-hermeneutic character of human life, or of the internal relations between the biological and the cultural. As such, Freud is a theorist of drives and the possibilities and limitations inhering in their indeterminacy. He is a theorist who can advance our understanding of the human need for what, following Julia Flower MacCannell, I call cultural parenting, or, in his terms, for a reality principle which shapes the drives in relatively determinate ways through a process whereby emergent subjects cathect (occupy and become occupied by) 'representatives' (which we necessarily encounter as we are culturally 'completed') of a worldly world. In all of this, sociability is a necessity, whether as an innate human potential (Marx, Arendt) or as a cultural imposition (Freud). In this study, I shall understand cultural parenting, or, the need for a reality principle which is taken in a worldly way, to be the fundamental human need. However, I shall also want to stress that human enjoyment of the potential associated with our incompleteness or indeterminacy (the potential for 'indeterminable development') is enhanced by a reality principle which strikes a balance between determinacy and indeterminacy, or, which allows the emergence of new needs and powers in a way which nurtures individuality without risking atomism. Let us now turn to capitalism to begin to understand it in terms of these human potentials and needs.

2 Capitalism
Culture of worldlessness

Dialectical critical realism is the unifying framework which supports and integrates the Marxian, Arendtian and Freudian concepts in which my theory of humanity is grounded. As expressed in Roy Bhaskar's philosophy of science, this is a realism which insists upon the distinction between potentials and their actualization, and between closed and open systems. In chapter one these concepts were adapted to enhance our understanding of the human organism as a necessarily open system. The concept 'open system' connotes the historico-cultural character of an organism which is at once indeterminate and capable of indeterminable development. Indeterminacy is understood as a nexus of powers and needs; the former associated with imagination, as theorized by Marx and Arendt, and the latter associated with the need for a 'world' or sense of reality as theorized by Arendt and Freud. Manifestations of imagination with which this study will be concerned are praxis and natality (both connoting an active orientation to the world) and fantasy (connoting withdrawal from the world). As imaginative creatures, we humans are capable of imposing form on nature, in the process of which we also impose form on ourselves, or, the making of objects involves also the constitution of subjects. We have begun to understand that because of our indeterminate nature the constitution of subjects should take place in a worldly (sociable and intelligible) habitat, and have begun to explore this constitution in terms of an encounter between drives and representatives, an encounter which is experienced initially through parenting relations.

Closed systems exhibit predictable behaviour; open systems do not. Human organisms are open systems upon which culture works to effect closure (lawfulness) of different kinds. Cultural lawfulness (regularity of occurrence sufficient to the nurturing of a sense of reality) is an essential attribute of human habitats. Natural lawfulness (a lawfulness of causal powers which may or may not be experienced as regularity of occurrence, as noted in chapter one) does not determine, but rather constrains, the lawfulness of culture. So, regularity of occurrence (both natural and cultural) requires, to a greater or lesser degree, the help of intentional human action. The peculiarity of capitalism is that its mode of lawfulness, the law of value, is such that even where actualized in practices it secures only temporary regularity of occurrence. It is important to consider this from two points of view: from the point of view of capital as value (the 'objective' point of view) and from the point of view of the subjects of capital (the 'subjective' point of view).[1] Where capital successfully actualizes itself as capitalism, or, it secures a lawfulness sufficient to the reproduction of value, we may say that it secures regularity of occurrence of those practices and processes which it needs for this reproduction. However, lawfulness in this objective sense does not necessarily secure subjective lawfulness (experiential predictability or relative determinacy) such as cultures normally secure for their members. Beyond this, though, the peculiarity of the law of value is that the more it is actualized, the less likely is regularity of occurrence (either subjective or objective) to be found. Expressed otherwise, in attempting to attain closure, capital-supportive collective action can be (at best) only temporarily successful (Aglietta 1998: 50; Arrighi 1994: 330). Regularity of occurrence as an objective matter of the reproduction of value's law is secured only for the moment, and in a way which is bound to endanger this closure sooner or later (Harvey 1982; 1996).

The nature of this very peculiar lawfulness can be understood with the help of the concepts of totality, of dialectic, of contradiction and of overdetermination (Althusser 1990a; 1990b).[2] However, because the primary interest in this study is capitalism from the point of view of citizenship and subjectivity, this objective dimension of capitalism will merely be sketched in here. The focus is on capitalism's potential to constitute different manifestations of worldlessness (an experiential unpredictability which undermines sociability and intelligibility) and on the different actualizations of this potential during capitalism's history to date. This potential will be more or less actualized depending, first, on the specific cultural context into which capital is attempting to insert itself or within which it is seeking to reproduce itself and, second, on capital's own changing needs.

To say that capitalism (capital actualized) is governed by the law of value is to say that capitalist cultures are compelled to produce objects which are both usable and exchangeable.[3] This compulsion sets in motion an expansionary, colonizing dialectic of use and exchange which moves more or less speedily and more or less erratically, as will be seen. In fact, as Postone (1993: 271) points out, value is a 'totalizing category' which, once instituted in practices, seeks to subsume cultures as a whole under its law, or, it requires a 'regime of accumulation' (Aglietta 1987) composed of related modes of production, of consumption and of knowing, all of which have a peculiar abstract character.

The result of successful subsumption is the transformation of the world into a single culture having the character of a totality.[4] At this point, it is worth noting that while there has existed, in some sense, a 'world system' for centuries (Wallerstein 1979), much of the world was, until recently, subsumed formally rather than really under capital. Where cultures are subsumed formally under capital they remain tool-using cultures and therefore retain much of their pre-capitalist distinctiveness (Marx 1976a: ch. 14; Appendix). The concept of real subsumption connotes the revolutionary change in working practices which emerges with their mechanization and the enhancement of capital's power through its institution as capitalism (an institution whereby capital subsumes pre-capitalist cultures as social formations). At this point, capital is present in a form which induces 'industrial pathology' (Marx 1976a: chs 7, 10, 15). Capitalism has recently rendered its scope both more intensive and extensive in ways which will be discussed in later chapters. For the moment, we should note that it has been progressively subsuming the globe under one division of labour, one mode of consumption and one mode of 'truth'.[5] It is therefore coming to constitute the peoples of the world as 'humanity' by subsuming them directly under its contradictory functioning, thereby rendering them more obviously affected by its own periodic crises and more immediately subject to the transformations which have effected the temporary resolution of these crises (Jameson and Miyoshi 1998).

The different modes of capitalism which will be discussed in this study are manifestations of the fact that in order to reproduce itself capitalism is under constant pressure to innovate technologically and organizationally (Albritton 1991; Arrighi 1994; Harvey 1982; 1996; Postone 1993). This unceasing innovative pressure is what renders worldlessness a necessary characteristic of cultures once these have been subsumed under capital and have shed their pre-capitalist relations and practices. Worldlessness is deliberate and willed rather than the (not necessarily intended) temporary outcome of intentional human activity such as war, or of unintended and/or natural activity such as famine or plague. As the willed result of considered human activity, worldlessness will be understood here as a result of the abrogation of the duty of parental care which cultures owe to their members. As noted previously, this duty of care derives from human biological 'incompleteness'.

The purpose in this chapter is to lay out in very general terms, not primarily why capitalism is necessarily contradictory, therefore indeterminate and subject to periodic transformations, but, rather, the subjective effects of this contradictory nature.[6] In the first section of the chapter capitalism's 'deworlding' of the world will be understood as the institution of an abstract mode of domination necessitated by its totalizing division of labour. Here, a short discussion of the concepts of totality, of dialectic, overdetermination and contradiction will be undertaken. The second section will introduce the critical categories which enable a closer examination of the subject effects of this deworlding, namely, commodity fetishism, worldlessness, narcissism and rationality. The third section focuses on the topic of capitalism and citizenship.

I Culture as totality

Marx's *Capital* (1976a) is an indispensable source for understanding the peculiar nature of capitalism as a totalizing culture. The concept of totality is used here largely in the sense developed by Althusser (1990; 1990a), on which more below. Following Althusser and Balibar (1970), I take *Capital* to be a realist work which theorizes 'capital' as a complex of powers and needs.[7] As a realist work, it does not require us to assume that these powers will necessarily be actualized or that these needs will necessarily be met.[8] All that can be said (and this is to say a lot) is that up to now capital's powers *have* been actualized and its needs *have* been met, through the subsumption of cultures under capital as capitalism. Through this unevenly achieved, often resisted subsumption, capital has managed to reproduce itself, in various forms over a period of several centuries (Arrighi 1994). This – for capital – happy eventuality has involved the successful imposition of capital's 'form' on human and non-human nature, 'form' here being understood in terms of a particular kind of knowledge, namely the Baconian strand of science preoccupied with the 'performativity' of human and non-human nature (on which more in chapter eight). The first systematic expression of this science was classical political economy, which set itself the task of identifying the causal powers of an emergent culture of 'industriousness' (Marx 1951) and of ensuring through scientifically-informed collective action the more widespread, effective and efficient actualization of these causal powers throughout the nineteenth century in England (Halevy 1972; Kanth 1986; Polanyi 1957).

Classical political economy as the theoretical self-consciousness of the emergent 'industrious' class is a dazzling example of the particular kind of power/knowledge complex required for the actualization of capital as capitalism, or, the translation of emergent powers and needs into necessary, rather than merely possible, practices. However, because of capital's peculiar nature (open, contradictory, therefore crisis-prone) recurrent transformative episodes involving new power/knowledge complexes have been required. So, whereas we can consider the activities of those early scientists as attempts to ensure 'closure' for capitalism by subsuming all activities under capital's law in a reliable, predictable way, capitalism itself resists such closure, despite the best intentions of its directing intelligences (Arrighi 1994: Harvey 1982). It is necessarily, rather than contingently, dialectical, therefore contradictory, or, it is a totality.

Totality: dialectic, overdetermination and contradiction

The concept of totality is used here in an historico-culturally specific sense to theorize the character of cultures once the law of value has been instituted really rather than merely formally. Capitalism is totalizing in the sense that it is inherently expansionary and necessarily seeks the subsumption of all cultures, as well as of all non-human nature, under the law of value. It is a totality in the sense that, in subsuming cultures which are spatially separated, it constitutes a division of labour whereby necessary activities or parts are separated in time and space. If we are to resist totalization we must understand capitalism, and the world, as a totality (Jameson 1992: ch. 10).

Understanding this capitalist totality in an anti-totalizing spirit is a matter of understanding it as decentred (Althusser 1990a; Balibar 1996; Cullenberg 1996). To say that capitalism is a decentred totality is to say that it is neither determined nor teleological in its movement, but, rather, overdetermined. So, the law of value is a law which lacks the linearity of cause and effect posited by (some) liberal sciences. Lacking this linearity, it is not susceptible to the predictions implied by economism.[9] Whereas linearity connotes external relations between a simple cause and its effect, overdetermination connotes a multiplicity of causes (which are also effects) and effects (which are also causes). Overdetermination is here not merely a matter of a simple plurality of causes, as Callinicos (1993), for example, claims, but the necessary, internally related plurality of 'causes/effects' needed to effect the reproduction of capital as a necessarily totalizing (contradictorily differentiating, dialectically moving) culture. This is the way in which the peculiar lawfulness of value will be understood here.

Once a culture has been subsumed really rather than formally under value's law, it becomes a unit (social formation) within capitalism and becomes subject to this dialectical, contradictory, overdetermining movement. The concept of dialectic is here ontological (therefore relational) rather than metaphysical, or merely epistemological.[10] It concerns the specific nature of capitalism as a totality of internally related parts and/or practices and is therefore, as Althusser argues, a 'materialist dialectic' (Althusser 1990b). As a materialist dialectic, it cannot be understood in terms of 'inversion' of, or extraction from, the Hegelian dialectic. It does not replace a one-sided idealism with an equally one-sided materialism. Rather, it understands and builds on the Marxian understanding of the inseparability of the 'ideal' and the 'material' in human activity (Marx 1976b), or, the materialist dialectic is a dialectic of practices rather than of 'matter' in motion.

The dialectic, then, is here understood as the form of movement of capitalism as a totality which, aided by collective action informed by the science of classical political economy, emerged out of a culture which was originally an experiential unity, or, a unity whose constituent activities were coordinated through face-to-face artisanal activities. It is the spatio-temporal separation of these activities which brings about the peculiar kind of internal relatedness of 'many determinations' connoted by the concept of overdetermination. It is important to note that real internal relatedness is here combined with empirical, experienced, separateness. This is the source of contradictoriness as the tendency of these internally related but spatio-temporally separated parts to forget their function in the totality.[11]

As the concept of totality connotes this necessary separation of necessary parts, the concept of contradiction connotes the tendency of these necessary, internally related parts to act 'as if' they were autonomous, or, to forget that behind empirical separation lies real interdependence (Althusser 1990a; 1990b). This 'forgetting' is one important source of crisis since, while the reproduction of capitalism (and of its constituent social formations) depends on the prompt and effective responsiveness of myriad, spatio-temporally separated parts, such responsiveness is difficult, sometimes impossible, to achieve, and even where it is achieved the kinds of contradictions (within rather than between parts) discussed by Harvey (1982) ensure that its achievement will lead only to a temporary resolution of crises. Note too that the resolution of crisis is never only the result of the 'free market'. It is a matter requiring the kind of political power embodied in the state (Althusser 1984a; Poulantzas 1978) and, increasingly, in supra-state institutions (Arrighi 1994). Such supervisory, co-ordinating institutions are necessary precisely because the causality characteristic of capitalism is overdeterministic rather than deterministic.

Capitalism's vulnerability to crisis (therefore the vulnerability of its constituent social formations) is, as noted previously, a function of its totalizing structure, crisis being, as Marx puts it, a manifestation of 'the unity of the phases which have become independent of each other' (Marx 1951: 377; Carver 1998: ch. 3). The resolution of crises requires reconfigurations of production, consumption and knowing. Because of the overdetermined character of value's movement, it is impossible to predict the nature of future reconfigurations (or, indeed, the demise of capitalism).

The dynamic and crisis-prone tendencies which different kinds of contradictions bring with them will be assumed rather than explored in this study. The important point to note is that the different forms of activity to be discussed are internally, dialectically related. They are mutually constitutive in a manner which precludes both predictions about future outcomes and identification of a fixed hierarchy of causes (Jessop 2002; Resnick and Wolff 1987). So far, capitalism has managed to resolve the crises through which it has passed.[12] However, it is not assumed here that this had to happen. It happened because humans engaged in effortful imaginative activity intended to resolve various crises. What we are particularly interested in here is that such crisis resolution has involved transformations involving changes in modes of subjectivation. These modes will be explored in terms of differently abstract modes of labouring, consuming and knowing (or not knowing) which are related to one another dialectically.[13] These, rather than the particular dynamics of crisis, will be the focus of attention in this study. I shall now go on to discuss the critical categories which will enable us to understand the subject requirements for, and effects of, these abstract activities.

II Totality and worldlessness

The realization of surplus value demands the commodification of social relations, activities and objects, or, it demands that the world be dedicated to the production of objects, services and messages which have both exchange value and use value.[14] This compulsion necessitates the reduction of human activity to abstract forms of working, consuming and knowing. Abstraction here connotes an impersonal, 'systemic' mode of constituting relations, subjects and objects, or, a mode of 'abstract domination' (Postone's phrase) in which different parts are identified as the kinds of parts which are susceptible to quantification and which are mediated by money/capital and bureaucracy. While all cultures are engaged in abstractions of different kinds, it is only the peculiar mode of abstraction characteristic of capitalism which produces the worldlessness which is criticized by Arendt. Here abstraction is compelled by value and is 'analytic' or fetishistic in form (Keenan 1993).

The law of value institutes a condition of worldlessness the dehumanizing effects of which will be understood as a condition of commodity fetishism (Marx 1976a: ch. 1), Lukács's theory of which will be elaborated with the help of Arendt's conception of worldlessness and Freud's account of narcissism.[15] Different manifestations of capitalist worldlessness are understood as modes of commodity fetishism as these emerged with the transition from the formal subsumption to the real subsumption of labour under capital. These modes of commodity fetishism are more or less marked by reification or dereification. What they all share is the abstract forms of working, consuming and knowing in which is implicated a worldless form of rationality: the everyday rationality of *homo oeconomicus*, on the one hand; the specialized rationality of the scientific expert, on the other.

Worldlessness as commodity fetishism

Commodity fetishism is a concept which enables theorization of the experiential condition which pertains once the world has been subsumed under the law of value. Here the concept's meaning, as developed by Lukács (1971), is merely sketched in, and will be elaborated in chapter six. It is important to note that the condition in question involves not only the reifications of which Lukács speaks, but also the dereifications whose character Arendt enables us to understand (1958: ch. 3). As manifestations of the law of value, both reification and dereification engender world loss through draining the world of its sociability and intelligibility. The concept of reification draws our attention to the improper displacement of 'thingness' onto what is in movement, and what therefore is changing. It also alerts us to the fact (which capitalism allows, even encourages, us to forget) that movement is the result of co-operative human activity. Given this conception of reification, dereification might seem a desirable corrective to a debilitating condition. However, as used in this study, dereification is also a critical concept which focuses on the improper displacement of process onto what is (or should be) thinglike (in the sense of relatively durable). It is a concept which enables the theorization of a cultural indeterminacy which debilitates creatures who are born 'prematurely'. The key point is that neither reification nor dereification, as constituted by the law of value, can be constitutive of either the sociable and intelligible habitat needed by indeterminate creatures or the relatively autonomous form of subjectivity needed for public-spiritedness. Each debilitates in a different way, as will be argued in

32 *Theoretical foundations*

later chapters (although the contradictions borne by dereifying relations and practices may be yielding conditions of possibility for the emergence of public-spirited citizenship).

Commodity fetishism as reification

Following Lukács, commodity fetishism is used in this study as a category of culture, rather than of political economy, or, of a particular culture which has the character of a totality (Lukács 1971: 83). As a cultural category, the concept of commodity fetishism directs our attention to the fact that the law of value (borne by the commodity) has penetrated all spheres of life and has reconfigured them according to its own needs. This reconfiguration involves impersonal forms of mediation which begin with the abstraction of 'labour' (Marx 1976a: ch. 7; Postone 1993: ch. 4). As Thomas Keenan puts it, 'abstraction is the name of what goes on in exchange' (1993: 181) and, as such, it is informed by the need to fragment and reconfigure activities and objects to render them more efficient and more controllable. Susceptibility to quantification is an essential dimension of these activities and objects. Indeed, abstraction is carried on in an analytical mode intended to ensure the quantifiability of that which is abstracted.[16] Once originally unified activities and objects are fragmented through an analytical mode of abstraction; they are reconnected via impersonal mediations. These impersonal mediations (money and bureaucracy) constitute a particular, impersonal way of imposing form on the human organism and the world and a particular and peculiar purpose in doing so: the production of commodifiable use values.[17] Once capitalism has industrialized production, parts are necessarily differentiated abstractly by means of these impersonal mediations.[18] These abstract differentiations give capitalist cultures their 'systemic', impersonally imperative character.[19]

The activities and processes which advance value's law constitute an everyday world which is both unsociable and unintelligible. Unintelligibility and unsociability are conceptualized in the Lukácsian analysis of commodity fetishism as reification, as the solidifying of activity in fixed forms which conceal from actors the human, imaginative and co-operative sources of their world.[20] This is a concealment which turns the world upside down in that it fosters the objectification of human activity through the autonomization of human artefacts and the concealment of human interdependence.[21]

Commodification, or the transformation of 'objects' into objects of both use and exchange, involves a multiplicity of internally-related activities and processes including advances in the division of labour (initially from workshop to factory), the reconfiguration of money as capital and the universal monetization of social relations. These developments render the everyday world both unsociable and unintelligible by constituting individual subjects as buyers and sellers of 'labour power' and by reducing sellers to their capacities to labour, consume and know 'abstractly'. While abstract labouring is most starkly manifested in the unskilled or semi-skilled industrial labour of machine-minding, abstractness is a necessary characteristic of all 'labour' (and indeed of consumption and knowledge) once capital's law of value has become necessary rather than merely possible (Lukács 1971: esp. 92–103).

Being required to labour abstractly (having to put one's person at the disposal of value's changing needs) transgresses the principle of autonomy which capitalism proclaims, but, more than this, it atrophies sociability by reconstituting interdependence as individual dependence on an impersonal, unknowable and indifferent power. This reconstitution is achieved to the degree that relations become contractualized and monetized and the division of labour has advanced beyond that effected in the workshop, or, until 'labour' becomes subsumed really, rather than only formally, under capital (Marx 1976a: pt 4, Appendix; Rattansi 1982; Sayer 1991). At this point (the point at which mechanized production in factories has become necessary), conception and execution of tasks will have been split and production of whole objects will have yielded to a fragmentation which involves for the individual worker a 'loss of the object' (Lukács 1971: 86–92). This object loss is a cognitive-affective loss which separates workers from human as well as from made objects, and from the activities of relating and making which engagement with objects normally involves (Marx 1977: 61–74). It engenders a loss of reality whose nature will be explored more fully with the help of the Arendtian concept of worldlessness (connoting the dereifying imposition of a process character on the world) and the Freudian concept of narcissism (connoting the experience of a fetishized mode of life).

Commodity fetishism, dereification, worldlessness

Reification is not the only manifestation of commodity fetishism, whose appearance in contemporary capitalism is marked also by dereification. For Arendt, dereification is what worldlessness is all about. Since dereification is becoming progressively more consequential in contemporary capitalism, Arendt's account of capitalist-induced worldlessness is an essential complement to the Lukácsian understanding of commodity fetishism as reification.

Dereification, or the dissolution of world to process, was a potential or tendency in capitalism from the start which is being actualized today as never before (Arendt 1958: 54–8; 1968a; Marx and Engels 1998; Berman 1982). Whereas Marxists use the concept of process in an objectivist sense to connote the character of movement and necessary inter-relatedness of apparently autonomous activities (Althusser 1977: 117), the concept is used in this study to theorize the worldlessness imposed on subjects by capitalism. So, we want to understand the ways in which appearances having the character of process educate the five senses.

Process, Arendt wants to insist, is a capitalist-induced reduction of the human world to an endless cycle of production and consumption which leaves nothing worldly (durable or tangible) behind; a reduction which deprives humans of the sense of a shared and reliable reality and which renders us forgetful of our capacities and responsibilities (Arendt 1958: 79–93).²² The concept of process here connotes a denaturing naturalization of creatures who have the potential for natality and praxis; creatures who can act imaginatively, intentionally or 'non-naturally'. This is a denaturing naturalization which draws us into a compulsive flow of worldless experience, or, which seeks to reduce us to matter which moves in accordance with value's law (Arendt 1958: 130; Ring 1989). It is the manifestation of the obsolescence and substitutability that accompanies the subsumption of use under exchange; a subsumption which has the potential to render human experience indeterminate (Arendt 1968a: 11) though, as will be seen, this potential is realized more or less depending on the character of the production process which predominates at a particular time (Albritton 1991).

Arendt's triadic classification of human activity in terms of labour, making and action will enable us to elaborate on her concept of process. This classification is used here to draw our attention to the unprecedented character of modern impermanence and worldlessness (Arendt 1958; Hansen 1993: ch. 1; Curtis 1999: ch. 3; Ricoeur 1990), not to claim either the desirability or actuality of empirically 'pure' forms of activity. It is the basis of an important understanding of the nature of capitalism's deviance. I assume the distinctiveness and essential character of activities labelled as labouring, making and action only for the purpose of understanding the culturally unprecedented form of activity initiated with capitalist industrialization.²³

Capitalist-induced worldlessness is understandable to begin with in terms of the invasion of the sphere of making by labouring. Labour is the activity whereby our animal needs are satisfied; it is activity oriented to the production of things which are to be destroyed through consumption. Making is an activity which expresses our human distinctiveness in that it is action informed by a plan, or, it is imagination imposed on nature for the purpose of producing durable things. Action is the activity which expresses natality, or the human capacity to begin something new through action in concert. One key difference between making and action is that, unlike making, action does not require the intermediation of things but is carried on directly between humans and is mediated only by speech. It is therefore oriented to the expression of human plurality or distinctiveness, and it is what introduces radical novelty and contingency into the world. Action is therefore a risky endeavour which cannot guarantee outcomes.

As natural creatures we need to labour for the maintenance of life; we are compelled to produce in order to consume, or, necessity compels an activity intended for the destruction of things produced. Labouring is therefore an unworldly activity in the sense that it is not capable of producing, by itself, a habitat suitable for humans. It is making, rather than labouring, which does this. Unlike labouring, which expresses our purely animal nature, making is a distinctively human activity undertaken for the purposes of filling the world with durable objects, that is, of objects which survive across the generations. It is also, though, an inherently destructive activity governed by instrumental rationality. The maker as subject approaches nature as raw material to be destroyed or transformed according to the intentions of the subject. In adopting this instrumentally rational stance towards non-human nature, the maker engages in an activity which is necessary for a truly human world.

It is necessary, but, like labour, not sufficient. While making is expressly human in being strongly intentional activity informed by a plan (although the plan may be kinesthetically rather than reflexively borne in the sense that it is transmitted inter-generationally and in mimetic mode[24]), it is, potentially, dehumanizing in that it is an essentially solitary and speechless activity which does not necessarily involve relations with other humans. It is in action that humans achieve truly human status because it is only in action that humans are immediately, personally and necessarily interdependent in a specifically human way, i.e. in a way requiring speech.

Most human activity displays aspects of labouring, making and action. In any case, a truly human life, one which respects the human capacity for 'indeterminable development', needs all three kinds of activities. However, the activities needed to reproduce capitalism combine them in a way which is detrimental to human flourishing. As will be seen, activity intended for the reproduction of value's law is a destructive mixture of aspects of labouring (its necessity and destructiveness), of making (its instrumentality and destructiveness) and action (its disruptiveness).

Where making takes place in the mode of labouring, objects are produced in a compulsive way for consumption and destruction rather than for use. Therefore making in the mode of labouring is a mode of activity which undermines the durable character of the world. Moreover, this making-as-labouring becomes, through the capitalist division of labour, an activity which is directed by a kind of 'systemic', rather than individual, intentionality (Gorz 1989; Kosik 1976), this being a manifestation of intentionality which is impersonal and which instrumentalizes all social relations as subject–object rather than subject–subject relations. This is an intentionality which intends us to remain in an unnecessarily necessitous condition which drives us to produce and consume with an urgency unwarranted by the available surplus (Arendt 1958: 118–35). In short, through the subsumption of making under labouring, capitalism extends and intensifies the compulsive 'lawlike' character of labouring and the instrumental subject–object orientation of making into new domains. Moreover, through its need to engage in permanent revolution, capitalism introduces a dimension of action (its unpredictability) into domains which should be relatively stable, thereby rendering the everyday world not only unintelligible (at least outside the specialized domains of scientific expertise), but, eventually, experientially volatile and unsociable.

As capitalism came to impose industrialization on the world, it constituted novel forms of indeterminacy or rootlessness which were deeply implicated in the emergence of 'totalitarianism' (Arendt 1973b: chs 10, 13). During the organized stage of capitalism, determinacy prevailed, whereas today we are experiencing an indeterminacy of the kind connoted by the Arendtian concept of process. This indeterminacy (partly willed) is what renders the contemporary world progressively unfit for human habitation (Baudrillard 1993: chs 1, 2; Bauman 2000; Sennett 1998).

To summarize, in instituting commodity fetishism capitalism is instituting its need that all human activity be undertaken compulsively as dictated by value's law. This is a compulsion to produce as quickly as possible objects which can be exchanged and to consume as quickly as possible these exchangeable objects. This is the institution of a logic of obsolescence and substitutability; a logic which involves both reifying and dereifying characteristics. Reification, which is most thoroughly explored by Lukács, is a matter of placing under a naturalizing compulsion creatures who are cultural, who therefore have more room for manoeuvre than the logic of compulsion allows. Dereification endows compulsion with a process character, so that the individual feels swept along, as opposed to being pinned in place, by an irresistible force.[25] Through dereification the world loses the character of stability and durability with which 'thingness' endows it. It becomes dissolved into an unintelligible and unsociable 'process' oriented to production for the sake of surplus value. Where human activity has been transmuted into production, human habitations cease to have the character of a world; they become incapable of resisting the 'consuming life process of the people dwelling in [them]' (Arendt 1977c: 210). In the universalization, therefore irresistibility, of process and production lies the key to modern worldlessness; a condition whose psychic effects can be understood as a condition of narcissism.

Worldlessness as narcissism

Where the world has been reduced to process, a condition of object loss through relational and object degeneration becomes endemic, therefore a sense of reality becomes impossible to achieve. This claim will be elaborated in later chapters. For the moment, we need to note that, as we know from Freud, narcissistic subjects are subjects who lack this sense of reality (Freud 1984a; Brennan 1992). Therefore capitalist subjects are narcissistic subjects (Kovel 1988b; Lasch 1978; Piccone 1980). This is a culturally-induced manifestation of narcissism. Indeed, the universalization of commodity fetishism renders narcissism a normal fate of the human animal. Narcissism is incompatible with the practice of public-spiritedness. In fact, it is the 'other' of anaclitic rationality, as we have noted before. Where anaclisis connotes world engagement and sociability, narcissism, in the sense used in this study, connotes world avoidance and atomism.[26]

Narcissism is the Freudian concept which will enable us to trace the psychic effects of the loss of reality (of worldlessness) which the successful actualization of capital as capitalism induces necessarily rather than contingently. As used here, the concept connotes a condition induced by the absence of a reality principle which would afford the reality-testing whereby individual subjects gain the sense of a world held in common with others. From the point of view of relative autonomy, worldly reality-testing is possible where cultural representatives are good objects, these being objects which, when internalized, constitute within the emergent subject the psychic strength required for effective engagement with a complex world (Freud 1984b; 1984d). In ways to be explored in chapters three and four, early bourgeois parents were good objects. What contemporary capitalism offers is bad objects which provide temporary consolation for the absence of such good objects; bad objects being objects which are incapable of nurturing the emergent subject's capabilities in any way. The absence of good objects leaves emergent subjects without achievable ideals; the presence of bad objects leaves them with unachievable and/or worldless ideals. Or, in ways to be explored in later chapters, the narcissistic subject is the subject governed by an ideal ego rather than by ego or superego (Chasseguet-Smirgel 1985; Lacan 1980: 2; Laplanche and Pontalis 1973: 201–2).

The narcissistic subjects constituted by a world-dissolving capitalism are subjects reduced to the debilitated condition of subjectivism; a condition marked by the intense self-preoccupation of subjects who have been deprived of the cultural resources for developing psychic strength in a culture in which psychic strength is taken for granted as a cultural good. While this condition is induced by an already worldless world (a world which does not yield a sense of reality), it is exacerbated by the inward turning which marks the narcissist's response to this worldlessness. It is worth pointing out that this inward-turning is a tendency, rather than a necessity, but a very powerful tendency under the conditions to be discussed in later chapters. It is understandable as an 'involution of drives' on the part of a 'subject in jeopardy'; a subject seeking to protect and nurture a fragile sense of self (Brennan 1992: ch. 4; Flax 1990). This involution of drives constitutes an avoidance of the world impelled by the world's neglect of the activity drive, the drive which originally takes a world-oriented form, or, which is experienced as a need for imaginative world-engagement and sociability (Benjamin 1990: ch. 1; Schachtel 1963: ch. 7). Narcissism of this kind enters this study in the shape of the late nineteenth-century domesticated capitalist wife in whom the unavailability of appropriate cultural nourishment provoked this response. This inward-turning is one possible, indeed likely, response to worldlessness. Another response is to direct attention towards the world in a wholly self-referential way. The capitalist husband was also a narcissist in the sense that he viewed the world in a self-referential way, but he did so in the mode of mastery rather than escape. In both cases, what was experienced was a radical detachment from the world; a detachment which dictates either avoidance or mastery. In both cases, there was a loss of worldliness in the political sense of a sociable recognition of interdependence which supports public-spiritedness. In the woman's case, this was also a loss of the conditions of possibility for gratification of her activity drive.

Of course, capitalism involved an earlier, catastrophic loss of reality for peasants and artisans (Hill 1967; Thompson 1968; 1978), as well as for those faraway others without whom bourgeois subjectivity would not have emerged (Bartolovich 2000; Gilroy 1993; Venn 2000).[27] The capitalist example is relevant here because it is part of the history of different modalities of specifically capitalist forms of subjectivity, and because it draws our attention to a form of deprivation which has been intensified today when individual subjects are experiencing a contradictory condition marked by the two manifestations of narcissism experienced within the capitalist household: the involution of drives experienced by the capitalist's wife and the worldless drive to mastery experienced by the capitalist.

It is worth noting that narcissism may take an atomized or communal form (Whitebook 1995: 35–40). The former is the notable achievement of capitalism which has naturalized a condition which Freud took to be an exceptional (or at least avoidable) individual fate. The latter was, we may say, the normal condition of human groups in the pre-modern world. It persists in the modern world in the form of nationalism, which attempts to restore the sense of worldliness destroyed by capitalism.[28] Both atomized and communal forms of narcissism involve, by definition, a politics of (individual or group) egoism; a politics which is without the generosity to attend to others (individual or group) as entities worthy of interest and understanding in their own right; a politics of sameness rather than of plurality. This is a politics which is wholly incapable of dealing with the global problems which now call for resolution. Before turning briefly to the question of capitalism and citizenship, an initial specification of capitalism's fetishized mode of (ir)rationality will be useful. This will open up the topic of capitalism's abstract mode of knowing (science), a topic to which we will return in chapter eight.

Capitalism and rationality

Rationality is an abstraction which refers to human potentials whose actualization requires cultural conditions of possibility. As an abstraction which has emerged out of western cultures, it tends to be naturalized and universalized in a mode which is, in fact, historico-culturally specific and fetishized. This is an individualistic mode involving a preoccupation with, on the one hand, the law of non-contradiction, and, on the other hand, the calculative instrumental rationality which is theoretically manifested in the scientist and practically manifested in *homo oeconomicus*. These modes have, as Marx noted of the abstraction called labour, their 'full validity only for and within [historico-culturally specific] ... relations' (1973: 105). To forget that this is the case is to fall into serious error; to forget that rationality may be (has been) an attribute of groups as well as of individuals; that it has been (continues to be) either fused with or internally related to the other human faculties (of imagination, affect). The rationalities that are describable as, for example, 'disengaged' (Taylor 1992: ch. 8) or 'economic' (Dryzek 1996: ch. 1) must be understood in these historico-cultural terms.[29]

On the question of rationality, capitalism is an unprecedented form of human culture in that, as noted previously, it renders the everyday world both unintelligible and unsociable to most of those whose task it is to reproduce it. This happens through the division of labour required for the implementation of the law of value, a division of labour which reconfigures cultures as totalities whose necessary parts are separated in time and space.

Behind the impersonal mediations of bureaucracy and money lies the abstract, fetishizing mode of knowing which is science; science being the sense of a totalizing culture which, as a totality, is crucially dependent on 'absent' (unexperienced) causes, or relations at a distance. This dependence on absent causes becomes a dependence on a stratum of specialist knowers whose task it is to 'stop and think'. Stopping to think involves contemplative rather than practical knowing, or, more accurately, it involves the reorientation of contemplation towards an understanding of the world in terms of its more efficient and effective practical manipulation. This withdrawal from the world constitutes a mode of rationality which will later, following Arendt, be understood as determinant judgement (chapter eight below). For now, we need to note that, unlike the anaclitic kinesthetic rationality which characterized pre-capitalist social relations, this rationality is cold and monological, or, it is worldless.

Science (both social and natural) is the form which knowledge takes as absent causes (causes which are not directly experienced) become necessary for cultural reproduction. Now, of course, in a particular realist sense, all cultures are dependent on absent causes (on the functioning of real powers which cannot be directly experienced). However, prior to industrialization, knowledge of these absent causes was acquired mostly unconsciously, as it were, or, by a slow process of practical, situated trial-and-error involving multi-sensual immersion in a habitat which was experienced as a world (Bernal 1954: pts II, III; Merchant 1989: chs 2, 3).[30] Knowledge acquisition was part of the everyday practical world; it was not the business of specialists (the knowledge of priests and shamans apart). Capitalism is dependent on absent causes in a much more radical sense (Lukács 1971: 186). There are two aspects to this dependence. First, being governed by the law of value, capitalism must constantly expand its geographical reach, or, attempt to subsume the globe under one division of labour. In doing so, it becomes a totality, as noted previously. As a totality, it is composed of social formations which become themselves acutely dependent on absent causes, or, on processes, practices and events that take place beyond the experience of members of these social formations. Second, the quest for ever-growing amounts of surplus value leads capitalism to search out new exchangeable objects and more efficient means of producing these. By the second half of the nineteenth century, capitalism could no longer be reproduced through the artisanal knowledge of engineers and came increasingly to rely on the technology which comes from the natural sciences (Bernal 1954: ch. 8; Kargon 1977; Landes 1969). As, through technology, the results of scientific knowledge were fed into the everyday world, a second kind of absent cause became necessary. In this case the cause was experientially 'absent' not because of spatio-temporal distance, but because it was accessible only by means of the theoretically-guided use of prosthetics (Arendt 1958: ch. 6). Here the 'beyond' of experience is beyond all direct (in the sense of prosthetically-unaided) sense experience and is cognitively accessible only to those who have undergone years of specialist training.

Through these two kinds of absent causes, the everyday world became drained of its sense from the point of view of its inhabitants as the activities of these inhabitants became mediated by the expertise embodied in science, as well as in money/capital and bureaucracy. As the need for scientific expertise came to penetrate more areas of life, there emerged a split between a common sense which was drained of significant cognitive content and a scientific expertise (possessed by a minority) without which capitalism and its constituent social formations would fail to reproduce themselves. This, very briefly, is what I mean by the unintelligibility of everyday life as constituted by capitalism. Unintelligibility (at the level of everyday experience) is a property of totalities, or of cultures which are differentiated in such a way that they are necessarily interdependent in ways which are not cognitively accessible through direct experience (Lukács 1971: 107).[31] It is in this way that the capitalist 'regime of truth' contributes to the constitution of a worldless world.

This is the point of view from which I want to trace the movements of capital since it began the injection of value's law into the cultural body. As noted previously, these movements will be described from a realist (therefore non-determinist, anti-teleological) point of view in that I describe different modes of capitalism in terms of capitalist and human powers and needs without assuming that powers will necessarily be actualized or needs necessarily satisfied. It is also important to note that neither capitalist nor human powers or needs remain unchanged over time, although there remain in place the identifying criteria discussed above: humanity's power for natality, praxis and indeterminable development and the related need for sociability and relative determinacy; and capitalism's power to produce unprecedented quantities of resources through its need to realize surplus value as profit. The successful actualization of capitalism's power, the satisfaction of its need, renders the world, over time, indeterminate. This indeterminacy transgresses against the human need for relatively determinate cultural shaping in ways that we have begun to explore. Before concluding this chapter, let us open up to discussion the topic of capitalism and citizenship.

III Capitalism against citizenship

An understanding of the contradiction between capitalism and citizenship requires attentiveness to capitalism's 'forming of the five senses'. Attentiveness here involves the writing of a brief history of capitalism and its modes of subjectivity. This work was begun by members of the Frankfurt School, whose critical theory posited a distinction between the relatively autonomous form of subjectivity constituted by, as they saw it, competitive, liberal, family-based capitalism and the subjectivity of the functionary to which all, including capitalists, were reduced, as 'monopoly' capitalism took the place of its liberal manifestation (Adorno 1967; 1968; Marcuse 1970).[32] In this study it will be important to make a distinction between hybrid bourgeois and liberal industrial capitalism so as to enhance our understanding of the sources of bourgeois public-spiritedness, thereby also, it is hoped, correcting some of the deficiencies of critical theory as discussed by Jessica Benjamin (1977). It will be necessary, therefore, to adopt a four-fold periodization of capitalism as follows: first, hybrid, bourgeois capitalism, the form of capitalism discussed by Marx in terms of the formal subsumption of labour under capital; second, liberal, industrializing capitalism involving the real, as opposed to merely formal subsumption of labour under capital (Marx 1976a: Appendix); third, organized, and fourth, disorganized capitalism (Lash and Urry 1987).[33] In terms of subjectivity and rationality, I shall argue that these modes began with male bourgeois, relatively autonomous subjectivity; a form of subjectivity which was knowledgeable in the mode of *sensus communis*, therefore rational in the mode of anaclisis. The concept of *sensus communis* is used here to differentiate between a shared sense which is kinesthetically rational (common sense), and one which encompasses a theoretical understanding of the world (*sensus communis*). This *sensus communis* constituted a novel mode of politicized sociability, or public-spiritedness. From our contemporary point of view, the bourgeois mode of public-spiritedness was limited because it was parasitic on necessary exclusions, as noted previously. At the same time, artisanal rationality retained its vitality into the nineteenth century (Bauman 1982; Calhoun 1982; Thompson 1968). As industrialization advanced, bourgeois was replaced by capitalist and artisan was replaced by proletarian. The capitalist remained relatively autonomous, but now, unlike the bourgeois, lived 'as if' absolutely autonomous and came progressively to treat the proletarian as a 'thing'. Moreover, and relatedly, the rationality of *sensus communis* was being replaced by that of *homo oeconomicus*. Expressed otherwise, rationality was becoming delinked from sociability in a way which dried up the sources of public-spiritedness. As liberal capitalism ceded via monopoly to its organized form, the rationality of scientific expertise became 'systemic' and capitalists lost their relative autonomy (Adorno 1967; 1968; Horkheimer 1947; Marcuse 1970, 1982). Differentiations now took on an abstract character which required that all become bearers of a systemic rationality in the occupational sphere while being encouraged to exercise an atomized form of calculative rationality (the rationality of *homo oeconomicus*) in 'private', although, as will be seen, contradictions within organized capitalism produced counterforces in the case of the organized working class. The organized mode of capitalism was marked by a stabilization of the use/exchange dialectic which was temporarily secured by a combination of state activity and mass mechanized production. In spite of the tendencies towards economic rationality just mentioned, this mode was conducive to a general readiness to contribute (albeit passively) to the provision of public goods. By the 1970s this exceptionally stable mode of capitalism was under threat and was coming to be reconfigured in disorganized and disorganizing mode. It is arguable that this reconfiguration is constituting experiences which are more strongly contradictory than any that have gone before. A word about these experiences will be useful at this point.

From worldlessness to worldliness?

The present dialectic of exchange and use is engendering contradictions which could be in some respects supportive of public-spiritedness. Among these is the contradiction generated by processes and institutions that have both psychologizing and depsychologizing effects. Or, expressed otherwise, individual subjects are required to be both autonomous (narcissistic in the mode of mastery) and heteronomous (narcissistic in the mode of escape), as noted previously. At the same time, we are required increasingly to be our own experts at a time when the conditions which supported expertise (relatively stable differentiations) are being dissolved.[34] This is what I shall argue in the course of addressing questions about citizen capacities and capitalist actualities. It is through the examination (necessarily sketch-like rather than exhaustive) of the forms of capitalist subjectivity that answers to these questions will be sought.

The purpose of this examination is to gain a sense of the gap between where we are and where we want to be. I take it that where we want to be is in a place where mature, relatively autonomous individuals learn how to act collectively as citizens so as to take responsibility for the problems of injustice, environmental degradation and general human misery which we cannot fail to notice today. Such individuals will possess a globally-oriented public-spiritedness directed not by economic, not by communicative, but, rather, by anaclitic rationality. The return to hybrid bourgeois capitalism is intended, not to seek a model of public-spiritedness for today, but to enhance our understanding of the conditions of possibility for an autonomy which is actual rather than illusory. Understanding the conditions which yielded the relative autonomy of the bourgeois will be fruitful in this respect.

Summary and concluding remarks

Capitalism is a novel mode of life (or culture) whose novelty consists in its necessarily totalizing, expansionary dynamic. This dynamic is necessary because capitalism is governed by the law of value, or it requires the production of objects which are both exchangeable and usable. This requirement has now resulted in the constitution of the globe as a totality, or, as one division of labour consisting in a contradictory unity of diverse, spatio-temporally separated parts. It is contradictory in the sense that these necessary parts tend to 'forget' their place and function in the totality, thereby generating crises of various kinds. The division of labour is understandable as a regime of accumulation involving specific modes of working (abstract labour), of consumption (abstract consumption) and of truth (abstract knowledge, or science). As manifestations and servants of the law of value, these are modes of activity which constitute a worldless (unsociable, unintelligible) world.

The concepts of commodity fetishism, worldlessness and narcissism have been offered as the means of elaborating on the worldless 'taking in' of culture which the law of value necessitates. This taking in is imposed by a culture which has today abrogated culture's fundamental task of parenting; the task, as it is conceived of here, of providing humans with a reality principle constitutive of an intelligible and sociable world, or, of providing the drives with relatively determinate shaping. The way in which capitalism renders the experiential world unsociable and unintelligible has been explored through an initial specification of the capitalist reduction of anaclitic-kinesthetic rationality, or, its subsumption under an abstract, fetishized form of rationality which takes both systemic and atomistic forms.

It is important to remember that capitalism is a culture which needs to transform itself in order to reproduce itself. Successful periodic transformations have been productive of different modes of capitalism whose different subject effects will be discussed in later chapters. The reader should bear in mind that these modes are treated here as 'real' (not 'ideal') types in that I take it that each mode has its own specific tendencies and needs which may or may not be actualized or satisfied in specific social formations but which had to be actualized or satisfied if capitalism were to reproduce itself. Such actualization includes among its conditions of possibility intentional collective action oriented to the resolution of crises. Each mode has emerged following different combinations of (multiple) contradictions and the (always temporarily) successful resolution of these contradictions via collective action.[35]

As will be seen, the different subject effects of the different modes depend in part on the character of differentiation (the ratio of personal to impersonal mediations, the relative consequentiality of personal mediations) required for the reproduction of value's law, on the degree to which the division of labour needs scientific expertise for its reproduction, as well as on the stability of differentiations and the speediness with which they can be reconfigured. The public-spiritedness which I shall identify in the bourgeois public sphere was due to a mode of differentiation in which personal mediations (sensuous presencing) remained strongly consequential while being balanced by increasingly consequential impersonal mediations, most importantly, print. This is what is discussed in the next chapter.

Part II

The bourgeois public sphere

3 The worldly world of the bourgeois subject

Our brief history of capitalist subjectivity begins with its hybrid bourgeois form. Hybridity is the attribute of a mode of capitalism in which capital subsumes labour 'formally' rather than 'really' (Marx 1976a: Appendix). It is the characteristic of an emergent capitalism in which work is carried on in artisanal rather than proletarian mode; a capitalism, therefore, whose identifying 'law', i.e. the law of value, is retarded and limited in its motion and scope by the presence of consequential pre-capitalist relations and practices and the underdevelopment or absence of those later innovations and inventions (mechanization, money, bureaucracy, railway, telegraph, etc.) which would eventually enable the subsumption of individual and intersubjective intentionality and activity under a 'system', thereby effecting the unintelligibility of the world (at the level of common sense) and rendering sociability optional rather than imperative.[1]

Formal subsumption did not have the power to dissolve the anaclitic-kinesthetic rationality of artisanal making, which remained consequential for the reproduction of everyday life. Yet it demanded, through the civilizing differentiations of which Norbert Elias speaks, a new mode of intelligibility which would eventually emerge as science but which, for the moment, constituted a novel form of *sensus communis*. What enabled this mode of intelligibility was the hybridity which maintained a balance between sensuous and non-sensuous presencing and between personal and impersonal social relations, or, between involvement and detachment. As I shall argue (largely though not wholly following Habermas) this balance, along with a novel mode of ownership of 'means of production', constituted a novel form of cultural parenting which nurtured individual bourgeois relative autonomy. It is in order to mark the presence and absence of this balance that I want to make a distinction between bourgeois and capitalist. Unlike the bourgeois, capitalists approximate to the subjectivity sketched in by Marx in *On the Jewish Question* (1994). Unlike capitalists, the bourgeois were capable of a class-specific sociability which also had a public character. Or, they were capable of a public-spirited manifestation of social love.[2]

While following the early critical theorists in taking seriously the relatively autonomous character of (male) bourgeois subjectivity, I do not share completely their understanding of its sources and am, in any case, trying to understand how we can move beyond a condition, not of reification, but of dereification, that is to say, of an irrationality in some respects quite different from the perversions of functional rationality with which the critical theorists were concerned (Adorno 1973; Adorno and Horkheimer 1979; Horkheimer 1947; Marcuse 1982; 1986). What is sometimes missed in depictions of bourgeois subjectivity derived from the critical theoretical perspective is the importance of hybridity to the constitution, not only of relative autonomy, but also public-spiritedness; an importance which is elided in the preoccupation with individual bourgeois family ownership and control of means of production; a preoccupation which fails to take seriously the distinction between bourgeois (formal subsumption) and capitalist (real subsumption).[3] We will only understand the nature of individual (always relative) autonomy if we keep this hybridity in mind so as to understand the ways in which, once the transition from formal to real subsumption has been effected, capitalism and autonomy are incompatible.

So, our interest in hybrid bourgeois capitalism is motivated by the need to understand the conditions of possibility for the practice of public-spirited citizenship. We will find that (hybrid) bourgeois subjects were characterized by a strongly individuated sociability (in this case a specifically bourgeois form of anaclitic rationality) which was grounded in a reflexive or theoretical form of common sense, or *sensus communis*. It is this combination of affective and cognitive attributes which renders bourgeois relative autonomy of such interest in the present conjuncture. This is the point of view from which we will return to material which is already well-worked, namely Habermas's (1992a) analysis of the bourgeois public sphere; an analysis which, despite the many criticisms to which it has been subjected,[4] provides the historical-sociological evidence for Marx's conviction that capitalism actualized new, and newly-potent, forms of human agency (Marx and Engels 1998; Forbes 1990; Gilbert 1981; Maguire 1978).[5] We can enhance our understanding of how this came about if we bear in mind the novel viewpoint that Arendt's concept of worldliness opens up.[6]

The claims about bourgeois subjectivity made in this study apply insofar as individuals were constituted by the institutions to be discussed in this, and the next, chapter. In writing about the bourgeois I assume actualization, on the side of individual human organisms constituted as bourgeois, of the potentials to be discussed through the institutions to be discussed.[7] These potentials are conceptualized in terms of the drive theory whose very general characteristics were discussed in chapter one. They include the potential for world-engagement as a happily active orientation to the world and to humans who inhabit the world, and the needs connoted by the Freudian concepts of ego and sex drives. In assuming full actualization of potentials and satisfaction of needs, I am abstracting from the dense particularities and pluralities which characterize any mode of life. Such abstraction is unavoidable if we are to say anything at all. The point is, when discussing subjectivity and citizenship, to choose a level of abstraction which retains a connection with the experienced world. In this respect, Habermas's early work is exemplary.

We can begin to understand the cultural specificities out of which emerged the novel form of subjectivity manifested in hybrid bourgeois subjects using the theoretical lenses provided by Norbert Elias's (1994) concept of 'civilization', with the help of which I shall begin to discuss differentiation and subjectivity in the first section of this chapter. The concept of civilization connotes a differentiating culture which places heavy demands on individuals for self-direction and introspectivity, and for an orientation towards other humans as similarly self-directed introspective subjects. Understanding the peculiar differentiating dynamic which constituted this emergent introspectivity will enable us to grasp some of the cultural conditions of possibility for the enjoyment of relative autonomy. Narrowing the focus in section two, I shall elaborate on the character of specifically bourgeois institutions so as to consider a worldly, non-abstract mode of differentiation: or, a differentiation which, through a specific balance of personal and impersonal mediations, retained the place-like character of the experiential world (for the bourgeoisie) while also constituting a public sphere marked by civic rather than formal relations. What was in question was a new kind of worldly world which was becoming differentiated in such a way as to demand new modes of intelligibility without, for the moment, atrophying the sociability which was a necessary dimension of all pre-capitalist cultures (Lefort 1978). Moreover, these new modes of intelligibility did not implement the expert/laity differentiation which would follow upon industrialization. Although the conditions of possibility (literacy and access to the relevant literature) remained beyond the means of most, a theoretical, reflexive orientation and knowledgeability could be acquired without undergoing intense periods of specialized training. This orientation is understood here as a manifestation of what Freud describes as secondary process functioning; a mode of mental functioning which requires a 'taming of drives' and splitting of the psyche. In section three I shall use a specifically Freudian lens to understand the psychic splitting which bourgeois differentiations constituted and to begin to think about the parental relations involved in this novel form of subjectivation.

I Differentiation and subjectivity: the civilizing process

Differentiation takes different forms in different modes of capitalism. In this chapter I am concerned with the characteristics of the earliest form of modern differentiation as described by Norbert Elias, a form whose significance for us here is that it constituted 'psychologized' subjects who were coming to know an increasingly complex world (as well as themselves) in a new, individualized way.[8] Elias enables us to understand the significance of a form of differentiation under which could be actualized the human potential for self-reflexivity and for a new kind of bourgeois individualized intentional and practically efficacious activity. This is the form of differentiation connoted by the concept of 'civilization', a theoretical, non-prescriptive concept which refers to a long-term directional change in human thinking, feeling and acting which first began to emerge during the sixteenth century in western Europe.[9] As a nexus of subjective capacities and orientations, the direction of this change was from spontaneity to discipline; from unself-consciousness to self-consciousness; from externally imposed disciplines to self-discipline.[10] What interests me specifically about this process is its contribution to the dissolution of common sense as a kinesthetic-anaclitic rationality which had, up to this time, sufficed for the reproduction of everyday life. Kinesthetic rationality begins in practical imitation and is refined and enriched by experience. It is largely non-reflexive but highly sensitive to the material quality and texture of the things towards which the individual's attention has been directed through imitation (Sahlins 1976; Strauss and Quinn 1997). It is, then, strongly embodied in practices which are concerned with the direct imposition of form on matter by individual artisans responsible for the making of whole objects, and is, moreover, anaclitic, or, it is a rationality which is 'between' rather than 'within' individual subjects, as well as between subjects and non-human nature.[11] It is a form of rationality which is unmarked by the abstracting, atomizing effects of industrializing fragmentation/differentiation. This is the rationality of pre-modern common sense which the modern world renders 'stupid' (Arendt 1994: 313).

This happened as activities and processes which were consequential for particular peoples came to take place increasingly beyond their experiential reach so that the untheoretical, taken-for-granted knowledge embodied in common sense became increasingly inadequate for the reproduction of everyday life and came to be replaced by the abstract, theoretical rationality of the sciences, which, as the social science of political arithmetic, first directed its attention to the functioning and effects of long-distance trade (Appleby 1978). As the effects of this trade came to impinge more on everyday life (as these effects moved from the fringes to the centre of communities), differentiation and the enhanced division of labour created longer chains of interdependencies going beyond the experiential. These processes also created a greater variety of occupations and greater need and scope for individual self-direction. This self-direction involved an 'internalized' splitting of the self; a kind of withdrawal of self from self, but also from world; a withdrawal which could be either self-centred or world-oriented (or world-oriented in a self-centred way). To the degree that this withdrawal took place, social relations became cooler, slower, more distanced, more deliberate and calculating. This was the beginning of those abstractions, both theoretical and practical, of rationality from sociability, of society from individual, of structure from agency, of objectivity from subjectivity, and so on.

Calculation and the 'muting of drives'

The 'civilizing' of the drives involved their 'muting', or, the slowing-down of responses to stimuli and inculcation of bodily decorum through, for example, the elimination or inhibition of habits such as spitting, or eating by cramming food into the mouth with the hands (Elias 1994: 475).[12] The most obviously politically significant of these inhibitions, which was implicated in the process whereby the emergent state gained a monopoly of the means of violence, was the prohibition on responding immediately and violently to provocation. However, what we are mainly concerned with here is the muting of drives involved in, and nurtured by, the need to think reflexively and to calculate costs and benefits before acting. This need was impelled by the increasing salience of the unprecedented (the absence of the expected, the presence of the unexpected) in the face of which individuals were forced to stop and think, rather than to react in an habitual manner. Yet this new calculating reflexivity was not yet the atomized rationality which came to have canonical status in the works of Descartes (in which rationality was conceptualized as abstract and disembodied) and Hobbes (in which it was conceptualized as atomized and calculating).[13] Rationality remained multidimensional, or, more accurately, human faculties and dispositions had not yet been fragmented in the way assumed in the fully modern world. Norbert Elias is insistent on this point, stating that it was not the elimination but the more even control of affect which was in question (Elias 1994: 186). So, for the moment, rationality remained enriched by the other human faculties.[14] However, it was becoming individualized or 'psychologized' as kinesthetic rationality proved its insufficiency in the face of a fragmenting world, a practically-adequate understanding of whose connectedness now needed to take on a theoretical form.

While pre-civilized behaviour had been, from a modern point of view, emotionally undisciplined or 'unpacified', and therefore potentially explosive and unpredictable, it was embedded in slowly changing repertoires of practices which, as artisanal practices, were highly skilled but which did not involve encounter with the unprecedented. In this sense, these practices engendered kinesthetic rather than reflexive conformity to cultural requirements. As noted before, kinesthetic rationality was attained through the imitation of sensuously-present examples of making and repertoires of practices were passed on from one generation to another with minimal change. It was the rationality of the 'practice' theorized by Bourdieu (1992). What was in place was a combination of emotional 'disorder' and practical-functional predictability. In this sense, the pre-civilized world was a place of sensuously present, speaking social relations and of kinesthetically known individualized but manifestly co-operative working practices. It was in this sense worldly (durable and intelligible), but, for almost everybody, worldliness was constraining rather than enabling; it constituted a very narrow range of practices which left the human potentials for praxis and natality underdeveloped.

Differentiation and relative determinacy

The civilizing process instituted a new combination of relative, worldly determinacy (constituted by successful pacification of aristocrats and of everyday life) and unprecedented cultural innovation (released by the increasing mobility and productivity engendered by long-distance trade).[15] Both constituted and required for their reproduction unprecedented forms of individual self-discipline of the kind described briefly above. It is important to think of this in class terms. The self-discipline involved in pacification as the inhibition of immediate violent response to provocation was to be imposed on everyone, whereas the self-discipline required for the cultivation of *sensus communis* was acquired largely by bourgeois subjects. Both were important, although I shall be concerned here with the latter more than the former.

The change from emotionally explosive and culturally repetitive practices to emotionally cooler (but not yet unsociable) and culturally innovative practices was enabled by the pacification of social relations engendered by absolutism's emergent monopoly of physical force, which was, in its turn, enabled by developments in the 'mode of production', or, to express the matter more accurately, there was a dialectical, internal relationship between these processes and practices. What was in question was a kind of spiralling, dialectical movement which Elias refers to as 'figurational change' (1994: 184). The state's emergent monopoly of physical force proceeded where redundant warrior-aristocrats found alternative and desirable occupations as commercial landowners, administrators or courtiers. As this monopoly of physical force became more effective, it rendered individual violence both unnecessary and extremely foolhardy, thereby contributing to the conditions needed for 'commodious living', therefore nurturing the new commerce which in turn 'fed' the absolutist state, and so on.

On the one hand, the emergent civilization was emotionally and cognitively demanding; it required unprecedented control of affects, as well as new forms of individualized mental functioning. Doing the right thing now required emotional self-control and, moreover, could not be determined in formulaic or commonsense terms, but required the exercise of hindsight and foresight, the ability to make judgements under novel and increasingly complex conditions. On the other hand, state-engendered order freed individual energies for the development of the novel psychic abilities needed to respond effectively to these novel demands.

Psychologization as psychic differentiation

Civilization was (in the beginning) a process of transition from a warrior to a courtly ethos and social structure; from physical combat to conversation; from martial fervour, impulse and bravery to caution and calculation, self-control and foresight (Elias 1994: 497). Warriors-turned-courtiers were required to relate to an ever-growing number of others in new ways and, in the process, were 'becoming more complex, and internally split in a quite specific way' (Elias 1994: 477). This internal splitting marked the emergence of the psychic dimension of relative autonomy as the ability to take a distance from the self for the purposes of self-knowledge and self-making. Such self-discipline was becoming an imperative for those who needed to maintain a position at court. It was a matter, not only of 'self-examination', but of imagining the 'selves' of others whose actions and reactions needed to be understood and anticipated in ways which would render foresight happily consequential. In this case, imagination was put at the service of understanding others for the purposes of their more successful manipulation; self-knowledge and self-making were oriented only to social success; they were manifestations of agonism (self-display and competitiveness) and ego-needs rather than of public-spiritedness.

What is in question is a top-down, long-term process of change the temporary resting place of which was the apparently (relatively) autonomous, introspective bourgeois subject (Elias 1994: 203). The generalization of the courtly model of self-discipline beyond the nobility required a multiplicity of interconnected developments, including increasing differentiation and improvement in living standards of broad sections of the population. These are the developments described by Marx in terms of early capitalist relations constituted by the formal subsumption of labour under capital.[16] Having noted the importance of large-scale structural changes, as manifested in pacification and differentiation, and of the 'space' that this afforded for the cultivation of new, strongly individuated, self-conscious practices, and for a new kind of attentiveness to an increasingly complex world, let us now consider the class-specific public-spiritedness constituted by hybrid bourgeois capitalism, a capitalism on the cusp of labour's real subsumption under capital.

II The emergence of bourgeois *sensus communis*

The emergent bourgeois world was constituted by a culturally unprecedented mode of differentiation whereby necessary, internally related processes and practices were becoming separated both spatially and temporally. This was the beginning (but only the beginning) of a condition which would eventually require scientific rather than artisanal expertise for the reproduction of everyday life.[17] At the beginning, though, it nurtured, rather than starved, the human potentials of bourgeois subjects. Unfortunately, this nurturing was at the cost of other social classes, as noted before, since, as it constituted a new (partly theoretical) world at the fingertips of bourgeois capitalists, it removed a world from the fingertips of peasants and artisans (Clark 1995; Hill 1967). In doing so, it opened up the possibility of a new, expansive, post-traditional form of worldliness which its participants conceived of (in unworldly terms) as universal.

During the period in question, the differentiation of spheres was becoming experientially significant for the emergent bourgeois class but it was doing so in a way that did not as yet atrophy worldliness. While common sense was under serious assault, change was sufficiently slow and mediations were sufficiently concrete and experiential to enable the constitution of a bourgeois *sensus communis*. *Sensus communis*, a kind of critical, self-conscious, yet shared orientation to and knowledgeability of the shared world, was a new and challenging mode of intelligibility enabled and necessitated as the everyday world was coming to lose its self-evidence. It was enabled through a combination of a novel kind of reading in private and novel forms of public association, which combination effected the acquisition of theoretical knowledge in a way that enabled it to retain a worldly character. (I shall return to this point later.)

The cultural survivals which rendered bourgeois capitalism hybrid consisted in the continuing importance of sociability as expressed in the necessity and prevalence of face-to-face and (mostly) personal social relations.[18] The necessary relationality of human life was experienced directly, through the sensuous and speaking presence of other humans. However, these face-to-face relations were coming to be differentiated in terms of their location in public or private spheres; family, 'culture' and 'economy' in the private sphere; state in the public sphere. Mediating the two was the bourgeois public sphere; the sphere in which relatively autonomous subjects met and deliberated in a way which constituted a 'public opinion' sufficiently confident to hold the state to account (Habermas 1992a: 236–50).[19]

Bourgeois private life: intimacy with a public face

Bourgeois private life began in the intimacy of the bourgeois house, which was a place in which a non-privative form of privacy could be enjoyed. A non-privative form of privacy is a privacy to which one withdraws in order to prepare for 'seeing and hearing others', for 'being seen and being heard by them' (Arendt 1958: 58). It was because the intimacy enjoyed in the bourgeois household had this non-privative character that it enhanced, rather than undermined, the relative autonomy of the bourgeois, and could be a source of public-spiritedness.[20]

The house was, for the moment, the kind of property which Arendt considers to be indispensable for citizenship (1958: 58–67). It was a place into which the family could withdraw as a unit, but within it were dedicated rooms into which individual family members could further withdraw for the practice of silent solitary reading (Ariès 1965: 390–403; Davidoff and Hall 1987: ch. 8). This was necessary both for self-cultivation and for the development of a theoretical understanding of the emergent totality; the world as experienced (the everyday world) and the world beyond experience which was coming to be needed for the reproduction of the world experienced. Privacy and silent solitary reading were essential for the nurturance of the new kinds of mental capacities needed for attainment of such theoretical understanding.

As an activity which imposes strenuous disciplinary demands on the individual, particularly at the learning stage, reading served to cultivate self-discipline in the process of cultivating a sense of self. The practice of reading requires the 'muting of drives', or, to anticipate a little, it is secondary process functioning in action.[21] This was particularly the case where reading was active and educational, oriented to self-improvement through the critical absorption of philosophy and literature, of moral weeklies and critical journals. Moreover, the content of this material also nurtured a form of imagination conducive to worldliness. It was, in addition to the cultural products of concert-halls, theatres and museums, the vehicle whereby bourgeois individuals developed a subjectivity marked by introspection and self-consciousness. This introspectivity was balanced by a world-oriented interest in the theoretical literature which, at that time and given the level of the intellectual division of labour, remained accessible to educated non-specialists (Brewer 1997; Gay 1998; Heyer 1988; Porter 2000; Williams 1961).

Bourgeois subjectivity was nurtured in the specific family form of the intimate oedipal family. This family instituted 'permanent intimacy' as against older forms of communality found in the extended and directly productive family. Relations between parents and children were becoming intimate in the sense that they were drained of their productive-functional character so that they became at once more private and individualized and more emotionally charged. In ways to be explored later, these relations cultivated in the small child the psychic dispositions needed to prepare him (but also, to a degree, her) for effective participation in the adult bourgeois world. This participation was a matter of active rather than passive conformity. It was secured by individual self-discipline rather than habituation. Self-discipline requires that the individual not merely do the right thing, but do it for the right reasons. Doing the right thing requires reflexiveness because the right thing is no longer embodied in routinized practices. In chapter four, we will see how the bourgeois family engendered the dispositions which would enable the maturing adult to adapt to these very challenging cultural requirements in a manner compatible with the subject's well-being.

The privatization of the bourgeois family, as well as the emphasis on self-cultivation, held the potential for worldlessness, but, for the moment, this was not actualized (Ariès 1965: 390–8).[22] Self-cultivation was not yet an end in itself, since the practice of self-cultivation in private was experientially related to the practice of self-presentation in public. Moreover, self-presentation in public came to have a distinctively and increasingly political character. This is the dialectic of 'inwardness and publicness' which sustained a form of subjectivity not yet driven into subjectivism (Habermas 1992b: 426).[23] Members of the intimate bourgeois family housed in an individuated habitat conducive to the nurturing of self-reflexivity moved out of that habitat on a daily basis into a forum of politicized sociability.

The bourgeois public sphere

The bourgeois public sphere was a sociable, rather than formal, public sphere in which face-to-face deliberation about matters of shared interest was an important activity. This was the kind of speech-mediated communication advocated by Arendt as the bearer of natality; a mode which was also necessary to balance the possibly 'deworlding' effects of that print comunication which was necessary for cultivation of the theoretical intelligence needed to comprehend the new cultural complexity.

This novel institution mediated between 'society', made up of 'private', directly-interacting individuals, and the newly depersonalized state, i.e. the state which was coming to encompass an impersonal apparatus of professionalized, bureaucratized practices which would persist behind and beyond monarchical succession.[24] As the state apparatus began to assume an independence from the personal sphere of the monarch, the courtly society began to drift towards the town, where it would influence the emergent bourgeoisie. What might be described as the bourgeoisie's organic intellectuals acquired the art of critical, rational public debate through its contact with the courtly world. It was when the court lost its central position in the public sphere that 'reason' could 'shed its dependence on the authority of the aristocratic noble hosts' and 'acquire that autonomy that turns conversation into criticism and *bons mots* into arguments' (Habermas 1992a: 31).[25]

At this point, with the end of its tutelage, the bourgeoisie could begin to assert itself against both monarch and aristocracy through the emergent institution of the public sphere. This was a novel place in which individuals who had cultivated their intellect in the private sphere came together to discuss matters of shared importance and to form a 'public opinion' which would be heard and responded to by the state (Habermas 1992a: 25–6). In contrast to the 'public opinion' elicited by opinion poll surveys, this was a public opinion which emerged out of the deliberations of worldly subjects; a public opinion, therefore, which was an expression of anaclitic, rather than economic, rationality; a rationality constituted by a balance of the private educational reading just discussed, and the daily practice of public face-to-face discussion. It was the latter which ensured that bourgeois intimacy and solitariness would not degenerate into subjectivism. So, bourgeois rationality was not yet 'cleansed' of sociability and opinion was not yet expressed as an apparently unmediated individual preference shaped by apparently unmediated individual interests. It was, rather, an opinion which manifested that sociable and political form of imagination which Arendt conceives of as natality.

At the same time, this opinion, being significantly concerned with relations between the emergent economic sphere which, increasingly engaged in production for exchange and, therefore, in the development of formal contractual relations between capitalists and labourers, had a decidedly class character (Habermas 1992a: 27). However, the 'freedom' of the emergent economic sphere remained at this time more aspirational and theoretical than actual. The task of persuading monarchy and aristocracy that this sphere practically should be free was an important part of the 'universalist' public sphere. So there was a tension (which would quickly become a contradiction) between the class character of the bourgeois public sphere and bourgeois self-interpretation as representative of humanity as such. For the moment, individual bourgeois entered the public sphere in the dual guise of bourgeois 'man' and universal 'citizen'; but 'citizen' was not yet the misleading and inappropriate labelling of humans who were necessarily self-interested rather than public-spirited. This would not become the case until industrialization had begun to subsume the world under commodity fetishism, thereby rendering even the class-specific public-spiritedness of the bourgeois impossible (Arendt 1973b: ch. 5).

Relatively autonomous subjects were subjects constituted by a culture which enabled withdrawal into privacy without at the same time allowing total escape from sociability.[26] Given this balance and the very important matter of the power endowed by ownership of the means of production, bourgeois (male) subjects could experience themselves as self-determining while at the same time remaining (necessarily) sociable. The appearance of self-determination was partly authentic and partly inauthentic.[27] It was authentic in the sense that it constituted a genuine form of psychic strength which enabled individual subjects to function in a relatively autonomous way. Such subjects did, in fact, participate in a culturally-enabled self-conscious practice of self-constitution which, in sociological terms, was unprecedented. It was inauthentic insofar as subjects thus constituted misrecognized their condition as solely self-generated, or insofar as they took their autonomy to be absolute rather than relative to the historico-cultural. Even where this illusion of absolute autonomy pertained, it was not expressed in atomism, since its potentially debilitating effects were counteracted by the unavoidable experience of sociability. Here the contradiction between the real nature of autonomy and the individual's interpretation of that nature did not yield atomism because that atomism could not yet be lived. The result was a worldly form of strongly individuated subjectivity.

As relatively autonomous subjects constituted by an experience of differentiation which was both (for the moment and on the whole) non-contradictory and predominantly personal in its (experienced) mediations, bourgeois subjects moved without any abrupt change of orientation from the private to the public and back again.[28] Or, we might say that much of the reality of internal relations between the different spheres was experienced also in the world's appearances. This was possible because the role of impersonal mediations was minimal – monetization not yet universalized through effective capitalization, modes of transport and communication not yet mechanized.[29] Not only were differentiations not abstract (because mediations remained largely personal), but change proceeded at a pace which (for bourgeois, although not for peasants and artisans) could be experienced in a worldly way. In social terms, we may say that 'systematicity' was not yet in place, or, to adapt Lockwood's (1964) distinction, social integration was also system integration. In cognitive terms, we can say that differentiation had not yet come to constitute an unbridgeable gap between the totality and its parts.

In this case, the constitution of a specific kind of public-spiritedness, or, of a collective political actor of the kind required to act on and in the world with self-awareness and commitment to the collective goal (bourgeois self-assertion – expressed as the demand for universal human emancipation – against monarchy and aristocracy) required a combination of 'private' and 'public' institutions having mutually reinforcing effects. That is to say, the different spheres within which the bourgeois subject acted (the intimate or familial, the economic, the 'cultural', the public) constituted a relatively stable and predictable (but not wholly predictable) form of appearances, not yet overwhelmed by systematicity or contradiction. By means of this unprecedented combination, bourgeois subjects could experience themselves as coherent, originary subjects without lurching into atomism. Expressed otherwise, they could experience autonomy while simultaneously living interdependence.

III Relative autonomy and the differentiated psyche

In the final section of this chapter, I begin to discuss the specifically psychic dimensions of this experience of reality in terms of Freud's late model of psychic differentiation; a model which will enable us to theorize the psychic splitting needed for the 'taming of drives' associated with self-discipline, and with the experience of a 'bounded' strongly individuated psyche. I shall do so under the assumption that the self-discipline imposed on emergent bourgeois subjects served to expand individual potentials in ways which were gratifying for the individual as well as useful for the culture.

When Elias speaks of civilization as a matter of 'muting' the drives, he is speaking of an historico-cultural process that 'binds' or disciplines psychic energy, or, that cultivates in the emergent subject the disposition to stop and think before acting or reacting. Expressed otherwise, he is referring to the possibility and necessity of delayed gratification. Subjects on whom the state has effectively placed its disciplining hand cannot give immediate expression to feelings of pain or outrage but must wait for the state to act on their behalf. In this instance the muting of drives can take place behaviouristically, or, it can be induced through simple stimulus/response mechanisms of habituation. Similarly with the discipline required for unskilled labour in the factory. However, the discipline in which we are interested in this chapter is self-discipline, or a discipline involving individuals' direct attentiveness and mental effort. This is the kind of discipline conducive to the development of the mental attributes needed for participating in a *sensus communis*, and it is no small part of the interest of Freudian psychoanalysis that it provides us with the resources for understanding both the difficulties and the satisfactions which such attentiveness and effort involve. In understanding these, we are understanding the centrality of the split psyche to the cultivation of relative autonomy.

The differentiated psyche with which I am concerned is the psyche of a subject whose drives have been 'tamed' through early parental care of the kind provided by the hybrid bourgeois family. This is the psyche composed of three agencies – the id, the ego and the superego – among which different quantities and qualities of psychic energy are distributed (Freud 1984e). It is more useful to think of the three agencies as related and contradictory dispositions or tendencies to behave in certain ways, expressed in (and constituted by) relations and practices, rather than as intrapsychic 'spaces' (Lichtman 1982: ch. 6; Schafer 1968). As I shall understand these, the tendencies associated with id and superego are worldless; those associated with the ego are worldly. The id connotes worldlessness in the very strong sense that it has no awareness of a world apart from its own existence. The superego is worldless in the sense that, as the product of repression, it takes a harsh, judgemental stance towards subjects who therefore become either harshly judgemental themselves or passively adaptable to the world.[30]

The id is the oldest part of the psyche, present in the infant from the beginning and conceptualized by Freud as a chaotic, unorganized cauldron of free psychic energy seeking instant release through the gratification of two kinds of drives: ego and sex drives, the former concerned with individual reproduction, the latter with group reproduction. The id has no conception of time or space or of logic. To be governed by the id is to be governed by an uneducated pleasure principle, or by primary process functioning, and therefore to be doomed to a foolhardy (because normally unachievable or, if achievable, destructive) quest for speedy gratification. This is the fate from which the emergent subject is rescued by the emergent ego, formed through the infant's dawning realization of the existence of an external, independent world. The ego protects the id from its own self-destructiveness, but, not only that, it enables the subject to achieve the best possible balance between id gratification and the harsh cultural demands conveyed by the superego (Freud 1985a: 336–9). As the harsh and judgemental source of repression, superego was during the bourgeois period of capitalism overruled by the ego.

In the mature subject (the reflexive 'psychologized' subject of whom Elias and Habermas speak) the ego is in command so that the subject has become capable of secondary process functioning, that is, of cathecting (investing with psychic energy) objects in the world in a self-reflexive, sustained and world-engaging fashion. What this means is that the subject has achieved a state of being which enables the ego to resist both unsatisfiable id demands and overly harsh superego demands. Subjectivation has been effected more by sublimation (a compensatory form of instinctual renunciation) than by repression (uncompensated instinctual renunciation) (Freud 1984e; 1984g). For reasons to be explored further in chapter four, it is this combination of secondary process functioning and sublimation that secures a rationality that is anaclitic rather than cold, abstract or narcissistic.

The constitution of this form of subjectivity is a labour-intensive undertaking whose successful outcome cannot be guaranteed and whose maintenance, where successfully initiated, needs constant cultural replenishment. The process of emergence involves a painful separation from a mother whose continuous intimate ministrations have provided the small child with a secure and interesting world. This separation is a matter of the resolution of the oedipal complex, or, the child's acceptance of this separation, along with its recognition that the mother 'belongs' to the father rather than to itself. Acceptance is rendered less painful (for the boy) through a compensatory identification with the father and the promise of future love from a mother-like object.[31] Identification is here a matter of internalizing admired characteristics of the father and it is undertaken under the dual compulsions of love (a wish to please parents) and fear (of punishment from parents), though where bourgeois subjectivity is concerned love is the predominant motivation, as I hope to make clear (Freud 1977a: 144–6).[32]

As understood in 'The dissection of the psychical personality' (Freud 1973a), this mode of identification involves the internalization of 'good objects', meaning the dispositions and capacities which will constitute a psychically strong subject, or, a subject whose ego is in command.[33] Internalization is in this sense a strongly affect-laden 'interactive' process invoked by a sensuously-presenced experience of parenting; an experience in which the emergent subject plays an active part, on the one hand through the activity drive, on the other through resistance to the demands of a civilized culture, in particular, the demands to cultivate bodily decorum and to become literate. Over time, where all goes well, the latter becomes transmuted into a conformity which is active and reflexive. Here subjectivation involves a dialectical rather than a one-way linear relationship between emergent subject and cultural representatives; one whereby eventually the child manages to reconcile its need for gratification with specific cultural requirements.

It is important to note that for the bourgeois this reconciliation did not require the major sacrifice of gratification which would be demanded of capitalist subjects and which coloured Freud's conception of subjectivation. Contrary to Freud's rather grim depiction of the painful and conflict-ridden character of the emergent understanding of 'otherness' on the part of the infant, there is an abundance of evidence that infants are, in fact, predisposed to be interested in their surroundings almost from the beginning of life. They display zestful curiosity about objects (human and non-human) as they come into view and reach out to grasp them (Benjamin 1990: ch. 1; Schachtel 1963: ch. 2).[34] While Freud is not unaware of this dimension of infant experience, he tends to neglect it in his theorization of emergent subjectivity. We have good reason to believe that the experiences of bourgeois infants were particularly rich and satisfying (in comparison with what went before and what would come after), and that the potential for active engagement with the world would have been strongly nurtured by bourgeois parents. This will be discussed further in chapter four.

The bourgeois subject was the subject with a strongly 'organized' and worldly ego. That is to say, cultural appearances afforded a reality principle which provided unprecedented opportunities for the gratification of the activity drive through the emergent diversity of practices and through the opportunities afforded for a sociability which had enjoyable agonistic (expressive and competitive) but also public-spirited elements. I follow Schachtel and Arendt, and indeed Marx, in considering these gratifications to be of importance in themselves, and not just substitutes for more intensely desired immediate sexual gratifications, although undoubtedly, given the imposition of 'civilizing' disciplines on the emergent bourgeois subject, these more directly bodily gratifications would have been strongly constrained, as in, for example, learning to read. Much was demanded but much was also given. It was because of this balance that anaclitic attachment was effected and that anaclitic rationality in the mode of *sensus communis* was a possibility. That this novel form of rationality was also considered necessary (due to the cognitively challenging character of the emergent capitalist world) is clear from the increasing importance and length of periods of formal education (Stone 1979: 273–4).[35]

Conclusion

In this chapter, I have returned to capitalism's bourgeois past to seek an example of public-spiritedness. In doing so, I have sought to understand the ways in which the differentiations of emergent European civilization effected a particular kind of psychologization involving the constitution of the differentiated (and apparently bounded) psyches of relatively autonomous subjects. As we have seen, this psychologization was related to a differentiation of functions which, on the one hand, allocated the function of pacification to the emergent absolutist state, thereby removing from the individual the need for physical, violent self-defence and demanding of the individual the self-control which this implies, and which, on the other hand, through the development of capitalism, demanded that the world become known in a new reflexive or theoretical manner. Both of these involved the 'muting of drives' so that, for one thing, individuals no longer erupted in explosive, strongly emotional behaviour and, for another, they were prepared to stop and think in the face of the unexpected; dispositions and capabilities which were becoming essential as the unexpected was now more frequently to be expected as absent causes became more salient in the mundane world. Common sense, as handed-down, kinesthetic, taken-for-granted knowledge, was becoming inadequate either to cultural reproduction or to the flourishing of individual subjects. Hence the emergence of relatively detached, calculating subjects; of self-disciplined, reflexive subjects capable of delayed gratification but not yet experiencing themselves as completely self-made or self-sufficient; subjects capable of 'control of affects', not of 'affective neutrality' or cold rationality. Affective neutrality (what I describe as the splitting of rationality and sociability) was not yet possible because the everyday experience of personal interdependence remained unavoidable. These were worldly subjects, in the sense that they were capable of active and confident engagement with external reality, but, more than this, as bourgeois, they engaged in a public-spirited, anaclitically rational way with that reality.

We have seen that the new intellectual competences being acquired by bourgeois subjects encompassed the ability to withdraw psychically from the self, or, to take a mental step back from self for the purpose of self-examination. This is the significance of the id–ego differentiation in Freud's theory of the split psyche. The significance of the superego is that cultural prohibitions had been 'internalized' so as to effect a form of disciplining which involved 'conscience'. However, for reasons that will be explored more fully in chapter four, the worldlessness of superego was mitigated by the worldliness of ego. These were the psychic conditions of possibility (the ego-governed split psyche) for the relative autonomy which marked the emergent bourgeois subject. In chapter four we will come to understand the significance of personally-authoritative, sensuously-present parenting in ensuring that this relative autonomy was anaclitic rather than atomistic or narcissistic in character. These relations formed a worldly world for emergent subjects; a world which, while placing heavy demands on these subjects, did so in a way that nurtured activity and imagination of a relatively autonomous kind. The result was a novel balance of sociability and individuality (of attachment/detachment) which produced a novel kind of social strength, a social strength consisting in social bonds not based on kinship and politicized through practices in a new kind of public sphere. Capitalism had arrived but, for the moment, the culture (for the bourgeoisie) remained a parenting culture; a parenting culture, moreover, which enabled individual directly-experienced parenting of a personally authoritative kind. The significance of this matter will be discussed in chapter four.

4 Parenting and the constitution of bourgeois *sensus communis*

Bourgeois subjects were relatively autonomous subjects who were also anaclitically rational. They were relatively autonomous in that they were capable of self-direction and were afforded the space for consequential individualized activity. They were anaclitically rational in that they were guided by a multidimensional rationality that was relational rather than atomized; a rationality that was 'between' as well as 'within' subjects. This combination of autonomy and sociability was the result of a culture which maintained a balance between withdrawal and attachment. Note here that withdrawal and attachment have both physical and psychic referents. When used for the purpose of silent, solitary reading, the physical withdrawal of individual bourgeois enabled by the privatized bourgeois house nurtured a kind of psychic withdrawal constitutive of introspectivity. At the same time, this withdrawal had a public dimension, as we have seen. It was withdrawal as preparation for sociable and/or public engagement. Where the engagement was for public purposes, it needed the theoretical education for world-reflexivity which the concept of *sensus communis* connotes. Here self-direction and self-engagement were internally related to self-presentation (possibly for public purposes) in public. Preoccupation with self was here worldly (anaclitic) rather than worldless (narcissistic).

What rendered bourgeois rationality worldly was the continuing functional necessity of sociability, which meant that interdependence was experienced directly and personally. What enabled the replacement of common sense by *sensus communis* were the differentiations which enabled new, strongly individuated and intimate familial relations, together with the related opportunity to withdraw into solitariness so as to engage in silent reading. What prepared individuals for the disciplines of such withdrawal was the new intimacy which consisted in a prolonged period of parental attentiveness to the emergent subject. This laid the psychic groundwork for engaging fairly happily in the difficult tasks of learning to read and write; tasks which require considerable, sustained self-discipline because they are forms of activity which do not yield the immediate gratifications of more practical and dramatic explorations of the world in which small children happily engage. Having learned to read and write, the subject was in a position to absorb, on the one hand, the new theoretical knowledge necessitated by 'civilizing' differentiations (i.e. abstract, impersonally-mediated differentiations involving necessary relations at a distance, or absent causes), and, on the other, the humanistic texts intended for the cultivation of self. Both forms of reading were necessary but not sufficient to nurture a *sensus communis*. What rendered them sufficient was the sociability which remained imperative. Even as the civilizing processes of which Elias speaks took on a strong bourgeois character, the 'human use of human beings' (Wiener 1989) had not yet replaced the human need of human beings. Human needs continued to be satisfied through the sensuous speaking presence of face-to-face social relations. In short, the particular bourgeois combination of presencing and withdrawal was what enabled a novel psychic balance of attachment/detachment constitutive of individualized consequential activity not yet reduced to atomism. However, the potential for atomism was already present in the privatization of the bourgeois individualized household and in individualized ownership of a new kind of property, capital.

Having set out my understanding of hybrid bourgeois worldliness as that of a 'civilization', that is, of a specific kind of reality in which relations at a distance are constitutive, or, a kind of necessary absent 'cause' of the reproduction of everyday life, and having explored the institutional supports needed for the constitution of *sensus communis*, I am now going to discuss this *sensus communis* as a kind of emergent, individuated mindfulness cultivated with the help of parental relations whose pattern of responsiveness to infants' wishes was such as to enforce on those infants the need to think. This need was generated by the absence of anticipated comforts or the presence of unanticipated discomforts; a need which was manifest in an infant reality-testing which laid the basis for reflexivity or secondary process functioning. Insofar as infant need was driven by the absence of the expected, the infant began to think about a reality which was capable of resisting it. It began to engage actively with happenings whose reliable occurrence was essential to the infant's feeling of well-being. In this case, reality-testing was a matter bound up with the infant's most imperatively-felt needs, which were necessarily a matter of both ego and sex interests, since these interests are, in their original state, fused rather than separate.[1] It was also, however, a matter of the activity drive. These are crucial points, as will be seen.

In discussing the emergence of individual capacities for secondary process functioning, I shall be stressing the centrality of the pre-oedipal stage of child development to this outcome.[2] Freud's best-known version of the oedipal complex and its resolution neglects the pre-oedipal phase of child nurturing and seems to assume as a necessity for adequate adult rational functioning that the (male) child be rescued from regressive maternal engulfment. Or, it assumes a gendered division of labour between the father as bearer of masculinity, activity and rationality and the mother as bearer of femininity, passivity and affect. This is what Jessica Benjamin terms the 'oedipal riddle' (1990: ch. 4). Her discussion of this riddle provides important resources, including an insistence of the centrality of the pre-oedipal experience, for understanding the parental relations needed for public-spiritedness.

The connection with citizenship here is that I am theorizing the reflexive anaclitic rationality of *sensus communis* as sublimated secondary process functioning; a functioning which I take to refer to the individualized 'mindfulness' which civilizing psychologizing differentiations made sociologically significant for the first time.[3] Sublimation here connotes both activity and sociability. My argument is that where drives are sublimated, secondary process functioning will be compatible with anaclitic rationality. Where they are repressed, secondary process functioning will involve 'abstract', disengaged or 'cold' rationality. The possibilities of repression or sublimation are given in the extra-familial context.

This chapter comprises two sections. In the first section I elaborate on the nature of bourgeois *sensus communis* in terms of Freud's account of the contrast between first, primary and secondary process functioning and, second, two possible fates of the drives: repression and sublimation. The purpose is to show that the constitution of *sensus communis* involved the kind of psychic development connoted by sublimated secondary process functioning. Having dealt with this matter, in the second part of the chapter I focus on the question of parental relations, making the argument that the pre-oedipal process of reality-testing is crucial for the transition from primary to secondary process functioning and for the child's ability to attain the potential for sublimatory rather than repressive adaptation to cultural requirements. What this means is that the bourgeois child's emergence out of maternal dependence was not marked by a psychically violent wrenching away from the mother, as some accounts of the resolution of the oedipal complex would have it. Both parents were tender towards the child, so we do not find the coldly rational father confronting an affect-saturated mother from whose arms he must rescue the male child (i.e. the child who was expected to engage successfully with the world beyond the family).

I Sublimated secondary process functioning

As noted before, I am following Ricoeur (1970) in interpreting Freud as an 'energetic-hermeneuticist' who provides the groundwork for understanding how culture enters into the individual human organism. Having opened up the topic of psychic differentiation in the concluding section of chapter three, I shall now begin to elaborate on the theme of rationality. This elaboration begins here with a consideration of the drives and their vicissitudes. We have seen in chapter one that the drives are potentials and needs coming from the individual, potentials which are shaped by culture's representatives. The drives with which I am concerned in this study are the activity (zestful exploration of the world), ego (need for self-reproduction) and sex (need for attachment to others or species-reproduction) drives. The representatives of disciplining cultures were oriented to the 'muting of drives' as we noted in chapter three, this being a matter of binding psychic energy so that it moves more slowly and more purposefully than before. This involved the taming, but not crushing, of idness via the emergence of ego and superego; a taming which is understandable as the ability to delay gratification. By idness I mean the dispositions of newborns in a world which is not yet present to them as a separate, external reality. Infants are in an unworldly condition marked by the experience of a wholly unintelligible world which has yet to demonstrate its sociability. Newborn dispositions include the quest for total and immediate gratification in the absence of knowledge of what might constitute its sources. This absence of knowledge is also an absence of understanding that the world exists independently of the infant and can, in fact, resist its demands. Coming to an understanding of this fact is a matter of slowing down the movement of energy so that the infant takes time to think about its appetite and the real possibilities of gratification in the world. In taking time to think, the infant is learning to tolerate delay between experience of a need and its satisfaction. While all cultures impose some form of delayed gratification on subjects, the specifically civilized or disciplined ability to tolerate delay has been crucial to the reproduction of capitalist totalities as well as for the functioning of relatively autonomous subjects.

A comprehensive understanding of the sources of bourgeois public-spiritedness demands attentiveness, not only to sexual and ego drives, as stressed by Freud, but also to the activity drive. At the beginning of human life, we find these three drives present in an undifferentiated state. As the first important activity in which the infant engages, reaching out for the breast involves all three (Schachtel 1963: ch. 2). So, in the infant, sexual, ego and activity drives, therefore love and gratification, are fused. This means that the primary carers of infants are also their earliest 'sexual objects' (Freud 1984a: 80–1; 1984d: 123). In intimate hybrid bourgeois families, attachment to such 'sexual objects' would have been intense and, in fact, Freud considers that 'the fear of loss of love is greater than the fear of punishment' (1984a: 97).[4] I take the statement to be true for the bourgeois family whose relations were marked by a novel combination of intimacy, affection and longevity which rendered its parenting 'good enough' to shape relatively autonomous adults. It was this combination of intimacy, affection and longevity which would render love so important and the thought of its loss so fearful. Retention of parental love would have been a crucial consideration in the formation of emergent bourgeois subjects.

At the same time, the opening up of the bourgeois world through the remarkable cultural innovations which Habermas discusses yielded significant gratifications beyond those connoted by the Freudian drives; gratifications which, along with the enjoyment of affectionate intimate parental relations, would compensate for the pain inflicted and the self-control demanded by the disciplines of a civilizing culture. In this way the experience of subjectivation was less difficult than it would subsequently become. Here again, Freud's account must be historicized if it is not to be a source of misunderstanding. Where historicized, that account enables us to understand not only bourgeois worldliness but also the psychic effects of its post-bourgeois capitalist dissolution.

Children who have experienced a satisfactory intimate relationship with parents will become capable of fulfilling the demanding tasks required for the development of *sensus communis*. They will be open to the nurturing of the civic virtue whose source is social love. Social love (whose existence signals the presence of anaclitic rationality) is a derivative of the love one feels for the mother who feeds and the father who protects and for the 'succession of substitutes who take their place' (Freud 1984a: 81, 84). It involves a libido which is desexualized through the successful resolution of the oedipal complex. The emergence of desexualized libido depends on the indeterminacy of the sexual drive in terms of changes of pressure, aim and object, an indeterminacy which leaves scope for the culturally constituted parental shaping of these drives (Freud 1984b). Because of this indeterminacy, these drives are capable of functions far removed from what Freud conceives of as their original purposes. Desexualization involves the redirection towards non-sexual objects of energy or libido deriving from the sexual drives. While Freud (1985a) considers this desexualized energy to be what fuels the work of civilization in a way which necessarily engenders suffering and frustration for individuals, it is important to correct his unduly bleak judgement by remembering that the infant is well-disposed towards the world at the beginning and remains so, so long as the world does not demand too much from it (Schachtel 1963: 5). In particular, the bourgeois infant was the happy beneficiary of new parenting practices which focused on that infant as a source of wonder and interest in its own right. Growing up in a world more affectionate and relaxed than would be its capitalist successor, and surrounded by myriad objects of stimulation and delight, the emergent subject could meet the demands of a 'civilizing' culture without feeling crushed under their weight. Under these circumstances the desexualization of libidinal energy was beneficial to the individual because it constituted the basis for the individual achievement of longer-term and more durable forms of gratification than that enabled by sexuality as narrowly conceived. The name for this more durable and satisfying form of gratification is sublimation, an understanding of which will be enhanced by a discussion of its 'other', namely repression.

Repression: the rule of superego

The fundamental difference between sublimation and repression is that the former involves individual reflexivity and the latter does not. That is to say, the presence of sublimation (in the strong sense in which I wish to use it here) signifies that the ego is in command so that the subject is capable of taking a critical distance from culture's demands. Where repression is in question, adaptation to these demands takes place behind the back of the subject (Freud 1984g). Repression involves the enforcement of culture's requirements upon the individual in a manner which is largely incompatible with the individual's well-being. While repression may be an unavoidable vicissitude of the drives in the sense that some repression seems necessary if the infant is to become human, civilization, in the disciplinary sense used here, has been based up to now almost wholly on repression and has, therefore, been excessively cruel in terms of the sacrifice of gratification which it extracts from its members (Freud 1985a: ch. 5; Marcuse 1987: ch. 4). Sublimation, insofar as it exists, is enjoyed only by a minority.[5] All are not equally repressed, and those who are repressed sense that their unhappiness (of whose repressive sources they are necessarily unaware) is unjust (Freud 1985a: 191–2; Schneider 1975).[6]

In Freud's account, the fate of the drives is related to the organism's need, first, to relieve tension by maintaining a bearable level of energy, and second, to comply with (or evade) cultural demands. In the bourgeois case, drives must be 'muted' in accordance with the needs of a civilizing, disciplining culture. As we have seen, this involves an internalization of cultural rules through the constitution of the superego. However, I am arguing that, for bourgeois, the harshness connoted by the concept of superego was itself diluted by the presence of a benign form of parenting conducive to the formation of a strong ego. For this reason, sublimation was a probable fate of the emergent subject's drives.

We can begin to think about repression in terms of internal and external stimuli. If these are experienced as unwelcome cultural demands, evasion of those coming from outside is possible up to a point, but evasion of those coming from within the organism (demands already internalized) is not. The unavailability of the option to flee leaves the possibility of repression, judgement or condemnation of an impulse which is forbidden by the culture. Repression is midway between condemnation and flight. Repressed items are either items which fail to emerge from the unconscious into consciousness, or which have been pushed down from consciousness into the unconscious. The original or foundational repressions are of incest and patricide, both being, for Freud, direct expressions of the oedipal complex (Freud 1985e).[7] In relation to these two related impulses, it is clear that the individual is in a contradictory situation since gratification of these impulses is almost bound to lead to punishment (whether inflicted by oneself or by the culture) and therefore a simultaneous loss of gratification.[8] If the overall balance is likely to be loss, the forbidden impulse will be repressed. From the individual point of view, repression is the most undesirable fate of the drives since, unlike sublimation, it involves renunciation without compensation and produces painful symptoms whose precise nature need not concern us here (Brennan 1992; Freud 1984g). In terms of the id–ego–superego relationship, it leaves the ego ill-equipped to fulfil its role of rendering the subject's life more tolerable, since its energy is squandered on the task of attempting to maintain repressions which are themselves seeking entry into the conscious mind (Freud 1986: esp. 405). Subjects constituted by repression will tend to be fragile, guilt- and anxiety-ridden subjects whose repressions are likely to erupt in various forms of neurotic behaviour. They will tend to experience cultural relations as punitive rather than nurturing and will be without the resources needed for public-spiritedness.[9] While this will not prevent them from attaining the mental competencies connoted by secondary process functioning (to be discussed below), these subjects will be, in the Arendtian sense, worldless.

Sublimation: the rule of ego

Sublimation is a concept which enables us to theorize a form of subjectivity which is neither atomistic nor oversocialized. As a manifestation of subjects' ability to love socially, sublimation is, unlike repression, an eminently worldly fate for human drives (Freud 1985a: 267–71, esp. 268, n. 1). It is worldly in the sense not only that it connotes sociable attachments, but that it provides maximum satisfaction of the activity drive. Whereas repression involves the victory of superego over ego (ego depletion and uncompensated sacrifice of drive gratification), sublimation is an ego-strengthening vicissitude of the drives which can afford intense satisfaction to individual subjects while at the same time advancing the work of culture. In contrast with repression, which is an evasive, reality-avoiding tactic bound to end in frustration, sublimation involves the acknowledgement of reality, or, the representation in the mind of what is real, even if it is 'disagreeable' (Freud 1984c: 37). Further, this representation of reality is for the purposes of active engagement with a reality which, while presently less than satisfactory, has in the past been responsive to one's wishes; thus there is a point to such engagement. In fact, sublimation is nurtured where the world has not been experienced as a radical and indifferent 'otherness', or, where there is not a sharp distinction between 'subject' and 'object'. This kind of indifferent otherness was absent from the immediately experienced world of the bourgeois subject, for whom the world had shown early concern through the attentiveness of the bourgeois family (on which more below). It had shown its concern through attentiveness, not only to the sex and ego drives, but also to the activity drive.

Thus sublimation is a worldly individual condition in that it involves a strongly relational experience of the world; one marked by recognition of the significance of other humans to one's own well-being.[10] Unlike Ricoeur, who associates sublimation with superego (1970: 489) and Róheim, for whom it is associated with id (see Marcuse 1987: 208–9), I understand sublimation in terms of the ego which (it is worth repeating) is here associated with voluntary self-discipline.[11] I judge that the sublimation of the bourgeois subject was governed neither by id nor by superego. It could not have been governed by id because of the muting of drives effected by civilizing differentiations, and, for reasons which I have discussed at some length and shall return to later, it would not have been governed by superego, where superego is equated with the coldly admonishing or harshly judgemental, because it was a matter of anaclitic rather than abstracted rationality. Sublimation as a condition of the relatively autonomous, anaclitically rational subject is ego-directed and enmeshed with the strongly individuated mindfulness connoted by the Freudian concept of secondary process functioning.

While a less individually demanding, more pleasurable form of sublimation may become possible in the (at present unforeseeable) future, for the moment the difficulty of the tasks with which citizens are faced demands an ego-directed form of sublimation. This form of sublimation becomes possible through infants' early experience of 'good enough' nurturing; an experience which constitutes an ego strong enough to engage in the kind of self-disciplined activity in which this sublimation consists. However, preparedness for sublimation will only ensue in a sublimated life if the cultural conditions productive of a variety of occupations and activities, from which individual subjects can choose in accordance with their own particular orientations, are available, although, even where this is not possible, the availability of sociable relations will compensate in part for the sacrifice of gratification which work generally requires (Freud 1985a: 268, n. 1).

Where the particular familial conditions which set the foundations for sublimation and the broader cultural conditions which enable the adult choice of sublimatory activity co-exist, the intra-psychic contradiction between atomism and sociability on which Freud (1984f) insists will be rendered less acute, or even experientially insignificant. If we accept the existence of this contradiction (and I think we must, pending more evidence than we presently possess of its non-existence), the importance of this point cannot be over-stressed. What the contradiction informs us is that sociability and atomism are both human potentials. Sociability can become more consequential than atomism and it must do so if we are to nurture responsible citizenship. Through sublimation, the ego's capacities are turned outwards and an active, individualized form of sociability becomes possible in a culture which is *at once* attentive to the satisfactions of its individual members *and* very demanding of these individuals. Much is given but much is also expected in return.

Given a civilized culture, sublimation is the most satisfying 'fate' for human beings in the sense that it provides adequate compensation for the sacrifice of drive satisfaction which the reproduction of civilized cultures requires. In becoming capable of sublimation, we come to cultivate our potentials for sociability (social love or libidinal bonding) and for a particular kind of disciplined and sustained self- and world-conscious attentiveness. We become capable of a kind of anaclitically rational secondary process functioning, and therefore of thinking in the manner required for participation in public deliberation about a differentiated world.

Two principles of mental functioning

The two principles of mental functioning with which I am concerned here are those conceptualized by Freud in terms of primary and secondary processes

(1976: chs 6, 7; 1984c). While Freud (1966) tends to naturalize these as necessary properties of all human mental functioning, I am reading them here as oppositions rendered thinkable through the historico-culturally-specific experience of the mature mindfulness nurtured in bourgeois subjects.[12] The broader conditions of possibility for the sociologically significant nurturing of this particular kind of mindfulness (a mindfulness rendered possible by a particular kind of cultural forming of the brain) include the institutions discussed in chapter three, among which the cultivation of an advanced level of literacy was crucial. Cultural changes may dissolve the conditions of possibility for individual cultivation of this mindfulness, as I shall argue in later chapters. For now, we need to understand the differences so as to grasp how it was that individual bourgeois subjects became capable of cultivating a theoretical understanding of a civilizing culture which was beginning to take on the attributes of a totality.

The primary process, or, the worldlessness of the immature subject

Primary process functioning connotes the immature, thoughtless and helpless mode of functioning of a being for whom the world is both unintelligible and unsociable; a subject who cannot tell reality from fantasy. For Freud, this is a universal and irrational state of (infant) human beings characterized by infants' hallucinatory reaction to stimulation (Freud 1984c; Cavell 1993: ch. 8; O'Shaughnessy 1974). It is a state of being which involves the undiscriminating, instant and speedy cathexis of psychical energy to hallucinatory objects. To cathect an object (an idea or doctrine, a part of the body, an object – human or non-human) is to adopt an active orientation towards it. Cathexis of hallucinatory objects is effortless and yields temporary and imaginary satisfaction. Here we can scarcely speak of attention or of intentionality, since energy slithers from one object to another without lingering to take in their reality. So, the cathexes of the primary process are made effortlessly. They do not require or enable the cultivation of memory, judgement or attention. They are cognitively empty, and therefore irrational. They are also a-social, since they consist in 'attachments' which are not experienced as attachments by the newborn, who has no sense of a world beyond itself, and therefore, no sense of relationship. There is not the sense of space between infant and others which is necessary for relationship. The 'world' is merely an undifferentiated source of gratification or frustration. In Freudian terms, the newborn is in a condition of 'idness' whereby psychic energy is highly mobile, therefore 'connectedness' (not experienced as such by the infant) is either virtual (hallucinations) or momentary (the instant gratification of the breast). What is in question is the intra-psychic functioning of immature and helpless creatures who are unable to satisfy their needs by their own unaided efforts and who fantasize gratifications which are lacking in the experienced world.[13]

The extreme mobility of id-derived energy led Freud to speculate in 'The dissection of the psychical personality', that the energy of the 'instinctual impulses' rising from the id is different than that found in other regions of the mental apparatus, being 'far more mobile and capable of discharge' (Freud 1973a: 107). It is free energy which 'flows towards discharge in the speediest and most direct fashion possible', as opposed to bound energy which accumulates and remains within particular neurones or systems of neurones (Laplanche and Pontalis 1973: 171). Its deployment signals immaturity, worldlessness and the inability to achieve durable and truly satisfying gratification. It connotes the existence of a subject in the grip of urgent needs whose satisfaction is beyond the subject's own powers, and who, in the absence of attentive others, can resort only to hallucinated gratification.[14]

The secondary process

In contrast to the mobile energy deployed by the immature and worldless subject, the bound energy of the mature, worldly subject 'holds fast' to its cathexes (Freud 1984f). The movement which binds mobile energy is a movement from ignorance, indiscipline and thoughtlessness to knowledge, self-discipline and thoughtfulness. It is also a movement from frustration to relatively enduring satisfaction, therefore a movement which enhances sociability. Moreover, it involves the emergence of a kind of mental functioning which endows this sociability with a particular kind of intelligibility and effectivity. This is the capacity to attend in a particular way to both 'external' and 'internal' reality (Brennan 1992; Hamilton 1993). Attention here connotes the self-conscious, active and sustained direction of psychic energy towards specific objects, purposes or projects.

Attention is related to the function of reality-testing and both are concerned with assessing correctly the possibility of gratification in one's environment. Correct assessment can take place only if there is a delay between the point of stimulation and gratification.[15] Immediate gratification would prevent the infant from becoming aware of an independently existing world (of an inside/outside relationship). Delayed or occasional non-satisfaction forces the infant to an awareness of such a world.[16] Regular satisfaction of needs allows the development of memories of occasions of past satisfactions. These memories are a kind of record of the nature of both the world and of the infant's experience of the world. They are what enable the psyche to discriminate between hallucinated objects of satisfaction (bad objects) and real objects of satisfaction (good objects). More than this, the repeated experience of a time limit to frustration enables the infant to develop a tolerance of frustration. The world is experienced as usually, but not always, responsive to the infant; therefore as neither wholly predictable nor neglectfully unreliable. Serious neglect would provoke infant withdrawal from the world: instant, wholly expected responsiveness would leave the infant engulfed in the world (Bion 1962).

To say that the primary process has ceded to the secondary process is to say that the pleasure principle has ceded to the reality principle, or, that the 'initial pleasure-ego' has ceded to the 'definitive reality-ego'. However, this is a development which advances, rather than negates, the purposes of the pleasure principle, as noted previously. It does so by aiding the correct identification of objects which are not only 'good' (or, potentially satisfying from the point of view of the emergent subject) but which are also 'real' (available in the external world so that the child has access to them whenever necessary). Moreover, these are objects which have become lost but which 'once brought real satisfaction' (Freud 1984d: 439). The pleasure of hallucinating gratification of the need (the indulgence of wishfulness) cedes to the real satisfactions obtainable by active, knowledgeable and loving engagement with the real world outside of the hallucinating psyche (the psyche disposed towards idness, or primary process functioning).

I judge that the account just given is in general terms accurate regarding the interactions between emergent bourgeois subjects and their environment. As an account of the transition from primary to secondary process functioning, it shows the necessary fusion of rationality and affect in origin and functioning of the thinking in question. Another way of expressing this is to say that, where libido becomes desexualized as social love, the splitting of rationality and affect does not occur. More specifically, rationality and sociability are fused in the form of social love, which becomes the basis for public-spiritedness.[17] Moreover, sociability remains a cultural imperative in the mature subject, since it remains functional in the sense that it remains a necessary dimension of 'utilitarian' activities. (It is also functional in that it takes a form which nurtures psychic health.) Before completing this chapter I need to say something about the parental relations which enabled the nurturing of this social love. This will lay the basis for understanding the significance of the divorce of rationality and affect which accompanied the differentiations of industrialized capitalism.

II Bourgeois parenting: a parenting for citizenship

Freud's particular object of knowledge is the declining bourgeois (or emergent capitalist) subject. Therefore he is dealing with a degenerating form of oedipal family. For this reason he considers the interactions involved in subjectivation to be largely a matter of infant resistance to cultural impositions and the repression of drive demands, rather than as an expression of the infant's openness to the world. He therefore stresses the ambivalence of the child's feelings for its parents as culture's message bearers and tends at times to stress the role of fear in securing its compliance to cultural demands. This stress on ambivalence and fear is appropriate to an understanding of capitalist rather than bourgeois familial relations. In the bourgeois case, the message bearers were powerful individual figures (relatively autonomous subjects) who were also authoritative. That is to say, love and protection predominated over judging and threatening. Ambivalence may have been present, since the relations were intimate, but in this case parental tenderness towards the emergent subject would have rendered the ambivalent character of bourgeois family relations less acute and burdensome than that experienced in capitalist families. Bourgeois parents provided their children with good objects whose internalization endowed emergent subjects with psychic strength. It was this which enabled the transition, by means of sublimation rather than repression, from primary to secondary process functioning.

This transition involves the 'muting' of drives, or the 'binding' of psychic energy so as to effect durable relations between that energy and the drive representatives. This is possible only where emergent subjects experience relative determinacy, or, a balance between total predictability (determinacy) and unpredictability (indeterminacy). Expectations must have a high probability of being met, but they should not be met instantly or on demand. Where all expectations are punctually met, the need to stop and think does not arise. Where expectations are rarely met, the motivation to stop and think will not be present. What is in question here is a reality principle which provides the reliability of experience needed for emergent subjects to test reality and the unpredictability of experience which renders it necessary to do so. This is what I mean by relative determinacy; that happy cultural condition which enables the nurturing of relatively autonomous subjects; of subjects who have enjoyed responsible parental attentiveness to their activity, sex and ego needs; subjects, therefore, who have the basis (in the form of emotional and intellectual maturity) for the practice of public-spiritedness under demanding and complex conditions.

Relatively durable relations between energy and drive representatives are the ground of psychic strength, a ground which is developed along with the ability to build up a store of reliable memories of real as opposed to hallucinated gratifications; a store on which infants can draw to evaluate the 'reality' of possibilities of gratification. In learning to evaluate these possibilities infants become capable of paying attention in a sustained manner so as to judge whether the objects in view are part of an internal or external world. They begin to get a sense of an inside and outside, and to experience the outside as a world of relations with separate others who are satisfactorily responsive to infant needs. They experience a dependence which yields neither frustration nor humiliation. However, not only must this experience of dependence be available, but it needs to be such as to prepare emergent subjects for the cultural expectations that at some point they will become relatively autonomous.

In the bourgeois case successful management of the difficult transition from intimate dependence to adult interdependence of a relatively autonomous kind was a matter of identification with the parents, identification with the father signalling the male child's emergence into the wider, less intimate world; an emergence for which it would have been prepared by earlier identifications with the mother (Brennan 1992; DiStephano 1991: ch. 1). Identification led here to imitation which in turn led to empathy, as Freud notes (1985c: ch. 7). Identification with the father was undertaken by the male child with the guarantee that, by abandoning his desire for the mother, he would in future come to enjoy a mother-like object. Here the intense wish for immediate and total satisfaction of sex and ego needs was transmuted into loving family relations which constituted in the emergent subject the psychic strength needed for the unprecedentedly demanding form of cultural membership which the 'civilizing process' involved for the bourgeois.

Rationality and the pre-oedipal phase: bourgeois mothering for relative autonomy

In the Freudian account of the oedipal family, the constitution of relatively autonomous subjectivity involves the dramatic and masterful abstraction of the (male) child from the clammy embrace of the mother; the movement of the child from the safe, but confining haven of unquestioning maternal love into the invigorating and challenging paternal world (Freud 1984e; 1986). This account of oedipal resolution assumes a gendered division of labour, and therefore the splitting of rationality and affect (the former being an attribute of the father, the latter of the mother), but the implications of Freud's own work are that the pre-oedipal phase (insofar as it is expected to lay the basis for sociable relative autonomy) cannot possibly have this engulfing, rationality-free character (1984b; 1984c).[18] We need to think of this matter historically so as to understand that while the gendered division of labour implicit in this account is true to the actuality of liberal industrial capitalist family forms, matters were quite other in the constitution of anaclitically rational bourgeois subjects; subjects who had not yet experienced the rationality/affect split. This was the case because commodity fetishism and the domestication of bourgeois women were as yet more aspiration than actuality. As noted before, I shall understand the differences between bourgeois and capitalist families in part through the critical use of Jessica Benjamin's account of the 'oedipal riddle' (1990: ch. 4) and I shall take Freud's interpretation of the rather neat resolution of the oedipal complex to be applicable, up to a point, to capitalist, rather than bourgeois, male subjects.[19]

The bourgeois family was an oedipal family. That is to say, it was a privatized, 'nucleated' family in which familial relations were intimate, i.e. 'defunctionalized' and saturated with affects. In these respects, it is similar to the capitalist nuclear family to which it ceded later in the nineteenth century. In both families, the triadic (intimate, privatized) relations between mother, father and child were what distinguished it from previous family forms.[20] However, the contexts within which these formally similar families were situated were quite different, therefore so too were intra-familial relations. This will only become clear in chapter five. For the moment, let me repeat that, while privatized, the bourgeois family remained sociable because sociability remained a functional necessity. That is to say, most social relations were carried on through communicative speech; or, through a mode of speech which had not yet been subsumed under bureaucratic or monetized relations.

They were directly experienced, or personally mediated. Because sociability was taken-for-granted as a matter of everyday life, atomism was not yet possible, although fears about its emergence were becoming expressed, or, atomism was by now identifiable as a potential which had not yet been actualized. At the same time, while sociability remained a functional necessity it was more relaxed, more 'even', as Elias would put it, than earlier forms of sociability which could explode into joy, boisterousness, anger or grief. Moreover, the steady prosperity of the bourgeois released the family from anxiety about the satisfaction of ego-needs which would have rendered non-bourgeois family relations more 'utilitarian' (Clark 1995). In short, the broader context described by Elias is significant here. Improvement in living standards together with political pacification yielded the assurance of 'commodious living' which gave living a kind of spacious character conducive to intra-familial generosity (Hamilton 1978: 41–2). This was expressed in the companionate marriage and in a new attentiveness to children as individuals meriting careful nurturing (Ariès 1965; Stone 1979).

The companionate marriage

While the companionate marriage may be seen as a 'sentimentalization' of the institution (Shorter 1975), we should be clear that this sentimentalization did not yet involve the splitting of rationality and affect, because commodity fetishism was not yet more than a possibility and the domestication of bourgeois women had not yet been secured. This is an important point in relation to the quality of parenting that mothers could provide. Wives in companionate marriages were, by definition, educated for companionship (Wahrman 1995: 395–9). Moreover, upper bourgeois women also benefited from the aristocratic acceptance of a modified role for women in public life (Davidoff and Hall 1987: ch. 10; Landes 1988). Overall, women had not yet suffered the catastrophic loss of status which would be their fate once domestication had been (for the moment) achieved by the nineteenth century's end. By comparison with what had gone before, bourgeois marital relations were warmer and more intimate; by comparison with what came after, they were more equal.

At the same time, these women, not being required to participate actively in the sphere of work, began to take on a mothering duty which (in the case of prosperous women) had been previously carried out by wet-nurses, namely breast-feeding. Simultaneously the practice of swaddling began to die out. Both of these changes were significant in enabling the novel physical and emotional intimacy which characterized bourgeois mother–infant relations (Stone 1979: ch. 9). As a maternal practice, breast-feeding became an intimate matter involving the infant's taking in of both biological and psychic nourishment (Stone 1979: 273). Or, in Freudian terms, ego and sex drives were simultaneously satisfied in this activity.

It was important to the psychically nourishing aspect of breast-feeding that the mother's calling was not the bourgeois mother's only calling; that she had a relatively fulfilling life outside the household. Only where this was the case, as it was with bourgeois mothers, could intimate mothering breed the social love on which public-spiritedness rests. For the bourgeois, as noted in chapter three, the myriad specifically 'cultural' activities were an important constituent of the emergent *sensus communis*, available to women as well as men at this time, and one which many of them enthusiastically experienced. The bourgeois mother was an individual subject in her own right in that she moved relatively freely between the public and the private spheres. Moreover, as a formally educated woman, she was also capable of nurturing her children by tutoring them at home.[21]

In effect, not only did bourgeois women enjoy companionate relations with their husbands, but their drive towards active engagement with the world was not yet frustrated in the way it would become once domestication had been achieved. This was what enabled them to provide their infants with the psychic nourishment they needed to gradually detach themselves from their mothers and to find substitute gratifications for the loss of maternal intimacy through identifications with the father. The infant was protected from engulfment by an over-demanding mother love because the infant was not the only possible source of its mother's gratification. For this reason, the infant could not expect the intensely dedicated nurturing that it might get from a psychically deprived capitalist mother. Yet, as we have seen, this was not a bad thing but resulted in a 'good enough' mothering which opened up a space (an absence of the expected) which forced the infant into thinking and which laid the foundations for adult intellectual and emotional maturity. Regarding the latter, the 'neglect' of the good enough mother was not such as to render the experience of dependence odious. In fact the balance attained between total dedication and neglect contributed to the balance of attachment and detachment which would be needed for adult relative autonomy. In short, as a good enough mother, the bourgeois mother provided her infant with a good object for internalization

Bourgeois mothering was a movement towards the 'vocation' of mothering, that is, towards the conception of mothering as the mother's only calling (Rich 1977). It was only the beginning, though. Women were not yet required to be, on the one hand, an ornament on the arm of husbands, and on the other, totally dedicated domesticated mothers. They were therefore not the cloying narcissistic mothers who came to be viewed contemptuously by coldly rational men. They would be deserving of respect as active persons in their own right. This is not to argue that bourgeois women were, in any sense, equal to bourgeois men. It is to claim that they were less unequal than would be their capitalist equivalents. To express the matter rather simplistically, bourgeois wives and mothers had more 'for-' and 'in-itselfness' than had capitalist wives and mothers.

The nurturing of bourgeois public-spirited subjects required mothers who were themselves anaclitically rational and who were themselves actively engaged in worldly pursuits. Such mothers did not provide the kind of hothouse atmosphere of total maternal-feminine devotion from which the paternal-masculine father rescued the (male) child.[22] We have noted the centrality of the mother's responses to the child in enabling or impeding reality-testing. On the quality of the mother's attention depended the child's ability to function according to the dictates of the secondary process; to lay the psychic foundations for attainment of sublimatory gratification rather than repressive deprivation. This is the logic of Freud's own account of mental functioning, which implies a rational-affective, rather than 'purely' affective form of pre-oedipal care if the necessary basis for sublimation is to be provided. In the absence of this relational and 'mixed' rationality, what will be developed is a repressive form of secondary process functioning constitutive of the cold rationality which does not, indeed cannot, be the basis of public-spiritedness. While in this case subjects will be capable of reflexive rationality involving close and continuous attentiveness to objects in the world, this will be the abstract or cold rationality of atomistic subjects rather than the anaclitic variety with which we are concerned.

Conclusion

Bourgeois worldliness was a reflexive form involving *sensus communis* rather than common sense. As a form of *sensus communis*, it predated the splitting of rationality and affect; a splitting which would debilitate the latter and pervert the former into a dehumanizing source of world mastery. *Sensus communis* was possible because the civilizing differentiations effected during the hybrid bourgeois phase of capitalism were largely actualized through personal, rather than impersonal mediations. They had therefore not yet effected the world alienation which would give differentiations the character of abstractness, or, which would effect the fragmentation of human dispositions connoted by the splitting, not only of rationality and affect, but also of individual and society, of masculinity and femininity, of object and subject, and so on. Using Freud's analysis of mental functioning, I have sought to clarify the internal relationship between rationality and affect in the development of infants' mental functioning and in the optimal functioning of the mature adult also. For the bourgeois, rationality was a fused, multidimensional rationality of the anaclitic type which emerged out of the activity of reality-testing in a world which was relatively determinate, rather than determinate or indeterminate. It was this balance that impelled the emergent subject into forms of mental activity which laid the basis for the later nurturing of secondary process functioning. At the same time, parental attention was such as to assure the child that the world was not a malign or indifferent place. The result was a nexus of abilities and dispositions connoted by the concepts of anaclisis, of secondary process functioning and of sublimation. These included the psychic strength needed for delayed gratification and for tolerance of complexity and contingency, plus the habits of mind needed to comprehend complexity in an active, confident way, and a sociability adequate to the enjoyment of lived, directly-experienced interdependence.

The bourgeois family provided the emergent subject with good objects in the shape of parents who were relatively autonomous in that their civilizing culture afforded opportunities for new kinds of individualized, consequential activity which did not yet have atomizing characteristics. Identifications with these parents put in place the ability to form lasting ties through the desexualization of libidinal demands and, therefore, the ability to love socially. Situated as they were in a nexus of necessarily sociable relations (of relations mediated by the sensuously present, speaking presence of other subjects) the activities which engendered these identifications received the kinds of institutional supports which effected, in the maturing subject, the split psyche in which ego-functioning was in command. Superego was present, but was constrained by ego. In any case, for bourgeois, superego was not yet the harshly judgemental voice of conscience that it would become in the course of the nineteenth century. The world was in general amiably disposed towards bourgeois and provided them with myriad meaningful opportunities for individually-chosen efficacious, consequential activity. This is what sublimation implies and requires.

While equality did not govern relations between bourgeois parents, the mother, as well as the father, was relatively autonomous in the sense that she could take a place (never unchallenged, and admittedly more modest than that of her husband) in the public sphere. At the same time, she was also becoming more dedicated to mothering than had previously been the case. This new dedication to the child was expressed in the increasing tendency to breast-feed, in the past the task of wet-nurses, as well as more active participation in the education of growing children. These unprecedented and long-term forms of careful attentiveness of mothers to their children enabled a form of intimacy with worldly rather than worldless consequences. It meant that while we may continue to characterize the bourgeois family as oedipal it was distinct from the late nineteenth-century oedipal family the effects of which gave Freud his object of study.

In the bourgeois family, while there was, undoubtedly, a gendered division of labour, the mother was not confined to the domestic sphere and sociability remained a necessity for all family members. Moreover, the world had not yet become cognitively opaque at the level of individual functioning. Both parents were authoritative in their own right. Both had a strong sense of self and were active in the world outside the family home. All of this would change once capitalism became 'really' rather than 'formally' instituted; that is to say, once successful industrialization set commodity fetishism in motion. This is what I examine next.

Part III
From place to space
The death of worldliness

5 The institution of commodity fetishism

The world of the hybrid bourgeois subject was worldly; it was, for the most part, a world which could be experienced 'with the fingertips'. That is to say, direct relations and personal mediations remained significantly consequential, so that what individuals did *as* individuals, but also *with* other individuals, could be seen to make a difference. This kind of individuality was nurtured by the new practices of silent, solitary reading which, served by the output of a flourishing publishing industry, enabled the cultivation of, on the one hand, a sense of inwardness and, on the other, a theoretical knowledge of the functioning of hybrid bourgeois cultures. The latter was possible because, until the late nineteenth century, science had not yet penetrated the everyday world. At the same time, individuality was protected from atomization due to the balance maintained between sociable engagement with and withdrawal from the world. The technologies of communication and transport which would disrupt this balance had not yet emerged. For these reasons, the bourgeois world had the character of a place, rather than of a space, that is to say, it constituted for its members a strong, experientially shared sense of reality.[1]

Another way of making this point is to say that the drives were represented in a relatively determinate, rather than a determinate or indeterminate way. This balance between determinacy and indeterminacy was conducive to human flourishing of the kind (eudaimonistic rather than hedonistic) associated with sublimated secondary process functioning. Thinking in the manner connoted by the concept of secondary process functioning was here a matter of worldly, sustained and theoretically-informed attentiveness to a complex and demanding (but for the bourgeois not yet harsh and indifferent) world. This was a world whose mode of differentiation was such as to require new kinds of individualized responsibilities which, given the character of worldliness which marked hybrid bourgeois culture, were meaningfully imposed on bourgeois subjects in that these subjects possessed the financial independence and intellectual and emotional maturity adequate to their fulfilment. In a very real sense, the strength of the class depended on the strength of its individual, relatively autonomous members. What this means is that the 'in' and 'for' itselfness of the class was radically democratic. Moreover, conditions of life were not yet such as to lead 'each man to find in the others not the *actualization*, but much more the *limit*, of his freedom' (Marx 1994: 45 [emphasis in original]), or, the human use of human beings had not yet replaced the human need of human beings. In intra-bourgeois relations everyday rationality was of an anaclitic, rather than economic, kind. Culture, for the bourgeois class, was a good enough parent in that it provided unprecedented opportunities for gratification of the activity and ego drives which compensated for the strong disciplining of the body to which Elias draws our attention and which is naturalized in Freud's account. The result was a libidinization of cathexes such that public-spiritedness as a particular bourgeois manifestation of social love became possible.

Having discussed the unprecedented historico-cultural experiences that enabled this temporary and fragile condition of worldliness, let me turn in this chapter to consider the pure capitalist institutions which would effect its dissolution. Commodity fetishism is the concept used here to connote the peculiarly capitalist manifestation of worldlessness; of worldlessness necessitated by the law of value. As a specifically capitalist form of worldlessness, commodity fetishism refers to two things: the quantification of particularity and, relatedly, the transmutation of differentiation into abstraction. As noted in chapter two, in referring to abstract differentiations I am referring to differentiations which involve a division of labour whereby the impersonal mediations of money and bureaucracy have come to predominate over the personal so that interdependence becomes experientially inconsequential. What is in question is what Postone (1993: 30) describes as an 'abstract structure of domination', abstraction here involving a worldless form of reification. Reification here is a humanly-debilitating tendency in that it induces forgetfulness of our potential for imaginative agency through rendering thinglike phenomena which are (or should be) in movement and therefore, possibly, susceptible to change through intentional human activity, and it institutes interdependence in impersonal forms which render sociability unnecessary and which nurture blindness to the necessity of co-operation in human life. The equally debilitating capitalist tendency towards dereification will be examined in later chapters. For the moment, I concentrate on the reified character of capitalist cultures as theorized by Lukács (1971) on the basis of Marx's *Capital* and I shall elaborate on reification as this was borne by liberal industrialization through commodification as instituted in abstract labour and money/capital. Commodities are things which are intended to fulfil two functions: use and exchange. Where most or all things have these two functions, we will necessarily find abstract labour and money/ capital and most or all institutions will tend to have the subject effects which will be discussed in this and subsequent chapters.[2]

The culturally unprecedented experience of abstract differentiation or impersonal mediations was rendered possible, and eventually necessary, by means of monetization, bureaucracy and inventions such as the railway and the telegraph (Buchanan 1992; Carey 1989). These inventions advanced capitalist purposes through overcoming spatio-temporal constraints on value's reach. In doing so, they introduced the possibility that the world beyond Euro-America would become subsumed 'really' rather than merely 'formally' under capital, as has happened today. To the extent that institutions became implicated in this abstract mode of differentiation, cultural parenting was threatened. As will be seen, however, different modes of capitalism have, up to now, been more or less incompatible with cultural parenting.

Commodity fetishism will be understood here as a dehumanized condition whose character will be elaborated in terms of the psychoanalytic theory which informs my understanding of worldliness and its absence. Using Marx and Arendt (as well as the work of post-Freudian psychoanalysts such as Ernest Schachtel and Jessica Benjamin) I have identified the importance of an activity drive (praxis in Marx's terms; natality in Arendt's) as an active, happily curious world-oriented potential seeking actualization (a potential experienced as a need), and of a sociability to which the activity drive is internally related. As was suggested in chapter two, the activity drive may be turned inwards as a result of painful or frustrating infant or adult experiences, or, through an encounter with parents or others who are indifferent to the subject's needs. This is how I am conceptualizing narcissism, a condition to which humans are vulnerable because of our essential 'prematurity' and consequent acute dependence on mature humans for our development. (We will consider an important example of narcissism later, that of the capitalist wife.) Where the ego and sex drives are formed in a relatively satisfiable way, emergent subjects will turn towards, rather than away from, the world which has nurtured them. Relative satisfiability involves the (relatively) determinate shaping of drives through cultural representatives. Following Freud, I have understood Arendt's claims about the human need for relative determinacy in terms of the reality principle which enables emergent subjects to test reality so as to learn to think and judge, or, to identify good from bad objects. Commodity fetishism prevents and/or perverts the relatively determinate shaping of these drives in ways to be explored in the remainder of this study.

In section one of this chapter I shall discuss commodity fetishism as the actualization of value's law so as to render abstract labouring and monetized relations necessary rather than possible or optional. This development rendered both bourgeois *sensus communis* and artisanal common sense progressively redundant and tipped the balance between personal and impersonal social relations in favour of the latter. It thereby secured the splitting of rationality from sociability. We can understand this in terms of a division of labour which, first, abstracted the ideational and the communal from the manual; second, dissolved useful things into component parts; and third, distributed the production of these parts over time and space. Added to these is the increasing ratio of dead to living labour, which brought the past into the present in an impersonal, opaque form.[3] The significance of these developments in relation to our interest in citizenship is considerable, since the unavailability of the experience of indebtedness to the past (in addition to the loss of awareness of the fact of interdependence in the present) eliminates sources of public-spiritedness.[4] In the second part, I consider the related and no less significant effects of commodity fetishism on the capitalist family, a family which became trapped in a privative form of privacy constitutive of narcissism rather than anaclisis. Here Jessica Benjamin's argument has enabled me to understand the woeful effects of the gendered rationality/affect split, instituted through the domestication of capitalist women, on both men and women. Domestication induced in capitalist women a condition of feminine narcissism; fetishism induced in capitalist men a condition of masculine narcissism. Neither women nor men were capable of the parenting needed to constitute sublimation. As the world became colder, social love became increasingly rare, and so, also, the sociable sublimation which nurtured anaclitic rationality. Whereas bourgeois subjects were sublimated, capitalist subjects were repressed. The former were governed by ego, the latter by superego.

I The law of value instituted

The transition from formal to real subsumption of labour under capital

During the early nineteenth century, the transition from formal to real subsumption of labour under capital was speeded up with the help of successful collective action on political, 'cultural' and economic fronts.[5] Classical political economy was the emergent self-consciousness of a novel culture. This science informed the collective action which was intended to make England fit for industrialists who were portrayed by their organic intellectuals as the most progressive class (Kanth 1986; Polanyi 1957). It was productive of a tortuous, dialectical and uneven process, but it is generally agreed that by the 1850s, artisan had ceded to proletarian (Bauman 1982; Calhoun 1982).[6] What this means is that hybrid bourgeois had ceded to capitalist, or, the satisfaction of value's needs resulted in the dissolution of conditions of possibility for the development of (a specifically bourgeois) public-spiritedness.

Where this change had taken place, commodified social relations and the intensified gendered division of labour (involving the domestication of bourgeois women) effected the institutional abstraction of rationality from the emotions, including the emotion of sociability. In relation to artisans, it began the dissolution of commonsense rationality and its replacement by, on the one hand, a systemic functional rationality in the sphere of work, and, on the other, an atomized rationality in the 'private' sphere.[7] At the same time, affect became confined to the sphere of the family. This splitting debilitated both rationality and emotions. Rationality became 'cold'; it lost its relational character. It became the property of the individual, rather than that which emerged between individuals, and it was directed towards mastery of, rather than engagement with, the world, both human and non-human. In effect, it became unconcerned with worldly matters and lost awareness that all human activity is, however indirectly, activity with one's fellow humans.[8] In becoming delinked from rationality, the emotions were trivialized and reduced to sentimentality. Deprived of their rational content and directionality, they were channelled into debilitating forms of intimacy and 'destructive *gemeinschaft*' (Sennett 1977).[9] These developments were manifestations of potentials (commodification of social relations, privatization of the bourgeois family, the removal of bourgeois women from directly productive tasks) that had emerged during the hybrid bourgeois stage of capitalism, as noted in chapters three and four.

The transfer of production from workshop to factory illustrates the way in which the law of value becomes culturally dominant rather than merely emergent and possible (Postone 1993: ch. 7; Sayer 1991). This transfer cut the limiting direct relationship between the pace of production and the bodily abilities of the worker which had ensured the everyday intelligibility and sociability of the working world (Marx 1976a: chs 14, 15, Appendix). It also required that money be transformed into capital and that the wage contract become the predominant form of social relationship between capitalists (a new class of owners of the social power to produce) and proletarians (a new class of owners of labour power and of nothing but labour power). Whereas money as capital exerted an abstract compulsion and constraint, money as individual possession rendered sociability unnecessary and interdependence invisible. From this point on, strenuous and systematic efforts would be made to ensure that the primary object of production would be exchangeability and that the primary character of 'labour' would be docility.[10] Expressed in terms of subjectivity, from now on, both bourgeois-becoming-capitalist and artisan-becoming-proletarian would become reduced as their respective rationalities became disabled and as sociability became a matter of choice rather than cultural imperative. This remarkable change came about as commodification was effected through monetization and changes in the division of labour which rendered abstract labour actual.

The fetishism of abstractions: the abstractions of fetishism

Abstraction is another way of talking about differentiation; one which draws our attention to the worldlessness inherent in processes of differentiation once they have gone beyond the point at which individual cultural members can comprehend their effects either kinesthetically or theoretically. This 'going beyond' involves affective as well as cognitive deprivations related to the divorce of rationality from affect which commodity fetishism institutes. The concept of commodity fetishism marks this 'beyond', which was experienced first in nineteenth-century England. At this time, and in this place, the world was becoming, slowly and unevenly, an impersonal totality of spatio-temporally fragmented, interdependent and contradictory processes and practices. Civilization was coming to be effected through a division of labour which baffled the senses so that the animation and autonomization of things which humans themselves had co-operatively produced was becoming a fact of life.

Where commodification has become universal, the 'treadmill effect' or 'a dialectic of transformation and reconstitution' comes into force (Postone 1993: 289). This dialectic is a matter of instituting substitutability and obsolescence, and therefore, a matter of rendering the world intangible and processual in character, as noted in chapter two. Subjects and objects become open to the calculations and fragmentations of the capitalist division of labour; they become means to ends which in turn become means, and so on. 'Use' as a realm of durability and predictability becomes the servant of 'value' as the realm of exchangeability and volatility. Expressed otherwise, particularity (quality) becomes subsumed under a form (quantity) which wishes to remain blind to its particular characteristics, or, value views particularities only from its own point of view (Harvey 1982: ch. 1). It ignores as far as possible any aspects of particularities which might conflict with its interests. This is the logic of the commodity, whose production requires the reconfiguration of human activities as abstract labour and the mediation of human relations by money.

The commodity

As the form of an 'object' which must be both useful (qualitatively distinct) and exchangeable (quantifiable), the commodity form is the 'cell-form' of capitalism, the entity which is the basic unit out of which the whole system is constructed (Marx 1976a: ch. 1), or, it is, as Lukács (1971: 83) puts it, 'the central structural problem of capitalist society in all its aspects'. Commodification requires the fragmentation and reconstitution of (a) social relations and human activities as quantifiable, calculable and exchangeable economic entities and (b) human needs so that they become experienced as the desire for commodities. Fragmentation and reconstitution either inhibit the actualization of activity drives or actualize these in the anti-social, instrumental form of mastery. Here fetishism is a matter of rendering the subjective objective and the objective subjective, as it were (Lukács 1971: 83). Or, more accurately, commodity fetishism removes the sense from sensuousness by instituting practically for the first time the split between subjectivity and objectivity, thereby rendering possible two kinds of beliefs: one, that agency is the property of the objectified result of human action (structuralism); two, that individual humans have, or should have, complete agential freedom (ontological individualism). Regarding the former, in a very real sense as the division of labour comes to cut the link between individual activity and object produced, as it comes to rob individual activity of its worldly intelligibility and relative autonomy, human beings do become bearers of a compulsive systemic logic which is incomprehensible to them (Althusser 1990d). At the same time, the ideology of autonomy, as expressed in ontological individualism, remains in place, even as industrializing capitalism renders autonomy obsolete.

The delinking of individual activity and object produced is an appearance of capitalism. That is to say, this delinking enters into everyday experience so as to 'form the five senses', or constitute subjectivities (capacities or incapacities). So it is mistaken to take the magical or religious fetish as an analogy here if in doing so we intend to argue that the effects of fetishism are purely 'in the mind' and might be dissipated relatively easily by revealing the irrationality of the fetishized condition. It is only partly true to say that in fetishizing the commodity we are investing it with powers which it does not possess (Cohen 1978: ch. 5), as when the religious fetish attributes intentionality to nature and mechanism or automaticity to humanity (Pietz 1988).[11] Since fetishization is given in the culture (Marx 1976a: 125–31), it is not simply mistaken to attribute intentionality to 'structure'. (The mistake occurs when this condition is naturalized as it tends to be in structuralisms, on which see Benton [1984].) For this reason, it is not wholly satisfactory to talk of commodity fetishism in terms of mystifying appearances rather than illusory beliefs (Geras 1971).[12] Certainly the appearances are mystifying, but mystification is not here 'merely' a matter of inducing amnesia regarding 'the facts of the matter', i.e. that the built world is the result of human action. The point is that capitalist appearances have constituted subjects who have been rendered passive in the sense conveyed by the structuralist conception of humanity (Althusser 1990d: 231–40). Humanity has been unnaturally naturalized in that it has been reduced (apparently) to matter in motion according to the law of value. The potential for imaginative activity on the world and with one's fellow humans has been either suppressed or subverted to the needs of that law. In effect, commodity fetishism effects the unnatural humanization of the world (the world becomes active) and the unnatural naturalization of the human (the human becomes passive). Since we are culture-dependent creatures, this unnatural naturalization was effected in its industrial manifestation through practices which *did* reduce humanity in this way. That is to say, through the advance of that division of labour which capitalism initiated with the detailed division of labour in the workshop, humans and their worlds became fragmented and reconstituted as elements of a (now global) culture having the character of a totality, or, as mainstream sociology used to have it, a 'system' (Luhmann 1982). Our reduction to the status of elements in this system was needed if the system, and therefore its component parts, were to be reproduced. And it has been reproduced.

To repeat, since we reproduce/transform ourselves in reproducing/transforming our world, this particular capitalist making of a world (which divides the world into subject and object while at the same time fragmenting objects for the purposes of more efficient production) is also a making of subjects (Althusser 1984a; Amariglio and Callari 1993; Postone

1993). The appearances constituted by commodity fetishism are not 'mere' in any sense, since they are constitutive of subjects who, for the moment, are the necessary bearers of the peculiar mode of (ir)rationality and (in)activity which the law of value requires. These are appearances which impede the nurturing of human potentials for imaginative activity and sociability. As such, they constitute narcissistic, disabled forms of subjectivity (Kovel 1988b). I shall now consider how this disablement is effected through the institutions of abstract labour and money.

Abstract labour[13]

The commodification of labour involves the fiction that 'labour' is something which can be abstracted from the body of the worker and sold at a price to a capitalist. The abstraction of labour in this sense was an eighteenth-century conceptualization and a nineteenth-century aspiration which has been actualized today as never before, as will be seen in chapter six. It is only with the beginning of industrial capitalism that simple labour, labour without description or qualification – in a word, abstract labour, – became thinkable through the application of human imagination to emergent phenomena to render these more systematically comprehensible. '"Labour"' says Marx, 'is as modern a category as are the relations which create this simple abstraction' (Marx 1973: 103). It was Adam Smith who first threw out 'every limiting specification of wealth-creating activity', thereby departing from the physiocratic concern with particular, concrete labour, i.e. agricultural labour. What this means is that abstract labour was theorized before it became institutionally significant since it was theorized at the start of that phase of capitalism during which workers were abstracted from communities and workshops and brought together in larger numbers to work in mechanized factories. At this point, human beings, in their idiosyncratic individuality of selves, places and relations, were reduced to elements of a system of factory production whose purpose was the realization of surplus value. At this point, indifference became a principle of organization and of social relations.

Indifference has here both an objective and subjective dimension. As an objective matter, it refers to the contradictory character of relations between parts of the totality: their 'indifference' to their relations to each other and therefore their tendency towards 'auto' development as discussed in chapter two. This is an important dimension of capitalism's crisis tendencies. As a subjective matter, the effects of indifference include the 'privatization' of sociability through the requirement that individuals relate to one another impersonally through contract, and transfer from one occupation to another, from one place to another, in accordance with the changing requirements of value's law (Marx 1973: 104–5). As industrialization proceeded, workers were freed from the constraints within which pre-capitalist cultures had confined them and were required to take on new responsibilities for self-maintenance. These new responsibilities inhered in their status as owners and sellers of labour power and as makers of contracts with capitalists as buyers of that commodity (Marx 1976a: 271). However, in entering 'freely' into this contract, workers were being subsumed under value's law. Or, the 'freedom' which was given with one hand was taken away with the other.

(It is important to note here that different modes of capitalism institute different combinations of objective and subjective indifference. For example, the organized mode minimized both for a short period in ways that will be discussed briefly in chapter six. Objective indifference can be minimized through effective supervisory activity of capital, for example that of the post-1945 nation-states in Euro-America. Subjective indifference can be minimized through various forms of worker association, but also through the intended or unintended effects of capitalist activity.)

In its industrial manifestation, the institution of abstract labour involves the abstraction of the potential to expend energy from all other individual potentials. It separates that potential out and actualizes it in a form which requires nothing from the individual possessor of labour power but the ability to obey orders and adapt to the mechanical movements of a machine. It imposes a form on that labour power which refuses the engagement of individual workers. That form involves a rationality and an imagination which are not those of the worker. In a real sense, individuals as factory hands are reduced to their biology, since abstract labour is 'work' reduced to its biological energetic dimension (Doray 1988: ch. 5).[14] However, this is a culturally-specific reduction compelled by a particular manifestation of the law of value (Postone 1993: 144–8). The result is that each individual labourer is considered to be identical to all the others and the great differences between individual labourers can be ignored. What is in question is an instituted indifference to the particularity of humanity, and to the particularity of individual 'specimens' of humanity.[15]

Abstract labour is 'one-sided' labour, as noted previously. In its industrial manifestation it is one-sided in the sense that the manual has been abstracted from both the conceptual-imaginative-rational and the communal-interdependent dimensions of the total work process. The former become the business of experts (capitalists, engineers) with whom labourers are unlikely to have any contact. Co-operative interdependence becomes transmuted into monetized or bureaucratized relations between buyers and sellers, or between experts and their clients or patients (Marx 1977: 32; Colletti 1976: 84). Hence the perception on the part of individual labourers that 'society' is an independent, active, producing entity which rules over them. As noted previously, this perception is not an illusion but is the correct perception of the appearances of commodity fetishism which does, in fact, dissolve consequential individual agency into the spatio-temporally and cognitively fragmented division of labour which commodification requires. Once this division of labour has been successfully instituted, the activity of any one individual becomes negligible in relation to the totality of systemic requirements, and 'collective labour' does indeed become an alien, indifferent power over and against individuals as individuals (Marx 1973: 242–3).

Having sold their labour power to the capitalist, workers are ruled over by capital as by a *thing*. That is to say, the means of life, the conditions essential for labour to take place, are alienated from the worker and become 'thinglike'. They assume the solidity and irresistibility of a world which is both all powerful and indifferent to individual labourers: hence 'alien powers'; hence worldlessness. This 'thingness' of the world enhances the dehumanizing effects of the loss of a world of durable humanly-made objects. The world of durable use objects is an artisanal world in which the marks of individualized human agency are quite clear. That is to say, it is an intelligible world in which human interdependence is directly experienced through the context-specific production and exchange of artefacts by the individual makers and users of those artefacts (Marx 1976a: chs 7, 14).

Abstract labour is crucial in the displacement of durability from the world of individually-made use objects to that of a dehumanized objectivity of systemness, or, of an impersonally co-ordinated mode of spatio-temporally separated differentiations which reduce subjects to nothing but ' "supports" of functions' (Althusser 1990d: 237). This is the worldless effect of a dual movement of reification/dereification. Reification of activity and relations and dereification of the world are internally related and overdetermine the worldlessness of subjects as bearers of value's law.

Monetization

Where monetized relations have become necessary rather than possible, that is to say, when money is present in the dual form of capital and of exchange medium, money has taken on the power to constitute subjectivities. Money here is the third commodity which is necessary for the exchange of commodities to take place (Marx 1976a: chs 3, 4; 1973: ch. on money; Rosdolsky 1977: chs 4–8). As noted previously, money in the form of capital exerts an impersonal and unintelligible compulsion through abstract labour and, as personal possession, is the impersonal mediator of social relations which tends to render sociability unnecessary (Marx 1977: 120–5; Simmel 1990: ch. 4). In these two functions, money is a conveyor of unintelligibility and a destroyer of sociability as well as a condition of possibility for subsuming needing under desiring (Haug 1987: 105–6).[16] Without money, the lived dichotomies which characterize reified forms of capitalism (rationality/affect, subjectivity/objectivity, individual/society) would be impossible. It is worth repeating that these effects are achieved by money only where it appears in the form of both capital and medium of exchange.[17]

The possession of money allows of the apparent evasion of the concrete, particular, embodied character of individuals and their social relations (Simmel 1990: 297–303). In money, needs and potentials come together in an abstract way in that the only needs recognized as real are needs which can be secured through money (commodified needs), and conversely, only those potentials are recognized which possess the money needed for their actualization. So 'what I am and am capable of is by no means determined by my individuality'; rather it is determined by the extent to which I *have* money (Marx 1977: 94, 96, 138; Simmel 1990: 303–12). The obsession with *having* as opposed to *being* and *acting* becomes increasingly prevalent, or rather, being and acting become subsumed under having (Gagnier 2000; Slater 1997). This obsession does not lead to the development of diverse forms of life through the proliferation of diverse forms of needs, but rather to the homogenization of needs as having. 'Having' here becomes a kind of universal under which are subsumed all particular needs, money being the necessary facilitator of this universal (more on this can be found in chapter seven).[18]

Where needs have been subsumed under having, relations necessarily have become monetized, which means that culture begins to impose itself on individual subjects in an impersonal and unintelligible way. The need to have is the overwhelming need produced by pure capitalism; a culturally constituted rather than innate human need which, once constituted, shapes the potentials for world-engagement in particular, impoverished ways, since it encourages the atrophying of sociability and engenders calculative, economic forms of rationality. Money is the ultimate fetish, the necessary fetishized form on which all other capitalist fetishisms are based. It is the means of injecting abstraction and fetishism into every sphere of activity, into every social relation. It is that which enables impersonal attachments which are experienced in the mode of detachment; that which enables us to relate without feeling and act without knowing.[19] In short, money connects in a way that separates us from one another and baffles our senses. It renders us oblivious to the fact of human interdependence and increasingly dependent on a world experienced as 'system' or 'alien power'. Before concluding this section, it will be useful to consider another aspect of this 'systematization'.

Fetishized co-operation and the end of cultural indebtedness

Artisanal objectifications which constituted cultures as worlds or places were objectifications in which interdependence was directly experienced. Individual human beings knew from their own experience that the world (suffered or enjoyed) was humanly made (although ordained by a god or gods). The division of labour was clearly a form of co-operation between individual contributors. Moreover, the past existed in the present in the form of a seamless inter-generational continuity which rendered generational indebtedness transparent. With the increasing mechanization of labour, this inter-generational continuity was destroyed as the build-up of the mechanized products of past workers effected a redistribution of labour from the living to the dead such that unintelligibility was intensified and the sense of inter-generational interdependence was atrophied (Marx 1976a: 1054). Now dead labour (machinery) predominated over living labour. From having been transmitted inter-generationally as a body of practices and objects over which individual mastery is both possible and desirable, the past, as world of work, became reified and was transmitted in the shape of the world of machinery as a world of alien powers or things whose human origin became obscure.[20] Both past and present produced a predominance of impersonal, unintelligible and apparently intransigent forces over against the individual worker.[21] The past as reified, systemic impersonal presence does not demand the remembrance or gratitude of the present.[22] So dead labour is not only the 'objectification of historical time', as Postone puts it (1993: 356) but is also the objectification of human interdependence and need. In effect, both past and present lose their human character as both are objectivated as indifferent, intransigent, impersonal presences.

As manifested in the industrial production process, the present is an 'objectivity' which is indifferent to (does not require the active engagement of) the intelligence of individual workers and is in general indifferent to their well-being unless that well-being can be commodified. The 'functional' is separated out from its 'other' (the expressive, the imaginative, the 'cultural') and becomes impersonally imperative in an unprecedented way (Castoriadis 1997: ch. 5). The 'a-functional' apparently optional or inconsequential becomes the arena of individual choice. Having had their labour power institutionally abstracted and divorced from their imaginative, affectual and rational faculties, workers become subjected to the objective/subjective split. Their intelligence, no longer required for life's most consequential activities, becomes transmuted into subjectivism as the 'other' of the objectivism constituted by commodity fetishism. This subjectivism is that a-social (or even anti-social) privatized condition which is antithetical to the needs of public engagement and which finds itself most comfortable in the intimacies of family or friends. This is also the subjectivism of 'rational choice' as the elimination of the experience of social co-operation and the logic of contractualism lead workers to conceive of relations with one another, as well as with the capitalist, in instrumental terms. Calculation becomes the predominant activity and orientation. The age of economic rationality, therefore of narcissism, has arrived (Marx 1994; Jacoby 1980; Piccone 1980).

To sum up, the processes of commodification effected by the successful institution of abstract labour and monetization rendered the differentiations which had been engendered by the 'civilizing' process more numerous and more complex than before while also transforming them through abstraction. Abstract differentiation changed the character of relations between the differentiated activities, the character of processes and, thereby, of human dispositions. As industrialization advanced, as abstract labour became prevalent, and as more relations became necessarily monetized, the balance between personal and impersonal social relations which had preserved the necessary sociability of hybrid bourgeois capitalism, was disturbed. Impersonal mediations began to predominate. Sociability became optional. At the same time, and relatedly, the shared theoretical sense (*sensus communis*) which had been possible during the bourgeois period of capitalism was dissolved as knowledge came increasingly to take the form of scientific expertise, meaning that the gap between experts as scientists and laity was beginning to open up. One effect of this was that while capitalists continued to concern themselves with self-improvement, the nature of self-improving activity began to lose its public character, and the absorption of theoretical knowledge in a worldly form became increasingly difficult (more on this in chapter eight). Self-improvement became narcissistic in character in that it was impelled by intense anxiety about the status of the self as the self became shorn of its capacities for sociability and the world became more cognitively opaque at the mundane level. Capitalist selves began to experience themselves as 'individuals' set against other 'individuals' and against 'society'.[23] Having discussed the occupational changes which contributed to this atomization, let me now move on to consider the familial changes to which these changes were dialectically related.

II Value and the capitalist oedipal family

Privative privacy and the differentiation of masculinity and femininity

The human need for cultural completion is the need for an intelligible sociable world and for a developmental process of taking in the world which equips us with the capabilities to act effectively in the world in the company of others. With the emergence of those abstract differentiations which characterized the industrial manifestation of commodity fetishism, such taking in became increasingly rare as indifference became the most salient attribute of cultural institutions. I want now to give a brief account of the way in which this indifference was manifested in the 'far-reaching cultural shifts' which took place between the 1850s and 1890s (Gay 1999a: 3) and which constituted distinctively gendered manifestations of narcissism: that of the capitalist and his wife.

Following up the clues provided by Jessica Benjamin (1990), I argued in chapter four that bourgeois mothers were persons who experienced their own kind of relative autonomy so that both parents were personally authoritative. Neither parent was debilitated by the rationality/affect split and both engaged actively and sociably with the world beyond the family. What this means is that from the beginning the infant encountered a mother who had a sense of self. She had had opportunities to develop her potentials outside of the privatized familial sphere but was also ready to devote herself to caring for her baby. She was equipped to take on the very great responsibility of drawing the infant out of its dependency in a way which would prepare it for the demanding tasks of bourgeois adulthood; to ensure that the infant's drives would be shaped and directed in ways that would secure sublimatory gratifications.

Commodity fetishism and the domestication of capitalist women dissolved the conditions of possibility for this kind of mothering. Both involved the splitting of rationality and affect; a splitting which, as this was manifested in the capitalist familial sphere, involved the splitting of masculinity and femininity (Zaretsky 1976). I follow Freud in conceptualizing masculine and feminine as culturally constituted dispositions which may be allocated to either men or women, although the passivity of femininity has been suffered overwhelmingly by women in modern western cultures, while the activity of masculinity has been enjoyed (although also suffered) by men (Freud 1977a: 141–2, n. 1). That is to say, activity and passivity are culturally nurtured dispositions grounded in but not determined by biology (Brennan 1992: 6).[24] The strongly gendered distribution of these characteristics was the outcome of a form of differentiation which not only abstracted the family from its productive and educational functions, but abstracted mothers from the world through domestication. Furthermore, this family was part of a nexus of institutions increasingly marked by the commodity fetishism discussed in the first part of this chapter. The differentiations of industrial capitalism were producing a culture which was more fragmented, more monetized and more impersonal than the hybrid bourgeois culture explored in chapter three. They were also constituting subjects markedly more self-interested, unsociable and anxious than had been bourgeois subjects (Gay 1999b: ch. 6). The relative autonomy of the capitalist was not mediated by the sociability which, for bourgeois, neutralized the atomizing potential of this experience. This was the capitalist who, as head of the nuclear family, had the task of extracting the small male child from maternal influence so as to put him on the road to masculinity. This would be a father (more formidably strict and judgemental than the affectionate bourgeois father) who would contrast so sharply with the debilitated, narcissistic mother who, as capitalist's wife, was expected to be nothing more than a 'pretty, ignorant and idiotic slave' (Hobsbawm 1975: 279). The result was a family in which, to borrow a phrase of Jessica Benjamin's, 'the ego, and reason, grow in opposition to love' (Benjamin 1977: 62).

However, the whole logic of psychoanalysis centres on the undesirability (if not the impossibility) of separating rationality from affect.[25] If, having demonstrated (or, perhaps more accurately, implied) the necessity of intelligent, responsible and sensitive mothering, Freud nevertheless insists upon the need to rescue children from their mothers, this may be due to his judgement of the quality of maternal care available in capitalist families. This is undoubtedly the case, but, more than this, Freud seems to expect parenting to be little more than an expression of parents' secondary narcissism. That is to say, children are to desire to become what the parents wished, but failed, to become.[26] While this is true to the situation of capitalist families (for reasons relating to the impoverishment of life effected through commodity fetishism), it is not, contrary to what Mark Poster (1978: 9), for example, claims, applicable to the bourgeois family.

It is true to the situation of the capitalist family because, for one thing, capitalist women did not receive the nurturing which would have rendered the necessarily selfless quality of motherly dedication supportable (or even possible). They could not be selfless because they lacked a strong sense of self. This is what feminine narcissism (in the sense used here) means. Bourgeois mothering was the task of a woman who had a sufficiently strong sense of herself to become self-forgetful in her parenting. That strong sense of self was fed by worldly activities enjoyed outside the household. She was not only a mother; she was not only an adjunct of her husband. So, while being dedicated to mothering, mothering was not her only calling. The outside world called her too. For this reason, she did not smother her child with narcissistic longings and, at the same time, she was not permanently on call. She was a 'good enough' mother, or, in other words, the best possible mother under fairly benign circumstances. While deeply attached to her infant, her worldliness would have been such as to take her away from the overwhelming attentiveness which debilitates through attachments which perpetuate dependence beyond necessity.

During the nineteenth century, women's worldliness came under dedicated and systematic assault as the privacy available in an increasingly 'fortified' family sphere became privative (Gay 1999a: ch. 6). As capitalist women's lives became straitened and confined, the possibility of sublimatory gratifications became remote. Repression became women's fate. This was a repression which involved an ideal ego, rather than superego, as suggested previously.[27] This was the case in England from the middle of the nineteenth century at which time economy and politics became 'masculinized' (Hobsbawm 1987: 200) so that women experienced a shrinking of the world within which they could move and act. They were expected to be neither intelligent nor knowledgeable (Hobsbawm 1975: ch. 13). This shrinkage was more striking in relation to capitalist women who, in being stripped of their political and economic activities, were left to devote themselves to cultivating the arts of the 'perfect lady', to becoming 'the Victorian ideal of the completely leisured, completely ornamental, completely helpless and dependent middle-class wife or daughter, with no function besides inspiring admiration and bearing children' (Perkin 1985: 159).

The successful institution of the domesticated, intimate capitalist family effected a gender differentiation more marked than that of bourgeois life, so that the mother became more emotional and the father became colder. This family form both expressed and reproduced the gendered psychic reconfiguration which left capitalist men with a superego-governed psyche and capitalist women subordinated to an ideal ego. The predominance of superego signifies the predominance of repression over sublimation, hence a coldly judgemental orientation towards the world. The predominance of an ideal ego signifies the absence of internalized objects which would enable the woman to engage with confidence with the external world. (This dimension of narcissism will be discussed in greater detail in chapter seven.) Both parents lacked something in a way which encouraged narcissism, but the mother's lack was expressed in an 'over-tender and over-anxious regard to the child, to whom she transfers her need for love', as Freud put it (quoted by Poster 1978: 13–14),[28] while that of the father was expressed in a coldly active and judgemental orientation which was interpreted as a manifestation of his rationality. Now only the father was authoritative, and he was so in a coldly rational way (Benjamin 1990: ch. 4). So, he was dominant rather than authoritative, domination being a form of power without love (Poster 1978: ch. 1; Sennett 1993b). What this means is that dependence had become obnoxious and ambivalence was experienced more intensely and destructively than had been the case for emergent bourgeois subjects. Identification with the father now involved internalization of domination, as Jessica Benjamin insists, since what was being internalized was the superego, as noted previously. Activity was now expressed in the urge to mastery and sociability was downgraded to optional status.[29]

Another way of making this point is to say that gendering was now more strongly marked in terms of the distinction between masculine and feminine. Males were expected to be masculine: to be rational, active and autonomous. Females were expected to be feminine: to be caring, irrational, passive and dependent. As reason became 'mono-dimensional', as it was successfully shorn, through institutional change, of affect, and as imagination became subsumed under the needs of commodification, or practised in a 'cultural' rather than 'human' mode (i.e. in relation to 'art' as an apparently autonomous activity in its own right), it did indeed become cold and worldless. Correlatively, love became sentimentality. At this juncture, it became necessary to remove the male child from the debilitating atmosphere of the feminized household if that child were to cultivate the dispositions needed for masculinity, therefore for world mastery.

Regarding the daughter, in one sense she was not required to make the absolute break from the mother demanded of the son. She could (indeed, must) remain within the household. In another sense, she was expected to break much more thoroughly from the mother in that she was required to transfer her libidinal attachment to a father-like object (Brennan 1992; Mitchell 1975). We might say that the daughter experienced the worst of both worlds. She was confined to the household, therefore her activity drive received minimal gratification, and she had to repress much more thoroughly than her brother her libidinal longing for her mother.[30] So, the absence of world-engagement was experienced by women along two dimensions: physical isolation through domestication and psychical isolation through the cathexis of a fragile self, rather than of objects in the world (Benjamin 1990: ch. 3). Cathexis of self was a matter of activity turned inward as an attempt to shore up the inadequately formed self; an attempt which was doomed to exacerbate rather than mitigate the problem in question (Brennan 1992: ch. 4). Hence the gendered distribution of orientations: detachment, independence, activity to the male as masculine; attachment, dependency, passivity to the female as feminine. Both daughters and sons, though, experienced the contrast between a supposedly regressive narcissistic mother and a civilized, active, masterful father, with the mother representing the principle of 'oneness' and engulfment and the father representing that of difference and autonomy (Benjamin 1990: 148).

In this case the resolution of the oedipal complex was one which pushed the boy towards the rational/independent/autonomous pole (the 'public' sphere of occupational and professional activity) and the girl towards the irrational/dependent/nurturing pole (the domestic sphere). Rationality was taken to be the prerogative of the former; irrationality the inevitable characteristic of the latter. In short, the capitalist nuclear family served to actualize a series of dichotomies which map onto one another; rationality/affect, detachment/attachment, public/private, subject/object, or, as Benjamin (1990: 177) puts it, 'icy paternal outside/regressive maternal warmth'. To the degree that this uncomfortable and debilitating condition had come about, the public and the private had become degenerate in the way discussed by Arendt (1973b: chs 5, 10).[31]

In relation to this point, individuals were coming to valorize personal independence (as freedom) and to view 'society' as their oppressive 'other'. Freedom was becoming freedom from the burden of sociability. This conception of freedom was becoming not only thinkable but, apparently, practicable, as living in a sociable way was no longer a cultural imperative. More than this, the cultivation of sociability was becoming both unnecessary and increasingly difficult as the indifference intruded into social relations through commodification began to take effect. Interdependence was coming to be lived by the capitalist as independence and by the worker as dependence upon an indifferent and intransigent 'system'. For the capitalist, independence was also nurtured in a specific way in the family sphere. But this independence, as Jessica Benjamin makes clear, while it may have been factually grounded for the moment in individual ownership of capital, was psychically fragile. The sources of capitalist autonomy were becoming drained of their sociability, which was an important element in the constitution of bourgeois psychic strength. Since, in contrast to the bourgeois, the capitalist was no longer required to live interdependently, his psyche was beginning to lose that strength. In the absence of this necessary, lived interdependence, the capitalist became incapable of acting 'intersubjectively'. His independence now rested on individual ownership of capital alone; hence, it was the independence of the 'atom'.

The self-discipline of the coldly rational masculine man could be the strongly moral self-discipline of the man of conscience who acknowledged allegiance to God or to a secular analogue of God (such as 'justice') rather than to actual human beings inhabiting a shared world.[32] Or it could be that of the instrumentally, economically rational capitalist oriented to success in the economic sphere (or a combination of both). In both cases, the small male child would have been expected to identify with a stern and distant father who would be a model for the contemptuous evaluation of the 'feminine' activities of nurturance. Masculinity was here expressed in an abstract, impersonal ethos, in indifference to personal need.

Neither the cold rationality of the active-masculine (whether this be expressed in economic rationality or in 'conscience') nor the warm affect of the passive-feminine is adequate to the tasks of public-spiritedness. Both rationality and affect are here worldless in that they are different modes of self-regard. Atomism involves a relentlessly egoistic instrumental orientation to the world, or, in psychoanalytic terms, the perversion of the activity drive via the imperative to mastery and the uneven development of the ego drive at the expense of Eros (social love). Conscience is here understood as a manifestation of the ego drive in that it involves a worldless concern with the preservation of one's personal purity (Arendt 1972: 64–6). Regarding the passive-feminine, this, too, is self-regarding in that the passive is a matter of invisible activity and attentiveness, i.e. activity and attentiveness turned towards the self, as noted previously.

Conclusion

Capitalism is a dehumanizing mode of life in that it has a strong tendency to abrogate the parenting task which is culture's essence. This tendency is related to its own need to realize surplus value. In this chapter we have begun to consider this matter from the point of view of reification: a shaping of drives which debilitates sociability for all, removes the possibility of imaginative activity from an emergent class of proletarians and from capitalist wives, and constitutes this activity in the mode of mastery in an emergent class of capitalists. We have considered these developments in terms of commodity fetishism as instituted through abstract labour and money/capital, on the one hand, and the capitalist oedipal family, on the other. Once existing practices have been subsumed under these institutions, differentiation takes on an abstract character; it is manifested in a worldless form in that it drains the world of its sociability and intelligibility. Now the abrogation of cultural parenting (begun in relation to artisans and peasants under hybrid bourgeois capitalism) comes to affect capitalists themselves.

As commodity exchange moved from the margins to the centre of communities, the nexus of social relations constituted by capitalism's commodified division of labour was coming to produce a cognitively opaque and depersonalized culture in which intelligibility and sociability were under serious assault. As the division of labour advanced, the production process became steadily more opaque to participating workers, who became indifferent to the character of work undertaken and ignorant of the purpose of the totality of a production process of which their activity formed a minuscule part. As contractual relations between buyers and sellers of labour power became more prevalent, direct and personal social relations were replaced by direct and indirect impersonal social relations. The result was that rationality was split between the impersonal systemic 'functional' form and the atomized form connoted by the concept of *homo oeconomicus*. Sociability was shorn of its functional character and withdrew into the non-economic spheres where it became a matter of choice rather than cultural imperative. In short, both rationality and sociability (as individual attributes) shrank to fit the atomized form of life that capitalism was coming to demand.

The fetishizing effects of this relational (therefore psychic) reduction were enhanced by the increasing ratio of dead to living 'labour' consequential on advancing industrialization. Both of these engendered amnesia regarding the necessity of inter-generational interdependence. The presence of the past as 'dead' labour, or labour from which the traces of individuality and agency had been erased, reconfigured relations between the generations so that indebtedness to the past could be cancelled, or never registered in the first place. These are the developments which render atomizing interpellations both intelligible and welcome. They are intelligible because they resonate with the lonely experience of dependence upon an indifferent, cognitively opaque and impersonal system of social relations experienced as 'things' (the frozen activity, or 'dead labour', of a mechanized and rationalized world). They are welcome because they apparently authorize individual protection from, and rights against, cultural 'thingness' conceived of as 'society'.

It was by these means that cultures became opaque to common sense (as they were transformed from particular cultures to constituent social formations of capitalism) and that science became essential. As noted in chapter two, science (both social and natural) becomes necessary as the culture becomes fragmented through abstract differentiations which transform it into a totality of 'many determinations', only a fraction of which can be directly experienced and known by particular individuals. What was coming into being was an unprecedented human condition whereby individuals were being required to act without knowing and were encouraged to relate without feeling, or even, to become unaware altogether of the necessity of human interdependence.

The worldless effects of the commodified division of labour were enhanced by those of the gendered division of labour. In the course of the nineteenth century, bourgeois (turning capitalist) women became domesticated. This meant that, not only were these women not required to work outside of the family, but they lost those opportunities for worldly pursuits which hybrid bourgeois culture had afforded them. Domestication reduced women to nothing but husband's ornament and child's mother; to specialists in beauty and caring. To the degree that this domestication was secured, rationality became masculinized and affect became feminized. Men became incapable of the nurturing abilities which bourgeois fathers had begun to acquire; women were expected to be specialists in nurturing but their own stunted development left them ill-prepared for this demanding task. Too much was asked of them; too little was given.

102 *The death of worldliness*

Once capitalism becomes the sole, or dominant form of life, this division of labour reduces adult subjects to an immature condition marked by the illusion of (or desire for) absolute individual autonomy combined with the experience of total dependence on an impersonal, indifferent and unknowable world. The indifference of the world breeds the indifference of individuals towards the world and towards others who share this world, which is no longer experienced as 'common'. Thus is set in motion a kind of worldless, downward, dialectical spiral whose effects have become so potent today. I begin the discussion of this new potency in chapter six.

6 Abstract labour and the network society

Industrialization initiated a mode of differentiation which culminated in the divorce of rationality and sociability and which reconfigured rationality as, on the one hand, the 'objective' or systemic rationality which is described as functional (Gorz 1989; Habermas 1989), and, on the other, the 'subjective' rationality of *homo oeconomicus*. Expressed in class terms, bourgeois was reduced to capitalist and artisan was reduced to proletarian. Expressed in terms of the reality principle, reality-testing became a systemic function rather than an individual or experientially co-operative activity, or, secondary process functioning migrated back to the cultural level from which it had 'descended' to the bourgeois individual through the civilizing psychologizing processes discussed in chapters three and four. It did not trickle down to the proletarian level, since proletarians need be no more than bearers of a functional rationality which works upon, rather than through, them. That is to say, functional rationality did not require the active, intellectual engagement of proletarians for its effectiveness. It did not actualize their human potentials for the kind of psychic functioning required for relatively autonomous forms of subjectivity. Out of this transition came a mode of differentiation which subjected proletarians to an impoverished form of psychologization and which reconfigured the capitalist psyche so that ego and id were subsumed under superego. Proletarians would not be allowed the opportunity to develop relative autonomy; that of capitalists was at risk through atomization. These were the psychic effects of the liberal industrial manifestation of commodity fetishism

Industrializing capitalism initiated a process of abstract differentiation whereby individual human powers were 'collected up', fragmented and redistributed in a way which rendered a minority of humans (capitalists) active and a majority (proletarians) inactive in relation to the most important arenas of life. This involved a novel kind of systematizing of culture in the sense that impersonal mediations became more consequential than the personal. Once impersonality had trumped the personal, individual subjects (first proletarians, later capitalists) began to experience themselves as bearers of structures (Althusser 1984a; 1990d). This was beginning to be the case by the nineteenth century's end, as the scale of industrialization rendered corporate forms of capital ownership necessary (Hilferding 1981). From this time on, the dichotomous differentiations which were inherent in liberal thinking (such as ideal/material, subject/object, individual/society) became experiential categories. These categories are, in fact, categories of a worldless world and they are directly relevant to questions about rationality and citizenship. They capture the experience of subjects who come after the relative autonomy enjoyed by bourgeois subjects and who have been encouraged to expect this relative autonomy (interpreted as absolute) as a right.

What I want to explore in the remaining chapters of this book is the way in which neoliberal capitalism constitutes new kinds of subjects who experience a wholly novel kind of worldlessness. This is the worldlessness which is engendered by a dereified mode of commodity fetishism which institutes contradictory requirements within the occupational sphere by demanding that individual subjects be simultaneously autonomous and heteronomous. This requirement is expressed in an unprecedentedly demanding reality principle whose only 'reality' for the subject is the demand for 'performance'; performance here being the imperative placed on subjects to labour abstractly so as to produce surplus value (Marcuse 1987: 45–50). I say this because, while placing high performance expectations on individuals now, capitalism is refusing, first, to guarantee satisfaction of the ego drive ('interests') and second, to provide the enabling relatively determinate appearances which are needed to render human indeterminacy bearable. For this reason I shall argue that the present capitalist configuration has abrogated the role of cultural parenting; that its cultural principle is not a reality principle but a virtual reality principle (Dean 2000). In the sense that this abrogation involves uncertainty which is designed rather than being the result of war, pestilence or famine, it is unprecedented (Sennett 1998: 31).

Designed uncertainty has been effected through an apparent return to the free-market practices valorized by nineteenth-century English liberal capitalism as manifested in the transition from organized to disorganized capitalism. This 'designed uncertainty' has begun to dissolve the conditions of possibility for the calculating practices of *homo oeconomicus*.[1] This is because the dialectic of use and exchange is now unprecedentedly speedy and unpredictable so the rules of cost–benefit analysis are difficult (sometimes impossible) to apply, or, cost–benefit analysis is a kind of reality-testing of a modest, atomized kind which is presently losing its conditions of possibility.

I shall make this argument by way of a contrast between 'organized' and 'disorganized' modes of capitalism (Lash and Urry 1987) which will be discussed in terms of their subjectively organizing and disorganizing dimensions as effected through their different manifestations of abstract labour. During the organized phase of capitalism, the inherently dynamic and contradictory (unpredictable) character of capitalism was kept under control through the effective supervision of the state (Althusser 1984a; Poulantzas 1978). Since the 1980s the state's supervisory touch has been lightened and commodity fetishism has been let off the leash, as it were. We have moved from a reified to a dereified totality. In a reified totality differentiations are relatively fixed and clearly bounded (in part due to the effective political supervision of the state); in a dereified totality they are not.

In section one of this chapter I evaluate the culturally-parenting character of organized capitalism (its reality principle) by taking as its exemplary organizing principle the institution of the factory; an organizing principle which informed, not only factories, but also offices; therefore, an organizing principle which comprised both manual and 'white collar' workers (Braverman 1974). This organizing principle, which is expressed also in the Keynesian welfare state, was the systemic bearer of secondary process functioning. As such, it left room for an individuated, privatized kind of reality-testing conducive to a passive conformity which, while inimical to the gratification of the activity drive, was not wholly incompatible with a sense of well-being. This is the condition characterized by Marcuse as 'one-dimensionality' (Marcuse 1986). As manifested during the organized phase of capitalism, this one-dimensionality did not leave individual subjects altogether deprived of sociability. In fact, the reified, durably-differentiated place which was the factory (or the office) afforded the possibility of durable sociable relations which tended to counteract the most debilitating effects of commodity fetishism. Today one-dimensionality remains a requirement but it is under threat at a time when it has become imperative for individuals to take on new responsibilities for their own well-being. In the second part of the chapter I shall consider this threat in terms of the transition from factory to network as principle of organization (Castells 1996). Whereas the factory tended towards reification (determinacy), the network tends towards dereification (indeterminacy). As will be seen, dereification is being effected by a revitalized laissez-faire working through a combination of organizational and technological innovations which enhance the worldlessness first introduced by the liberal-industrial form of commodity fetishism. The nature of the worldless form of dereification effected by capitalism will be understood with the help of Arendt's conception of process. The class and occupational dimensions of contemporary dereifications will be explored with the help of Castells's account of the network.

I From liberal to organized capitalism

From capitalist to functionary: from culture to totality

In discussing the movement from culture to totality I shall take as the clearest manifestation of the latter the post-1945 quarter-century of relative stability in the Euro-American world; the quarter-century during which capitalism was most experientially 'systemic' or 'organized' (Lash and Urry 1987).[2] During this period the institutions discussed in chapter five – abstract labour and monetization – were carried forward from the liberal industrial mode of capitalism theorized by Marx, but some of their anticipated effects were eliminated or modified through the modestly 'socialized' character of organized and mechanized mass production. Partly as a result of this, the dialectic of use and exchange took on a stately pace which rendered reification more salient than dereification. At the same time, the impersonal disciplinary character which had at first impinged only on proletarians, became, in some respects, experientially significant for capitalists and their intellectuals (knowledge producers). The difference between proletarians and capitalists/intellectuals was that whereas secondary process functioning remained a necessity for the latter, it was optional for the former, who would need to be strenuously upwardly mobile to achieve this culturally constituted form of mindfulness (Bernstein 1977).[3]

Universalist claims notwithstanding, effective participation in the bourgeois public sphere required a form of cultivation beyond the resources of most non-bourgeois (Habermas 1992a: 125). For the majority, individual conformity to the new disciplinary requirements of emerging industrial production was induced in a variety of ways ranging from early paternalistic arrangements whereby social relations were based on the principle of kinship, to later, more large-scale and impersonal institutions which sought to fabricate disciplined, docile individuals through surveillance, or the 'gaze'. This could be the 'falsely loving' gaze of paternalism (Sennett 1993b: ch. 2), or it could be the cold, distant, impersonal gaze of the Panopticon (Foucault 1979). As further differentiation followed with the development of industry, and as mass politics came to replace the elite politics of the bourgeois public sphere, the problems of functionality and co-ordination became acute and bureaucratic forms of co-ordination became increasingly necessary. Now discipline was imposed increasingly through drilling; it required no sense of an individual 'interior' or 'consciousness' of which the disciplined behaviour was the direct expression (Dreyfus and Rabinow 1983: chs 6, 7). What was in question was the passive conformity of the functionary (bearer of structures) rather than the active conformity of the relatively autonomous. As capitalism was transmuted into its organized form, capitalists too began to take on the role of functionary. However, one class of functionary required the mindfulness of secondary process functioning; the other did not. Increasingly, though, this was a repressive rather than sublimatory manifestation of secondary process functioning, although where working conditions were conducive to the enjoyment of sociability an element of sublimation would be available, as noted previously.

Abstract labour: the organized mode

The institution of abstract labour, as manifested in mechanized industry, requires the division between mental and manual labour and the reduction of individual labourers to appendages of machines. The factory (and, beyond this, the office, as Braverman makes clear) was the place in which abstract labour was instituted and functional rationality operated on individuals as bearers of functions.[4] That is to say, it was a manifestation of systemic secondary process functioning in the sense that it necessarily subsumed individuals under its purposes and in that its own purposes were, in addition, subsumed under those of a larger system in which it was a 'cog' (Godelier 1988: 4, 5). In theory, if not in practice, the individuality of workers was effaced; in theory, if not always completely in practice, the consciousness of individual workers ceased to be a constitutive element of the production process (Doray 1988; Gorz 1989). Continuity between subjective and objective (or, more accurately, the absence of a sense of subjective and objective) became unnecessary, and even impossible, as individual workers were reduced to minute and interchangeable elements in myriad different production processes whose overall character they were not required to comprehend. As bearers of functional rationality, workers were required to be passive rather than active. They were required to carry out, without question, and as efficiently and as speedily as possible, sets of instructions of which they needed to have little or no understanding.[5] Furthermore, the machines which they minded in accordance with these instructions were seen by workers as the property and power of *capital*, as *objective*, impersonal power, rather than as the outcome of the *social* power of past workers. The past was present in a way which impeded understanding of the world-making powers of co-operative human activity and of the contribution made by previous generations to the constitution of the present. In this way, the culture was taken in through impersonal, systemic sources which engendered individual passivity and atomism.

This passivity was enhanced through the bureaucratization of collective action in the economic sphere and its atomization through electoral politics in the political sphere. Electoral politics is a link in the chain of that bureaucratic action which characterizes organized capitalism. Bureaucratic action is action carried out by elites as experts on behalf of, or upon, the population at large or targeted strata of the population. What it requires from individual subjects is compliance rather than active involvement. In fact, such action can be carried on with minimal conscious engagement on the part of the (represented, taxed or administered) groups in question. What this means is that bureaucratic action intensifies the disjunction between subjectivity and objectivity. It constitutes subjects as passive recipients of (and passive contributors to) public welfare. Here fulfilling one's public responsibilities is passive rather than active (Aglietta 1998: 61); it requires no reality-testing. It requires neither the exercise of individual thought and judgement nor the deliberation of citizens (Keane 1984).[6]

At the same time, we need to note that the institutions of organized capitalism mitigated some of the dehumanizing effects which Marx expected from pure capitalism. This mitigation came about in two related (although also contradictory) ways. First, the socialization of labour through mass production produced some of the effects of association expected by Marx

(1978: 168). It reinstituted sociability of a kind. Second, the decommodification put in train through state-directed activity rendered interdependence visible and, up to a point (at least compared with what was to come after it), benign (Thomas 1984).

Regarding the first point, while organized capitalism instituted commodity fetishism, it did so in a modified form productive of a reality principle which constituted a relatively stable form of appearances. Stability was instituted through career structures for professional strata, jobs for life for manual workers and 'cradle to grave' provision of welfare services for all (Baldwin 1990; Sampson 1995). The relative stability of the production relations instituted through the factory rendered these relations more sociable than the demands of abstract labour would lead us to expect. Remember that what is demanded from workers in theory is the indifferent selling of characterless labour power as the simple preparedness to be set to work at whatever the law of value happens to require at any moment. According to this criterion, what characterizes the relationship between buyer and seller of labour power, between worker and worker, and between worker and labour process, is indifference. However, the durability of work relations during the organized stage of capitalism neutralized for the moment this indifferent logic of abstract labour and rendered factories and offices (possibly) sociable places. Individual subjects experienced relatively stable and embodied (face-to-face) social relations in the sphere of production. In this way they could cultivate their sociability, so, while the labour contract was in place, the form of production was such as to counteract (up to a point) the calculating, atomizing effects to be expected from this. The worst effects of commodity fetishism were not experienced.

Regarding the second point, commodity fetishism was also modified through the decommodification effected by class politics and the welfare state (Baldwin 1990; Offe 1984). While both of these functioned technocratically, they also exemplified a relatively benign form of human interdependence. As the state was visibly involved in welfare activities on behalf of people who, for the moment, imagined and experienced themselves as a 'people', the social bond was visibly expressed through a range of bureaucratic measures which served to roll back the market. In these ways, interdependence of an admittedly tenuous kind was nurtured in the shape of the odd kind of kinship surrogate that is the nation. However, as this interdependence was effected technocratically rather than co-operatively, therefore in a mode which tends towards indifference (Herzfeld 1993), it was itself vulnerable to the erosion of the minimal active political commitment needed to keep it in being. In any case there was a contradiction between technocratic paternalism and working-class collectivism, on the one hand, and between these and an emergent working-class atomism, on the other. The first was expressed in England in the workplace through shop stewards' movements and grassroots rebellions against the English version of corporatism (Goldthorpe 1984; Jefferys 2000; Lash and Urry

1987: 269–79). The second was expressed in an enthusiastic response to parts of the Thatcher agenda during the early 1980s and, increasingly, in a reluctance to pay the price of maintaining the technocracy itself. Individualized cost–benefit analysis (an atomized, calculating form of reality-testing) was being encouraged for the purposes of challenging the authority of technocracy.[7]

Such reality-testing was supported also by the increasing commodification, therefore monetization, of workers' wants. Consumption was becoming transmuted into consumerism (Baudrillard 1981; 1993; Haug 1987); workers who were becoming affluent were workers who were turning to the joys of consumption and to the 'private' intimate familial sphere (Goldthorpe *et al.* 1968). This was a world-evading form of privative privacy enjoyed by workers as consumers of individually-secured gratifications. The private was becoming an escape from and a compensation for the experience of life on the assembly line or in the office, not an arena in which the individual prepared for public engagement with fellow citizens. Increasingly-privatized affluent workers were workers who were receptive to interpellations promising more affluence and greater individual freedoms. As reluctant bearers of structures, they were also receptive to the message that the state would no longer nanny them (Gamble 1994); that they would be allowed to grow up.

During the organized stage of capitalism, what was in question was a nexus of impersonal, but not wholly worldless, institutions which constituted passive subjects who were 'supports' or 'bearers' of systemic secondary process functioning (functional rationality); subjects which, as supports, did not need to develop those thinking, judging and acting abilities demanded of the bourgeois during the hybrid stage of capitalism. Subjects as bearers of functional rationality were feminized subjects in the sense that they were rendered passive, rather than active.[8] We might say that they were parented in a way which impeded the emergence of the maturity connoted by the concept of autonomy. Yet the principle of autonomy informed the culture of which they were members. At the same time, sociability was not completely shredded under organized (welfare state) capitalism and the most debilitating atomizing effects of unintelligibility were kept at bay through guarantees about future well-being. The nexus of institutions produced by this mode of capitalism constituted a kind of stability which facilitated the cultivation of directly experienced, fairly stable personal social relations. It was, moreover, not completely indifferent to the needs of individual subjects. So long as the welfare state was in operation, and reliable and relatively well-paid work was available, the environment was not experienced as wholly unresponsive to individual needs, for a sociable and intelligible world. This world did not constitute the conditions of possibility for relative autonomy since it disregarded the needs connoted by the activity drive by instituting a reified, determinate form of life. It was, moreover, cognitively opaque to proletarian bearers of structures and was only partially transparent to individual intellectuals. At the same time, it muted anxiety about ego interests by promising and delivering rewards for good behaviour. In effect, neither objective nor subjective indifference was fully instituted during the organized stage of capitalism, which minimized the former through a combination of the standardization effected by mass mechanized production and effective state supervision and, in relation to the latter, rendered sociability more consequential than atomism. This is not to say, though, that the 'work of culture' was achieved by means of sublimation as the earlier analysis of social love might lead us to expect. While there were sublimatory aspects to the occupational sphere in the sense that sociability could be enjoyed, the thoroughgoing suppression of the activity drive precluded anything which could be meaningfully identified as sublimation. At the same time, while the activity drive was seriously frustrated, the sex drive was beginning to receive new permissions for apparently untrammelled gratification; gratification, it is worth noting, not at all conducive to the nurturing of social love (Marcuse 1986: ch. 3). Nevertheless, public purposes (in the limited sense of care of the poor, the sick, the old) were fulfilled up to a point by such subjects, but not in an active, knowledgeable, relatively autonomous way.

The dynamic of organized capitalism was a contradictory dynamic of socialization/atomization. Socialization by means of association in the factory faced a two-fold threat: first, the technocratization of collective action as the action of bureaucratic union officials on behalf of a membership; second, the atomization (privatization) of increasingly affluent workers. This two-fold threat involved the redirection of individual attention from the public to the private sphere, or, the reduction of public to 'spectacle' (Debord 1994). Over time, it produced either indifference to the public realm or a limited kind of interest group politics of the kind conveyed by the concept of economic rationality. The latter was a one-dimensional rationality which was, for a time, adequate to the reproduction of a way of life which, while humanly impoverishing compared to the hybrid bourgeois form, was relatively comfortable. The privatized enjoyment for which workers began to cultivate a taste during this period paved the way for neoliberal interpellations of individuals as self-interested and self-reliant subjects. These interpellations invited individuals (as fathers of families, at any rate) to take back responsibilities of which the state had deprived them.[9] Individualized one-dimensional rationality was to increase its scope. As capitalism moved from organizing to disorganizing mode, self-interest and self-responsibility became a duty the fulfilment of which was explicitly urged by political leaders (Gamble 1994). However, this self-interest will be misunderstood if we understand it purely in terms of 'economic rationality'. This is what I now begin to show through an analysis of contemporary capitalism's organizational logic and occupational forms.

II Capitalism and disorganization

Disorganization as process: an Arendtian perspective

With the advent of disorganized capitalism, the process character of the law of value which was first described by Marx and Engels (1998) and first experienced by workers who were drawn into the new industrial process (through the contrast between making with tools and making with machines) returns to prominence. Here, a brief recapitulation of the nature and necessity of process will be in order.

As we noted in chapter two, the reduction of world to process is effected through the subsumption of human activity under labouring; a subsumption which is necessary to reconfigure production for 'use' as production which is also for exchange. To say that the world has been reduced to process is to say that a worldless form of dereification has taken place; one which, far from correcting the reifying dimensions of capitalism, exacerbates the worldlessness which these dimensions induce. We can begin to understand the psychic problems induced by process by recalling Freud's concept of the reality principle which must provide for emergent subjects objects which are fairly stable and sensuously present if psychic health is to be established. Through the experience of such good objects, subjects in a civilized culture acquire the intellectual and emotional strengths needed to function in such a challenging environment. Since capitalism necessarily reduces the world to process, it must fail to provide its subjects with such objects.

Capitalism must reduce the world to process because it must ensure that objects are exchangeable as well as usable. That is to say, objects must be produced for consumption rather than use, therefore for destruction or obsolescence. Expressed in Arendtian terms, making must be reduced to labouring. The essence of labouring is that it comprises activity oriented to consumption needs. The importance of this is three-fold. First, activity undertaken in labouring mode is a compulsive activity, in the absence of which life cannot be sustained. Second, the objects produced by labour-governed activity are intended for immediate consumption, therefore for destruction. Third, in contrast to making, which connotes individually controlled, skilled, imaginative activity, labouring connotes mass activity (Arendt 1958: 123). So process connotes a denaturing compulsiveness of human activity as activity determined by the urgency of bodily needs. It also connotes the dissolution of both subjects and objects under the specific compulsion of value, or, the experience of life as flow into which individuals are submerged rather than as activities in which they are involved.

To elaborate, industrialized making is making reduced to labouring in the senses that, for the purposes of efficiency, whole objects are decomposed into parts and those parts are produced through a flow of mechanized operations which is experienced by individual labourers as a process within which they function as machine minders. Dereification of the object is here accompanied by a reification of the means of making objects as machines and a dereification of the (artisanal) subject as an element in a 'collective labourer' in such a way as to 'make a speciality of the absence of all development' (Marx 1976a: 470), or, the body becomes, apparently, pure matter in motion according to the needs of the machine (Doray 1988: ch. 5).

So, the logic of labouring is a compulsive and destructive logic which serves to obliterate the individualized distinctiveness of human activity, subjects and objects. This is the logic under which more and more activities become subsumed as the law of value makes its way in the world; a logic which dictates that we labour abstractly and consume abstractly (more on the latter in chapter seven). As this happens, more and more objects are produced for consumption (the sooner, the better). The more that objects are produced for consumption, the more does the thingness of the world dissolve, or, commodity fetishism takes on a dereifying character. With the advent of disorganized capitalism, the process character of capitalism intensified and entered new domains. This intensification is associated not only with the subsumption of making under labouring, but with the reduction of property to wealth. Both making and property are oriented to use. As making is what produces the durable useful objects which turn the earth into a world held in common, property is what provides the durable place within which individuals may prepare themselves for activity in public (Arendt 1958: ch. 2).

Capitalist ownership dissolves property into wealth by changing the nature of ownership and of what is owned (Arendt 1958: 58–67; Bowles and Gintis 1986: chs 6, 7). Property is tangible; unlike wealth, it has a clear use value (Arendt 1958: 69). The subsumption of the former under the latter is, in effect, the subsumption of use under exchange. This is manifested in the transformation of money into capital and of capital into finance capital; finance capital being the most fluid form of capital whose unregulated flows in recent years have contributed so much to the unintelligibility and unsociability of our world. While, as Arrighi (1994: ix) reminds us, 'financialization' is a recurrent feature of capitalism, the consequences for everyday life depend on the mode of capitalism in which financialization is embedded (or the point of transformation at which it occurs). As facilitated by electronics, financialization is reducing the world to process in unprecedented and bewildering ways.

The dereification involved in labouring and wealth has become more intensive (it reaches the psyche) and extensive (it penetrates areas which in the past have been protected from value's remit) in recent years. Let us consider now the organizational and class dimensions of this contemporary dereification, which will be approached via the concept of the network as developed by Castells (1996).

Disorganization as network

The network, rather than the factory, is the exemplary organizational principle of the new mode of capitalism. This is not to say that factories disappear or that production becomes secondary to consumption, but that both become reconstituted (Castells 1996; Negri and Hardt 2001: 280–303). This reconstitution is a matter of the different modes of materiality implicated in the shift from mechanics to electronics. We will begin to understand the subject effects of this shift in terms of an unprecedented mode of materiality which reconfigures places as spaces, thereby effecting an experience of 'weightlessness' or 'dematerialization' (Coyle 1997; Tapscott 1995).[10] Here weightlessness and dematerialization are characteristics of an acutely worldless condition associated with the unprecedented speeding-up of the dialectic of exchange and use.

Keynesianism plus mass mechanized production slowed down and rendered relatively predictable the use/exchange dialectic. Neoliberalism demanded its acceleration. This was effected initially through the deregulation of capital and the organizational innovations intended to enhance 'flexibility', meaning the totality's prompt and effective response to value's changing requirements. These new organizational features engendered the experience of disorganization. They included the 'rolling back' of the welfare state[11] and the 'rolling forward' of the big corporations (Radice 1999). In addition, changes in production processes which had been initiated during the 1970s began to dissolve the determinacy experienced in the mechanized factory. These include just-in-time delivery systems, small-batch production, as well as the 'vertical disintegration' effected by sub-contracting, outsourcing, self-employment and temporary work (Castells 1996: ch. 3; Harvey 1989: chs 9–11; Lash and Urry 1987: chs 4–7).[12] Now dereification would become intensified, loosening the connections between exchange and use and increasingly privileging the former over the latter. Thus the process character of experience to which Arendt draws our attention becomes ever more consequential. This institutionalization of process as intangibility would have high psychic costs (Bauman 2000; Sennett 1998), to be discussed in chapter seven. The combination of these changes constitutes social relations of the kind conveyed by the concept of the network.

As the neoliberal implementation of the law of value effects dramatic experiential changes in the occupational sphere, it also effects its entry into areas of life previously barred to it; a movement which is overseen by the state.[13] Accompanying these changes is a rhetoric of globalization exhorting the reconstitution of individuals as subjects suited to the new mode of life, a rhetoric in which is reiterated the importance of education and of a revitalized work ethic. Capitalism's new mode, we are assured, requires more educated workers than its organized predecessors (Knights and Willmott 1990). It also requires that individuals become actively engaged and entrepreneurial (O'Malley 2000); that they put their imaginations and their emotions at the disposal of capital accumulation (Aglietta 1998). As possessors of labour power, humans must remain available (as human resources) for systemic subsumption, but now some must await in educated and active mode (Castells 1996: ch. 4; Delanty 2001; Pijl 1998: ch. 4). However, while we may be required to be more or less resourceful (on which more later), we are all reinterpellated as self-interested, self-reliant, active, knowledgeable and flexible subjects capable of taking charge of those matters hitherto under the direction of the state, and of responding speedily and effectively to the requirements of the market. In effect, individuals are given new responsibilities for self-maintenance; responsibilities which tend to inculcate a sense that, while we can make demands on, and have obligations towards, others with whom we have contractual relationships, beyond this we owe nothing to, and should expect nothing from, our culture (Massing 1999; Solow 2000).[14]

From place to space: from factory to network

In claiming that disorganization intensifies the process character of experience I am claiming that locations became more like spaces than places. This is evident in the contrast between factory and network: a contrast which is immensely significant for our understanding of the different subject effects of the two modes of capitalism. The mechanized factory is a 'place', in Goffman's (1971) sense of the term, or, it has some of the attributes associated with worldliness. It involves visible processes which constitute fairly stable appearances. It is a 'concrete', clearly bounded system of directly experienced social relations within which individuals interact with solid, durable, directly experienced industrial machines productive of solid, durable, directly experienced things. The network is a space; it is an 'immaterial' (or, more accurately, a less weightily, less reliably material) system of flexible, speedily and unpredictably changing social relations within which individuals interact with rapidly changing electronic machines productive of apparently immaterial, fleeting (non)objects (services and messages). Where the network is in question, processes are less visible and therefore more mysterious than those found in the strongly-material, relatively durable mechanized world; they constitute evanescent and seemingly ungrounded appearances (Sennett 1998: ch. 4). We may say that while the conception and execution of tasks is split in factory production social processes are visible, embodied, stable and durable, as are social relations. What this means is that sociability is not antithetical to the experience of factory life, in spite of its abstract and impersonal principles of organization and the increasing ratio of dead to living labour. At the same time, stability and durability (which are relative to the conditions produced by disorganizing capitalism) may themselves be experienced (indeed have been experienced) as oppressive and stultifying. However, the point is that the appearances constituted by industrial-mechanical practices are experienced as 'real'. That is to say, subjects constituted by such practices could locate themselves in time and place, even if only in passively-conformist mode. At the same time, these subjects will have been promised that, as good subjects, they will be rewarded by a life of peace and security. Intense boredom and lack of stimulation are compensated for by security of conditions of life (experiential predictability), by the sociability enabled by factory production, and by the new delights of private consumption. The situation of the subject constituted by the network is quite different.

Places are like printed texts; they are resistant to the imprinting of new meanings. Spaces are like electronic texts; they are hospitable to the imprinting of new meanings. As a space-like mode of organization, the network is an extraordinarily flexible form whose purpose is to secure the speedy distribution and redistribution of objects across the globe. It thereby effects an unprecedented speediness of the use–exchange dialectic, a speediness which is facilitated by electronics (Castells 1996: 471) and underpinned by the enhanced power of finance capital (Castells 1997: ch. 5; Harvey 1989: ch. 11). The resultant institutional and organizational mix induces experiential instability (indeterminacy) of an unprecedentedly intense kind.

Prompt responsiveness to value's demands is at once a function of the revalorization of competitiveness and that which enables the intensification of competitiveness. The result is 'an extraordinarily variable geometry that tends to dissolve historical, economic geography' (Castells 1996: 106). The willingness of capital to threaten flight, and the swiftness of such flights once decided upon, force governments into competition for capital's favours (Castells 1996: ch. 4).[15] So the experience of place and reality constituted by the factory cedes to the experience of space and virtuality constituted by the network (Castells 1997: ch. 5).

In approaching the difficult question of virtuality, we are coming to the heart of the unprecedented worldlessness instituted by contemporary capitalism and of the intensification of that dereification to the dehumanizing character of which Arendt alerts us.[16] The specific psychic effects of virtuality (a strange kind of presenceless presencing) will be discussed in chapter seven. For the moment, we can consider it as an emergent property of a combination of commodity fetishism and electronics. We noted in chapter five that the abstractions of commodity fetishism render the world increasingly opaque at the experiential level (the level of common sense), and noted also earlier in this chapter that, as manifested in organized capitalism, commodity fetishism engendered a reified form of worldlessness which was not wholly incompatible with sociability and predictability. Electronics deepens opacity by aiding the speeding up of the dialectic of use and exchange and by rendering processes and practices less experientially material than in the organized past (Sennett 1998: ch. 4). It enables the ever-speedier apparently dematerializing reconfigurations of use that the concept of 'information' connotes (Castells 1996: ch. 1). 'Information' as product and process connotes the possibility and necessity of changing spatio-temporal separations and re-fusions of different elements of production processes, as well as the speeding up of the dialectic and the reconfiguration of modes of material so as to produce novel objects of exchange. Thus the preoccupation with information signals an increase in the importance of 'messages', of 'services', of electronic images whose production, in parts of the West, comes to take on more significance than the production of 'things'.[17] In this way, the world becomes, not only less 'material', but also less transparent in its functioning.[18]

For Castells, though, virtuality is constituted not primarily by electronic media but through the occupational structure which requires individuals to live 'in the space of flows and in timeless time' (Castells 1998: 370).[19] It may be tempting to dismiss this language as extravagant or vacuous. Far from this being the case, it expresses something quite profound about contemporary capitalist intentions and about the experiences engendered by the successful implementation of those intentions. To live in the 'space of flows' and in 'timeless time' is to live in a dereified world in which place and time are required to empty themselves of their particularities and to offer themselves as empty spaces and durations for the imprinting of value's law. This experience renders us incapable of 'cognitive mapping', or, of locating ourselves in thought in a mappable space (Jameson 1992: chs 1, 10; 1994). The language ('space of flows', 'timeless time') is a language expressive of the locationally and temporally unbounded ambitions of neoliberal capitalism as it goes on its globalizing way. In experiential terms, these ambitions require that individuals and places maintain themselves in a state of permanent openness to unpredictable and unintelligible rearrangement. Expressed in psychoanalaytic terms, what is in question is a volatile and unpredictable relationship between 'representatives' and drives, or between form, energy and matter; the relationship connoted by the concept of primary process functioning. For this reason, and in relation to subjectivation, contemporary capitalism may be more appropriately characterized as 'disorganizing' rather than as 'disorganized' and, for this reason, as noted previously, I want to argue that its reality principle is 'virtually' rather than 'really' real (more on this in chapter seven). A word about the occupational structure of the network society will be useful at this point.

The network society and abstract labour

The network society requires a reconsideration of the concept of abstract labour explored in chapter five. There, abstract labour was conceptualized in simple terms as the mere readiness to put one's energy at the disposal of capital, the exemplar here being the unskilled machine-minder. In this case 'abstract' referred to the paring away of skilfulness and sociability from workers' activities, as well as the splitting of objects into component parts; paring and splitting being for the purposes of efficiency, flexibility and control of both worker and work process. While abstract labour of approximately this kind remains a necessity, the thoughtlessness and docility which would have best equipped abstractly labouring workers for their tasks is no longer adequate for a large minority of workers who constitute a new aristocracy of labour (Pijl 1998). Of particular interest here is the nature of what have been differently described as 'symbolic analysts' (Reich 1991) and 'self-programmable workers' (Castells 1998). Castells's concept is more appropriate here since it captures quite well the kind of 'autonomy' enjoyed by these workers. The 'programme' connotes the insertion of software into a machine which, once set in motion, works automatically. 'Self-programmable' in fact implies a contradiction between autonomy and heteronomy (between reflexive self-direction and passive adaptation) which as it becomes increasingly lived may prove eventually to have serious politicizing effects.

As 'symbolic analysts', self-programmers engage in occupations (the provision of services as messages and the attempt to constitute new needs for new services) which require them to be expert manipulators of symbols and/or of persons.[20] They are engaged in an endless process of redefinition of skills and of tasks, and, to this end, of themselves also. Or, as Castells puts it: 'Whoever is educated, in the proper organizational environment, can reprogram him/herself toward the endlessly changing tasks of the production process' (1998: 361). I shall return to this very important matter in a moment. First, though, let me note that in addition and in contrast to the self-programmables, the network society also requires a stratum of 'generic' labourers.

Generic labour manifests many of the characteristics attributed in chapter five to abstract labour, in that it is a form of labour which demands that individual labourers behave as 'human terminals' (Castells's term) which are easily interchangeable with machines or other human terminals at the behest of capital. In order to carry out their tasks, individual generic labourers need do no more than receive and execute signals. Their function is to adapt promptly (but unthinkingly) to changing systemic requirements. Generic labourers live in a condition of acute commodity fetishism in the specific sense that they have been reduced to their potential to expend energy. As such, they are not required to cultivate their most human potentials in any way and are, therefore, as individuals, wholly interchangeable and disposable. These are the holders of 'McJobs' (Ritzer 1996) for whom work remains as paltry as ever it was under organized capitalism, or for some of whom it has even become more paltry (Judt 2001). For these labourers, the split between mental and manual labour remains in force. Docility and passive conformity remain the requirement. But, now, no guarantees of future security are given for satisfactory fulfilment of these dreary dehumanizing requirements. On the contrary, what instigates conformity today is the awful possibility of becoming 'structurally irrelevant' or part of the significant minority of those who are (for the moment at least) surplus to both the production and consumption requirements of capitalism (Castells 1997: ch. 4).

In contrast to generic labourers, self-programmable workers are required to display openness to challenging novelty and preparedness for ongoing self-transformation. Aspirants to self-programmable status must undergo an education which equips them with the dispositions and skills needed to carry out the most demanding and constantly changing tasks. Maintaining themselves in this condition through 'life-long learning' and the acquisition of 'transferrable skills' (Delanty 2001: 112; Slaughter and Leslie 1997: ch. 3) is an imperative if they are not to slip down into the ranks of generic labour or, worse, become structurally irrelevant. So they, as well as generic labour, must adapt to capitalism's requirements, the difference being that this is an active form of adaptation requiring a self-initiated process of (possibly unending) self-transformation (Castells 1998: 361). In a very real sense, self-programmable workers must maintain themselves in a condition of 'vacant possession', in the sense that they must contain no important and resistant remnants of (commitments to) earlier activities (or particularities) which might impede value's flow.

The personal qualities valorized by disorganizing, networking capitalism are detachment and flexibility, or, in effect, indifference in the sense discussed in chapter five. At the same time, the sociability of 'teamwork' is asserted as a necessity. However, this is the sociability of 'weak ties' (Kotter 1995) since it is a sociability of serial, rather than sustained, attachments. The functionally effective subject becomes a kind of empty screen on which can be written, with little effort, new messages which can be equally effortlessly erased and replaced by newer messages, and so on. At all levels, workers must be indifferent to their occupations in the sense that they must be willing to abandon those occupations on no other grounds than that the law of value dictates it. Attachment to colleagues, to occupation, to place, is now out of place (Bauman 2000). Detachment, or, more precisely, the ability to engage in serial, temporary attachments in 'teams' (to act as if attached while remaining innately detached) is what is functional for capitalism now (Sennett 1998: ch. 6). Yet self-programmable subjects must be highly motivated. They must energetically pursue whatever it is that is currently considered to be exchangeable and they must put their minds to the production of endless streams of new forms of exchangeability. They must refuse to make judgements about the quality of activity to which they will become (temporarily) devoted.

Reality-testing and the network: from reification to dereification

While self-programmers do not suffer from the cognitive deprivations of assembly-line or office workers or holders of 'McJobs', their way of life is such as to prevent the kinds of reality-testing which the experience of autonomy requires. That way of life is marked by the revitalization of commodity fetishism through the insinuation of the law of value into areas previously protected from its writ, and the dereification (reduction of world to intangible process) which networking effects. This is what is expressed in the language of flux and flows.

The popular appeal of this language, which is used by Castells, albeit not only by him,[21] lies in its power to express the experiential character of disorganizing capitalism. Its theoretical significance is that it implies the impossibility of individual reality-testing, as will be argued later. Today, differentiation is borne by swiftly, unpredictably moving processes yielding the experience (sometimes exciting, sometimes unintelligible – sometimes exciting because unintelligible) of flux. This is a world which requires self-programmable workers to be at once entrepreneurs of subjectivity and docile bearers of value's law. It requires individual subjects of all kinds to be self-responsible in a self-interested way and under unprecedentedly volatile, unintelligible conditions, to which the proliferation of risk theories testifies (Bauman 1999; Beck 1992). These volatile conditions constitute disorganized (depsychologized, heteronomous) subjects as a functional necessity, but they also require those subjects to act 'as if' they were psychologized or autonomous.

Unlike the concrete differentiations experienced by the bourgeois subject, and the abstract, but relatively stable, differentiations experienced by the 'organized' subject, the differentiations which confront self-programmers are very much 'for the moment'; subject to the reconfigurations enabled and required by incessant innovations in production processes, labour markets, products (tangible and intangible) and patterns of consumption (of tangibles and intangibles). The potential to melt 'all that is solid into air', noted by Marx and Engels a century and a half ago (Marx and Engels 1998; Berman 1982), has been actualized with unprecedented enthusiasm and vigour today. The result is a tendency towards ego disorganization of the kind connoted by the concept of primary process functioning; towards an immature, narcissistic mode of psychic functioning the characteristics of which will be discussed further in chapter seven. For the moment it is worth recalling that, in the case of self-programmers, this is a contradictory narcissism which combines within one subject the tendencies towards both mastery of, and escape from, the world associated respectively with the capitalist and his domesticated wife.

Enhanced powers of flexibility include enhanced demands for worker mobility, at least among the new aristocracy of labour. For the moment the practice of this geographical mobility appears to be enhancing the narcissism of already-detached subjects by facilitating their 'secession' from responsibilities to the less fortunate.[22] Such mobile workers become 'flexible', rather than public-spirited, citizens (Ong 1999).[23] In terms of property, they tend to retreat into private enclaves in which their needs are supplied largely through 'market forces' and so, apparently, by means of their own autonomous efforts. When self-programmers stand still they do so in spaces which are increasingly likely to take the form of gated communities, often with their own private schools, police force, etc. (Blakely and Snyder 1997; Curtis 1999: ch. 1). Rather than the tolerance of plurality which territorial mobility might be expected to cultivate, the withdrawal from the world which these communities allows nurtures a strong distaste for encountering the unexpected, in whatever form it takes. Here the very worldlessness of the wider world stimulates a new kind of collective subjectivism or indifference which intensifies, rather than corrects, the worldlessness of the outside world's relentless indifference and objectivism. Inhabitants of gated communities can remain oblivious to the external conditions of possibility of their protected, but also impoverished, way of life. This condition of oblivion is rendered the more likely in that, increasingly, responsibility for adaptation to capitalism's demands is the subject's own duty and concern. It follows logically that since they can demand nothing from their culture apart from what is enforceable by contract, such subjects cannot be expected to feel a sense of responsibility for the conditions of life of the heterogeneous 'others' whose activities (or whose loss of activity) may be conditions of possibility for their own.

Compared to the bourgeois way of life, that of self-programmables is both unintelligible and unsociable. The speediness of change and the increased complexity and fragmentation accompanying that speediness result in an opacity beyond the cognitive grasp of the most highly educated. In ways that will be explored further in chapter eight, it is now becoming impossible for individuals to engage in calculations about the chains of interdependencies and division of labour whose emergence in early modern Europe initiated a process of psychologization. Yet individuals need to be able to do this if they are to 'know how to go on'.

Conclusion

In this chapter I have set up a contrast between organized and disorganized capitalism so as to explore the different subject effects of different manifestations of abstract labour. Taking the factory and network as the organizing principles of these two modes of capitalism (organized and disorganized respectively), I have argued that the reifications which marked the factory were not wholly debilitating, since they served to counteract the atomizing effects to be anticipated from the institution of abstract labour. Moreover, the factory principle was accompanied by a welfare form of capitalism which retained a parenting dimension. We may say that organized capitalism was characterized by a reality principle which, as Marcuse correctly notes, was also a performance principle (it demanded compliance with the requirements of value's law). However, the willingness to comply was rewarded fairly predictably so that the effects of the unintelligibility introduced into the production process through the industrial division of labour were mitigated by stability and the predictability of experienced conditions of life.

The principles which inform contemporary institutions and which are now borne by electronic technology are those of the free market and of the network. These principles are mutually supportive in that they both tend towards volatility and unpredictability. They are dereifying principles in that they tend to constitute de-differentiation rather than differentiation. De-differentiation is not in any sense a return to a predifferentiated world as place. Far from it. It is, rather, a process which demands vacant possession of places and individuals which/who must offer themselves as empty spaces awaiting the imprint of value's law. In constituting spaces, capitalism dissolves both private and public as places (directly experienced domains of relatively stable practices) within which the self can be nurtured (the private) and in which such nurtured selves can appear and have their voices heard (the public). Private now comes to connote not that which nurtures individuals and prepares them for public activity or sociability but *either* the value of economic, as opposed to political, practices *or* a narcissistic retreat from the world. In either case, it is a privative rather than worldly privacy. In fact, Meyrowitz (1985) shows the ways in which the value of privacy becomes more and more irrelevant as the boundary between public and private dissolves along different dimensions. We appear to have arrived at the point at which privacy means nothing more than freedom from responsibility, or, a retreat from the demands of our fellow human beings and the obligations of world care.[24] This absence of a self-constitutive privacy will be explored in chapter seven in terms of the immiserating psychic effects of fantasizing. For the moment, we should recall the importance of such privacy in the constitution of relatively autonomous bourgeois subjects.

As noted previously, capitalism now requires 'autonomous', self-responsible subjects. Having examined the institutional sources of such self-responsible subjects in chapters three and four, we are in a position to begin to understand that contemporary capitalism is imposing contradictory requirements on its subjects. It is, if anything, even more demanding than was early bourgeois capitalism, but it is failing to provide the nurturing which would make the fulfilment of its demands bearable. This is what accounts for the prevalence of economic rationality in contemporary capitalist democracies, but this economic rationality is a disabled rationality which seeks, necessarily unsuccessfully, the clear objects and rules of calculation which economic rationality requires. I shall return to this question in chapter eight. Before doing so, I shall go on to consider the extra-occupational practices which intensify the worldlessness that working in the network induces. These are the fantasizing practices associated with consumerism and virtuality; practices which are intended to reconfigure need as desire through the institution of abstract consumption and which, in doing so, constitute an unprecedentedly privative form of privacy.

7 Abstract consumption and the dissolution of the ego

Pure capitalism is an abstract culture which cultivates subjective indifference as a matter of principle and of daily survival: the indifference of capitalists to the particularity of labourers and the indifference of labourers to capitalists, other labourers, and process and objects of production. Indifference towards human particularity is expressed in the abstraction of 'labour power' (the capacity to expend energy) from the particular bodies of individuals, and in the labour contract. 'Unformed' energy must be at the free disposal of capitalism in that individuals must be prepared to respond promptly, efficiently and effectively to the changing and increasingly unpredictable demands of the law of value. This energy is 'sold' to capitalists through an impersonal, instrumental relationship mediated by money. Indifference towards worldly particularity is expressed in the reduction of place to space, this being a matter of dissolving the boundaries, within and between cultures, which had protected particularities from value's rule. Having considered the reduction of place to space through occupational relations in chapter six, it is now time to explore the ways in which, through abstract consumption, private place cedes to privative space. As place becomes space, the non-privative privacy needed to constitute a sense of self becomes unavailable. The individual becomes disorganized, or, psychic boundaries begin to dissolve.

Indifference is particularly pronounced in capitalism's contemporary manifestation which has been largely freed of the concrete, substantial and retarding freight carried over from the pre-capitalist past and, more than this, is served by a technology of extraordinary flexibility, lightness and speed. Electronics has been immensely important in speeding up and intensifying the process character of life, whose initial impetus is the need to subsume all activities under a labouring logic so as to realize ever-increasing amounts of surplus value. It has done this by transforming the ways in which commodities are produced, as well as the range and character of 'things' considered appropriate for commodification. In effect, electronics introduces new modalities of matter and renders one – virtuality, which first made its institutional appearance with the advent of the telegraph (Carey 1989) – in myriad new forms which endow it with novel forms of consequentiality (Hayles 1999; Heims 1993; Landow 1997; Langan 2000). Our interest in consequentiality here is an interest in the ways in which the culture is taken in and reproduced through its individual human 'units'. Where abstract consumption is in question, this 'taking in' is strongly mediated by fantasy in a way that nurtures desires rather than needs or wants. It is of the essence of capitalism that need and want be constituted as desire, since without desire as a kind of insatiable wanting (a desire which is temporarily sated by means of exchange objects) capitalism would be unable to reproduce itself (Hillman 1994). This necessity of desirousness is what Haug (1987) describes as the commodity aesthetic.[1] It is what introduces process into the psyche. We can understand this by considering desire as kin to the infant wishfulness analysed by Freud, therefore as a manifestation of psychic 'processing' which has much in common with the primary process functioning attributed by Freud to the infant. Recall that primary process functioning consists in instantaneous cathexes and de-cathexes of misperceived objects in the groundless hope that these will bring gratification. Such objects are bad objects. The increasing prevalence of such bad objects and the relative absence of good objects is what I mean by psychic 'vacant possession', a condition which inhibits the emergence, not only of social love, but of the mental abilities connoted by the concept of secondary process functioning.

The tendency towards primary process functioning can be understood in terms of the dissolution of attachment or, more accurately, the reconstitution of attachment as serial attachment to constantly changing objects (the subsumption of being under having, in Marxian terms). In effect, the dissolution or unbinding of our attachments is necessary along two dimensions. First is capitalism's need for 'vacant possession' of possessors of 'labour power' as the 'abstract' potential for expending physical or psychic energy which I discussed in chapters five and six. Second is its need for free access to 'consumption power' as an abstract free-floating neediness (desirousness). This neediness sets in motion a vicious cycle of fantasizing of a peculiarly debilitating kind; a fantasizing caught up in the dialectic of use and exchange.

Insofar as privacy becomes a refuge within which the activity of fantasizing takes place, it becomes bereft of resources which might serve to counteract the worldlessness experienced in the occupational sphere. Therefore, in contrast to the privacy enjoyed by bourgeois subjects, it is no longer an institutional support for the particular manifestation of social love which is public-spiritedness. In this chapter Lacanian psychoanalysis, in the shape of Lacan's concepts of imaginary, symbolic, real and lack, will be used to enhance our understanding of the relational combination in which contemporary privative privacy consists. What is in question is a combination of relational absence and presence: absence of authoritative personal parenting relations; presence of a combination of indifferent impersonal relations and virtual relations. This relational configuration nurtures the dispositions associated with the concepts of imaginary and symbolic (worldless desire for an unattainable self-perfection, helpless subsumption under an impersonal and intransigent law of culture, respectively). This combination of imaginary and symbolic, which is configured in different ways by organized and disorganized capitalism, as will be seen later, constitutes an experience of lack or desirousness which, in turn, disposes individual subjects towards 'explosions' of the real.

The chapter is in three parts. Part one sets the scene for an understanding of the privative character of contemporary privacy by recapitulating the understanding of bourgeois and capitalist families developed in earlier chapters. On the basis of this recapitulation, it goes on in part two to use the Lacanian categories (imaginary, symbolic, lack and real) to theorize the character of social (including parenting) relations once culture has become a totality of abstractly differentiated and contradictorily related parts ruled by the law of value. This, I suggest, is what is conveyed by the concept of the symbolic, or, what Zizek refers to as the 'big Other' which he describes as a 'disembodied rational machine' (1996: 144). However, as a 'disorganizing' machine, the symbolic is irrational rather than rational. In effect, the Lacanian categories are interpreted historico-culturally to enable an understanding of psychic functioning as it emerged in a culture almost wholly freed of pre-capitalist social relations (Brennan 1993; MacCannell 1986; Zizek 1989; 1996). The imaginary, symbolic and real connote the degeneration of the ego-directed, relatively bounded psyche (discussed in chapters three and four) consequent on the transition from the formal to real subsumption of labour under capitalism, and, following that, the systematizing of social relations (through impersonal mediations) as liberal industrial capitalism ceded to its organized form. As we shall see in part three of the chapter, this psychic functioning is a significant capitalist asset. It is a source of abstract consumption in the form of a narcissistic flight from the world (involution of drives) consisting in fantasizing an unattainable self-perfection. Abstract consumption is a worldlessly dereifying institution which, present as a potential in capitalism from the beginning, has been actualized more intensively and extensively now than ever before since its effects are now less likely to be counteracted by either authoritative personal parenting or reifying institutions such as the welfare state. The ways in which this actualization impoverishes subjects will be understood from the point of view of the differential effects of internalizing good and bad objects, and with the help of Freud's account of daydreaming. Having understood the different subject effects of organized and disorganized capitalism in terms of the withdrawal of parenting by the latter, we will be in a better position to understand the differential effects of abstract consumption under the two modes. As will be seen, the lack experienced by subjects now is more intense, because more contradictory and indeterminate, than that constituted by organized capitalism. Contradiction inheres in the simultaneous demand for autonomy and heteronomy; indeterminacy inheres in the nature of representatives encountered by subjects.

I Capitalism and reconfigurations of the oedipal family

A recapitulation

The development of bourgeois subjects was dependent on the experience of long-term, stable relations with parental figures who, between them, through a certain kind of disciplining love, enabled emergent subjects to develop their powers of active engagement with the world without becoming atomistic or instrumentally rational. As is clear from Freud's account of mental functioning, the foundations laid down during the pre-oedipal period are crucial to this development. This period initiates a process of reality-testing which affords the possibility for developing those higher psychological faculties which endow individual subjects with a sense of competence and an active orientation to a differentiated world which requires of subjects the ability to stop and think before acting. This involves the dispositions and capacities associated with secondary process functioning, which, in a sublimated form, constitutes *sensus communis*. These capacities and dispositions, memory, attention, judgement and self-discipline, will only be nurtured if the reality principle (the representatives encountered by the emergent subject) is intelligible: if the infant has at its fingertips objects which are sensuously and psychically (fairly constantly) present. Such sensuous and psychic presencing is a requirement if the emergent subject is to experience dependence as benign rather than malign. Beyond this, the balance between total and instant satisfaction and serious and regular frustration is needed if the infant is to begin to think about the world, since it is the absence of the expected which initiates this activity. Expressed otherwise, emergent subjects need a world at their fingertips, but not wholly predictably at their fingertips, if they are to develop their potentials for secondary process functioning and sublimation; if they are to develop *sensus communis*.

Bourgeois parenting enabled the internalization of good objects, these being objects which were really there and available to the infant, and which had in the past provided real satisfaction. This was a mode of internalization which endowed emergent subjects with the psychic strength to engage in the arduous but ultimately rewarding activities required by 'civilization'. It matters that the parents enabling this mode of internalization were relatively autonomous; that their culture had nurtured a balance of attachment/separation and of determinacy/indeterminacy such that individuals were strongly individuated without being atomized, and that they were allowed the scope for relatively free movement without suffering the anxieties of formlessness. In fact, it was the availability of these good objects, through changes in family relations towards intimacy and individuality, that constituted the individual's form. What was in question was internalization of cultural requirements through personally authoritative parental relations. Contrary to what is argued by Jessica Benjamin, for example (1977; 1990:

42–8), I take it that internalization is not necessarily a bad thing; that it takes different forms and may be necessary for the kinds of arduous duties of self-reliance that contemporary capitalism is placing on subjects today. It may also be necessary for the assumption of responsibility for the duties of world care which global public-spiritedness now requires.[2]

It matters too that *both* parents possessed personal authority, since the pre-oedipal stage of subjectivation was crucial to nurturing in the emergent subject the dispositions and abilities associated with the adult enjoyment of relative autonomy. This was a pre-oedipal stage during which mothering was of a 'good enough' kind. That is to say, the mother was not yet domesticated but was active in her own right beyond the household sphere. For this reason, she had a personal authority which would be denied her capitalist daughter or grand-daughter. She was dedicated, but not dedicated exclusively, to care of her infant. 'Good enough' mothering was here a matter of nurturing in the infant, through the fairly benign experience of dependence, capacities for interdependence, or for social love, but also capacities for tolerating delayed gratification and, relatedly, the ability to stop and think about the world in an imaginative and attentive way

The erosion of motherly authority

In the capitalist nuclear family, only the father was authoritative and sociability had become an individual option rather than a cultural imperative. This was the family constituted by the liberal industrial capitalism of late nineteenth-century England, first among capitalists themselves and, later, up to a point, among workers (Zaretsky 1976: chs 3, 4). It involved a distribution of labour and of faculties and dispositions which allocated women as dedicated mothers to the privatively private family sphere and men as moral authority and breadwinner to the 'public' sphere. This distribution debilitated both men and women, as we have noted. On the one hand, the replacement of multi- by one-dimensional rationality effected an atomized form of masculine capitalist subjectivity which was experienced as absolute rather than relative autonomy. Capitalist men became narcissistic in an active world-mastering way. On the other hand, women, being deprived of any satisfaction of their drive towards activity and world-engagement, became more obviously worldless in that they moved in a confined and constraining environment. This constraining mode of life induced a tendency towards the 'involution of drives', or the inward-turning of psychic activity, as well as the temptation and tendency to use infants as compensatory objects whose perfection and attachment to the mother would console her for the inadequacies of her own life. The work of the father was here to remove the male child from maternal influence and to ensure that he cultivated the masculine dispositions needed for successful world mastery. Identification with the father – internalization of domination, as Jessica Benjamin (1977) puts it – was the source here of a sense of independence as detachment from others; a detachment which was enhanced by the impersonal and often invisible forms of necessary attachments in the extra-familial culture. The capitalist's world became divided between those who thought and those who felt. However, as thinking became increasingly a matter of scientific expertise, and as ownership of productive property became collective (with the increasing prevalence of corporations), secondary process functioning and reality-testing drifted back to the 'systemic' level from which it had descended onto bourgeois individuals during the hybrid stage of capitalism. So now the capitalist was required to think as determined by the totality and to act as its functionary. In this way, fathers lost their authority and became, in a sense, feminized (more on this below). As bearers of functional rationality, they could no longer serve as role models for sons. They had 'less to offer, and therefore less to prohibit' (Marcuse 1987: 97).[3] In this way the promise of relative autonomy was withdrawn (in fact but not in theory) not only from proletarians and women, but also from capitalists themselves.

From oedipal to nuclear family: totality as symbolic

Recall that I am using femininity and masculinity as cultural categories which connote passivity and activity respectively. The withdrawal of the possibility of autonomy effected through organized capitalism involved the feminization of all men and, therefore, the transition from oedipal to nuclear family. However, because the promise of autonomy had not been explicitly withdrawn but remained as an important cultural item, women began to claim autonomy as their gendered 'others' began to lose it. Or, they were claiming an autonomy which had become an illusion as fathers, following mothers, became 'domesticated' in their own way. The result was the family criticized by some as a fatherless family (Lasch 1977) and advocated by others as a 'democratizing' family (Brenner 1999).[4]

The absence of personally authoritative parental relations means the absence of those cultural resources needed for the individual enjoyment of autonomy. However, during the organized phase of capitalism, cultural parenting was not abrogated. Organized capitalism imposed a reality principle on subjects which, as noted before, was also a 'performance principle' (Marcuse 1987: 44–5). At the same time, it provided most people most of the time with the class-specific resources needed to 'perform'. In the case of unskilled labour, these 'resources' would be very paltry indeed (Willis 1979). In any case, for everybody, although for some more dramatically than for others, performing in the particular organized sense transgressed against the human potential for imaginative, skilled, individualized activity and, moreover, involved the breaking of culture's promise to deliver individual autonomy. Lacanian psychoanalysis conveys the sense of frustration and betrayal induced by the contradiction between promise and experience.

II The dissolution of the ego: imaginary, symbolic and real

The Lacanian categories

The first point to note is that the psyche marked by the tendencies associated with the imaginary, the symbolic and the real is the psyche of a narcissist.[5] Before this claim is elaborated, I provide a brief description of these categories as (sometimes[6]) used by Lacan. The concept of the imaginary connotes an experience of specular, virtual relations which yields the illusion of absolute individual autonomy, or, it refers to a condition in which the emergent subject is unaware, not only of its own immaturity and helplessness, but also of a world which is capable, not only of resisting its demands, but of imposing itself on that subject (Lacan 1980a). This is the condition exemplified by the moment at which the infant, between the ages 6 and 18 months, 'still sunk in his motor incapacity and nursling dependence' as Lacan puts it, catches a glimpse of itself in the mirror and becomes entranced at the sight of this ideal ego, or, an ego which endows the infant with an illusory belief in its own autonomous powers and splendour. For Lacan, this striking moment 'situates the agency of the ego ... in a fictional direction' (1980a: 2), a direction which guarantees that the symbolic as the voice of culture, or Law of the Father, will be experienced as an alien, oppressive obstacle in the way of the independence promised by the ideal ego. The symbolic (the law of culture) introduces the small child to the 'order of objectifying language' whereby cultural membership is secured as the child is drawn out of the family and into the wider world. Note that bodies here are merely the materials on which the law inscribes its commands (Forrester 1981; Jameson 1988; Lacan 1980b).

The attainment of cultural membership through insertion into a linguistic structure forces the emergent subject to face up to the abyss between the grand illusions of the imaginary and the harsh actuality of the symbolic, yet the subject never abandons the impossible desire for autonomy. Beyond the imaginary and the symbolic lies the real, this being the 'substrate' on which form is imposed by the symbolic; a substrate, it is important to note, which can never be wholly captured by form. Hence the process of subjectivation leaves a 'remainder' or 'lack' in which resides the individual potential to 'refuse' or 'rebel' (Stavrakakis 1999: ch. 1). As Lacan notes, the real 'is there ... ready to burst in and submerge what the "reality principle" has constructed under the title of the "external world"' (Lacan, quoted in Dews 1987: 104). The idea here is that the symbolic (culture) is apparently all-powerful but really incapable of totally capturing the subject. In imprinting its form on the raw biological material (the real), the symbolic necessarily leaves something over which may return to haunt it. In this way, the logic of the real is a logic of disruption, of resistances to a symbolic which is always somehow lacking in something from the point of view of the subject (Zizek 1989: 122).

Historicizing the categories

This bleak sketch of subjectivity and its miseries is read here as true to the experiences of subjects constituted by the law of value (culture as totality or symbolic) particularly as this is expressed in a disorganized capitalism which has rendered pre-capitalist survivals inconsequential.[7] In adapting the Lacanian categories to my purposes, I shall use the imaginary, symbolic and real as critical concepts which enable us to understand the inadequacies of both the 'pre-oedipal' (the imaginary) and the 'oedipal' (symbolic) stage of subjectivation once parents have lost their personal authority. Moreover, I shall understand the imaginary as a mode of relating virtually to 'objects' which nurtures the disposition to fantasize; fantasizing fulfilling (apparently) subjects' needs to escape a harsh and indifferent reality but fulfilling (really) capital's need to reproduce itself. At this point, the personal relations required for the constitution of psychic strength begin to disintegrate under the impact of a combination of specular, or virtual relations (the imaginary) and impersonal relations (the symbolic). It is this combination of imaginary and symbolic that constitutes 'lack' or desirousness and which nurtures the dispositions to rebel connoted in Lacanian psychoanalysis by the concept of the real. I am understanding this concept in realist terms (as understood from the Marxian/Arendtian/Freudian point of view outlined in chapter one). That is to say, I take it to connote innate human indeterminacy and the potentials and needs associated with this indeterminacy. This understanding coincides with that of Lacan up to a point (Lacan 1980a: 4–5). It goes beyond Lacan in that it infers from innateness the need for relative determinacy and keeps in mind the possibilities of a restored worldliness inhering in the human potential for world-transformation. From this point of view, the disposition to 'rebel' on which Lacanians insist is related to the dearth, in capitalist cultures, of good objects capable of completing prematurely-born human creatures in a relatively determinate way.

However, in adapting Lacan's categories in this way, I shall want to distinguish between the psychic effects of organized and disorganized capitalism in terms of the two registers in which lack is experienced. In relation to organized capitalism, lack is experienced in relation to culture's pinning down of subjects under a performance principle whose rigorous disciplines leave little room for enjoyment of the activity drive. This pinning down is a transgression against its own alleged principle of autonomy. This is the condition criticized by critical theorists such as Marcuse.[8] Lack here comes after the 'fall', or, after capitalism's withdrawal (in practice, not in theory) of the promise of individual autonomy which, during the hybrid bourgeois phase of capitalism, had been kept (to the bourgeois). It is the experience of subjects who have registered this promise, who are eager to experience its fulfilment and who find themselves captured (the term is here used in a strong sense) by a culture (symbolic) in which commodity fetishism has become unavoidable.

For the subjects of disorganized capitalism, the experience of lack is more fundamental and acute and is implicated in the culture's refusal to provide the drives with the relative determinacy which indeterminable creatures need. Recall that this is the need to inhabit a sociable and intelligible world; one which constitutes a reality principle from which emergent subjects gain the sense of a testable, therefore knowable and responsive, reality; a responsiveness adequate to the cultivation of social love in the absence of which the human animal becomes 'sick' (Freud 1984a: 78). Failure to satisfy this need is the willed failure of the network principle of organization which we have considered in chapter six; a principle which, as has been seen, demands that subjects maintain themselves in a condition of alertness to the changing demands of value's law; demands for an ever-speedier dialectic of exchange and use, therefore for ever-speedier obsolescence of objects and practices. To the degree that these demands are satisfied, process has come to mark not only the occupational sphere but also the psyche itself. Process is in this case a matter of the unintelligibly moving cathexes and de-cathexes of bad objects by subjects whose culture reduces them to a condition of primary process functioning. At this point we have a Law of Culture (that of the disorganized symbolic), which has abrogated the Law of the Father (that of the organized symbolic).[9] Before elaborating on these claims through an unpacking of the Lacanian categories I should point out that the categories can be interpreted from two points of view: the point of view of the emergent subject and that of the adult subject. From the first point of view, they connote the replacement of personal by impersonal authority and/or power and the psychic damage effected by this replacement. From the second point of view, they connote the different kinds of contradictory experience (constitutive of contradictory subjective wishes or tendencies) with which organized and disorganized capitalism provides the adult subject, i.e. the promise of autonomy (the imaginary) and the actuality of heteronomy (the symbolic).

Desirousness and the imaginary

As interpreted here, desirousness is the disposition to fantasize impelled by a profound sense of lack. At the same time, the fantasizing which lack provokes involves a loss of reality which is necessary for a particular and peculiar manifestation of 'reality', namely, disorganized capitalism. Here fantasizing becomes a requirement of the performance principle as this is applied to consumption (Baudrillard 1993: ch. 1; 1998). For organisms which need worldly cultural completion, it is an attempt to escape a painful reality which is, in fact, a flight back into the source from which escape has been attempted, since it is a flight effected by the commodification of imagination (Appadurai 1991; Honneth 1995). As such, it involves a new kind of perversion of the human need for relative determinacy, for sociability and for intelligibility.

Desirousness is the disposition which is nurtured once the 'pre-oedipal' phase of parenting takes on the character of the imaginary. As we have noted, the imaginary is the specular moment at which the emergent subject experiences the illusion of wholeness and autonomy. It is worth considering the implications of this specularity here since I take it to be the mode whereby virtual objects are taken in in such a way as to nurture immaturity, or the psychic volatility or 'vacancy' needed if subjects are to do their consuming duty. The mirror is an object from which the subject gets a reflection of itself. Now, while we know that human infants (unlike other infants, apparently) do in fact find great interest and delight in viewing their image in a mirror, it is rather odd to reduce the mother–child relation to this 'moment'. The implications of this reduction are as follows: that the decisive infant experience is of primary narcissism, rather than that zestful exploration of the world associated with the activity drive and sociability, and that, moreover, the mother is wholly unable to coax her infant out of this debilitating self-absorption by drawing its attention to the worldly delights which await its exploration. These are implications that no significant, consequential face-to-face parenting is available. Yet, since the mirror stage takes place before the age of 18 months, infants should have had (might have had) opportunities to explore the world and will have had the experience of parenting through feeding and other activities, as discussed in chapter four. It is while feeding that the infant experiences (or not) the mother's attentive gaze; the gaze which registers and accepts, indeed loves, the child's needs in a way which nurtures the capacities for relationship. It is the mother who draws the infant out of its primary narcissism (its illusions of wholeness and autonomy) and encourages it to aim for, and take delight in, more achievable ideals such as the taking of its first step and the utterance of its first word. It is thus gradually prepared for the less personal, less tender, and more challenging demands of the wider world beyond the family.

The imaginary concept captures nothing of this possible infant experience.[10] The world as mirror appears to give nothing back to the infant but a misleading external image (Frosh 1991: 114–15).[11] This may be the misleading external image of narcissistic maternal expectations, or it may be the infant's response to the absence of reliably present personal parenting (good objects). Such an absence provokes the inward turning, a kind of 'attention and activity in reverse' (Brennan 1992: ch. 4, esp. 155; Schachtel 1963: ch. 7) which we have found in the capitalist wife. The imaginary would here connote the presence of desires for self-perfection which emerge in the infant as a result of the absence of realistic wishes and suitable parental guidance in the external world. This is a condition whereby the psyche becomes governed by an alliance of id and ideal ago (Chasseguet-Smirgel 1985); a condition formed by identifications which provide a kind of compensatory fantasy for inadequate nurturing; a fantasy which blocks reality-testing and blurs the line between reality and fantasy. As will be seen later, this debilitated inwardness is encouraged by abstract consumption, as manifested in the practices of consumerism and virtuality, both of which nurture in both emergent and adult subjects expectations of wholeness for the attainment of which neither can provide any psychic support whatsoever. For the moment, and remaining with the Lacanian categories, I want to return to that of the symbolic to trace the emergence of the subject out of the imaginary phase (which is never completely left behind but continues to haunt the subject as a lost or not-yet-attained state of perfection) into the symbolic register of experience.

The symbolic: culture as totality

Having understood the imaginary moment as the experience of mirroring, or virtual, relations which are incapable of constituting the conditions of possibility for the attainment of psychic strength, let us now consider further the logic of the symbolic moment as a logic (which may or may not embody a parenting dimension) of impersonal cultural conditioning. The symbolic connotes that abstract impersonal mode of domination which enters the world with the law of value; a mode of domination which is unavoidable once cultures take on the character of a totality. It imposes itself upon the emergent subject through the power of language, a power inhering, remember, in an impersonal structuring ability rather than in sensuously-present speech.

Take the Panopticon as an example. Panopticism exemplifies the systematized, impersonal and disciplining ways in which capitalist industrial culture (including the welfare state) renders human bodies compatible with value's law. Directed at the human world, panopticist surveillance attempts to constitute a cultural lawfulness of predictable constant conjunctions where such lawfulness had not existed before (Foucault 1979: pt III; 1980: ch. 6). In doing so, it activates or reconfigures some causal powers (human activity reconfigured as mastery over nature; the separation of rationality from sociability) and suppresses others (the anaclitic, kinesthetic rationality of artisans; the *sensus communis* of hybrid bourgeoisie). The 'watcher in the tower' is the impersonal, anonymous, universal principle to which all must conform in 'objective' (stimulus/response) rather than 'subjective' (communicative, dialogical) mode (Foucault 1980: ch. 8; Dreyfus and Rabinow 1983: chs 6, 7; Owen 1994: ch. 9). Here form is imposed on human matter through a sustained, systematic, impersonal process of drilling and surveillance based on (Baconian, nomological) scientific discourses (on which more in chapter eight). This is the subsumption of individual human particulars under the disciplinary universal: or, civilization imposed on subjects who are required to be productive in a docile and passive rather than reflexive and active way.

So, the symbolic connotes an impersonal power to shape through naming; a power which over-rides whatever individual, embodied parents may say or do (Bowie 1987: 100–33). As a parental power, it involves the separation of the parental function from the biological parents and its allocation to the bureaucratically-mediated scientific expertise of state-supervised 'pastoral' care (Lasch 1977). In effect, the 'world of words' is not the communicative world of dialogical speech sought for by Arendt, but rather, the world of capitalist interpellations once commodity fetishism has become necessary (Goux 1994).[12] However, as we have seen in chapter six, the organized mode of capitalism constituted a reified world which, through its relative stability, facilitated the enjoyment of sociability and instituted, for a time, a relatively benign form of bureaucracy, thereby mitigating the effects to be expected from such abstract domination. Unlike the disorganized mode, organized capitalism did not abrogate the task of cultural parenting, although the parenting in question left much to be desired from the point of view of subjects who expected to be autonomous. It did not constitute the conditions under which consequential individual activity would be possible. Public activity was largely technocratic; private activity was becoming atomistic.

The symbolic imposed a determinate form on the subjects of organized capitalism, one which eliminated the possibility of autonomy. For this reason, the contradiction between imaginary as promise of autonomy and symbolic as experience of helpless subsumption under an all-pervading impersonal power was evident. Now, however, the symbolic requires subjects to behave as if the promise of autonomy had been actualized while also requiring us to function in a real sense in primary rather than secondary process mode.

Imaginary and symbolic: a distinction without a difference?

As we noted in chapter six, the subjects of disorganized capitalism are expected to retain as much as possible of that indeterminacy which leaves them open to (and wholly dependent on) cultural formation. Expressed in psychoanalytic terms, subjects are to be disposed towards the world in the mode of primary process functioning and to remain in a state of narcissism. The ways in which abstract consumption nurtures this form of subjectivity will be discussed in a moment. For now we need note only that insofar as cultural parenting has been abrogated in this way, and once subjects are expected to behave 'as if' autonomous while remaining desirous, the distinction between imaginary and symbolic is no longer sustainable since the symbolic now 'orders' the subject to remain within the imaginary moment, as it were (MacCannell 1991). It orders the subject to act 'as if' autonomous while simultaneously remaining governed by primary process functioning. This insupportable condition is what leads to explosions in the 'real'.

Lack, indeterminacy and the real

The real is that which not only can say no, but is bound to say no, apparently, to cultural imposition. At the same time, the human real is that which cannot function without cultural imposition. This is the way in which Lacan conceptualizes civilization and its miseries. However as both Freud and Lacan know, cultures may inflict greater or lesser degrees of misery on their members and, as noted before, I am interpreting the Lacanian real as the conceptualization of a culture which has instituted commodity fetishism so that impersonal, abstract differentiations have attained the kind of causal power associated with the structuralist interpretation of the world. So, let us think of the real as that complex of powers (indeterminacy, imagination, sociability, speech) and needs (the need for cultural completion via an intelligible and sociable world) which is the essence of humanity. What Lacan is insisting upon is that this real is both intransigent and impotent in the face of attempts to impose cultural form on it. Or, he is allocating, apparently, a wholly negative power to this human innateness (Rustin 1995). It can only react to what is experienced in a desperate and impotently desirous manner (Cascardi 1992: ch. 5). At this point it will be well to recall the more optimistic and positive conceptions of human powers to be derived, not only from Marx, but even from Arendt and Freud. From this point of view the human indeterminability connoted by the real is not only, or even mainly, a matter of lacking and desirousness. It is also associated with sociability and the activity drive, both of which are, when not corrupted or negated by deviant cultural institutions, conducive to experiences of, at least, modest satisfactions and, at most, joy and sustained love. So the Lacanian real is testament not to the inevitability of debilitating, because impotent, human desirousness, but, rather, to potentials unfulfilled, needs unmet and/or causal powers misunderstood.

To summarize this section before elaborating on contemporary experiences of lack, I have adapted the Lacanian categories of imaginary, symbolic and real to understand the predicaments of subjects in the cultures of organized and disorganized capitalism. The predicament for organized subjects is related to the withdrawal of the possibility of autonomy, and the inhibition of the enjoyment of the activity drive. The more profound predicament for disorganized subjects is that their culture refuses to provide them with a reality principle capable of 'representing' their drives in a relatively determinate way. The experience of lack, or of desirousness, is more acute in the latter than the former case. I have understood this experience in terms of the absence of good objects in the subjectivation process; an absence which is connoted by the concepts of the imaginary (the pre-oedipal phase reduced to a mirroring activity) and symbolic (the oedipal reduced to an impersonal structuring activity). Mirroring activity involves the debilitating practice of fantasy and inculcates in emergent subjects grandiose illusions of personal potency; illusions which render the subsequent experiences of the symbolic more unhappy than they might otherwise be. This unhappiness further exacerbates the tendency to fantasize. Because this fantasizing has now become essential for the reproduction of capitalism, I am claiming that the distinction between imaginary and symbolic is becoming obsolete, and that this is what accounts for the specific experience of lack of disorganized subjects. This is what I shall explore now.

III Abstract consumption, or, consumption as fantasizing

Fantasizing and the nurturing of indeterminacy

The culturally-engineered indeterminacy constituted by the fantasizing which has now become essential to capitalism's reproduction is a mortal transgression against the duty to complete human instincts by giving the drives the forms, directions and objects which would render them relatively satisfiable. In a very real sense, capitalism must now maintain a kind of infantile wishfulness in its subjects if it is to reproduce itself. This is a condition whereby drives are represented or constituted as unsatisfiable and as needs to have, rather than to be or to do; or rather, being and doing are subsumed under having. Capitalism needs that humans need in this desirous way, and it needs that humans seek satisfaction of these needs through particular kinds of objects, objects which generate illusory rather than real gratification.[13] Let me elaborate on this point by returning to the first object of gratification, namely the mother's breast as this was encountered by the emergent bourgeois subject. This breast exemplifies the good object which nurtures the dispositions and abilities associated with sublimated secondary process functioning. The hallucinated breast exemplifies the bad object which impedes such nurturing. Once abstract labour and consumption become instituted, objects, or 'representatives' offered to subjects (both emergent and mature), take on, increasingly, the character of hallucinated objects and the provision of good objects becomes progressively unreliable.

Objects: real and hallucinated

In the beginning, the breast is part of the undifferentiated flux (the 'oceanic fullness') which is the infant's experience of the world. Quickly, though, the infant learns to reach out and find the breast. It enters into an interactive relationship with the breast and, through the attentiveness of the mother's gaze, into a relationship with the mother also. As the infant becomes experienced, the world becomes differentiated into parts that provide satisfaction and those that do not. Hallucination is an infant response to the absence of satisfying parts. Hallucinated satisfactions are satisfactions involving the momentary cathexis of psychic energy to 'objects' which are abstracted imaginatively from the concrete world and considered only in terms of the individual's gratification. Such is the hallucinated breast, which becomes a kind of substitute source of that gratification which the embodied breast is at present unwilling or unable to provide (Castoriadis 1995). However, the hallucinated breast is quite unlike the breast of the mother, not only in the obvious sense that it can provide no 'material' nourishment for the child (it is calorie-free). It also provides no psychic nourishment. Detached from its embodiment in the mother the hallucinated breast requires of the emergent infant subject nothing but hallucinated consumption. That is to say, there is no need for interaction with a separate person and, therefore, no sense of an external world which may either recognize, accept and satisfy one's needs, or resist them. Expressed otherwise, there is no motive to engage with the world in the manner connoted by secondary process functioning. More than this, though, there is no basis for the emergence of social love since there is nothing in the external world for which the infant should feel grateful. Hallucinated consumption is worldless in the dual sense that it requires neither knowledge nor sociability. In addition, it provides no more than momentary and illusory satisfaction to the infant who remains as hungry and loveless as before the hallucination. In effect, nothing is demanded of the infant and nothing is given. After the hallucinatory episode, the infant remains just as infantile and just as hungry as before, and also just as unattached, psychically speaking.

This hallucinatory infantile moment conveys something of the condition of the desiring subject; a subject whose desirousness is not the result of individual failure, or of temporary absence of gratification, but of a cultural conditioning which fails to provide the resources needed to grow up. Such subjects are parentless children in that they are deprived of the possibility of maturing in the way described by Freud; that is, they cannot make the transition from primary to secondary process functioning.

Reality, virtuality and the mental functioning of daydreaming subjects

As noted in chapter four, reality-testing can only take place on the basis of accumulated memories fed by the experience of objects which brought real, rather than hallucinated, satisfaction. Freud judges this reality-testing to be impelled wholly by the striving for gratification of sex and ego drives (fused in the infant). However, following theorists such as Jessica Benjamin and Ernest Schachtel, I have argued that it is also a manifestation of the activity drive which impels the infant towards encounter with the world as an object of interest in its own right. In any case, the infant needs, for both kinds of gratifications (of the flesh and of the activity- and world-oriented imagination, as we might say) to encounter real, material objects; objects that can be experienced with the fingertips and subsequently imagined and thought about. On the basis of this experience, the ability to judge new experiences (to decide whether they are real or hallucinated, whether they will be a source of gratification or frustration) is cultivated. Where the ego and sex interests are in question, judging involves the willingness to stop, think and evaluate or, as Freud puts it, to postpone the moment of discharge of energy which will relieve the tension which arises from experience of the wish for gratification. Having stopped to think, the emergent subject is likely to be in a better position to act effectively on the world.

As we have seen, stopping to think involves a muting of drives, or, the slowing down and binding of energy. Under the culturally specific form of civilizing differentiation discussed in chapter three, this binding of energy was the beginning of a form of self-control which enabled the emergent subject to actualize potentials for constructive imaginative activity and (possibly) for social love. If the world does not present good objects to the emergent subject, these potentials will lie dormant or be actualized in a stunted form. Good objects are objects which have given real satisfaction, for example, the embodied breast as opposed to the hallucinated breast. With the embodied breast, the infant has a world at its fingertips; with the hallucinated breast it does not. Attached to the embodied breast is another human being with whom the infant must interact. Where the embodied breast (or its analogue) is attached to a 'good enough' parent, the infant will take in the material which will satisfy its biological needs, and the nurturing attention which will constitute it as a psychically strong, world-engaging subject (Benjamin 1990: ch. 1). In relation to the latter, it will take in the actuality of an object which is not merely an extension of itself. It will develop a sense of something which is separate and different from itself, but also (mostly) benignly disposed towards it. The hallucinated breast is mere object of desire, at once wholly compliant with the desiring infant and wholly incapable of providing what it needs, namely emotional and bodily nourishment.

The infant begins to gain a sense of the world, to cultivate common sense, by comparing the real to the hallucinated and by trying to understand what it is about the real that makes it sometimes present and sometimes absent. Putting its (emergent) mind to this, and other absences/presences, brings the maturing subject to a sense of independently existing others who are sometimes malign (they occasionally fail to appear as expected) but more often benign (they appear most of the time). The child is beginning to cultivate those dispositions which will, in future, enable the full emergence of the split psyche which, as I have been arguing, is the necessary basis for public-spiritedness as a particular kind of active engagement with a 'civilized' world.

The introduction of the reality principle involves the splitting off of one species of 'thought activity', namely 'phantasying, which begins already in children's play, and later, continues as daydreaming, abandons dependence on real objects' (Freud 1984c: 39). Where dependence on real objects brings the frustrations and humiliations of neglect and indifference, individuals may retreat from the real world into a dream world. This is what I referred to earlier as the 'involution of drives'. Here the potential for imagination is actualized as daydreaming, which comes to take over from the hallucinations of infants, as individuals come to depend more on fantasy than on real objects for their psychic nourishment (Zizek 1997a).

Daydreaming is a feminizing activity which involves a worldless withdrawal of attention from the world and its contents for the sake of the solitary enjoyment of a kind of 'private theatre' (Teresa Brennan's phrase). It is a prolongation into adult life of the habit of hallucinating compelled by frustration. In terms of psychic development, daydreaming involves the consumption of 'empty calories', or worse. That is to say, the inward-turning of attention involved in daydreaming results in a diminution of the capacity to engage in action (Brennan 1992: 99, 93). Since daydreams also provide instant although short-lived and illusory gratification, it may be further supposed that this is also a diminution in the capacity to exercise self-discipline. Finally, since satisfaction is sought from fantastic rather than real objects, sociability either fails to emerge or, where it is emergent or present as a capacity, is bound to atrophy. The capacity for thought, for sustained attention directed towards a given object, is constitutively related to the exercise of self-discipline, or the capacity to delay gratification, but also to the availability of (human) objects in the environment capable of, and willing to grant, satisfaction. Daydreaming arises where the development of these capacities is rendered difficult and it then becomes an additional obstacle to any further development of these related capacities. It is a condition of debilitating wishfulness involving fantastic relations with fantasized objects which are at once wholly compliant with the individual's desires and wholly incapable of satisfying needs. Such are the objects constituted by abstract consumption and virtuality.

From consumption to abstract consumption

The need to consume is a universal need whose purpose is life maintenance. Now, as we know, for humans consumption is never merely biological. It takes as many forms as there are cultures. Or, consumption is an instinct (it is rooted in our biology), which, as necessarily culturally constituted, has the character of a drive which is always experienced by the individual through 'representatives'. So consumption needs are necessarily met in a great variety of ways, but they always require a constant flow of objects which, as objects of consumption, are doomed to destruction. It is in this way that Arendt notes the necessity of consumption as destruction for the sake of life.

Once consumption becomes a duty impelled by the value needs of capitalism it becomes consumerism (Baudrillard 1993: ch. 1).[14] As such, consumption becomes corrupted through its articulation to capitalism's need for boundless consumption. In the process, it enhances the worldlessness of the world in two related senses. First, it intensifies the process character of the world through the speeding-up of the flow of objects intended for consumption rather than use, and second, it induces serial attachments to things rather than to humans (Arendt 1958: 126–35; 1977c).[15] We 'have' objects; we don't live among them. Not experiencing ourselves as living among them, we can dispose of such objects without regret. Or, commodified objects do not constitute a world. The momentary satisfactions which this kind of consumption affords effect a displacement of attention from the world towards the increasingly fantasized inner 'reality' which the possession of these objects constitutes for such subjects.[16] This is the significance of 'having' as a mode of attachment to the world.

Here the commodity becomes immediately implicated in the fetishism which was discussed in chapter five as a matter of abstract labour and money. Where consumption has ceded to consumerism, the worldlessness of abstract labour is compounded by that of abstract consumption. Those who labour abstractly must now also consume abstractly, or, the age of 'abstract desire' has arrived (Deleuze and Guattari 1983: 337). At this point, indifference has come to characterize relations without, as well as within, the occupational sphere, or, relations have come to take on the character of either imaginary or symbolic (or of different proportions of imaginary and symbolic dimensions). The imaginary here connotes virtuality, fantasizing and narcissism; the symbolic connotes the impersonal systemic relations (relations mediated by money) which yield access to virtuality and fantasizing.[17]

Once the consumerist orientation has been internalized, fetishism becomes a dimension of every activity (Leiss 1978; Marcuse 1986). All needs become satisfiable in the monetized mode of having. The world becomes a world of 'manipulative semblance' (Haug 1987: 103). It is at this point that bad objects begin to become more consequential for subjectivation than good objects, or, that lack becomes, not only the culturally specific experience of loss of autonomy (contradiction between imaginary and symbolic) but the culturally induced experience of indeterminacy (contradiction between real and imaginary-symbolic).

Abstract consumption as virtuality

I now want to consider an important variant on abstract consumption: namely, the virtual relations borne by electronic media of communication. These are also an important supplement to personal and familial relations. By virtuality I mean the odd kind of disembodied presencing of bodies which constitutes appearances incapable of endowing individuals with the psychic strength needed to undertake self-direction. This is the virtuality of relations between performers in and spectators of electronically-generated performances on television, on film, on video games and through virtual relations 'experienced' through electronic networking (Baudrillard 1993: ch. 2; Rodowick 2001: ch. 7; Turkle 1995; Zizek 1997a: ch. 3).

Virtual relations provide subjects with illusory sources of selfness through the taking in of objects as images (of celebrities, of film and sports stars) with whom (which?) subjects who lack can identify (Pitkin 1998: 272–3). This is a taking in of the virtual, presenceless presence of an otherness having the flat, unyielding character of the mirror; a taking in comparable in quality to the taking in of the fantasized breast in that it demands nothing of the individual subject and offers nothing in return but momentary, empty gratification (Frosh 1991: 76). These imaginary identifications take the form of 'as if' identifications (Reich 1953); identifications which are motivated, from the side of the subject, by an unrealizable longing to be like an admired object, the subject's ideal ego. They result in intense, short-term attachments which provide instantaneous ('as if by magic') compensations for the lack inflicted by inadequate parenting, and they are effected through superficial imitations rather than the internalization of capacities and dispositions. To borrow a Marxian analogy, 'as if' identifications are to bourgeois identifications as the lion skin is to the lion (Marx 1994: 37). They make the difference between playing at being someone or doing something and really becoming someone or doing something.

'As if' identifications are substitutes for the reality-testing which is a necessary condition of psychic strength. They are also identifications with fantasy figures with whom (which?) individuals may have the experience of a spurious intimacy (Meyrowitz 1985; Poster 1995).[18] As such they exacerbate subjects' inability to differentiate between self and other and to engage with the world in a way which affords the possibility of an enabling 'taking in'.[19] They are a way of taking in (a virtual reality) which obscures the distinction between the idea of an object and the external actuality of that object (Schafer 1968: 78). This is the form of internalization which disorganized capitalism nurtures most assiduously through its extensive and intensive actualization of abstract consumption and, therefore, of obsolescence and substitutability in 'public' and 'private' spheres. This is the experience to which I refer in talking about the strange presenceless presencing instantiated now. It is in such a world that 'culture' assumes a new kind of institutional significance which is expressed in the discipline of cultural studies.[20] Electronic media of communication at once exacerbate the experience of volatility and (seemingly) provide consolation for the frustrations experienced in the occupational realm (or in the absence of an occupational realm for the structurally irrelevant). This consolation consists in an endless stream of messages serving to encourage the habit of fantasizing which is now not only a temporary and solitary release from a tedious and unsatisfying reality but also an essential part of that reality itself. As noted before, in trying to escape from reality, fantasizing subjects are driven back into reality (a reality which cannot endow them with a sense of reality, or common sense). Even in their fantasizing, they are observing the performance principle. Such is the reality of the virtual reality principle. Such is the character of the privative privacy constituted by abstract consumption.

Conclusion

This chapter has traced the lineaments of that abstract consumption which is no less necessary for the reproduction of capitalism than the abstract labour which was discussed in chapters five and six. Abstract consumption transgresses against the human need for relative determinacy by refusing to provide emergent and adult subjects with the representatives (good objects) which our indeterminate nature requires. Where good objects constitute need as relatively satisfiable want, the bad objects provided by capitalism now constitute need as desire. Desirousness is a necessity where the speedy obsolescence of objects is a necessity. Up to now, capitalism has managed to obtain, overall, intensities of desirousness among sufficient numbers of people to ensure its own reproduction.

In turning need into desire, contemporary networking capitalism nurtures an acute form of wanting which has no tangible object of satisfaction in view and which, as such, is more akin to the uneducated, worldless condition of an infant than to that of the object-directed, relatively satisfiable mature adult. Desirous subjects are adult subjects who have not been afforded the opportunity to test reality in a way which would nurture the secondary process functioning needed for sustained, imaginative and critical attentiveness to the world as it is, as opposed to the world as these subjects would ideally like it to be. These subjects are maintained in this infantile, indeterminate condition through cultural parental neglect.

We have understood the psychic sufferings inflicted by cultural indeterminacy with the help of Lacan's categories of imaginary, symbolic and real. With the help of these categories we have grasped how capitalism as a culture of commodity fetishism is bound to engender lack as a condition of desirousness from which the subject can derive little but suffering. Desirousness emerges in the first instance out of the indeterminacy which is borne by parents who are bereft of personal authority so that they are incapable of providing the child with good objects for internalization. Here the 'pre-oedipal' phase has the character of the imaginary, meaning that it nurtures, rather than counteracts, immature, narcissistic tendencies. The oedipal 'resolution' involves, not the consolatory internalization of good fatherly objects, but rather, the imposition of culture's law via an impersonal structuring process. Neither pre-oedipal nor oedipal moment affords the resources needed for the later cultivation of relative autonomy, therefore neither affords the resources for the later cultivation of public-spiritedness.

In the concluding chapter we will return to the question of citizenship and consider the possibility that the real is now erupting in a way which resists the substitute gratifications of fantasizing and which could take the form of a citizens' movement intended to restore to the world its intelligibility and sociability. Before doing so we need to consider another kind of transgression against the 'real', namely, the cognitive contradiction whose effects we are presently beginning to experience. It may be that this contradiction, along with that between autonomy and heteronomy, will push us in the direction of such citizenship.

8 Abstract knowledge, or, disorganized capitalism and the vicissitudes of science

In discussing contemporary disorganized capitalism I have used the concepts of process, dereification and network to make an argument about the virtual reality principle which is encountered by emergent and mature subjects now. Contemporary capitalism is subjectively disorganizing in that it fails to provide its subjects with the resources for testing reality so as to know 'how to go on'. This is a matter of failing to provide the kinds of social relations (therefore objects) constitutive of the psychic strength required for relatively autonomous subjectivity. At the same time, individual subjects are expected to act autonomously or, they are to be responsible, as individuals, for self-maintenance. This responsibility includes self-education for occupational participation in the network society. Beyond this, though, it is coming to involve also individual responsibility for the provision of imperative present and future use values; a responsibility which leads many individuals, for the first time, into direct and directly commodified relations with scientific and technical experts of various kinds. In this case, the subsumption of consumption under value is taking place at a time when the trustworthiness of the knowledge which these experts purvey is under attack from different directions. An important example here is the retirement pension; a use value which, with the state's abrogation of its welfare task, is becoming part of the system of commodity exchange in which it is caught up in the logic of the stock market, therefore in a logic which, unlike that of state provision, is bereft of guarantees for the future (Harmes 2001). Moreover, this is happening at a time when confidence in the stock market is beginning to dissolve, due to a combination of factors, which include its volatility and the corruption of many of the most important stock-market players (Blackburn 2002; Kane 2002). This loss of confidence in a particular kind of expertise coincides with a general sense of unease (sometimes alarm) about natural science.[1] In this chapter I shall discuss the political implications of these developments in terms of the cognitive contradiction which underpins an apparent cognitive crisis which, since knowledge is now 'the main productive force' (Aronowitz 1990: 116), has fundamental implications for the reproduction of capitalism and therefore for the reproduction of its constituent social formations.

sciences suggests that they will be every bit as abstract and universalistic as their deterministic predecessors (Hayles 1990: 216; Rifkin 1998: ch. 7). Moreover, their translation into technology (effected in a more worldlessly instrumental manner than before) goes on as though nature possessed the cognitive transparency allocated to it by Baconian science. Or, postmodern science is Baconian science of and for an indeterminate, dereifying age. In the third section of the chapter, the experiential dimension of these dereifying changes will be considered as a transition from the 'law of insurance' (Giddens 1994) to the 'law of the lottery' (Neary and Taylor 1998). The latter brings the cognitive contradiction into the everyday world in a way which, through the requirement that we become our own experts, may yield the possibility of new kinds of citizen action.

I Totality and the two-worlds thinking of determinant judgement

The reality principle as I am interpreting it always requires a functionally adequate form of knowledge which may be the unreflexive knowledge borne by kinesthetic rationality which is reproduced with minor changes down the generations, or the reflexive, theoretical, scientific form which became necessary for abstractly differentiated capitalist social formations. In both cases there is an internal relationship between subjects who know and objects that are, or can be, known. The 'civilizing process' was in part a dialectical process of constituting new subjects and objects of knowledge: subjects capable of reflexivity and unexperienced objects which, as unexperienced objects, needed to be known 'theoretically'. Expressed in psychoanalytic terms, it was a process involving the transition from one reality principle to another. Chapters three and four were intended in part to remind us of the subjective changes required for a new kind of knowing of new kinds of objects as western European cultures began to undergo a new mode of differentiation such that absent causes (of a natural and cultural rather than supernatural kind) began to assume consequentiality for everyday life. Beyond this, all objects were to become known scientifically, or, to be susceptible to objectification (impersonal, fetishizing abstraction from context) and quantification (Foucault 1974; Porter 1992). Or, they were to be fetishized in a reifying way.

The question of the knowledge needs of totalities was introduced in chapter two. The account given there will be critically elaborated with the help of Arendt's conception of 'two-worlds' thinking, this being thinking which conceives of the world as composed of essence and appearance, hence 'two worlds' (Arendt 1978: ch. 1). Arendt uses the two-worlds concept critically in relation to the character of Platonic western philosophy which had endangered worldliness by engendering a differentiation in thought between a realm of perfection beyond experience (essence) and experience itself ('mere' appearance).[6] This orientation demoted the everyday world (the world of particularity that educates the five senses) and rendered it subject to the transformative or dismissive attentions of intellectuals; an orientation which when expressed in science effected the 'de-realization' of all that cannot be scientifically verified, as Marcuse noted (1986: 147).[7]

Two-worldness and the necessity of science

Once a culture has been transformed into a totality, scientific knowledge becomes a necessity for the reproduction of that culture. For capitalism as a whole (as opposed to the social formations of which it is composed) science is the necessary means of redesigning the world so as to reproduce value (Haraway 1991: 47). The reproduction of value does not necessarily involve the reproduction of constituent social formations and may now be endangering the reproduction of all human life. The reckless propensity which has brought this situation about is understandable in part as a manifestation of a two-worlds orientation. Here I adapt freely from Arendt's usage to understand two-worldness as both theoretical orientation and empirical, experiential condition. As a theoretical orientation it has been the mode in which we understand the functioning of totalities, on which more later. Practical two-worldness has been actualized as capitalism (as a 'universal' or 'essence') has successfully subsumed appearances or particulars (pre-capitalist cultures) under the law of value. Here appearance is a particular which is evaluated solely from the point of view of a universal. The universal is indifferent to those aspects of the particular which are irrelevant to its purposes. It seizes on what it needs and ignores or destroys what remains, as happens in the reduction of humanity to labour and consumption power.

Practical two-worldness has been effected in two ways. First, as discussed in chapter two, capitalism separates in time and space elements which are necessary for the reproduction of everyday life, so that 'absent causes' become increasingly consequential. In this way, the community loses its self-sufficiency in a way which requires it to attend to matters beyond its direct experience. There is the world as experienced and the world which, while not experienced, is essential for the reproduction of the experienced world. This is what I describe as empirical two-worldness, by which I mean the gap between empirical necessities and experienced actualities which opened up as the everyday world became saturated with absent causes and relations at a distance. This began to occur as long-distance trade became a matter of necessities rather than luxuries, so that the effects of this trade were experienced throughout rather than merely at the margins of communities. As more community activities became dependent on absent causes, social science became a practical necessity (Appleby 1978). In this case, we can think of essence and appearance in terms of a spatio-temporally differentiated totality (essence) and its parts (appearance). On the one hand, no one is capable of experiencing or observing the totality as a whole; on the other hand experience or observation of a part *alone* does not yield knowledge of the functioning of the totality. The point is that the experientially acquired knowledge of artisanal common sense is no longer capable of ensuring cultural reproduction (Giddens 1990).

The second way in which two-worldness is instituted relates to the saturation of capitalist cultures with the results of natural scientific knowledges. This began in earnest towards the end of the nineteenth century when the physical sciences began to demonstrate their power to advance value's law (Bernal 1954: pt VI; Manicas 1988: ch. 10). From now on the absent causes constituted by spatio-temporal separation were joined by another kind of cause which enhanced the cognitive opacity of the world at the level of experience. Whereas the significance of spatio-temporal separation of necessary causes could be understood, given the availability of relevant reading-matter, by anybody able to read, an understanding of the necessary causes of new processes of production required expert knowledge (of a scientific kind) built up over years of arduous training beyond that required for fluent literacy, therefore beyond the capabilities of an educated, lay public. We can understand this 'beyond' in terms of the increasing mathematization of science during the nineteenth century (Kuhn 1977: ch. 3). This mathematization was implicated in the splitting of expert and laity; a splitting which was institutionalized by the emergence of professional science (Hobsbawm 1977: ch. 15; Kargon 1977).

Science as determinant judgement or, a reified rationality for a reified world

Science exemplifies the theoretical expression of the two-worlds orientation. It prides itself on being knowledge which goes beyond everyday experience or the world of appearances. In doing so, it produces knowledge of the real powers of things, or, of what lies beyond appearances (Bhaskar 1989: 180–92). It is worth recalling that the 'know how' of artisanal common sense was also grounded, necessarily, in the real powers of things. However, knowledge of these real powers was unconscious in the sense that it was incorporated into practices which had emerged and evolved slowly over time through practical trial-and-error. With the institution of science the practice of trial-and-error is instituted within the study and the laboratory as spaces within which new kinds of experts 'stop and think' about 'objects' constituted as such through mental and/or practical abstraction from context. A novel kind of abstract knowledge is thus produced and eventually fed into nature on a larger scale and more quickly than was either necessary or possible in pre-capitalist cultures.

Science (of the kind considered here) is the institution of a particular kind of capacity to 'stop and think'; a capacity which requires a worldless withdrawal from the flow of everyday life. We can begin to understand the peculiar, dehumanizing logic which informed the practical implementation of science (both social and natural) in terms of Arendt's distinction, drawn from Kant's work, between determinant and reflective judgement (Arendt 1989). In making this distinction, Arendt is intending to draw attention to the destructiveness of the modern western manifestation of reason.[8] Unlike others who share her intentions, such as Adorno (1973), she is doing so for the purposes of clearing a conceptual space for understanding a specifically political form of thinking (reflective judgement) which will be explored in the conclusion when we return to the question of anaclitic rationality. More than this, though, through her account of process as worldless dereification, she is offering the conceptual resources for understanding the emergent contradiction between the law of value and modern science as well as the shared process logic of value and the emergent postmodern sciences.

Unlike reflective judgement, which is situated and self-consciously historico-cultural, and which attempts to transcend an individual viewpoint for the purpose of understanding those of myriad, different others, determinant judgement prides itself on its ability to take an 'unsituated' view. The unsituated view is held to be somehow uncoloured by history or culture and, for this reason, to be capable of gaining access to context-independent or 'universal' truths about the way nature works. As context-independent truths, these are truths under which particulars are subsumed. Subsumption involves mental and sometimes practical abstraction of an object of study from the relational context in which it has its being so as to consider it from the point of view of the universal. As a matter of determinant judgement, abstraction is effected analytically rather than dialectically.[9] In abstracting analytically, i.e. in ignoring the necessity of relations and change, determinant judgement is ignoring an essential element of nature and is also expressing and advancing the divorce of rationality and sociability. It is a monological mode of apprehending the world, or, it involves an impersonal, abstract form of rationality which thinks 'about', rather than 'with', appearances.[10] In thinking about rather than with appearances, determinant judgers are working on 'evidence' which is far from the everyday empirical in which we are all saturated. As noted by Arendt (1958: ch. 6) the scientific 'empirical' is quite different from that of the everyday world. Not only is the object of study conceptualized in analytical abstractions (as when psychologists conceptualize intelligence as a quantifiable property quite appropriately studied out of its everyday context), but it is often available only with the help of prosthetics such as telescopes and microscopes. This scientific method (analytical abstraction, prosthetically-aided observation) renders the scientific 'empirical' very peculiar indeed. This particular method is what makes scientists' withdrawal of attentiveness from the experienced world worldless. It is worldless because it ignores what is essential to experience, namely, its relationality and situatedness.

In effect, scientific mastery is gained through a cultivated blindness to the everyday world of appearances (the sensuous world which forms the five senses), a blindness which is linguistically expressed and advanced in the mathematical language which is the favoured language of science (Arendt 1958: ch. 6; 1977b: 266–77). Mathematical language facilitates inattentiveness to situatedness by eliminating all reference to the experiential. It enhances that forgetfulness of appearances in which the worldlessness of determinant judgement consists and, in the requirement that claims about the world be formulated as statistical probabilities, it enhances the atomizing, standardizing tendencies of industrial cultures (Arendt 1958: 43).[11] Increasingly, too, as mathematical modelling comes to supplement or even replace laboratory work, mathematics encourages attentiveness to similarities in pattern at the expense of differences in substance (Hayles 1999: 99).[12] To the extent that this happens, science becomes 'postmodern' and tends towards the dereification, rather than reification, of the world (more on this later).

Modern science, as manifested in determinant judgement, seeks to represent or 'mirror' objects (Rorty 1980), the implication here being that the unsituated view is the all-embracing correct view of the object in comparison with which other views are either wrong or trivial. From what has just been said, it will be clear that this is a very odd kind of mirroring. We will return to this point below. For the moment, let us consider briefly what is involved logically in the 'mirroring' of objects, regardless of how odd we may consider this mirroring to be. The 'mirroring' practised by science requires subject constancy (capacity to sustain a particular kind of educated attentiveness[13]) connoted by secondary process functioning and an object constancy which enables the observance of protocols relating to replicability and publicity. Repetition of experiments and/or observation of numerous possible 'instances' of a 'universal' are required to establish that a particular is, in fact, an instance of a universal. Only where the object is conceivable from one point of view, which is taken to be, if not the only conceivable, then the most consequential point of view (the universal point of view), is this repetitive practice meaningful, or, only then can scientists claim to have arrived at reliable (although always 'for the moment') conclusions about the part of the world to which their attention has been directed.

Culture is deeply implicated in the constitution and maintenance of constancy and intelligibility. As noted in chapter one, culture is an attempt to create 'closed systems' or the reliable reproduction of a particular way of life.[14] The constancy secured in pre-capitalist cultures had a repetitive character which allowed a modest form of practical experimentation, generally in relation to the provision of luxuries rather than everyday necessities (Bernal 1954: ch. 5; Merchant 1989: ch. 3; Zilsel 1945). This was an experiential constancy of relations, of practices and of objects which allowed of the smooth intrafamilial, intergenerational transmission of knowledge as common sense. The kind of constancy produced by value's law is quite different from this precapitalist constancy, since it is constancy in the production of commodities, therefore a constancy which may (and indeed now does) require loss of experiential or 'subjective' constancy. Moreover, as noted in chapter two, objective constancy is always necessarily 'for the moment', since capitalism is necessarily a crisis-prone culture. Since the 1970s, we have been experiencing a crisis which has endangered both subjective and objective constancy and is presently necessitating the dramatic forms of experiential inconstancy discussed in chapters six and seven. The postmodern sciences are dialectically implicated in this development, as will be seen later.

To summarize, both capitalism and science (as knowledge intended for impersonal and efficient mastery of the world) are expressions of a two-worlds rationality involving the evaluation of 'objects' from the point of view of a desirable or truthful state (reality) against which everyday objects fall short and to which they should conform. The capitalist reality is value; the scientific reality is truth. Where science becomes directly implicated in value's reproduction, as has been happening increasingly since the 1980s (Slaughter and Leslie 1997: ch. 1), the truth which scientists seek is one which will bring objects into line with the needs of value. In any case, both capitalism and science manifest an impersonal, monological, abstract form of rationality which proceeds by subsuming particulars (identifiable at the level of appearances) under a supposed universal (identifiable at the level of reality). In terms of our understanding of human flourishing, this is a world-dissolving rationality in that it is indifferent to particularity and to the needs of creatures who need completion through the constitution of a common sense. It attends to humanity in a way which is ignorant of, or indifferent to, this human need.

The dialectic of exchange and use has now moved on in a way which has engendered a contradiction between the need for nomological (determining) science and capital's tendency to reduce the world to process, therefore to undermine the specific subject/object constancy which modern science has both presupposed and helped, for a time, to reproduce. Beyond this, the innate inadequacies of science are becoming evident as scientific knowledge is practically fed into the world and, simultaneously, capitalism's need for science becomes ever more urgent. For the moment this need is being met in a remarkable way by postmodern sciences. This is what I discuss next. (The reader is warned that this discussion is intended to be exploratory and indicative of certain powerful tendencies in contemporary sciences, particularly the life sciences.)

II Disorganized capitalism and the emergence of postmodern sciences

The ways in which the process character of capitalism is exacerbated by the marriage of neoliberalism and electronics were discussed in chapters six and seven. Following this marriage, the 'social evaporation of the tangible' (Arendt 1958: 69–70), which was a capitalist potential from the point at which industrialization began, has, as we have seen, assumed an unprecedented intensity and speed. The deregulation of capital flows was one accelerator which enhanced the transformation of property into wealth; a transformation which 'dematerializes' consequentiality by instituting the rule of finance capital in electronic rather than mechanical mode, thereby endowing it with novel globalizing powers and movements whose complexity and speed begin to defy understanding (Harvey 1989: 161).[15] It is the rule of an unregulated, or lightly and ineffectively regulated, finance capital (Eatwell 2002) which accelerates the dialectic of exchange and use in a manner that seeks the rule of exchange over use, therefore the rule of substitutability and obsolescence over objectivity and worldliness. This is one dimension of the cognitive crisis. Another is science's own misconception of the world and of its own activities.

The 'design fault' of modern science

The 'design fault' of modern science consists in the fact that it conceptualizes the world analytically rather than dialectically (Levins and Lewontin 1985). This is not accidental, but is related to its theoretically nurtured blindness to context; a blindness which is the source of both the strengths and weaknesses of this science. We noted before that science claims to mirror or represent the world, or, to make present in theoretical knowledge what is the case in (part of) nature. As a matter of analytical abstraction, however, this 'mirroring' is never only mirroring (Bhaskar 1989: ch. 3). It is a highly selective concept-dependent 'mirroring' whose practitioners tend to forget the difference between what is 'mirrored' and the concept with whose help mirroring takes place (Althusser and Balibar 1970: 86–90). Bhaskar (1997) has enabled us to understand the way in which experimental logic contravenes nature in that it constitutes, through deliberate human activity, a closed system within which objects, having been taken out of context, are examined for the immediate purposes of establishing their causal powers and the ultimate purpose of reconfiguring the world by reinserting these objects into contexts which may be foreign to their origins. Feminist philosophers of science have been more concerned than Bhaskar to stress the way in which the mechanistic worldview which supports the practice of laboratory experimentation contravenes nature through blindness to its necessarily organic, relational character (Haraway 1991; Keller 1985; Merchant 1989).[16]

The analytical assumption guiding experimental practice is that we can gain real, useful knowledge of objects abstracted from context. Given the extraordinary practical efficacy of science, it would be foolish to deny that this is true. Real powers have been identified and acted upon successfully, at least in the short term. What this means is that scientists have provided explanations which are (for the moment at least) consistent with nature. In this sense, natural science has passed the 'pragmatic' test (Hesse 1978) since despite periodic 'revolutions' it has managed to accumulate a body of knowledge about causal powers which has enabled, up to now, the successful transformation of parts of the world according to this knowledge. However, as noted previously, the explanations which scientists have given us are not explanations of reality as a whole, but of a part viewed from a certain point of view and therefore constituted as a part from that point of view. Newtonian physics is a notable example of this fact. Relativity and quantum theory did not cancel out Newtonian physics but revealed the local nature of its applicability (Capra 1983: ch. 4). However, while the more philosophically-inclined physicists warned us that the world is not as simple and stable as the Newtonian viewpoint had encouraged us to believe (Schrödinger 1996), the mechanistic worldview has remained influential and is only now being seriously challenged in some sciences. For reasons which we will now explore, it would be premature to view the challenge as an advance towards a more worldly form of science.

Postmodern science: a dereifying science for a dereifying world

Postmodern sciences are sciences which rediscover those real attributes of nature to which modern science has been blind; such attributes include movement, complexity, relationality and situatedness. In addition, science is recognized as an 'active intellectual construction' (Prigogine and Stengers 1984: 55) rather than the transparent mirroring of an object. The shift of emphasis from substance to relation, from the uniform and universal to the specific and the unique, that the new sciences promise, the abrogation of the observer's god-like status, seem to promise respect for the richness and complexity of nature manifested in the possibility of a dialogue within nature rather than an instrumentalizing discourse *about* nature. Nature is apparently accepted in all of its complexity and determinism is recognized as exceptional and local rather than universal. For these reasons, critics of modern science have, as noted earlier, welcomed these developments as a move away from the 'totalizing totalitarian claims' of a science that applies only to simple, stable objects (Prigogine and Stengers 1984: 216). Unfortunately, these developments have, if anything, enhanced rather than minimized the practical hubris displayed by modern science.

It is not possible to do more than suggest the strange nature of the new knowledges outlined here. Having argued in chapter seven that consumerism is reducing the individual psyche to process, let me now go on to suggest that new configurations of matter and meaning are beginning to effect something similar within the more obviously material stuff of the body (both human and non-human). Genetics is one of those sciences which has proceeded under the banner of determinism (Rose 1997). Recently, though, the discoveries of molecular biologists have been leading geneticists to recognize the complexity (non-linearity, non-determined nature) of their objects of study (Capra 2002: ch. 6). This recognition pushes for a theoretical repositioning from a conception of genes as self-contained substances having identifiable and stable (determinate) properties to one which takes stability as a remarkable rather than taken-for-granted matter (Keller 2000: 14), and which seeks to understand the conditions of possibility for the maintenance of stability. This involves a systemic exploration of the cellular network within which the gene is situated. Conceptualization of the cellular network is influenced by cybernetics (Haraway 1991: ch. 3).[17] This influence encourages the conception of entities as nothing but relations, or, difference, not substance, is what now identifies entities.[18] Or, more accurately, the idea that matter is substance cedes to the conviction that it is pattern and life becomes a kind of constantly flowing indeterminate 'stuff' whose constant 'repatterning' is conceptualized as informational reconfiguration (Haraway 1991: ch. 10; Hayles 1999: ch. 3). Information, as Hayles points out, is an idealizing metaphor which nurtures blindness to embodiment, therefore to the limitations of time and place.[19] As a concept which was developed within the engineering sciences, it facilitates the fusion of mechanism and organism, a fusion which, expressed in the concept of 'genetic engineering' takes the instrumentalism of Baconianism to new depths. In effect, 'information' is the new scientific 'universal' under which can be subsumed virtually anything.

Indeed, genetics is immensely fruitful in terms of creating new materials through the reconfiguration of existing materials. As Rifkin (1998: ch. 1, esp. p. 14) points out, the 'recombinant possibilities' in biotech laboratories are 'near limitless' and encourage a view which dissolves organisms and species into their chemical constituents. Here, bodies themselves are reduced to process, or, we have the beginnings of a dereified form of rationality every bit as fetishized as its reified predecessor. Gene splicing exemplifies the logic of an activity informed by this reduction of matter to flows of information, flows into which the designing intelligence of the scientist can break without too much concern for the specificities of substances or the integrity of organisms (Capra 2002: 154–6).[20]

The important point here is that recognition of the fact that relations animate the objects of scientists' attention is leading to an undialectical demotion of organisms to mere matter in constant motion according to the unpredictable dictates of 'information'. Or, as Rifkin puts it: 'the door is opened to a thorough reinterpretation of existence as pure process devoid of any kind of ultimate, unchanging frame of reference' (1998: 220). Looked at from this point of view, a science practising under the sign of information can happily cohabit with a dereifying capitalism. And, indeed, this is what we find when we consider what is happening in the life sciences.

The demotion of organisms to flows of information is nurturing a scientific orientation which is, if anything, more hubristic and instrumental than that of modern science.[21] The difference is that whereas modern sciences normalized determinacy, postmodern sciences normalize indeterminacy. However, as it turns out, the latter opens up previously inconceivable opportunities for commodification as geneticists turned entrepreneurs begin to put science more directly and immediately at the disposal of value (Slaughter and Leslie 1997: chs 1, 2, 6). This may seem surprising, given geneticists' emergent understanding that the world is far from the simplicities of the mechanistic world, that it is not determined in its movements in any clear sense. This understanding should, as Capra (2002: 142) claims, put an end to the fantasy that genetics can, or should, produce 'tangible practical applications' in the near future. Far from this being the case, the new genetics manifests key features of the determinant attitude and practice in the biological field (Kaplan 2000; Winston 2002). That is to say, it is taking a view on the world which is every bit as universalizing in its ambitions as was modern science, and it is blind to the experiential realm which is subsumed under 'system', 'networks', 'information', etc. In fact, both nature and culture are reduced to the status of mere plaything of 'information', the expectation being that the 'information' perspective will yield reliable, practically-efficacious knowledge of that world.

From science to technology: from risk to uncertainty

As science becomes technology, the riskiness that accompanied science's false universalism becomes transmuted into uncertainty (Reddy 1996). There are two related reasons for anticipating problems once scientific theory has been translated into technological practice. One is the abstract character of scientific knowledge (whether abstraction takes a modern or postmodern form); the other is the failure to take sufficient account of the provisional nature of scientific findings when considering the practical usefulness of these. Scientists are not free from the human tendency to naturalize their specific experiences, or, as Rifkin (1998: 216) puts it, to 'inflate the tiny aspect of nature's reality that we are manipulating at a moment in time into a universal cosmology'. For these reasons, science was from the beginning a risky endeavour, but, for a time, its riskiness was 'latent' rather than 'manifest' (Beck 1992).[22]

Riskiness becomes manifest once a science is taken out of the laboratories and from the pages of professional journals and fed into the everyday world. The practical implementation of the theoretical results of undialectical abstractions was bound to have unintended, potentially disastrous, effects, since technological intentionality was misguided from the start (Lash and Wynne 1992: 5). Indeed, we are now experiencing outbursts in the non-human 'real' as nature says 'no' to our impositions or subverts our intentions in all kinds of unexpected ways (Aronowitz 1988; Beck 1992; Capra 1983; Fuller 2000). Through technology, in the last few years the uncertainty that began to seep into modern physics during the early part of the twentieth century, at which time it was expressed theoretically rather than practically or politically, has made its way into the practical world as the increasing intrusiveness of science into the everyday world has come to constitute that uncertainty anticipated by Arendt. So, not only does science reduce appearances to 'mereness' by rendering common sense 'stupid' (Arendt 1994: 313–14) but it also renders the world a more dangerous place than it would otherwise be. As science comes to be directly governed by value's law, the dangers become more immediate and more acute. Moreover, as noted previously, science itself becomes processual in character. It thereby begins to give new meaning to the 'social evaporation of the tangible' anticipated by Arendt some time ago (Arendt 1958: 69–70).

Science and the dialectic of exchange and use

Scientific success in the laboratory (confirmation of findings via replication of experiments) leads to the technological reconfiguration of science which brings science into the everyday world of appearances. In a sense, the more science succeeds, the more scientific mistakes have effects beyond the laboratory. At the same time, science's own failures become the basis of new market booms as, through the more extensive and intensive movement of value, their rectification takes a commodified form (Beck 1992: 175).[23] This last, most urgent development introduces the law of value (therefore the dialectic of exchange and use) more deeply and immediately into the 'space' within which scientific 'stopping and thinking' has taken place up to now.

Two developments are taking place simultaneously: recognition of the riskiness of scientific knowledges and an enhancement of capitalism's need for such knowledges. This enhanced need is expressed in the concept of 'informational' capitalism (Castells 1996: 18–22), a concept which connotes the replacement of 'things' by 'messages' as the prime source of exchange value. The preoccupation with 'information' which has come to saturate all spheres of life is in part an expression of the speediness and unpredictability of change in the network society and on the knowledge needs of subjects who, less than before, can rely on habit to know how to go on in the world. Knowledge becomes information as change becomes the norm (Rifkin 1998: 219). Information is knowledge rendered both transient and commodified, or, it is knowledge produced under the sign of exchange rather than of use; therefore it is knowledge doomed to speedy obsolescence; and therefore, in a real sense, it is not knowledge at all (Roszak 1988). Similarly and relatedly, as we have seen, information also connotes the reconfiguration of nature under the sign of change, rather than of stability. Or, from the informational point of view, nature and the world are transformed into a flow of matter which is susceptible to re-engineering and which must be re-engineered if a flow of new 'objects' adequate to the reproduction of value is to be secured. Expressed otherwise, the speeding up of the dialectic of exchange and use involves the imposition of new forms on existing matter and the constitution of new materials out of old. Both require new knowledges. Therefore the speeding up of the dialectic is the speeding up of knowledge production. Or, in Aronowitz's words quoted previously, 'knowledge has become the main productive force' (1990: 116).

Given that this is the case, the resistance among many practising scientists to warnings delivered by philosophically disposed theoretical physicists is disturbing. These warnings have not yet dissolved the 'logical empiricist and positivist *ideology*' which continues to inform the common sense of scientists (Aronowitz 1988: 239 [emphasis in original]). In any case, the possibility of 're-engineering' human and non-human bodies is pursued with unprecedented dedication by entrepreneurial scientists, and with the enthusiastic support of many governments (O'Hagan 2001).[24] What Susan Strange (1986) describes as 'casino capitalism' makes its entrance into the basic material of life. Indeed, the field of genetics exemplifies most clearly Lyotard's claim, made some time ago (1984: 41–7), that knowledge as use value is being replaced by knowledge as exchange value (Westphal 2002). Of course, some areas of science have been commodified since the 1880s but the universities have provided an uncommodified enclave within which more or less useful or useless knowledge could be produced. Now, however, commodification is entering the universities as the state abrogates its responsibility for the funding of knowledge (Delanty 2001; Fuller 2000: pt 2; Slaughter and Leslie 1997). As an example of the 'liberal excess' which accompanies this development, Fuller notes the 'tendency of laboratory scientists in particular to treat the university as little more than a relatively efficient space for doing business' (2000: 47).

As exchange value, knowledge must be fed into the world as speedily as possible, therefore the time taken to stop and think must be as short as possible, a practical development which is connoted by the concept of 'technoscience', or, a science in which basic research becomes entrepreneurial (Slaughter and Leslie 1997: 38, 21).[25] Now, value roams freely, and the obsolescence and substitutability which are borne by commodity fetishism have been let loose in new areas of life and have regained access to areas from which they had been excluded during capitalism's organized phase. Now, trial-and-error, which remained confined to the laboratory for long periods in the past, moves out into the world ever more boldly and swiftly, and at a time when supposedly pre-established general rules have demonstrated their unreliability through evidence of science's practical riskiness as well as the findings of the new sciences. Finding out that we have assigned nature a property that it does not possess will increasingly now occur after the practical damage is done and (possibly) is irreversible.

So, theory continues to be pumped out and translated into practical activity through technologies which act on the world in unprecedented and irreversible ways, or, ways which eliminate the possibility of learning through trial and error. Irreversibility is either ignored, treated as irrelevant given the enormous benefits to be derived from the new technologies, or legitimated through the imputation of a scientific truth in which we now have little reason to believe. The fact that philosophers of science, and sometimes scientists themselves, continue to proclaim the provisional nature of scientific knowledge does not change this practical orientation. In co-operating in reducing the gap between science and technology, scientists have not been prepared so far to act upon their avowed scepticism by arguing against the translation of their theory into technological practice (Kitcher 2001).[26] In any case, the pressure to find private sources of funding for research makes it increasingly difficult for them to do so. The result is a kind of overdetermined indeterminacy, or, an exponential growth in uncertainty as science's misperception of its own activity is multiplied by value's insouciance about the world.

Presently, the increasingly potent and irrational combination of science and value is becoming visible in the shape of a 'new political economy' involving scientists, businesses and governments. This new political economy is likely to render science more rather than less destructive. At the same time, as this new configuration of science, government and capital comes more clearly into view, and as anxieties about the genetic engineering of food become more acute, the possibility emerges that individuals forced to be 'autonomous' will turn from an increasingly impotent economism to public-spiritedness. In fact, given the present impotence and/or irresponsibility of states (Stein 1997), the politicization of science by citizens rather than by governments and special interest groups is needed if the practical efficacy (as opposed to destructiveness) of science itself is to be restored.[27] Let me turn briefly to this question before concluding the chapter.

III Science and citizens

In relation to the categorization of rationality which I have used throughout this study, determinant judgement is a manifestation of that systemic functional rationality which emerged over the 'civilizing' centuries but which became essential to the functioning of capitalism towards the end of the nineteenth century, at which time also the atomized economic rationality of *homo oeconomicus* had become possible. The latter was embodied in male capitalists, as depicted by Marx in *On the Jewish Question* (1994), and would be nurtured in proletarians as commodity fetishism came to characterize all social relations. We have seen this tendency at work in the privatization of working-class life during the organized phase of capitalism (although counteracted up to a point by the sociability enabled by organized production) which nurtured receptiveness to the reinvigorated atomism and economism initiated by neoliberalism during the 1980s.

There was an internal relationship between functional and atomistic rationality in that the successful actualization of the determinant judgements of scientists (natural and social) yielded, for the moment, a world of stable, therefore predictable, differentiations. The world (of differentiated 'objects') as pinned down under the knowing gaze of the scientific expert yielded knowledge which, when fed into the everyday world of appearances, yielded experiences which were susceptible to modest individual cost–benefit analysis regarding individual private goods. At the same time use values, such as pensions, insurance and healthcare, whose provision required the most meticulous and expert form of calculation, were ensured by the state. So, while scientific expertise rendered common sense redundant, it enabled, for a time, a modest form of atomistic rationality which was sufficient for the practices of everyday life under conditions of a reified form of commodity fetishism.

During this period, what Giddens (1994) calls the 'law of insurance' prevailed. This law has now been replaced by the 'law of the lottery' (Neary and Taylor 1998: ch. 3). The law of insurance connotes conditions of life sufficiently determinate to enable meaningful calculations regarding the likelihood of different possibilities. The law of the lottery connotes an indeterminacy which eliminates the possibility of such calculations. The movement from insurance to lottery is a movement from an instrumentally, functionally rational culture to one which is irrational, or, in which a surplus of volatility eliminates that regularity of expectation in the absence of which knowledge for a human world becomes impossible to produce. In 'subjective' terms, it is a movement beyond the rationality of *homo oeconomicus*. It turns out that the state has abrogated its responsibilities to control the risks inherent in value's law (or has become incapable of fulfilling these) just at the point that these risks are becoming resistant to cost–benefit analysis. Indeed, in seeking to extricate itself from welfare provision, the state is thereby enhancing risk by removing remaining constraints on value's movement. These constraints are removed not only at the point of provision of knowledge to individual clients, but in the process of production of knowledge itself, as the state withdraws from the public funding of science. At this point, the apparently extravagant claim that risks are being transmuted into 'uncertainty', or that they lie 'beyond the world of quantifiable redemption' (Neary and Taylor 1998: 53), becomes persuasive. For subjects expected to be their own experts, the result, for the moment, is an experience of 'lack' (in this case, lack of justified expectation of present and future vital use values) which may hold the key to the transformation of 'desirousness' into sustained and citizenly political engagement.

The loss of trust in experts of all kinds has a number of different causes, as noted previously. In addition to the degeneration of capitalist institutions which an unregulated neoliberalism has effected, there is the visibility and audibility of scientific disagreements as well as the publicity given to scientific mistakes and the proliferation of sensational and/or contradictory findings of a science caught up in the market logic of public relations. The term 'Enronitis' which entered the language in 2002 (Blackburn 2002) condenses all of those doubts, fears and the corrosion of that respectful lay attentiveness which (natural, and to a lesser extent, social) scientific experts could expect to receive in the past (Giddens 1990; 1994). The question is, what, if any, is the potential for public-spiritedness in this development?

The devolution of parenting (the welfare function) from state to individual has been undertaken in rational choice mode. That is to say, it has assumed an atomistic individualism as both necessary and sufficient for the making of rational choices in relation to matters which in the past have required expert knowledge and labour-intensive, institutionally supported calculations about the future. Yet rational choice involves a particular kind of reality-testing (the reality-testing of cost–benefit analysis) which needs to envisage clear objects and assume constant relations for its practice. The economic rationality of rational choosers requires that clear distinctions be made between subjects and objects and that these be viewed as quantities which can be calculated (Amariglio and Callari 1993: 208–10). That is to say, it requires a mode of differentiation which is becoming unavailable today, when, as Fredric Jameson noted in a succinct expression of our worldlessness, we are becoming incapable of 'cognitive mapping', or, of locating ourselves in thought in a mappable bounded space (Jameson 1992: 51–4).

Individuals, as supposedly free and rational choosers, are now being forced to become their own parents in the very strong sense that they are required to evaluate the risks of decisions whose spatio-temporal conditions and ramifications are beyond the knowing of any expert, since they are subject to the unpredictable de- and re-fusions and differentiations of which the network society, as the society of finance, is the bearer. These are decisions bearing on vital use values which are provided through mortgages, insurance and pensions. The difficulties of making good choices among a bewildering and ever-changing variety of mortgage 'packages' has been exacerbated by the mis-selling of these packages by the relevant experts (Hutton 2002b). A combination of genetic discoveries and insurance disasters associated with climate change is presently increasing the number of conditions, accidents and disasters which will be uninsurable in the future (Altman 2001; Rifkin 1998: 160–2). As for pensions, the occupational and state pension schemes which during capitalism's organized phase provided for the aristocracy of labour the assurance of a comfortable old age and which protected the less fortunate from penury, are now being reconfigured in ways which withhold assurance and protection (Blackburn 2002; Harmes 2001; Scott 2002).

The findings of postmodern sciences, as presently constituted, will do nothing to reconstitute cultural parenting. Far from it.[28] The practical implementation of these sciences will enhance the worldlessness of the world by enhancing its volatility. They are in any case also the bearer of an instrumentalist universalism more extensive, intensive and relentless than anything we have experienced before. This does not mean that we must, or can, forget science. It means, rather, that science must be reconceptualized in a way which avoids the violence of either reifying or dereifying abstractions, or, which avoids the equally misleading tendencies to reduce organism to either atom or information. Indeed, the proliferation of risk and the intensification of uncertainty through the unintended consequences of scientific activity urges the reconceptualization of science's basic presuppositions. It urges us to remember both that nature offers more than one option and that we have the power to organize rather than 'make' nature. Because we do not make nature, that power is limited by the real nature of nature itself. At the same time, the answers we receive from nature depend in part on the questions we pose (Bhaskar 1997; Haraway 1991; Hesse 1978). In identifying correctly particular causal powers, we are not thereby necessarily exhausting the possibilities of the 'objects' in question. A 'modest realism' (Kitcher 2001) is one which seeks knowledge of real natural powers without ever forgetting the historico-cultural conditions of possibility of their discovery. Recognizing the historico-cultural character of the questions will free us up to pose questions other than those dictated by the quest for mastery, questions to which answers compatible with worldliness may be heard

(Aronowitz 1988: 333, 330). This could be a matter left to scientists prepared to become reflective about the conditions of possibility of their own knowledges or it could involve an unprecedented citizen involvement in deliberation about the nature and future of science itself.

Conclusion

In this chapter I have elaborated on capitalism's 'regime of truth' (the abstract knowledge which is the correlate of abstract labour and consumption) in terms of the cognitive contradiction which has emerged in recent years. This contradiction has emerged out of a condition of indeterminacy which is overdetermined by (a) the transformation of the world effected by a dereifying form of commodity fetishism which begins to reduce 'thingness' to process, (b) the proliferation of scientific 'mistakes' as the results of a fundamentally misconceived science are fed into the world beyond the laboratory, and (c) the closure of gap between 'discovery' and practical implementation of scientific knowledges such that the time which was previously given over to 'stopping and thinking' before acting has been cut short. The latter has come about as capitalism's need for new objects of exchange becomes ever more urgent. This need involves the imposition of new forms on existing matters which, in some cases, is a matter of constituting new materials out of old, as in genetic engineering. The combined result of these developments is the loss of that 'objectivity' which in the (more organized) past yielded up relatively constant objects of knowledge. So, having begun to consider the ways in which contemporary capitalism impedes the constitution of the 'subject who knows (determinantly)' (or the subject governed by secondary process functioning), we have in this chapter viewed this matter from the point of view of the loss of objects to be known 'determinantly'. While noting the emergence of a dereifying postmodern mode of science (sciences of complexity rather than of unilinearity), we have noted the survival of a worldless universalism in these sciences and, moreover, have found little evidence that they are resistant to meeting the needs of value. Indeed, in their reduction of situatedness to system, and of relationality to information, they promise a worldlessness (the worldlessnes of indeterminacy rather than of determinacy) even more virulent than that which characterized the determinant mode of science.

Evidence of the cognitive contradiction which is feeding its way into everyday experience includes crises relating to climate, to the food chain, to the re-emergence of infectious diseases that science had relegated to the past, and the emergence of new virulent and deadly infections the treatment of which raises serious questions about the pharmaceuticals industry and the inequitable treatment of people in poor countries. These are issues in which the role of natural sciences appears to predominate, but in general, the distinction between the natural and social sciences is becoming difficult to sustain. Also of significance, though, are those matters in which the social sciences are obviously implicated; matters involving the reduction of politics to public relations and the loss of authority of both politicians and journalists consequent on this reduction (Mayhew 1997), and the provision of expert knowledges to individual clients in the form of mortgage, insurance and pensions advice at a time when, for a variety of reasons, the soundness of expert advice has never been more questionable.

So, scientific expertise becomes questionable at the moment that it becomes an important, individual use value in the sense that the individual access to such expertise is no longer mediated bureaucratically. Now expert knowledges are produced explicitly for the purposes of exchange and are increasingly directed at disorganized (contradictorily constituted) subjects who, abandoned by the shrinking welfare state, must seek their own individual present and future vital use values. For the moment, this state-enforced self-preoccupation is expressed in an economic rationality more intensive and extensive than anything that has gone before, hence the anxieties expressed by democracy theorists such as John Dryzek, as noted in my introduction, but hence also, via realization of the impotence of this form of rationality, the potential for the emergence of a new post-capitalist rationality.

Hope that the emergence of such a rationality might be in prospect is based on the fact that the subject-loss referred to before is not straightforward, since 'disorganized' subjects are in the grip of contradictory cultural demands for autonomy and heteronomy. These are subjects who feel entitled to be autonomous but who experience themselves as heteronomous. Yet they are also subjects who, in being forced into particular forms of self-responsibility (which demand a new kind of expert knowledgeability if the claims of experts are to be correctly evaluated), are also being forced to act 'as if' autonomous. However, unlike the 'as-ifness' examined in chapter seven (the 'as-ifness' encouraged by fantasizing), this 'as-ifness' exerts pressure on the subject to become reliably knowledgeable about the world beyond self. For this reason, it may become the source of a new kind of public-spiritedness as the two contradictions (of subjectivity, of knowledgeability) come together. Where new cognitive requirements are placed on contradictorily constituted subjects, the realization that these cognitive requirements are, in fact, part of an unsustainable and irrational world may induce more support for the radical questioning of capitalist and scientific business as usual than is presently being manifested. In the conclusion to this book, I shall consider the possibility that this radical questioning might be the source of a new anaclitic rationality having the character of a *sensus communis*.

Conclusion
Citizenship and the recovery of worldliness

The network society is a groundless world of flows which requires from the new aristocracy of labour peculiarly uncommitted social and cognitive commitments. That is to say, it requires serial attachments (to self, to persons, to knowledges and skills) which demand the ability to become temporarily attached while remaining detached. It requires self-programming subjects whose only commitment is to instant and unquestioning responsiveness to the emergent and unpredictable demands of value's law. Anticipating these demands, preparing to answer value's summons, becomes the all-absorbing task of individuals in this world. Success in this arduous endeavour brings (for the moment at least) large material rewards, but these rewards are not guaranteed and may dissolve at any time. For 'generic' labourers, meagre rewards, similarly without guarantee, are available. From both groups, self-reliance is demanded under threat of future impoverishment. The structurally irrelevant are just that: irrelevant. Their fate depends on the readiness of governments and their electorates to dole out ever more meagre and grudgingly offered sustenance.

Individual autonomy has now become official policy, since, as governments attempt to 'roll back' the welfare state, interpellations and practices are systematically designed to elicit individualized self-direction and maintenance. Autonomy is here conceptualized as atomism; as the self-interest of individuals who are in external relations with one another and with 'society'. This atomism is intensified by the unknowability of the world in which self-programmable workers find themselves. Standing readiness to change, and standing anxiety about the satisfaction of needs, together with the need for self-reliance without a sense of self are the characteristics of self-programmable workers. So, while the 'consciousness' of such workers is constitutive of the new labour process in a way not required of factory workers, the world remains an 'alien power' standing over self-programmable workers as *individual* workers. It is an objectivity against which individual subjectivity is insignificant. Reification in this sense remains a characteristic of capitalism but it now coexists with dereification. What this means, as noted previously, is that the subjects constituted by contemporary capitalism are split subjects who are at once 'psychologized' through 'privatizing' and individualizing practices related to the demand that subjects be responsible, as individuals, for self-maintenance and self-transformation, and depsychologized through novel manifestations of abstract labour and consumption which tend to constitute disorganized psyches governed by primary, rather than secondary, process functioning. The result of satisfactory fulfilment of these contradictory capitalist demands is self-absorbed subjects who lack a sense of self. That is to say, they lack the sense of groundedness which renders worldly, rather than worldless, flexibility possible. They are ungrounded because cultural parenting has come to an end.

Yet this is not the first time in the history of human cultures that cultural parenting has dissolved. The civilizing process which Elias (1994) describes is an example which testifies to human capacities to reconstitute cultures and therefore, by definition, cultural parenting. The emergence of hybrid bourgeois capitalism was, from this point of view, the replacement of one kind of cultural parenting (or one kind of reality principle) by another. Moreover, this replacement effected the expansion of human cultural horizons by enabling an unprecedented, but class-specific, nurturing of human potentials for activity, imagination and relative autonomy without (for the moment) incurring the cost of atomism. As noted previously, the principle of autonomy remains active in our political and theoretical 'common sense'. In political terms, neoliberalism in power has designed policies on the assumption that autonomy is both actual and desirable. In theoretical terms, various writers are persuaded in different ways that autonomy remains a desirable goal whose achievement is facilitated by contemporary capitalism (Castells 1997; Giddens 1991; 1994; Laclau 1990). More specifically, autonomy seems to be promised in the need for reflexivity which the proliferation of risk throws up and, for some, in the release from the kinds of cultural expectations associated with the concept of role (Castells 1998: 369; Giddens 1991: 75).[1]

From this point of view, capitalism's need for new kinds of active, educated and flexible subjects, together with the dissolution of patriarchy and of extra-familial social roles (or, more accurately, the reflexive rather than compelled choice of social roles), renders possible new forms of self-cultivation and self-direction. Indeed, this is the Marxian position. Marx, though, hoped that, eventually, these forms of self-cultivation would be compatible with public-spiritedness. This is implicit in his solidarity principle: 'from each according to his abilities, to each according to his needs' (Marx: 1974b: 347; Love 1995). The *Manifesto* remains an interesting narrative of how such public-spiritedness might emerge out of capitalist-constituted atomism. It anticipates a time when the whole world would have been transformed in the image of capitalism so that humanity would have become a lived category. As noted at the beginning of this book, something of this kind is happening at the moment through the expansion of wage labour, through new movements of peoples (enforced and voluntary), through new modes of communication, and through the everyday experience and emergent understanding of 'absent causes' and unintended consequences which are constituting unanticipated and unwanted

164 *Conclusion*

absences and/or presences. All of these are urging us towards reflexivity, or, a questioning of what has been taken for granted up to now. There is as yet, though, little sign that enforced reflexivity is taking a public-spirited form. In this final chapter, a discussion of public-spirited reflexivity will be undertaken with the help of Hannah Arendt's account of reflective judgement, the intention being to provide some content for the form and practice of a *sensus communis* adequate to the tasks of a global, rather than hybrid bourgeois, world. The chapter is in three parts. The first part unfolds the logic of the *Communist Manifesto* so as to consider the possibility that out of the experiential contradictions discussed in the third part of this study might emerge conditions of possibility for the transcendence of the expert/laity split. The second part elaborates on the character of reflective judgement as the embodiment of natality and a new kind of *sensus communis* (theoretical anaclitic rationality) relevant to the needs of world care now. Part three will elaborate on this global *sensus communis* in relation to the question of 'interests' and redistribution.

I Autonomy and heteronomy: beyond the contradiction?

My examination of bourgeois subjectivity was intended to remind us of the very demanding character of autonomy and of the cultural conditions of possibility for one of its manifestations. Where this is forgotten, the danger is that we will assume autonomy where it does not exist, and neglect the important political task of its nurturance. It may be that this task is beyond our present resources. Here I have begun to think about these resources in terms of two contradictions: the contradiction between autonomy and heteronomy, discussed in chapters six and seven, and the cognitive contradiction which is discussed in chapter eight. These are contradictions which are experienced most powerfully within the most intensively 'neoliberalized' Anglo-American world. Other kinds of contradictions are being experienced elsewhere and may signify the possibilities of more potent forms of collective action than any possible in capitalism's birthplace (Castells 1997: ch. 5). My interest in contradictions is deliberately parochial, for reasons which have been indicated in my introduction and which will bear repeating here.

The assumption guiding my focus on the West is that it is here that the greatest sacrifices will need to be made if the world is to become at once safer and more just. Here the Marxian solidarity principle will need to find its actualization if a non-coercive and non-coerced redistribution of resources from the West to the rest is to be effected and if a mode of life more in tune with human and non-human nature is to emerge. The further assumption is that moral exhortation is never adequate to engendering the willingness to make sacrifices; that the conditions of possibility must emerge out of the way of life of those whose 'abilities' must become the source of satisfying others' needs.

Public-spirited citizenship has conditions of possibility for its full exercise, including as necessary, but not sufficient, the ending of exploitation. However, there are different forms of exploitation which are experienced differently by different groups. The emergent exploitation which is manifested in the cognitive contradiction is generally experienced by the relatively wealthy. It seems insignificant compared to the life-threatening and often brutal forms of exploitation experienced beyond the prosperous parts of the Euro-American world. The reason for focusing on this form of exploitation is that it may hold the potential for the emergence of a public-spirited citizenship such that these relatively educated, relatively prosperous class fractions will take on responsibilities for world care, which would include the remedying of more virulent forms of exploitation and dehumanization than we ourselves experience. In doing so, we could come to enjoy a more meaningful form of autonomy than its present neoliberal manifestation.

Economic rationality and its transcendence

Neoliberalism as a matter of government policy has assumed the self-directing, self-contained liberal subject to be a fact of nature. It has therefore not had to concern itself about the psychic (therefore economic and cultural) resources needed for the practice of autonomy (which is, in effect, equated with 'rational choice'), and has been content to conceive of the necessary cultural resources in terms of sustaining a framework of 'choices' for possessive, entrepreneurial subjects. That is to say, government policy is informed by the belief that economic rationality is what characterizes subjects/citizens and that conditions are such that economic rationality can be practised and acted upon effectively. However, the possibility of making 'good' choices, that is, choices which enhance the well-being of individual choosers (however that well-being may be conceived), depends on the intelligibility of the world, on the degree of knowledgeability attained by choosers and on their ability to act in a forceful and effective manner in complex, constantly changing circumstances. This is a matter of reality-testing and of the dispositions needed to engage in reality-testing. But, as we have come to understand, reality-testing can only take place where cultural parenting has ensured the availability of a shared sense of reality. This is not the case in disorganized cultures in which the clear boundedness of subjects and objects which the concept of rational choice entails has been dissolved through the de-differentiations discussed in earlier chapters. In these unprecedented circumstances (circumstances in which neither expert nor lay rational choices can be meaningfully made) the need for a new form of rationality begins to assert itself. Moreover, despite its bleak portrayal in previous chapters, the present conjuncture is not bereft of the resources needed to rise to this challenge.

It is worth exploring the possibility that the irrationality of economic rationality will become clearer as it becomes more obviously impotent in face of the responsibilities presently facing the new aristocracy of labour. In being forced into the acquisition of new kinds of theoretical competencies (for the kinds of occupational reasons examined in chapter six, and in relation to the extra-occupational concerns discussed in chapter eight), individual subjects are simultaneously running up against the limitations of these competencies. Under these conditions, it is possible that such subjects will begin to question the modes of (ir)rationality which we are forced to adopt if we are not to sink into demeaning employment or the 'structural irrelevance' of unemployment. It is possible that as crises and scandals proliferate, as they are doing at the moment, our present mode of life will be judged as practically irrational, as well as unjust and destructive.

What I am suggesting is that the very practical anxieties and dilemmas discussed in chapter eight may provoke even the most self-absorbed into that thinking which Arendt considers necessary for the restoration of worldliness to the world. Thinking in this specific Arendtian sense is the other of the 'cognitive', monological thinking of determinant judgement. It is dialogical, self-consciously situated thinking oriented to the world, and to those with whom we share the world; thinking, moreover, which does not depend on preconceived frameworks which impose a pattern on the world. Such thinking becomes a necessity as cultures lose their way in the sense that appeal to existing theoretical or common sense is inadequate to discovering 'how to go on'. Thinking of this kind is a necessary preliminary to that acting in concert which is the business of public-spirited citizens and is, therefore, a manifestation of natality in that it is a use of imagination oriented to dialogue with others. Moreover, as preparation for dialogue with others (who, by virtue of their humanity, are simultaneously the same as and different from one's self) such thinking is also thinking about and for plurality, and therefore is thinking resistant to the abstract universalism that has marked determinant forms of thought (more on this later).

Two-worldness: the closing of the gap?

It is possible, given the kinds of globalizing changes and crises which are becoming apparent now, not only through media of communication, but also through mundane, direct experience, that in some real sense the gap between 'common sense' and science is beginning to close, as Ulrich Beck claimed as early as 1992.[2] What is also possible is that a global sense of connectedness is being developed through these same experiences. Marx and Engels looked for precisely these developments in the *Manifesto* which anticipated, first, the constitution of 'humanity' as a reality rather than abstraction through the socialization and mobilization of 'labour', and second, the closure of the gap between essence and appearances. Both of these developments would emerge out of capitalism's own changing requirements and were considered by Marx and Engels as the sources of an emergent global public-spiritedness; the public-spiritedness needed for actualizing the solidarity principle. As we know, humanization of this kind did not take place. What happened instead was that technocracy and capitalism effected the emergence of the 'social', which involved a debilitating depoliticization antithetical to public-spiritedness, but compatible with a certain conception of democracy (Arendt 1958: 38–49; Keane 1984). However, the conditions which made this depoliticization comfortable (a kind of class consensus which produced guarantees of rewards for good behaviour and the slowing down of capitalism's destabilizing dynamic) have been dissolving for some time as neoliberalism has come successfully to reshape the world according to capitalism's changing requirements. The world is becoming one culture through the increasingly intrusive activities of capitalism into places and activities that were up to now either excluded as structurally irrelevant to its concerns, or protected politically in value-free enclaves.[3] At the same time, places and activities which were previously structurally relevant have been rendered obsolescent, the obsolescence of places being as much a feature of capitalism as the obsolescence of persons (Castells 1998: ch. 2). The problems of superfluousness and rootlessness which Arendt identified as constitutive of totalitarianism have not been resolved, but have, on the contrary, been exacerbated by this apparently revitalized, triumphant capitalism.[4] In fact, we are all deracinated now. Furthermore, as discussed in chapter eight, capitalism and science are entering into new kinds of intimate alliances as knowledge acquires new salience in the generation of surplus value, and as scientists themselves become increasingly entrepreneurial. The problems identified at the start of this book are in part the result of this reshaping, but are also the effects of the longer-term developments discussed in earlier chapters.

The *Manifesto* was extraordinarily prescient about capitalism's future trajectory but it is misleading in two important respects in relation to the contemporary conjuncture.[5] One of these (the hope that the contradiction between classes would be manifested in empirical polarization and conflict) has received considerable attention and will not be discussed further here. The other (the belief that the knowledge gap would be closed so as to eliminate the expert/laity distinction) has received less attention.[6] This leaves a serious gap in the Marxist problematic, as Andrew Sayer (1995) has pointed out. Sayer writes in relation to the failure of radical political economy to ask searching questions about the division of labour. Here I want to explore the matter from the point of view of citizenship.

The very simple account of revolutionary change provided in the *Manifesto* rests on the assumption that as capitalism spread its laws over the globe, the world would become knowable as a unity; that, moreover, it would become cognitively transparent at the level of experience, or, as noted previously, that the gap between essence and appearance would be closed. This would come about through emergent capitalist needs for socialized, mobilized and educated 'labour'; needs whose satisfaction would restore sociability, as well as intelligibility, to the experienced world. Expressed otherwise, a new kind of post-capitalist *sensus communis* would emerge. The gap between capitalist and proletarian would be closed (the expropriators would be expropriated) when capitalists proved unable to provide these socialized, mobile and educated proletarians with the means to feed themselves, or, when the modest distribution of surplus value mediated by the wage contract would no longer be possible. Here economic immiseration would clearly reveal capitalism's irrationality and would be inflicted upon proletarians who had surpassed the educative immiseration inflicted on factory workers (Marx 1973: 325; Postone 1993: ch. 9). More than this, though, the psychic immiseration of atomism would have been transcended through 'association' by means of which workers would have recovered their capacities for sociability (Marx 1978: 168).

In effect, Marx and Engels anticipated the overcoming of capitalism's affective and cognitive damage through capitalism's own changing requirements; requirements which would humanize in a global sense by engendering an everyday experience constitutive of both sociability and theoretical knowledgeability (a recognition of the ineradicability of co-operation, as well as a happy acceptance of this fact, plus knowledge of the totality as a totality of many determinations). This was in anticipation that humanity would become a meaningful empirical and worldly category; that individuals would share a sense of a shared world; that we would come to know, somehow, how to go on together in a way which would respect individual plurality. On the question of future group plurality, Marx and Engels were silent (Nimni 1991). I shall return to this point later.

The networking informational capitalism which was discussed in earlier chapters certainly displays many of the characteristics anticipated by Marx and Engels. Labour is now, increasingly, required to be educated, mobile and sociable (although we have no reason to believe that the need for 'generic labour' and for the 'structurally irrelevant' will diminish[7]). In chapter six I concentrated on the humanly-impoverishing aspects of this education, mobility and sociability, pointing out that the narcissistic form of subjectivation which neoliberal interpellations constitute has configured self-programmers' experience of education, mobility and sociability in a worldless way. The combination of extraordinarily high rewards and of the punitive effects of failure to conform constitutes an intense anxiety which induces a narcissistically active orientation towards the world; an orientation whose nature I have been attempting to understand as a contradictory combination of the psychic characteristics of the late nineteenth-century capitalist and his wife. That is to say, activity turned outwards is wholly atomistically instrumental in form. Yet this apparently masterful and self-referential activity is undertaken by subjects who experience an intense lack; a lack which obliterates awareness of, on the one hand, the sufferings of others, and, on the other, the potential for enjoyable world engagement. Mastery is specific to the stratum of self-programmers whose lack has both actual (as in the psychic immiseration discussed in chapter seven) and potential (the threat of economic immiseration) dimensions. In the case of generic labour, individual subjects are the apparently docile means of mastery's implementation.

Nevertheless self-programmers are required to be active. Unlike the inward-turning activity of narcissistic capitalist wives, discussed in chapter five, and the docile form of narcissism instituted during capitalism's organized phase, self-programmers' narcissism is a narcissism which is world-active, albeit in a worldless way. Something of this is implied in Giddens's account of the reflexivity engendered by capitalism's contemporary form (1991; 1994) and in Laclau's analysis of its faulty 'structuration' (1990: 39–59). Each is pointing to something which is encouraging individual activity rather than passivity. Each of these positions deserves attention. However, in neither of them is there any real appreciation of the difficulties faced by individuals seeking meaningful active public engagement now.[8] Both court the danger of 'egoistic universalism' (Bourdieu 2000: 65) or, the suppression of the conditions of possibility needed for the enjoyment of practical and public-spirited (as opposed to formal-legal) autonomy. They are insufficiently attentive to the nature and distribution of means of autonomy and responsibility (Cooke 1999). In this respect, Arendt's political theory offers us a viewpoint which is at once more sober and more relevant to our present situation and its tasks. It is to that political theory that I now return.

II Thinking for citizenship: natality and reflective judgement

A rehumanized world would be a world freed of the rationality of determinant judgement discussed in chapter eight. At the same time, it would be a world freed of capitalism but not of science. A science for a rehumanized world would be an underlabourer of citizens. If this were to become possible, citizens would need to become capable of meaningful reality-testing. This would involve a kind of self-educative movement on the part of citizens that would equip us to begin to 'test' the claims of the new political economy of capital, government and science, and to do so, in part, in terms of the need to render the world less cognitively opaque by slowing down the pace of change. This self-educative movement is already under way, but not necessarily in a public spirit. Self-education is happening in response to the direct experience of two-worldness by increasing numbers of people (the experience of the necessarily interdependent character of the world at a global level; of the saturation of everyday practices by sciences which are not always benign in their effects). Travel, both embodied and virtual, is enhancing this two-worlds experience.

Accompanying this emergent experience of the totality *as* a totality is the emergent realization that in a decentred contradictory totality self-interest no longer works. Understanding that, since we live in a totality, our self-interest is bound up with the interests of others, holds the potential for an emergent *sensus communis* having global scope. Given this understanding, we might come to accept that autonomy is always also a matter of interdependence, or, more strongly, that autonomy is a gift of culture acting on human potential so that interdependence is a precondition for its enjoyment.

A worldly education would be one intended for the constitution of a post-capitalist *sensus communis*: of a common sense which is theoretical as well as practical. As we have understood from the analysis of bourgeois *sensus communis* in chapter three, the presence of *sensus communis* requires a combination of personal and impersonal social relations such that there is a balance in favour of the former over the latter. This balance is necessary not only to ensure the personal parental authority needed to nurture psychic strength in emergent subjects who, as adults, will possess the intellectual and emotional maturity in which relative autonomy consists, but to provide mature adults with the daily practice of a sociability which does not merely consist in the 'weak ties' encouraged by the capitalist model of 'teamwork'. I take it that *sensus communis* as a theoretically informed shared sense of a shared reality is necessary for the meaningful experience of individual (relative) autonomy since relative autonomy requires effective and responsible participation in public deliberation and decision-making. Meaningful freedom always involves freedom in public (Arendt 1973a: ch. 6). This is not to say that we should be 'forced to be free'. It is to say that we should be aware of the limited nature of freedom as 'liberation', or the 'negative freedom' about which Isaiah Berlin speaks (Arendt 1973a: ch. 1; Berlin 1969).

Since we all live in a totality the practice of political freedom now requires a theoretical, but also worldly, understanding; that is, the mindfulness which has been analysed in this study in terms of sublimatory secondary process functioning. Sublimation connotes the presence of that social love which ensures that the individuated rationality embodied in secondary process functioning does not become atomized or disengaged. In addition to the balance of personal and impersonal mediations mentioned above, a balance between determinacy and indeterminacy is needed if reality-testing conducive to this particular mindfulness is to be available. The 'relative' in relative determinacy here connotes a complexity and lack of regularity in the everyday world such that stopping to think is a necessity. The 'determinacy' in relative determinacy connotes the presence of a durability conducive to contemplation: to the concentration on and examination of 'objects' sufficient for the attainment of understanding. Poststructuralism was an early warning that the balance between determinacy and indeterminacy had tilted towards the latter and that, therefore, thinking theoretically was becoming impossible. However extravagant may have been the language in which these warnings (celebrations from a poststructuralist point of view) were expressed, they remain relevant to our present condition. They remind us that our present way of life is not conducive to the development of that secondary process functioning which is the precondition of science itself and therefore of the reproduction of our world.

Secondary process functioning: a reprise

I have been arguing that the secondary process functioning analysed by Freud was a particular manifestation of the individualized mindfulness constituted by the civilizing differentiations discussed in chapter three. This is the mindfulness involved in meticulous, sustained reflexive attentiveness to objects in the world; attentiveness which requires that individuals take a distance from the world, or, become contemplative. Becoming contemplative involves a taking in of the world which constitutes inwardness, or, the disposition to engage in an internal dialogue. The danger of this kind of taking in is that it risks a worldless rather than worldly disengagement from the world of the kind described by Arendt as two-worlds thinking, a tendency clearly manifested in Cartesianism (Arendt 1977e: 54–6; Taylor 1992: ch. 8). Or, it risks the splitting of sociability and rationality, as in determinant judgement. This is the splitting which was effected in practice through the capitalist differentiations discussed in this study and examined in chapter five as it emerged within the capitalist family as atomism and subjectivism. The rationality of public-spirited citizens needs to be 'attached' to, rather than detached from, the world and the plurality of persons and cultures which inhabit the world. This is the orientation which is captured by the concept of sublimation. Moreover, this attached anaclitic rationality is not incompatible with a science more worldly than we presently practice and may, indeed, be part of the conditions of possibility for the constitution of such a science.[9]

As a condition enjoyed by bourgeois subjects, sublimation involved the enjoyment of sociability and of relatively freely chosen, but demanding, activity. It was a matter of eudaimonism rather than hedonism in that it effected the development of human powers through effortful activity. Achievement occurred following the benign experience of parental care (therefore of dependence) discussed in chapter four. This was benign in that the infant was attended to as an object of interest in its own right by a mother whose worldliness allowed a maternal selflessness yielding the space within which the infant's individuality could begin to flourish. Attachment was here enjoyed rather than suffered. The world as otherness could be viewed as a source not of 'lack', but of what completed the subject. This is not to say that the experience of subjectivation was only or wholly benign. I take it that such an experience is impossible, particularly under demanding disciplinary conditions (Flax 1993: ch. 5).

The cultivation of secondary process functioning is necessary if the theoretical knowledge needed for the reproduction of totalities is to be attained. The enjoyment of sublimation is necessary if that theoretical knowledge is to be worldly. Disorganized capitalism has been dissolving the conditions of possibility for both secondary process functioning and sublimation through the constitution of a debilitating nexus of unauthoritative personal, impersonal and virtual relations. These are relations which do not afford the cultural nourishment which emergent subjects need to take in if they are to feel a sense of gratitude to their culture and if they are to engage with the world in the very disciplined, demanding way which meaningful relative autonomy demands. The acquisition of the mindfulness necessary for relative autonomy requires major sacrifice of drive gratifications, since it requires that fluency in reading and writing be attained. As an adult mode of functioning it requires withdrawal from the world since it is a mode of knowing which involves contemplation, as noted previously. Withdrawal is here both a physical and psychic matter depending upon the availability of a place in which the individual can be solitary. It requires 'a room of one's own', as Virginia Woolf put it a long time ago. Let us be clear that having a room of one's own involves the kinds of differentiations which render the public and private distinctions meaningful (Arendt 1958: ch. 2). Rendering them meaningful would involve restoring the place-like character of human habitations so that they would afford the conditions of possibility for self-constitution, self-renewal and reflection (Cooke 1999). It would involve reconstituting a privacy having some of the characteristics of that enjoyed by the bourgeois; a privacy centred on private property of the kind advocated by Arendt.[10] Only through this restoration would individual subjects be capable of attending attentively to both 'external' and 'internal' reality (Brennan 1992).

I shall now go on to elaborate on the concepts of anaclitic rationality and *sensus communis* in terms of the thinking involved in reflective judgement, this being a mindfulness which involves an attentiveness to plurality which will not seek its subsumption under sameness, and a rationality which refuses rationality and sociability (Arendt 1977a; 1989a). In other words, reflective judgement is the 'other' of the determinant judgement examined in chapter seven. It is a form of understanding rather than cognition, or, it seeks the disclosure out of citizen deliberation of a world-respecting truth, rather than the imposition upon the world of a scientific, worldless truth.

Thinking for a global public sphere

The thinking needed for the practice of global public-spiritedness is an anti-rationalist rational reflectiveness which is rendered possible through the re-fusion of those faculties which capitalist differentiations have fragmented (Arendt 1971; 1977a; 1994). In contrast to the monological character of the thinking of determinant judgers (of scientists and philosophers), the thinking of citizens must be dialogical and 'plebeian' in character. The former is worldless; the latter is not. The worldlessness of determinant judgement lies in its 'absolute abolition of relations to the appearing world' (Arendt 1958: 267). The worldliness of reflective judgement lies in making these relations (both subject/subject and subject/object) the prime objects of its attention.

Unlike the abstracting, rationalizing, logical thinking and language of science, the thinking and language of citizens (and of those who wish to advance the activity of citizenship) will be context-specific but also plural, or, it will take account of a diversity of contexts, not only its own. That is to say, it will be the thinking of an 'enlarged mentality' (Arendt 1979: 336–7) involving a 'self-taught concreteness' which will correct the abstractness which a western theoretical education nurtures (Arendt, quoted in Hansen 1993: 195); a concreteness which is needed if worldliness is to be regained through dialogue with other humans with whom the world, as well a responsibility of care for the world, is shared. In this respect, the orientation to communication as speech and to the use of a worldly language which relates directly to the appearing world is crucial (Hansen 1993: ch. 6; Villa 1996: 31–3).

The thinking advocated by Arendt is dialogical, therefore anaclitically rational thinking. Such thinking is dialogical in the sense, first, that it is undertaken by 'split' selves, i.e. selves who take a distance from their own self-interest so as to attend to the interests of the world and of a plurality of others, and second, it is 'anticipated dialogue with others' (Arendt 1968a: 10). It is mental activity undertaken for the purposes of engaging in action with one's fellow citizens in the public sphere. The judgement of anaclitic rationality is in this sense a manifestation of natality, or, it is imagination applied to understanding (an orientation of humans to other humans) rather than mastery of nature (praxis) or self-preservation (fantasy). It is imagination whose purpose is preparedness for participation in public deliberation (Arendt 1989a).

From commodity aesthetic to political aesthetic: thinking and taste

Being a worldly form of mental functioning (one which resists the abstract thinking of western science), reflective judgement is aesthetic in two senses. First, it refuses the mind/body dichotomy which informs abstract rationality and which is expressed in the suspension of the experiential which such rationality demands (Armstrong 2000; Marcuse 1987: ch. 9). Second, and relatedly, it involves the cultivation of taste as a faculty which establishes 'an active relationship to what is beautiful' (Arendt 1977c: 219; 1989: 58–65; Curtis 1999: ch. 4). What is beautiful is a matter of what is deemed necessary for world care, therefore for creatures who are incompletely 'natural'. In cultivating care for the world, reflective judgement intends to reject the theoretical abstractions whereby science comes to know the world determinantly and to transcend the violence which capitalism's practical abstractions have inflicted on humanity and non-human nature. Thus, as Beiner points out (1989: 103), the aesthetic is internal to politics; it is not its destructive other, contrary to what some commentators proclaim (Eagleton 1990; Harvey 1989).[11] The political aesthetic here involves the development of a passionate partiality for the world; a partiality which would motivate us to counteract the literally destructive effects of the production/consumption cycle initiated by capitalism. Far from leading us away from politics, it would take us to the heart of the matter of a global form of public-spirited citizenship. As a politicized faculty taste would seek the restoration of the world's durability. So, rereification of the improperly dereified and deceleration of change would be the preoccupation of an aestheticized rationality oriented to world care.

Thinking and the transcendence of self-interest

Whereas taste is concerned with the built environment, as it were, in the sense that it concerns itself with how the world needs to be for plural, fragile creatures who are born incomplete, imagination directs its attention at the present situatedness of those plural, fragile creatures. It connotes a mental activity which brings to awareness (in worldly rather than 'virtual' mode) the plurality and reality of the world beyond direct experience. It involves making absent what is present (my own self and self-interest) for the purpose of making present what is absent (the selves and self-interest of others) (Arendt 1977a; Hansen 1993: ch. 6). In doing so, it releases us from the internal exile that is modern subjectivism (Arendt 1968a; Sennett 1977).[12] What is in question here is not an identification which might involve the projection of our own identities onto others, but an effortful act of mental 'visiting' which would retain the distinction between self and others while at the same time relating self to others (Curtis 1999: ch. 5; Disch 1994: ch. 5; 1997). Putting ourselves in the place of others would be for the purposes of creating a web of commitments constituted by speech and action (Arendt 1958: 182; Bickford 1996). Here developing the enlarged mentality would not require that we submerge our selves under an overwhelming, absorbing principle of unity but that we recognize the humanity in others. Neither would it require that we replace one set of interests by another. It is important to note here that interests (as pertaining to the ego drive or the need for self-preservation) must be acknowledged and evaluated, but awareness of the cultural formation of such interests will alert us to the possibility, and in many cases the desirability, of reconstituting these.

So, the purpose of imaginative visiting would be to evaluate all interests in relation to the need for world care. Here imagination would not only counteract the subjectivist character of capitalist culture, but also contribute to the cultivation of a global public-spiritedness grounded in the fact that we now share the globe in an unprecedented way and that, therefore, worldliness can no longer be a property only of local communities but must be given, somehow, at a global level as well. In short, imagination is a vital faculty for the constitution of public-spiritedness where the 'public' exceeds the class (as in the hybrid bourgeois public sphere) and the nation (as in the post-1945 welfare state) as it is now bound to do. More than the bourgeois class or the twentieth-century nation, we now need to imagine the conditions of those absent others whose activities (or lack of activity) constitute the conditions of possibility of our own (Venn 2000). In terms of the requirements for the expanded public-spiritedness which the world needs now, the importance of imagination of this kind cannot be over-stressed, although, as we have seen in chapter seven, this is not the kind of imagination which is being nurtured by contemporary capitalism.

Having prepared ourselves for action in concert (dialogic face-to-face speech in the first instance), we would formulate and express an opinion about matters under discussion.[13] To express an opinion in the sense relevant to citizenship is not to express a personal or group-oriented preference or interest, but to make a judgement about the world shared with others from the 'enlarged' point of view, the point of view nurtured by taste and imagination. (However suspension of self-interest would here be possible only because no catastrophic sacrifice of 'interests' would be risked thereby. More on this below.) Opinions, as opposed to preferences, can only be formed with the benefit of a multiplicity of opinions held by others; they are intrinsically other-directed and concerned with the collective caring for a shared world (Arendt 1973a: 225, 227, 247; 1977a: 239–49; Habermas 1992a: 236–50). Opinion in this sense does not state a certainty but puts forward a view for the purposes of persuasion; it involves the context-specific knowledgeability of citizens who function in a plural world: a world of particularity and contingency rather than of 'universality' and predictability. Opinions are here the expression of cognitively enhanced reflective judgements previously formed through solitary, but worldly, contemplation; a contemplation oriented to understanding the sources of worldlessness so as to effect their elimination. Or, the 'life of the mind' (Arendt 1978) is inherently political and active in its purposes.[14]

III Solidarity, responsibility and the politics of redistribution

If worldliness is to be restored to the world, the sameness implied in the concept of humanity must rest, not on abstract universalism, but on the differences of its constitutive units. Or, sameness must be revealed through difference and difference will be revealed through dialogue (Arendt 1968b: 89, 90). Here the reconciliation of sameness/difference would nurture a form of solidarity unlike the narcissistic solidarity which depends on the presence of 'otherness' as enmity for its constitution; a solidarity resting on a shared sense of a shared human fragility and possibility.

Following my understanding of human need derived from Marx, Arendt and Freud, I take it that the sense of global responsibility will take a citizenly form only where human plurality is protected and that citizenship will be cultivated only through the cultivation of selves. This requires the recovery of world or community, i.e. of sensuously-present, relatively stable relations lived in a worldly place. This, rather than the worldless floating world of contemporary cosmopolitanism, is what yields the significantly different differences which Arendt calls plurality. We can only be plural in a sociable, situated way. At the same time, we cannot be citizens of the world in any meaningful sense unless we are simultaneously citizens of a sensuously-experienced place (Arendt 1968a; 1968b; Linklater 1998: ch. 4). So, while the only practically functional unit now is the globe, the reconstitution of worldliness requires the meaningful experience of sensuous presencing, therefore the reconstitution of community in a real, rather than rhetorical, sense. The particularity of community is not (necessarily) a threat to global citizenship, but, rather, its necessary prerequisite.[15] The important point is that this community or plurality be marked by a non-parochial worldliness, or, that it be characterized by anaclitic relations between communities rather than narcissism. At the moment, narcissistic pluralism is the norm since all plurality is under threat (Castells 1997). The great task before us is to attempt the cultivation of anaclitic forms of plurality; forms which do not relate only to the wider world in a competitive zero-sum game of interest group politics. This is not to claim that 'interests' can be ignored. The point is, as noted previously, not to ignore interests but to deliberate on them in a public-spirited way and, if necessary, to nurture their reconstitution. In relation to the 'interests' of the aristocracy of labour, the hope would be to persuade these subjects that the culturally-constituted interest in absolute autonomy, as expressed in freedom to 'choose' consumerism for example, is a world-destroying interest which has not been constitutive of individual well-being (Soper 1999).[16]

If the relatively privileged inhabitants of the Euro-American world are to assume collective responsibility for the damage inflicted on 'innocent bystanders' by the western way of life, that way of life must itself become worldly. In becoming worldly, it would become less destructive of the worlds of others. An emergent worldliness would here begin to restore the cultural parenting needed by fragile and vulnerable humanity (Turner 1993a). Only where this takes place will the possibility of bearable and meaningful global responsibility emerge in the Euro-American world. If the aristocrats of labour are to commit themselves voluntarily to the solidarity principle which will require from them significant self-sacrifice, they will do so only where persuaded that the results of doing so will not be self-obliteration. To expect fragile and imperfectly humanized humanity to be altruistic on an everyday basis is to expect the impossible. In fact, altruism is the undialectical 'other' of egoism.

The constitution of new communities will require as necessary, but not sufficient, the slowing down of value's flow so as to render the world more world-like. We have, potentially, the means to effect this slowing-down in the shape of pension funds which, according to some, point in the direction of a 'post-capitalist society' (Drucker 1993).[17] Pension funds represent a socialization of ownership of means of production which could yet become the basis for a new, post-capitalist mode of life. Reasons to be (just a little) optimistic regarding this possibility inhere in the politicization of this question which is presently under way (Blackburn 2002; Harmes 2001).[18] Along with questions about parenting and science, this related question of value's flow is of crucial importance. The question of justice (the implementation of the solidarity principle) is a question not only of the geographical redirection of this flow but also of its deceleration through the reconceptualization of use and the minimization of exchange. In this way, justice, worldliness and respect for non-human nature could be served.

Citizenship, democracy, lack

Contrary to what some democracy theorists seem to imply (Mouffe 1992), we cannot depend on an unreconstructed 'lack' or 'desire' for the necessary motivational resources of citizenship. Such 'lack' yields 'nomads' rather than citizens (Melucci 1989; 1996a; 1996b). If public-spiritedness is to be nurtured, the experience of lack must be interpreted as the loss of sociability and intelligibility as well as the presence of unwanted demands and social relations; a loss which diminishes us by impeding the possibility of acting relatively autonomously and responsibly. This would be a particular kind of politicization of lack; a politicization oriented to the constitution of a citizenry rather than merely a democracy, since democracy need mean no more than that all particular interests are entitled to be represented. Democracy in the sense of entitlement to political voice is an ineliminable dimension of public-spirited citizenship but democracy alone is insufficient since democracy implies nothing about responsibilities. It is associated more with claims on the group, or claims by one group on another, than with responsibilities for the world (Castells 1997; Laclau and Mouffe 2001).

In talking about responsibility I am not talking about duties which are passed down to docile group members, but, rather, an active, adult appropriation of responsibility for participating in the activity needed to reproduce, improve or restore a way of life. Responsibility in this sense is not a diminution of relative autonomy but rather an enhancement, since it involves active participation in the shaping of our world. In the beginning this participation is bound to be difficult, since we have been given few of the resources needed for the necessary world-engagement. In the absence of those resources, we have to teach ourselves to be responsible so as to reconstitute responsibility's conditions for future generations. As learning creatures who come after a long, rich history of human cultures, this unprecedented task need not be too much for us, particularly if we remind ourselves that the debility we presently experience is the work of a particularly destructive culture and that we will begin to overcome this debility as we recover a worldly sociability.

This debility is in part related to the specifically political history of twentieth-century Euro-America. In its liberal manifestation, democracy has tended to be conjugated with the nation rather than citizenship. The modest redistribution of resources from 'capital' to 'labour' which the welfare state effected was considered to be necessary for the meaningful enjoyment of citizenship of propertyless individuals (Linklater 1998: ch. 6; Marshall 1973). This was to be the functional equivalent of the ownership of capital which had endowed hybrid bourgeois and capitalists with the 'objective' basis of their relative autonomy. However, the desired effect (the experience of relative autonomy) would only have been constituted where those in receipt of welfare conceived of themselves as beneficiaries of resources which they had collectively agreed, as citizens, to redistribute (Habermas 1992b: 434). This effect was not secured during the crucial post-1945 phase of organized capitalism for reasons which have been indicated in chapter six. Citizenship as clientelism (a clientelism between individual and welfare state) became established and politics became the worldless politics of interests. As welfare-state clientelism fell into disrepute, citizenship became conjugated with consumerism or with entitlements to ownership and consumption of goods and services or even with victimhood, which seeks redistribution of resources by legal rather than welfare means (Heater 1991; Oliver 1991). In any case it is bound up with a legal and instrumental rationality which interpellates group members as clients or patients rather than as citizens (Katznelson 1988).

Citizen deliberation and the transcendence of scientism

On the substantial matters which need citizens' deliberation, among which we can include those economic, political, familial, 'cultural' and cognitive matters which have been raised in the course of this study, it will be clear that a discussion of these matters requires activity and orientations which encompass 'interests' and utility. Given my reliance on the Arendtian categories of labour, making and action to understand the deviant character of capitalism, it is worth stating here that the point of judging reflectively now is not to establish and maintain a politics free of 'making' and 'labouring' concerns, therefore free of the problems which determinant judging was supposed to solve, but, rather, to subsume making and labouring (therefore determinant judgement in both its theoretical and practical manifestations) under politics.[19] So, for example, the restoration of science's practical efficacy must be compatible with the relative determinacy which the optimal development of individuals' potentials for activity and sociability requires. As noted previously, this relative determinacy requires the politically supervised deceleration of the use/exchange dialectic; a deceleration which should also effect the slowing down of the rate of production of scientific knowledges.[20] Supervising citizens would be thinking citizens who had developed the form of rationality connoted by the concept of reflective judgement, but also the cognitive abilities needed to evaluate the claims of scientists.

Given the nature of our world (the fact of totality or two-worldness), thinking needs the 'banisters' provided by 'cognition' but the cognitive dimension of reality-testing must not be left to scientific experts.[21] This is because the restoration of world care demands that cognition be strongly contextualized and historicized, and self-consciously informed by the worldly concerns which render cognition 'critical' (Habermas 1974: ch. 6). As such, it would be a force for the constitution of an anti-technocratic, anti-commodifying science, offered for the judgement of citizens, rather than for the disposal of capitalists or the servicing or manipulation of subjects. It would be thinking and judging for the purposes of deliberating and forming opinions as to how, or whether, scientific knowledge should be used. In this way, science would become humanized because, as an object of citizenly attention, scientific claims would necessarily be translated into an everyday language which can be spoken and understood by non-experts, and its results would be fed into the world in ways which would not prevent care of the world.²² Here cognition would retain a central place, but would be subsumed under a *sensus communis* so as to minimize the risk of cognitivism and instrumentalism. More than this, such subsumption would (could) put an end to the irrationality which an increasingly science-nurtured manifestation of commodity fetishism has constituted. In this way, the enlarged thinking needed for citizenship would be such as to encompass the cognitive and productive needs of a complex world, and to ensure that these needs would be interpreted in anaclitically worldly rather than economistic and instrumentally rational mode.

We now have the electronic means (swift and flexible) of carrying on a political conversation of global membership and scope, but this cannot be sufficient to the purposes of constituting a meaningful sense of global membership, since virtual relations tend towards worldlessness, as I have argued in chapter seven.²³ Virtual relations depend for their public character on the pre-existence of an experienced sociability of the kind which is available only in worldly communities and on the availability of a private place for contemplation. Since, as argued by Meyrowitz (1985), they dissolve the boundaries needed for a meaningful public/private divide, electronic media are antithetical to the constitution of such a place, although they are essential for the speedy communication which is a necessary dimension of a global-spirited citizenship. What is needed, then, is a worldly nexus of different modes of communication: speech, print and electronics. This nexus would provide the basis and readiness to imagine the needs of radically different, and also more exploited, others, and to take some responsibility for their satisfaction. This is no less than the Marxian solidarity principle demands.

Conclusion

The potent combination of irrationality and hubris which capitalism currently displays has provoked an eruption of anger across the globe; anger which is expressed in novel forms of collective action. If this anger is to be translated into citizenly activity of a globally public-spirited, but also cognitively effective kind, we need to recover the individual abilities associated with the concept of the 'knowing subject', but we need to do so in a reflective rather than determinant mode; in a mode, that is, which is characterized by anaclitic rather than abstract or economic rationality, and by an anaclitic rationality which is part of a *sensus communis*. This is a matter that requires the cultivation of those subjective dispositions which, in earlier chapters, have been understood in terms of sublimated secondary process functioning and which has been viewed in this chapter from the angle of vision provided by Arendt's concept of reflective judgement. As we have seen, reflective judgement involves the cultivation of an imagination which will be tolerant of significant, consequential (rather than merely cosmetic) plurality and the preparedness to reconsider one's own distinctiveness as a possibly worldless source of unnecessary suffering to others. Beyond this, it involves the development of a knowledgeability which will rise to the task of judging the claims of experts.

Learning to judge reflectively would be a primary responsibility of individual citizens and providing the resources for such learning would be a primary responsibility of the community. Such learning would be essential for effective participation in public deliberation. Cultivation of the kind of 'enlarged mentality' required for effective reflective judging is essential for citizenship given that we live in a world which is (in the absence of some unimaginable return to small-scale, self-sufficient cultural units) irreversibly a two-worlds world. For the foreseeable future, we live in a world marked necessarily by dependence on absent persons and distant places. The great political task (which is also an economic and 'cultural' task) is to reconfigure this dependence as benign interdependence through a form of cultural parenting which, in providing emergent subjects with good objects for internalization, would nurture the emotional and intellectual maturity required for a global public-spiritedness; a public-spiritedness extended by imaginative and scientific understanding of the extra-experiential, or, of the totality which constitutes our own part of the world. Attaining the sense of worldliness adequate to a complex and fragmented world (one necessarily suffused with scientific knowledge of all kinds) means attaining the capacity to formulate opinions which are both non-egoistic and cognitively non-trivial. The attainment of this capacity is a requirement for ensuring the subordination of the scientific and economic to the well-being of human and non-human nature. Where the capacity is nurtured, subjects will not feel overwhelmed by two-worldness; we will have been prepared for satisfying participation in the totalized world which would otherwise be experienced as both unintelligible and unsociable.

The willingness to develop the capacities associated with reflective judgement will only be nurtured where face-to-face social relations become more durable and more consequential than they are at present. Only where such restoration takes place will mature subjects experience relative autonomy. This restoration implies a radical change in our way of life; a change away from indeterminacy and towards relative determinacy, therefore a change which requires the slowing down and eventually elimination of the dialectic of exchange and use. The practical resources for this may lie in the structure of pension funds which may afford the possibility of transcending capitalism. Membership control of pension fund income, which contributes significantly to capital flows, could be transformed into the power to control and retard flows of capital so as to render these compatible with the needs of worldliness and justice.

If there is to be a world government we must ensure that it is one which is meaningfully accountable to a plurality of communities through the active attentiveness of public-spirited citizens. This will only be the case if those of us who live in the privileged parts of the world direct our thinking attention at the many problems that press in on us now. If we are to think attentively and judge politically, we must regain a sense of reality as the combined activity of a plurality of humans with whom we share a world. We can begin to regain this sense of reality by thinking of our worldless world in a way which goes beyond our own sphere of activities and our own preferences. We can seek to verify our shared reality through the real or imagined presence of others rather than through the pronouncements and activities of politicians and experts. While imagination can be served (will need to be served) by electronically mediated messages, we will need to ensure that our capacities for citizenship are not atrophied through over-reliance on such messages. We will need to actively cultivate the virtues of a sociability which transcends the networking mode in which we are presently required to function. In doing so, we can begin to resist the pressures towards narcissism coming from capitalism, as well as from a corrupted form of politics, both of which encourage us to mind our own business rather than concern ourselves with the public in any meaningful way. We can begin to expand and transform our rationality. Citizenship is now not only a good in itself but has become the increasingly urgent means of correcting the hubris emerging from the revitalized marriage of capitalism and science.

Notes

1 Human nature: indeterminate and indeterminable

1 Best's introduction is a usefully succinct account of eighteenth-century critical reactions to Enlightenment thought.
2 For evaluations of these demonstrations, see Bromley (2001); Seymour (2001). Note also the importance of 'everyday' public activity of a kind which seems to escape the debilitating logic of economic rationality. In addition to the papers in Hill and Montag (2000), see Bickford (1996: 176–87).
3 The Marx–Freud nexus has been much discussed. For good examples of this discussion see Kovel (1988a); Lichtman (1982); Schneider (1975); Wolfenstein (1993). Marcuse (1987) remains essential reading. There is no corresponding literature on Freud and Arendt, but it is worth noting Arendt's own objections to psychoanalysis at this point (1978: 35; 1964: 297). See also n. 20, this chapter. See Moruzzi (2000) for a rare example of a psychoanalytic treatment of Arendt's political theory. On Arendt and Marx, see Parekh (1979); Pitkin (1998); Reinhardt (1997); Ring (1989).
4 The concept of culture is used here to refer to a necessary dimension of human life as argued by, for example, and most usefully, Carrithers (1992). This use does not involve the claim that there exist in the contemporary world any clearly-bounded self-sufficient cultures. It is the case, though, that capitalism is attempting (and with notable success at the moment) to constitute the world as one culture, albeit one which, having the character of a totality, is experientially heterogeneous. In later chapters it will be necessary to use the concept of culture in a narrower sense to refer to specialized practices of 'meaning-production' which emerge as a consequence of the capitalist division of labour. This second meaning will be indicated by the use of single quotation marks. See Friese and Wagner (2001) for a succinct discussion of different usages of the culture concept.
5 I adapt this notion of 'leaning on' from Castoriadis (1997), who in turn derives it from Freud. 'Leaning on' in this context involves the conceptualization of necessity in terms of conditions of possibility rather than determination. See the discussion in Whitebook (1995: 175–7).
6 For more on imagination, see Castoriadis (1995); Kearney (1998).
7 Althusser (1984a; 1984b; 1990c) is an attempt to initiate the intra-Marxist theorizing needed to understand this fact about humanity. See also n. 7, chapter two below.
8 Leroi-Gurhan (1993) is a thoughtful and thorough exploration of the emergence of culture out of a particular kind of biology. Woolfson (1982), drawing on Engels's *Dialectics of Nature* (1966), discusses this question as 'the labour theory of culture'. Bakhurst (1991) elaborates on the relevant work of early Soviet theorists, including Vygotsky, Lenin and Ilyenkov.
9 See also Mészáros (1975).
10 See Whitebook (1995: 264, n. 7) on the question of 'non-domineering mastery'.

11 Arendt herself makes reference to the work of Merleau-Ponty and to that of the zoologist Adolf Portmann (1978: ch. 1).
12 For more on kinesthetic rationality, see Sahlins (1976); Strauss and Quinn (1997).
13 Falk (1994) is a useful account of the recent return to the body in social theory. However, escape from embodiment remains a powerful desire which is presently being serviced by an extraordinarily rationalist manifestation of the life sciences (Hayles 1999). More on this topic can be found in chapter eight.
14 This stress on the importance of face-to-face speech is future, rather than past-oriented. It does not involve the wish to return to the relatively changeless certainties of past communities. See Boyte (1990; 1992) on the importance of face-to-face relations in constituting and enacting citizenship. Lee (1992) discusses objections to this position. It is worth noting here that, contrary to what Derrida argues in *Of Grammatology*, the 'metaphysics of presence' is to be attributed not to romantic arguments about speech, but to the actualization of a print culture (Ong 1982: 166–70).
15 Given the tentativeness and incompleteness of Arendt's remarks on natality, it is of use to read *On Revolution* (1973a) as a meditation on the category and the human faculty to which it refers. Bowen-Moore (1989) gives an extended discussion of the concept.
16 See Ball (1995: ch. 9) for a succinct discussion of the distinction which he makes in terms of artisanal activity (technē and communicative citizenly activity (praxis). I take it that Marx's preoccupation with 'labour' as, ideally, the imaginative imposition of form on nature, is intended to convey the centrality of individual imaginative activity to the well-being of humans. See Lobkowicz (1967); Postone (1993).
17 See Callinicos (1987) for a defence of the 'making' concept of history.
18 See Parekh (1979); Pitkin (1998: 134–9) for a discussion, and refutation, of Arendt's critique of Marx. Postone (1993: ch. 6) provides an extended refutation of Habermas's critique of Marx on labour.
19 On this question see Reinhardt (1997: ch. 4). As Lawrence Wilde pointed out to me in the early stages of my research on Arendt, she acknowledges Marx's commitment to a radically democratic model of Athenian citizenship (1958: 131, n. 82).
20 Arendt's disapproval of psychoanalysis has been noted previously (n. 3, this chapter). Her quarrel with psychoanalysis is in part that it brings into full view what should be kept in darkness (1978: 35) and that it excuses irresponsibility (1964: 297). The latter charge is not sustainable in relation to Freudian psychoanalysis which is grounded in the possibility of responsibility for self. This, surely, is the logic of the cure. The former objection need not hold where we are using psychoanalysis as a social rather than psychological theory; one which can guide us on the institutional requirements for individual relative autonomy. In fact, psychoanalysis enables the correction of Arendt's 'flight from inwardness' which is a significant flaw in her political theory (Ring 1989).
21 See also Collier (1981).
22 For Strachey's comments on Freud's sometimes ambiguous usage, see Freud (1984b: 108–9). Bettelheim (1982) provides a relevant critique of the English translation of Freud's work.
23 Greenberg and Mitchell (1983) is a useful discussion of the post-Freudian splitting of psychoanalysis into a drive model (biologistic, deterministic) and an object-relations model. In this study I want to reunite drives and relations and understand both as both culturally and biologically constituted.
24 See Marcuse (1987) for an historico-cultural conception of the reality principle.
25 Some Freudians relegate the 'energetic' dimension of Freud's theory to his 'pre-history' as manifested in *Project for a Scientific Psychology* (1966). See, for example, Lear (1998).
26 By 'object' I mean here any thing (human or non-human, found or made) which is perceived of as having an existence independent of the perceiver. For more on this, see Schachtel (1963: 83, n. 4).
27 In 'Beyond the pleasure principle' (1984f), Freud conceptualizes this antagonism as a contradiction between Eros and the death drive.

28 As Peter Gay (1998: 10) points out, Freud's 'chosen laboratory' was 'the long nineteenth century'. Gay's own four-volume account of the 'bourgeois' nineteenth century provides excellent background material on this matter (1995; 1998; 1999a; 1999b). Schorske (1980) is also of interest.
29 Freud himself begins to contemplate the possibility of a cultural theory of instincts and their vicissitudes in *Civilization and its Discontents* (1985a: 335–40), a work on which Marcuse relied heavily.
30 On his interest in the sex drives, Freud notes that this grouping of 'primal drives' is 'merely a working hypothesis' which may need to be overturned (1984b: 120–1).
31 Yet Freud's own work is in some respects hopelessly contradictory on this question, as his liberal preconceptions come up against clinical and historico-cultural evidence against the innate a-sociality of humanity. See in particular *Group Psychology and the Analysis of the Ego* (1985b).
32 From a psychologist's point of view, sublimation is a 'frontier concept' (Whitebook's phrase) by means of which the extra-familial world makes its appearance in psychoanalysis; the theory was, in any case, from the beginning a sociological theory, as Marcuse (1987: 31) correctly notes.
33 Heater (1990) discusses the requirements for citizenship in terms of the three sets of rights analysed by Marshall (1973). These are civil, political and social rights, in addition to which Heater adds a sense of obligation and civic virtue. Warren (1995) discusses capacities from the point of view of subjectivity. See also Balibar (1994); Turner (1986).

2 Capitalism: culture of worldlessness

1 The use of quotation marks is intended to remind the reader that the categories of objectivity and subjectivity are, like all categories, historico-cultural and make the kind of sense expressed here only in a fetishized culture. See Adorno and Horkheimer (1979). Having made this point, I shall forbear from further use of these warning signs.
2 For a more recent attempt to theorize the complexity of capitalism, particularly in its contemporary manifestation, see Jessop (2002).
3 It is worth pointing out here that I am using 'value' as a cultural rather than 'accounting' concept. On the latter see Harvey (1982: 35–8).
4 See Jay (1984) for a comprehensive and critical analysis of the concept of totality. My usage in this study is intended to avoid the traps which Jay brings to our attention.
5 Aglietta (1998: 63) discusses this new kind of 'globalization' in terms of the spread of 'paid employment which has enabled capitalism to penetrate into the very heart of non-Western societies'.
6 The importance of attending to the ways in which value constitutes subjects as well as objects has been stressed by Postone (1993).
7 Althusser is normally read (and abused) as a conventionalist. Following Resch (1992), I read him as a realist. See also the papers in Callari and Ruccio (1996). Going beyond Resch, I read him as a realist who understands the conventional as culture (conceptualized by Althusser as ideology) or, as that which completes the human organism (Althusser 1984a; 1984b). In this sense, all human life is conventional because of the real nature of the human organism. Althusser's appropriation of psychoanalysis is intended for the theorization of this matter. See also this book, ch. 1, n. 7.
8 In the study I assume that capitalism has been most fully instituted where English cultural influence has been strongest (as in, for example, parts of the United States). England is my implicit reference in much of what I write. See Esping-Anderson (1990) for a Eurocentric typology of modes of contemporary capitalism. These are the Anglo-Saxon or liberal model, the Rhenish or conservative Catholic model and the Nordic, or social democratic model. See also Hutton (2002a).
9 Athusser's expanded account of the dialectic and contradiction rules out economism and renders his own attempt to conciliate dogmatic Marxists through 'last instance' economic

determinism nonsensical. Of course, he knows this since as he says, 'the "lonely hour" of the last instance never comes' (Althusser 1990a: 113).
10 Bhaskar (1989: ch. 7) is a clear and succinct discussion of different understandings of dialectic. However, Bhaskar's misunderstanding of Althusserian dialectics (1989: 127) should be noted. See also Bhaskar (1993).
11 Wilde (1989) is an excellent analysis of Marx's use of contradiction.
12 Brenner (1998) provides a comprehensive analysis of post-1945 crises.
13 Transformation cannot be a dramatic, all-at-once revolution but must comprise a dialectical process, aided by deliberate human action, whereby one mode of capitalism comes to be replaced by another. The messiness of actual transformations is a fact of history. For the purpose of the argument to be made in this study however, the messiness will be ignored.
14 As Baudrillard points out, the concept of use value only makes sense in a culture which requires that things be exchangeable as well as usable (1975: ch. 1), or, the concept is internally related to that of exchange value. Unfortunately, Baudrillard's pertinent analysis of the dangers of economism in Marxism is marred by his failure to recognize that Marx knows this, as Postone points out. Postone's interpretation of Marx constitutes a refutation of Baudrillard's critique of Marx, a refutation which does not hold for all Marxists, as Postone (1993: ch. 2) makes clear.
15 Brewster (1976) is one of many Marxists who refuse to see the critical value of the concept of fetishism.
16 See Porter (1992) for a comprehensive discussion of the peculiarities of the modern preoccupation with quantification.
17 Beniger (1986) is a useful history of the emergence of some of the impersonal mediations which control subjects who inhabit the 'advanced industrial world', as he puts it.
18 Giddens (1990) is also relevant here. Luhmann (1982) is the most authoritative 'systems' theorist of differentiation.
19 However, we should beware in this context of using the contrast between system and lifeworld (Habermas 1989), with its implication that 'lifeworld' can be meaningfully protected from 'system'. The concept of totality, which is used here in preference to that of system, is intended to remind us that capitalism is necessarily a totalizing, therefore dialectically moving, contradictory mode of life rather than merely an 'economy'. This is something about which we can be sure, occasional confinement of value within politically-determined boundaries to the contrary notwithstanding.
20 See Arendt (1958: 139–44) for an account of worldly reification.
21 What is neglected in the Marxian account of commodity fetishism is amnesia regarding human dependence on nature as living rather than 'dead' matter. On this, see Brennan (2000).
22 Pitkin (1998) is the most comprehensive (critical) treatment of this aspect of Arendt's work.
23 Arendt's remarks on this matter are sometimes obscure (1979). Ricoeur (1990) offers an analysis which stresses the fundamental point about durability versus evanescence. For a critical discussion of Arendt's categories, which misses this point, see Zaretsky (1997).
24 See Adorno and Horkheimer (1979: esp. 180–2) on mimesis which, it is worth noting, does not involve 'slavish' reproduction.
25 This is the force which has been receiving the naturalizing theoretical attentions of post-structuralists in recent years. In chapter seven, Lacanian poststructuralism will be found to yield some important theoretical insights on the psychic effects of dereification.
26 This critical conception of narcissism is not universally shared, and is usually attributed to conservative social theorists, of whom Christopher Lasch is one of the most noteworthy (see Lasch 1978). Marcuse (1987) adopts a positive conception of narcissism.
27 Said (1993) is excellent on the 'cultural' silence which accompanied this 'deworlding' of the west's 'Other'.

28 The imagining of a community beyond the face-to-face is an attempt to fill the void left by the loss of a commonsense world. See Anderson (1991) for an account of the role of print capitalism in nurturing this form of imagining. What Anderson neglects to discuss is the need for a paternalistic bureaucracy or welfare state to ensure that this imagining would become more than fantasy.

29 Hirschman (1977) is an interesting account, from an history of ideas point of view, of the normative elevation of economic rationality over more 'passionate' motivations for action. Adorno and Horkheimer (1979), indebted to Lukács (1971), remain an indispensable source of understanding of capitalism's fetishized rationality.

30 I am aware that seventeenth-century scientific discoveries were intimately implicated in politics and commerce (Jardine 1999). However, these discoveries affected everyday life in Europe only on the margins, therefore, unlike twentieth-century sciences, they did not enter into the reconfiguration of subjectivities.

31 For this reason, tenderness towards modern 'common sense', such as is displayed by Giddens (1984), is misdirected. Bourdieu (2000) gives a more realistic and politically radical position.

32 See Baran and Sweezy (1966) for a discussion of monopoly capital.

33 The Marxian distinction between 'formal' and 'real' subsumption of labour under capital is an important source of my understanding of the differences between hybrid bourgeois and liberal industrial capitalism. Theorization of capitalism and its 'modes' or 'stages' began in earnest with the writings of Hilferding (1981), Hobson (1938), Lenin (1982) and Luxemburg (1963). While his use of the term 'late' is regrettable, Mandel (1978) is important on the post-1945 period. See also Brenner (1998). Albritton's particular approach, derived from Japanese Unoist Marxism, is crucial to the understanding which informs this study, since it affords the materials for enhancing our understanding of the experiential differences between different modes of capitalism (Albritton 1991).

34 Different attempts to encapsulate the peculiar character of the present conjuncture include Castells's concept of the 'network society' (1996) which will receive some attention in this study, Bauman's concept of 'liquid modernity' (2000), as well as the earlier 'disorganized capitalism' (Lash and Urry 1987). Sennett (1998) is an excellent phenomenological study of contemporary capitalism.

35 Aglietta (1987; 1998) is useful on this question. See also Jessop (1999; 2002). Both Aglietta and Jessop use the distinctions Fordism and post-Fordism to capture the differences between modes that I label as organized and disorganized. My choice of this label is dictated by the topic of subjectivity, for reasons which should become clear as the discussion proceeds.

3 The worldly world of the bourgeois subject

1 This is a theoretical claim for which evidence is scattered among the sources used for the study. Harvey (1982: ch. 5) is useful on the local, personal character (and absence of competitiveness) of early nineteenth-century capitalism. Deane (1973: 203–4) comments on the persistence of dependence on personal sources of investment until the late nineteenth century. Finally, as Sennett (1993a: ch. 7) shows, a significant indicator of the movement from formal to real subsumption in the sphere of 'circulation' was the arrival of large department stores in the latter half of the nineteenth century. Before such time, shopping would have been necessarily a sociable activity. With the advent of the department store, sociability became optional.

2 It is important to note also the many differences in modes of life which the label of bourgeois may conceal (Gay 1999a: 18–31). Maguire (1978: ch. 2) is useful on Marx's discussion of economic and non-economic bourgeoisie. Bauman (1982) and Calhoun (1982) are important sources of understanding (from the 'labour' point of view) of the experiential differences between formal and real subsumption of labour under capital.

3 The effects of the failure of critical theorists such as Adorno (1967; 1968) to consider the debilitating character of capitalist, as opposed to hybrid bourgeois, (male) subjectivity are usefully discussed by Benjamin (1977).
4 See the papers in Calhoun (1992); Hill and Montag (2000).
5 See Hamilton (1991) for a critical discussion of Marx's use of historical sources in his account of bourgeois 'revolution'. Mooers (1991) is more sympathetic to the Marxian position. The assumption in this study is that the period discussed by Habermas is key to understanding the transition from formal to real subsumption and, therefore, the transition to a value-governed culture of worldlessness. See also this book, n. 5, chapter five.
6 Although Habermas's work displays Arendtian influences, these are implicit rather than explicit (the preoccupation with 'congenial' talk in coffee-houses and salons; the recognition of the importance of the character of privacy) and retain only a 'residual' or ghostly presence in Habermas's subsequent work in the form of his concepts of communication and the lifeworld, on which see McCarthy (1991). See Benhabib (1996: 199–215) for a comparison of Arendt and Habermas.
7 That this actualization depended on the exclusion and even brutalization of others has been noted in chapter one. See Montag (2000) for a recent criticism of Habermas's silence on this question. Other dimensions of the bourgeois world which go undiscussed include the continuing and important political role of aristocrats (which enhanced the hybrid character of the culture) during the period in question (on which see Comninel 1987; Kramnick 1990) and religion, on which see Kalberg (1993); Wuthnow (1989). For an analysis of the contemporaneous 'plebeian' public spheres (also not considered here), see Thompson (1968). Clark (1995) and Scott (1988) discuss the gendered character of plebian and bourgeois public spheres respectively.
8 Giddens (1990) is also relevant here.
9 As Elias notes, 'the concept of "civilisation" ... expresses the self-consciousness of the West ... It sums up everything in which Western society of the last two or three centuries believes itself superior to earlier societies or "more primitive" contemporary ones' (1994: 3).
10 What marked the very beginning of this change, for Elias, is the publication (and enthusiastic reception) in 1530 of Erasmus's *De civilitate morum puerilium* ('On civility in children'). This was a work whose enormous circulation allows Elias to see it as both symptomatic and constitutive of fundamental social change. Erasmus's theme is 'outward bodily propriety' (Elias 1994: 42–7). Ariès (1965) is also relevant here.
11 Merchant (1989) is an important account of the erosion of this anaclitic relationship between human and non-human nature.
12 Elias's appeal to psychoanalysis should be noted at this point. However, while he deploys a psychoanalytic vocabulary of 'ego' and 'superego', of 'drives' and 'libido', to discuss the new kind of internally complex subject, Elias does not deal systematically with psychoanalysis and, in fact, produces an account of the psyche in some ways more congruent with behaviourism than with psychoanalysis itself. See Elias (1994: 487–8); also, the discussion in Honneth and Joas (1988).
13 Hobbes's preoccupation with calculation expressed the sense that 'interests' are more conducive than the 'passions' to a peaceful, orderly life. As Hirschman (1977) argues, this preoccupation was prescriptive for, rather than descriptive of, seventeenth-century actualities.
14 In Adam Smith's work we have, side by side, intimations of the 'free market' and therefore of economic rationality, and the taken-for-grantedness of the unity of rationality and the emotions (Smith 1982; Rothschild 2000). Mullan (1988) charts the increasing anxiety about 'sentiment and sociability' as the effects of the new commerce became more visible.
15 I stress long-distance trade because relations at a distance were what stimulated the need to think 'scientifically', and what therefore initiated the processes whereby common sense would be rendered redundant. However, I am aware that long-distance trade assumed

institutional weight only through domestic changes in the 'mode of production'. See the debate in Aston and Philpin (1985). 'Mode of production' is in quotation marks to indicate the misleading character of the concept which, as Raymond Williams pointed out some time ago, is 'a prisoner of the social orders which it is offering to analyse' (1983: 263).

16 Stevenson (1985) offers an account of some of the effects of differentiation on eighteenth-century English artisans. See also Thompson (1968; 1978). For an account of the role of the state in England's 'civilizing process', see Corrigan and Sayer (1985).

17 The need for (as opposed to possibility of) science (both social and natural) emerged along with the development of commodification, therefore it emerged at the margins of community life. This need did not become apparent at the everyday level until commodification had developed to the point at which exchange had become monetized and money had become capitalized (Appleby 1978; Marx 1976a; Rosdolsky 1977).

18 See n. 1, this chapter. For more on survivals see Althusser (1990a).

19 Wood (1981) is useful on the separation of the 'economic' and the 'political' in capitalism.

20 Both Arendt (1958) and Sennett (1993a) view intimacy as a threat to public-spiritedness. This is because they consider only its capitalist (as opposed to its bourgeois) manifestation.

21 As Elias notes: 'the transformation and regulation of drives that is demanded both to write and read books is always considerable' (1994: 479). See Ong (1982) and Vygotsky (1986) on the theoretical issues at stake here.

22 The contrast between the seventeenth and eighteenth centuries, pointed out by Ariès, is relevant here. Seventeenth-century households, unlike those of the eighteenth-century bourgeois, were dedicated to sociability rather than privacy. During the earlier century, the houses of upper-middle and upper classes were open to the world, with individuals coming and going without inhibition. However, it is also worth noting that the hybrid bourgeois household did not yet have that fortified character which would be secured by capitalists (Davidoff and Hall 1987: chs 7, 8).

23 Habermas makes this point in relation to his rejection of Sennett's account (in Sennett 1993a) of the 'fall of public man'. For Habermas, Sennett is confusing two distinct kinds of 'publicness': that of a pre-bourgeois period which consisted in 'forms of an impersonal, ceremonialised role-playing aesthetic of self-presentation' and that described by Habermas (1992b: 427). Sennett's publicness seems closer to that of Arendt, at least to her early strongly agonistic depiction of the public sphere (1958), on which see Moruzzi (2000). I consider Habermas to be more persuasive than Sennett on this point, for reasons which should emerge as the argument unfolds.

24 See Hanson (1970) and Loades (1974) on the history of this development in England.

25 In this distinctly unworldly formulation of Habermas we can hear resonances of the metaphysical authorization endowed on 'reason' as traditional cultural supports fell away.

26 Contrary to what Carpignano (1999) argues, it is not dialogical speech alone but the balance between speech and print communication which, for Habermas, secures the politically effective public-spiritedness of the bourgeois public sphere.

27 I use the terms 'authentic' and 'inauthentic' following Arendt (1978: 37–40).

28 Let me repeat: the hybrid bourgeois mode of life was contradictory in that exploitation, particularism and exclusiveness were necessary to its functioning. However, this contradictoriness was not yet experientially significant for most bourgeois. 'Cultural' silence on faraway conditions of possibility for bourgeois prosperity, of the kind discussed by Said (1993), is a symptom of this fact.

29 Carey (1989) discusses the 'collapse' of time and space enabled by the advent of railways and telegraph.

30 For more on the various interpretations of this difficult concept, see Laplanche and Pontalis (1973: 436–8). See Boothby (1991) for a different interpretation of these 'agencies'.

31 Mitchell (1975) gives an account of the much more complex and difficult trajectory of girls in oedipal families. See also Brennan (1992).
32 For a useful but also hostile and ultimately dismissive account of the Freudian concept of identification, see Borch-Jacobsen (1988).
33 I am using the concept of 'good objects' in a Freudian rather than a Kleinian sense here, i.e. as representations of 'real' objects which are vital for the emergence of a sense of reality, or, common sense.
34 Any parent knows this. However, note also the evidence provided by educational psychologists and culture theorists such as Jerome Bruner (1974).
35 The fact that this education took place increasingly in the home meant that teaching methods were less harsh and authoritarian than was the case in grammar schools. See Williams (1961) for a brief history of formal education in modern England.

4 Parenting and the constitution of bourgeois *sensus communis*

1 It is important to note that, when used in reference to the drives, 'ego' connotes the individual organism's 'interest' in self-preservation whereas 'sex' connotes the species interest in self-reproduction. For Freud, the former tends towards atomism or egoism, as the latter term is used in an everyday sense, and the latter towards fusion; hence his conception of an intra-psychic contradiction. As used in this study, the differentiations of id, ego and superego connote an historico-culturally specific mode of psychic differentiation which emerged in the first instance through the civilizing differentiations discussed in chapter three. When used in this context, ego connotes an individual disposition towards the reconciliation of self- and other-oriented tendencies ('ego' and 'sex' respectively) in a manner conducive to relative autonomy, and therefore, as I am arguing, to *sensus communis*. See Laplanche and Pontalis (1973: 130–43, 220–2) on the different conceptions and configurations of these concepts in Freud.
2 The correction of Freud's neglect of the pre-oedipal phase of subjectivation has been effected by the object relations school which includes Melanie Klein and D. W. Winnicott. For a discussion see Greenberg and Mitchell (1983). See also DiStephano (1991). It should be noted that the object relations school is developing, rather than departing from, the logic of Freud's own position on the pre-oedipal experience.
3 Before this time such mindfulness, dependent as it was on a sophisticated form of literacy, would have been available only to a tiny minority of intellectuals. See Graff (1987) for an historically informed discussion of different conceptions of literacy. Febvre and Martin (1984) trace the 'coming of the [printed] book' in western Europe. Cavell (1993) is an extended discussion of the 'psychoanalytic mind'.
4 From this point of view we can think of the fear of castration as a fear of separation from the loved parent rather than from the organ of pleasure (Bernheimer 1991; Poster 1978: 22). From this point of view, the phallus signifies the fullness of love rather than sexual gratification.
5 In speaking of the 'sublimation' experienced through the performance principle instituted by capitalism, Marcuse uses the term 'repressive sublimation' (Marcuse 1987: 207).
6 Schneider attributes repression wholly to capitalism and can therefore anticipate a time when it will be eliminated.
7 From this point of view, repression is an unavoidable, universal fact of human life. On the work of non-western cultures, see Kakar (1981); Malinowski (1922); Obeyesekere (1990).
8 Freud (1974) contains a clear account of this point.
9 The contradictions in Freud's work on the relationship between repression and superego functioning cannot be explored here. Brennan (1992) discusses these in relation to the question of (the absence of) superego functioning in women. See also Rowley and Grosz (1990).

10 Freud relates the phenomenon of sublimation specifically to social relations, as when he says: 'A certain kind of modification of the aim and change of the object, *in which our social valuation is taken into account*, is described by us as "sublimation"' (1973b: 129 [emphasis added]). It must be noted, though, that sublimation takes different forms and may involve an initial rejection of a painful reality, as is the case with artists. At the same time artists, by virtue of being artists, will 'find the way back' to reality by moulding their fantasies 'into a new truth which expresses the reality of [their] contemporaries' (Freud 1984c: 41–2). So, artists initially use their imaginations to escape from a painful world, but, as artists, they come to transform the worldless imagination of fantasy into a worldly imagination whose works may nurture the worldly imaginations of their fellow citizens. For an excellent discussion of post-Freudian uses of the concept of sublimation, see Whitebook (1995: ch. 5).

11 As Marcuse points out, in Róheim's account idness connotes connectedness to others; it involves unification, not isolation. More than this, it is productive of artefacts for the use of the group. Now, in the sense that sublimation is the 'other' of repression, and that it is in the service of (rather than at odds with) the pleasure principle, this conception of sublimation is not incorrect. However, from our contemporary point of view it is inadequate. As a matter of idness, the communality of which Róheim speaks would not require the strong sense of individuality connoted by ego functioning. Communality of this kind is unfeasibly utopian at this time, at least in Euro-American cultures.

12 Kakar (1981) is useful on the cultural specificity of the distinctions.

13 This account of primary process functioning will prove to be extremely helpful in enabling us to grasp the psychically immiserated condition of contemporary adult subjects.

14 This aspect of the infant's experience is taken up by Melanie Klein and her followers, among whom we must include Lacan. See Rustin (1995) for a discussion. It is worth repeating before moving on that this Freudian depiction of the intensely needy and a-social infant covers only one aspect of infant experience and needs to be filled out with the help of evidence gathered by post-Freudian psychoanalysts who insist upon the innate disposition of infants to reach out to the world in a happily expectant way (Benjamin 1990; Schachtel 1963). Historico-cultural conditions determine the degree to which neediness or happiness comes to the fore.

15 As Freud puts it: 'Instead of [hallucination], the psychical apparatus had to decide to form a conception of the real circumstances in the external world and to endeavour to make a real alteration in them' (1984c: 36).

16 'For something to be thought about, it must be absent from perception' (Hamilton 1993: 243). See also Marcuse (1987: ch. 1).

17 Whitebook (1995: 106) insists upon the importance of retaining a distinction between ego and sexual instincts, thereby, in my view, replicating a capitalist-induced dichotomy. The 'collapse' into a 'monism of desire' which, for him, the distinction helps to prevent, is in fact an artefact of contemporary capitalism, as will be argued in chapter seven.

18 This is the model which is taken for granted by critical theorists such as Adorno, who are in this respect insufficiently historical in their understanding of oedipal family forms (Benjamin 1977). See also Balbus (1982); Poster (1978: ch. 2).

19 Simon and Blass (1991) chart the intricate changes of view and emphases in Freud's development of his oedipal model.

20 See Hajnal (1983) and Seccombe (1995) for discussions of pre-industrial households in north-western Europe.

21 This is a description of one (not untypical) bourgeois woman's activities:

> On 9 April 1792 Anna Margaretta Larpent rose at 7.30, a little earlier than her usual hour, 'spent some time', as she described it, 'in self-examination', and then read two chapters of that blistering critique of the British constitution, Thomas Paine's *Rights of Man*, before sitting down to breakfast. During the morning she

tutored her two teenage sons, John and George, who were on holiday from their school in Cheam. In a ritual that was to be repeated throughout the holidays, she and John read passages from an instructive and improving work, Sarah Trimmer's *Sacred History*, a didactic anthology from the Scriptures written by a best-selling evangelical and advocate of Sunday schools. She taught George to spell, read and learn Latin.

(Brewer 1997: 56)

Brewer goes on to describe the rest of the lively and demanding day of a 'moderately prosperous' woman in London in the late eighteenth century. It is not too fanciful to suppose that Anna Margaretta Larpent was enjoying sublimation as well as suffering repression.
22 For later elaborations of this aspect of Freud's theory, see Hamilton (1993). Chodorow's (1978) work on this subject has inspired a 'difference feminism' which valorizes the supposedly female virtues of empathy and understanding. See, for example, Gilligan (1982). For a criticism of 'the binary logic of mutual exclusivity' which informs this kind of thinking, see Benjamin (1995). For the emergence of these debates in political theory, see Dietz (1985; 1987); Elshtain (1981).

5 The institution of commodity fetishism

1 On the concept of place, see Meyrowitz (1985); Relph (1976); Urry (1995).
2 Some of these subject effects have been captured in the dichotomous categories which are characteristic of the liberal social sciences, including rationality/affect, subject/object, individual/society (agency/structure being a 'critical' manifestation of the latter). As suggested in chapter two, these categories become experiential categories once differentiations take on an abstract character. They are the categories of a strongly differentiated, reified culture whose abstractly differentiated parts are in a contradictory relationship. What, for example, is the agency/structure dichotomy but a conceptual expression of that contradiction which the young Marx noted in *On the Jewish Question* between a political-legal sphere in which citizens are 'free' and an economic sphere in which they are subsumed under the compulsion to labour abstractly.
3 Pockets of pre-industrial or 'local' production remained in England up to the mid-nineteenth century, on which see Chandler (1962); Clark (1995). See also n. 7, this chapter.
4 Frisby (1985: ch. 2) discusses Simmel's account of the 'presentism' of 'modernity'. MacCannell (1991) attributes this to the Enlightenment, rather than to capitalism.
5 I am not implying here a bourgeois revolution of the clear and dramatic kind suggested in, for example, the *Manifesto*. See Hamilton (1991); Mooers (1991). Comninel (1987) has shown how complicated French 'revolutionary' action was. See his ch.1 for a useful discussion of the different positions on this. For evaluations of the English bourgeoisie, see Eley (1992); Perkin (1985). The latter considers that the English bourgeoisie was reluctantly radicalized by means of the Corn Laws of 1815. Mayer (1981) is useful on the persistence of pre-capitalist 'survivals' in Europe. See also n. 5, chapter three, this book.
6 Calhoun's book is an excellent analysis of the effects of the rationality/sociability differentiation in dissolving the social strength that had marked artisanal collective action.
7 The atomization of workers would proceed far more slowly than that of capitalists. As the nineteenth century progressed, workers' collective action increasingly took the form of defensive accommodation to capitalism (Bauman 1982; Perkin 1985: ch. 9). This accommodation might yield some protection from the most unsociable and unintelligible effects of commodification, but this would be a just-for-the-moment protection. To the degree that it was effected bureaucratically rather than communally, it was vulnerable to dissolution from internal as well as external sources. Offe and Wiesenthal (1985) provide a useful analysis of the logic of proletarian collective action.

Regarding survivals, we know from sociologists that as late as the 1950s in England there were communities which had not yet been subsumed under economic rationality (Young and Willmott 1962). Up to the mid-1950s, working-class families in Bethnal Green lived in a nexus of 'extended' relations enabling the co-ordination of three, rather than two, generations and the predominance of personal over impersonal forms of mediation. The transfer of people to new towns would bring this way of life to an end.

8 In fact, we are beginning to understand that, were it possible to cleanse rationality completely of affect, rationality would become disabled. Damasio (1994) explains why this is the case. The nature of the capitalist's apparently affectless state was more complicated than is implied by the simple idea of the divorce of rationality and affect, and needs more careful treatment than can be provided here. However, it is certainly the case that rationality was theoretically and practically reconfigured (in a way which impoverished women) as the property of masculine mastery and that it was thereby drained of sociability.

9 Following Sennett, I take 'destructive *gemeinschaft*' to be a form of community which has been shorn of its utilitarian functions and has nothing with which to occupy itself except 'emotional housekeeping' (1993a: 311). This can be the community of the family (Sennett 1977) or of ethnic groups (1993a: ch. 13). In other words, a destructive *gemeinschaft* signifies the draining of rationality from 'community' or family relations, leaving these relations vulnerable to irrational emotional outbursts.

10 We should note here capitalist attempts to reinstate paternalism in the factory (Joyce 1984; Sennett 1993b: ch. 2). Sennett refers to capitalist paternalism as 'an authority of false love' (1993b: 50).

11 Neither is it adequate to consider the concept of commodity fetishism as the manifestation of a capitalist-specific instance of a knowledge-deficit which is found in various ways in all previous cultures (Althusser and Balibar 1970: 216–19. See esp. 217, n. 8).

12 Geras's analysis of commodity fetishism is very useful up to a point, but is marred by its cognitivism.

13 I am discussing abstract labour here as a cultural rather than an economic phenomenon; that is to say, as a subject-constitutive activity. I am therefore not concerned with the strengths or weaknesses of the labour theory of value, for a discussion of which see Harvey (1982); Postone (1993); Rosdolsky (1977).

14 This is a controversial matter on which see Blauner (1964) and Braverman (1974) who stress the debilitating effects of abstract labour. For views which stress worker resilience and resistance, see Burawoy (1979) and Edwards (1979). Harvey (1982: ch. 4) evaluates the evidence.

15 For historical accounts of the emergent factory discipline, see Perrot (1979); Pollard (1963); Thompson (1967).

16 For example, where differentiation has reached the point of monetization, and where prices of goods become standardized, the sociability involved in 'trucking and bartering' is no longer a necessity. Trucking and bartering require speech; fixed pricing does not. Where there is fixed pricing, speech becomes an optional extra, which individuals involved in the exchange relation may decide to forego. Where the exchange relation is experienced as part of 'society', the individual becomes increasingly likely to give up on sociability in this form. The advent of the department store in the 1850s signalled the emergent atrophying of the sociability of shopping (Sennett 1993a: ch. 7). See also n. 1, chapter three, this book.

17 After Marx, Simmel (1990) remains the most fruitful point of departure on this topic. It should be noted that in addition to treating the problems attached to the monetization of social relations (ch. 5), Simmel (ch. 4) stresses its emancipatory character, or, its tendency to release individuals from a condition of personal dependence. See the discussion in Frisby (1985: ch. 2).

18 What this means is that much of what passes for diversity under capitalism is cosmetic rather than structural, analogous to the diversity attained by different styles of decoration in a terrace of structurally identical houses. For a discussion see Zizek (1997b).

19 Money, says Nigel Dodd, is 'altogether distinctive' in that it 'requires the pre-existence of minimum forms of information, extended through time and across space, in order to proceed' (1994: xxvi).
20 In attempting to understand what was lost in this change, we need to beware of romanticizing physical labour, as Baudrillard reminds us (1996b: 54, n. 33).
21 Today the past exists also in the present in the commodified form of the heritage industry (Urry 1995).
22 'To remember the dead is to remind ourselves that our individuality is dependent on and linked to the other' (MacCannell 1991: 77). See also Venn (2000: ch. 3). Venn refers to the 'repressive forgetting' of the shared past (2000: 191). The theme of remembrance is crucial to Arendt's political theory (Pirro 2001).
23 Wagner (2001: ch. 9) is useful on historical changes in the understandings of 'society'.
24 Nancy Chodorow (1978) and Dorothy Dinnerstein (1978) have offered proposals for changes in parenting practices which could eliminate these debilitating dichotomies. As noted before, Carol Gilligan (1982) appears to embrace them. Now, however, regardless of our fears of wishes, the world is dissolving the conditions which made the fragmentation of human faculties possible. Unfortunately, this is not presently happening in a way which is beneficial either to us or to non-human nature. I shall discuss this in later chapters.
25 Freud is generally criticized for his rationalism. See, for example, Cavell (1993: ch. 7). However, rationalism is antithetical to the logic of psychoanalysis and to Freud's conception of human well-being. As Freud notes, reason is to be put to work to replace the effects of repression by sublimation; it is to serve the interests of the drives, or, to replace an immature pleasure principle with a realistic pleasure principle. The former is loveless, the latter is not. Note the following key statement which expresses succinctly the centrality of emotions to rationality: '[W]e must begin to love in order not to fall ill, and we are bound to fall ill if, in consequence of frustration, we are unable to love' (Freud 1984a: 78). Note also, though, Flax's discussion of the contradictions in Freud's understanding of these matters (1990: ch. 3). Spence (1982) is useful on the question in relation to therapeutic practice and the logic of the transference.
26 This is clearly expressed in the following: '"His Majesty the Baby" is to fulfil those dreams and wishes of his parents which they never carried out, to become a great man and a hero in his father's stead, or to marry a prince as a tardy compensation to the mother' (Freud 1984a: 85).
27 Alford (1988) is useful on the relations between superego and ideal ego. I shall make use of Lacan's understanding of the ideal ego in chapter seven.
28 Note that Freud (1985d) attributes this to the absence of sexual gratification in capitalist marriages. While this was undoubtedly a factor, the woman's lack of worldly gratification would have been equally significant.
29 The example of shopping was cited above (n. 16, this chapter). Another example is the replacement of bourgeois coffee-houses by clubs for capitalist 'gentlemen'. The latter, unlike the former, were used by their members as retreats from world and family (Sennett 1993a: 83–4, 115, 117).
30 For a different view see DiStephano (1991: 44–5).
31 Arendt's comment on late nineteenth-century capitalism is relevant here. She notes of the liberal division between public and private that it 'had nothing to do with the *justified* separation between the personal and public spheres, but was rather the psychological reflection of the nineteenth-century struggle between *bourgeois* and *citoyen*, between the man who judged and used all public institutions by the yardstick of his private interests and the responsible citizen who was concerned with public affairs as the affairs of all' (1973b: 336 [emphasis in original]).
32 Benhabib (1992) discusses some of the problems with this position. See also Bernstein (1995).

6 Abstract labour and the network society

1 For this reason, if for no other, the arguments of social theorists such as Giddens (1991) and Lash and Urry (1994) regarding the emancipatory potential of uncertainty need serious modification.
2 It is this exceptional period which, as Sennett puts it, 'defines the "stable past" against which "disorganization" is identified' (Sennett 1998: 23).
3 This particular manifestation of class exploitation is discussed by Sennett and Cobb (1993). What these writers found in 1960s America was a strong sense of deprivation among members of the working class; a sense of deprivation related to their lack of opportunity to develop their 'insides' in the ways afforded to members of the middle classes. For relevant material on the situation in England, see Hoggart (1957); Williams (1961).
4 During this period the 'industrialization of intelligence', or, the mechanization of mental processes previously carried out by clerks, began to accelerate (Kennedy 1989).
5 Hence Taylorism's preference for unintelligent workers capable of performing as 'trained monkeys' (Gorz 1989: ch. 3; Kosik 1976: ch. II). See also n. 14, ch. 5, this book.
6 It is of interest to note here that Hannah Arendt found the 'job-holding' mentality which functional rationality induced in individuals in 1950s America to be as antithetical to citizenship as was unemployment in 1930s Germany (Barnouw 1990: 180).
7 During this period citizenship became associated with individualized economic entitlements to share- and home-ownership (Oliver 1991).
8 The outpouring of literature on narcissism is a response to this. See Lasch (1978) for an interesting example. Frosh (1991) provides a good general discussion of this literature and of the problems it was seeking to understand.
9 For a discussion of this deprivation, see Lasch (1977); Barrett and McIntosh (1982).
10 While Marxists such as Callinicos (1989) correctly remind us of the continuing importance of industry and of the material, their failure to investigate the new lightness of experience expressed in poststructuralisms is unfortunate. Castells's insistence on the importance of this development is timely.
11 Griffith (1999) discusses the 'privatization' of healthcare in Euro-American social formations during the 1990s.
12 Piore and Sabel (1984) consider the emancipatory potential of the new 'flexibility'.
13 Some states embraced this, some had it thrust upon them (Radice 1999). As Linda Weiss notes: 'the most ardent adherents and steadfast practitioners of free-market economics find their home in London, Canberra and Washington, not in Paris, Bonn, or Tokyo' (1999: 129).
14 Contractualism becomes a feature of trade union membership, in that, through legislation, trades unions are transformed from collective to individualized organizations in that private rather than collective voting becomes a requirement and membership is secured increasingly by individualized inducements rather than through (enforced or spontaneous) solidarity (Strinati 1990; Jefferys 2000; Western 1995).
15 This claim is controversial. Hirst and Thompson (1999) insist upon the undiminished power of states, as do Panitch (1994) and Weiss (1999). Nevertheless, some powerful examples of capital flight exist, among them the experiences of 1980s France under Mitterrand. Castells's evidence that the state has been undermined by the 'network society' and is now required to act more consistently and openly at the behest of capital is persuasive. This is *not* to say that the state is unimportant. It *is* to say that it is now much more obviously the 'functionary' of capital than it appeared to be in the recent 'organized' past when it was relatively autonomous. Beck (2000) insists upon the radical diminution of states' powers now. See also Jessop (1999).
16 In addition to Baudrillard (1993: ch. 2; 1996b), see Heims (1993) for a pioneering attempt to develop a philosophy of this new 'virtual' reality. See also Langan (2000); Rodowick (2001).

17 See also Roszak (1988) for a general and critical discussion of the 'cult of information'.
18 The concept of information is also implicated in the contemporary reconfiguration of the life sciences. This will be considered in chapter eight.
19 Castells does not cite Baudrillard, but his account of virtual reality is compatible in its essentials with Baudrillard's account of simulation which, while it may have appeared extravagant when first written (and still does to some), is an extraordinarily prescient expression of the experience of life as it is coming to be lived now.
20 Mayhew (1997) discusses this question in relation to the infusion of a public relations logic into a newly fusing politics, economics and social sciences. See Weir (2001) for British intra-governmental changes which both express and promote this new fusion.
21 Dews (1987) provides an excellent account of the language and 'ontology' of flux.
22 The possibility that such secession would come about was expressed by Robert Reich some time ago (Reich 1991).
23 Ong uses the concept of 'flexible citizenship' to refer to 'the cultural logics of capitalist accumulation, travel, and displacement that induce subjects to respond fluidly and opportunistically to changing political-economic conditions' (1999: 6). Clearly, flexibility is the radical other of the public-spiritedness with which I am concerned in this study. It is worth noting that Reich (1991) also expressed the hope that global mobility, together with the high educational requirements with which it is accompanied, would lead to a more thoughtful and responsible form of citizenship; one which would transcend the irresponsibilities of self-interested electoral politics. I shall return to this question in the conclusion.
24 See Moore (1984) for an historico-cultural account of privacy from this point of view.

7 Abstract consumption and the dissolution of the ego

1 On desire, see Stavrakakis (1999: ch. 1); Weber (1991: ch. 8); Agamben (1993: 26–8). For more on the concept of need in Hegel (and Marx), see Fraser (1998). On Marx, Heller (1976) remains essential reading.
2 Benjamin assumes that the dissolution of the patriarchal or nuclear family can only be a good thing, one which will leave the way open for the constitution of strong mothers, with whom daughters will identify. Her argument rests on the conviction that internalization is an impediment to the attainment of autonomy; that what writers such as Adorno (1967; 1968) identified as autonomy was nothing but unconscious subordination to external authority. Or, internalization is always internalization of authority and authority is necessarily a bad thing. As Whitebook notes (1985: 147), there is no room in Benjamin's theory for the concept of benign authority. On the need for parental authority, see Arendt (1977d) and MacCannell (1991). See also Sennett (1993b).
3 It matters here also that (as noted in chapter five) once industrialization was complete, the past would become present in the present in the frozen form of 'dead labour' or machinery.
4 Those who see an emancipatory significance in the release of women from domestication include Castells (1997: ch. 4). See also Beck (1992: 109–29). Ginsberg (2002) provides a brief history of the family in the west since 1968.
5 Flax (1990: ch. 4) criticizes Lacan for naturalizing, and sometimes apparently celebrating, a condition which is, in fact, historically specific and debilitating. See Brennan (1993); MacCannell (1986); Zizek (1989; 1996) for a more appreciative approach which stresses the historico-cultural character and/or critical potential of Lacan's work.
6 Lacan's categories and his usages are intentionally elusive. For a discussion, see the translator's note (Lacan 1980: vii–xii); Bowie (1987: 105–6). Dews (1987) is an excellent guide to the vicissitudes of Lacan's usages.

7 Althusser's 'Freud and Lacan' (1984b) is an extraordinary expression of the psychic suffering inflicted by the symbolic. Unfortunately, the essay is written in universalizing mode. This can be corrected by reading it in tandem with 'Is it simple to be a Marxist in philosophy?' (1990d).
8 Dews (1995) is interesting on the shared critical viewpoint of early Lacan and early Frankfurt School members.
9 Both Borch-Jacobsen (1994) and MacCannell (1991) elaborate on this theme of parental loss although neither attributes it specifically to capitalism.
10 I follow Finlay (1989) and Flax (1990) here. Boothby (1991) discusses this matter in some detail and provides an interpretation of the Lacanian position which differs from that offered here.
11 Finlay (1989) contrasts Lacan and Winnicott on this question. See Winnicott (1971).
12 Jameson (1988) provides a different interpretation of the movement from imaginary to symbolic, stressing the child's emancipation from familial relations through 'naming'.
13 Clearly, biologically driven needs must be satisfied if humans are to be maintained in a state of desirousness. In other words, a form of reality-testing (more or less impoverished depending on class and location) remains possible. However, even this is now under threat, as will be seen in chapter eight.
14 But see Stearns (2001) for a universalist conception of consumerism. Stearns also discusses the importance of consumerism as consolation for recent loss of status.
15 Marx (1977: 120–5) remains relevant here.
16 Slater (1997) discusses other interpretations of the 'culture of consumption'. See also Gagnier (2000).
17 This is a combination which yields 'simulacral economics' (Pecora 1988).
18 Clearly this kind of fantasizing is not new. Our grandparents and parents fantasized about Rita Hayworth or James Dean. The point is that now this fantasizing is not mitigated by the materially weighty and habitual daily commitments and practices required by organized capitalism. The point is that now, in every sphere of activity, volatility, or 'flexibility', is advocated and prepared for. Meyrowitz (1985) is excellent on ways in which television enhanced the institutional weight of the virtuality which had previously been borne by the cinema. Rodowick (2001) begins the vital task of theorizing (in a way which has significance for questions about worldliness) the different characteristics of analogue and digital technologies.
19 Turkle (1995: 200) notes the tendency of virtual communication to encourage the 'acting out' rather than 'working through' of personal difficulties.
20 For a discussion see During (1999a).

8 Abstract knowledge, or, disorganized capitalism and the vicissitudes of science

1 One issue which is attracting significant public attention is that of genetically engineered crops, on which see Robbins (2001).
2 Much that is important in modern science will be ignored in this chapter. For an account which emphasizes its exuberant and passionate character see Jardine (1999); Uglow (2002). See also Keller (2002); Kitcher (2001).
3 See Merton (1967) and Zilsel (1945) on the artisanal origins of this tendency in science.
4 See Megill (1991) for an analysis of different conceptions of objectivity.
5 As an example, we are arriving at the point at which the human body is becoming saturated by prosthetics to such a degree that writers can plausibly speak of its mechanization (Mazlish 1993). See also Haraway (1991: ch. 8). In analysing the effects of 'informatics' on the human body, Hayles (1999) talks about the 'posthuman'. Dickens (2001) shows the impossibility of retaining a clear distinction between the biological and cultural sciences even in the absence of these deliberate attempts to transform bodies into artefacts. Farr (1984) discusses Marx's approach to these questions.

6 See also Marcuse (1986: ch. 5).
7 See Lukács (1971: 130, 131) on the intellectual mechanization of the world which preceded the practical mechanization effected by capitalism. Sohn-Rethel (1978) finds the origins of intellectual mechanization in the economic practices of ancient Greece.
8 Wellmer (1997) criticizes Arendt's conception of determinant judgement on the grounds that it rests on a simplistic positivistic understanding of philosophy and science. We may accept much of Wellmer's criticism without abandoning the central insight of Arendt's account, namely, the worldlessly instrumental character of science, particularly in its Baconian manifestation. This is what Arendt is really interested in.
9 See Ollman (1993: ch. 2) on dialectical abstraction.
10 The privileging of sight over the other senses is an important factor in nurturing thinking 'about' rather than 'with' appearances. See Haraway (1991: 188–96) for a discussion which seeks to redeem the reputation of vision by stressing its necessary embodiment and particularity, something which is ignored in the ocularcentric use of vision by modern sciences. Jay (1993) discusses 'ocularcentrism'.
11 Andrew Sayer (1992: ch. 6) offers a realist analysis of the uses and misuses of quantification. See also Aronowitz (1988: ch. 12; Lukács 1971: 129–33). The conception of lawfulness as statistical probability is that of a science which remains at the level of appearances but which reduces appearances to impersonal, standardized abstractions. The assumption informing statistical 'laws' is that probabilities are underpinned by deterministic laws (Reddy 1996: 225).
12 Keller (2002: chs 8, 9) discusses the importance of computer simulations in the life sciences.
13 Kuhn is useful on the ways in which education in the natural sciences (an education for secondary process functioning) nurtures the clarity of vision which is required for the simplifying abstractions in which scientists engage (1977: 228–39).
14 In the absence of cultural lawfulness, a lawfulness in nature cannot be identified. Worldliness needs both cultural and natural 'lawfulness' (in the sense of regularity of occurrence).
15 Two examples from different 'parts' will be useful here. The first, from the world of finance (in which electronics is directly implicated), concerns the fall of WorldCom, America's second largest telecoms firm, in July 2002. The structural complexity of this and other big companies is now such that tracking the multiple flows of finance becomes close to impossible. One verdict on WorldCom is that it 'was a company struggling to understand itself' (quoted in Doward 2002). The second example comes from the world of agribusiness. In relation to livestock, it seems that as use becomes subsumed under exchange useful things begin to move about more frequently and to more places than ever before. This movement renders the identification of causes and the control of effects ever more difficult, as has been found recently by those attempting to establish the causes of, for example, BSE, and foot and mouth disease. As a result of the BSE outbreak in Britain, government regulations now require that every cow in Britain have a passport recording its place and time of birth and all of its movements (O'Hagan 2001). This is an attempt to restore 'thingness' to individual animals (to reify what has been dereified) so as to counteract the tendency towards cognitive opacity of a space-like, de-differentiating world.
16 See Keller (1983) for an account of a worldly and nature-respecting scientific practice.
17 Hayles (1999) provides a brief history of the strange partnership of cybernetics and life sciences, a partnership in which the work of Wiener (1989) is strongly influential. See also Rifkin (1998: chs 6, 7).
18 See Hayles (1990: chs 7, 8) on the ways in which postmodern sciences resonate with poststructuralisms.
19 See also Rifkin (1998: ch. 7).
20 The fact that this activity has a very low success rate does not prevent the biotech industry from acting as if the contrary were the case (Capra 2002: 156).

198 Notes

21 During the 1960s and 1970s, life scientists were meticulous about confining their experiments to the laboratory, given the uncertainties of releasing transgenic organisms into the environment. Responsibility of this kind is now rare (Capra 2002: 139–40)
22 As Kuhn notes, the 'mode of problem selection' adopted by scientists which makes short-term success 'particularly likely' also ensures 'long-run failure' (1977: 262). See Gee *et al.* (2002) for case histories of disasters associated with the translation of science into technology.
23 The Kyoto Agreement expresses this orientation in that it prescribes market solutions to the problems created by the thoughtless and/or misconceived application of science to nature (Wilbert 2001).
24 O'Hagan notes that the Blair government spent £52 million on developing genetically modified crops in 1999 and £13 million on 'improving the profile of the Biotech industry'. This contrasts with £1.7 million spent on promoting organic farming.
25 The theoretical and (up to a point) institutional distinction between science and technology is what has justified practising scientists' lack of reflection on the practical implications of their 'pure' research. See the discussion in Kitcher (2001: esp. ch. 1).
26 Ted Benton discusses an example: that of 'agriculture, pharmaceuticals and food processing', an alliance whose part in recent British agricultural crises he traces (2001: 7–11). See also Beck (1992: ch. 8). See Ahmed and Mackie (2001) on the public reaction to what was seen as the collusion of politics, economics and science in the BSE debâcle in Britain.
27 One theorist of democracy has made this point by claiming that politics must 'replace epistemology' (Barber 1984: 105). See also Fuller (2000). For a more sceptical view of the democratic supervision of science, see Kitcher (2001).
28 For example, Kitcher (2001: ch. 14) discusses the ways in which the availability of genetic testing is making everyday life more rather than less uncertain. At the same time, entrepreneurial geneticists are nurturing the quest for hitherto unattainable certainty by offering parents the apparent means of choosing their children's sex (Revill 2002).

Conclusion: citizenship and the recovery of worldliness

1 Beck (1992: 109–15) stresses the contradictory character of this release.
2 Delanty (2001) argues for such closure, but does not deal with the question of natural science.
3 It is worth re-stating that in claiming that the world is becoming one culture I am not claiming that it is losing experiential heterogeneity. Rather, experiential heterogeneity is being reconfigured as the manifestation of capital's totalizing nature.
4 See Canovan (2000) for a discussion of the contemporary relevance of Arendt's analysis of totalitarianism.
5 Hobsbawm (1998) discusses the *Manifesto*'s contemporary relevance in his introduction to the new edition published to mark the 150th anniversary of its publication. See also Ball and Farr (1984); Panitch and Leys (2000).
6 Cohen (1978: Appendix) is an unusual treatment of this question. See also Carchedi (1983); Farr (1984); Resnick and Wolff (1987).
7 In addition to Castells (1998: ch. 2), see Aronowitz (1990: ch. 4) on capitalism's 'development of underdevelopment'.
8 Melucci (1996b) is more attentive to the contradictory experience of contemporary subjects than is either Giddens or Laclau.
9 The search is on for a post-rationalist science. See, for example, Capra (1983) who looks to Chinese philosophy. Harding (1997) surveys non-European or 'Southern' sciences; Rose (1994) favours a feminist approach. For a discussion of different feminist approaches, see Haraway (1991: ch. 9). For the possibilities inhering in 'chaos theory', see Hayles (1990).

10 Writing against socialism, which she considers to be merely completing the work of capitalism, Arendt sees the recovery of property by the 'masses' to be the most important political question (1972: 214). What she has in mind here is individualized assured possession of a private place.
11 Note the contrast with the worldless aestheticization effected by Nazism, which facilitated the unnatural naturalization of the human, i.e. the subsumption of human plurality under the alleged (race) laws of nature. The political aesthetic proposed by Arendt is intended to overcome this tendency in the modern world (Curtis 1999; Villa 1996: ch. 3).
12 This use of the imagination is essential if we are to provide what Norman Geras describes as 'multivious care' (2002).
13 See Bohman (1998) and Buck-Morss (2001) on the practicalities of instituting a global public sphere. Young (1996) discusses the problems of 'speaking across difference'.
14 Unlike Beiner (1989), who interprets Arendt's late turn to philosophy as an abrogation of politics, I take her preoccupation with the solitary thinking of the 'spectator' to be, not a departure from the political, but an understanding of the requirements of the political when cultures have lost their way, so that they are forced to stop and think in contemplative mode. This is precisely our condition today. The life of contemplation is no longer the antithesis of, but, rather, a necessary moment in, the life of action. See Bradshaw (1989) for an elaboration of this position.
15 Advocates of 'cosmopolitan democracy' view the city as an appropriate unit for the cultivation of the necessary orientations. See Dagger (1997: ch. 10); Delanty (2000: ch. 4). For more on 'cosmopolitan democracy' see Archibugi (1995).
16 Indeed, evidence abounds to this effect. See, for example, James (1998).
17 See also Blackburn (1999); Clark (2000).
18 Harmes's pessimism on this question should be noted.
19 A strong and perennial criticism of Arendt's political theory is that she attempts to sustain an unsustainably pure conception of political action (as action free from labouring and making concerns). If she does, she is wrong, but her position is far from clear. See the discussion in Arendt (1979). The point for Arendt, I take it, is that political activity not be subsumed under 'householding' or economic rationality.
20 Fuller (2000: ch. 7) discusses an earlier attempt (that of the New Deal) to slow down the pace of scientific 'progress' so that innovation would not become socially destructive.
21 The significance of this is not always appreciated by radical theorists who look forward to a post-capitalist re-fusion of cognition and affect. See, for example, Maffesoli (1996: Appendix). Maffesoli applauds the emergence of a 'pluralistic knowledge, in which disjunctive analysis, the techniques of separation and conceptual *a-priorism* are giving way to a complex phenomenology which can integrate participation, description, life narratives and the varied manifestations of collective imaginations' (155). He looks for 'a logic of the passions' to replace the 'politico-moral logic to which we have become accustomed'. While Maffesoli's wish to see the surpassing of 'rational monovalence' (157) can be applauded, it is unfortunate that he neglects to discuss this question in relation to the continuing necessity of science. His lack of appreciation of this question allows him to dismiss Bourdieu's call for a 'popular theoretical sense' as nothing but intellectualism (163). Any insurrection of 'subjugated knowledges' (Foucault 1980: 81) needs to be aware of the ineliminable need for theoretical knowledge in a two-worlds world.
22 'We humanize what is going on in the world and in ourselves only by speaking of it, and in the course of speaking of it we learn to be human' (Arendt 1968a: 25). On this matter, see also Fuller (2000: ch. 8).
23 For reasons having to do with the differential subject effects of sensuously present and virtually present social relations, it is disastrous to insist, as does Castells (1996: 372–3), that all human communication is virtual in that it is all mediated by symbols. Barber (1997) discusses virtuality in relation to the constitution of a global public sphere. Rheingold (1993) is an enthusiastic advocate of the electronic global community.

Bibliography

Adorno, T. W. (1967) 'Sociology and psychology', Pt 1, trans. I. N. Wohlfarth, *New Left Review*, 46: 67–80.
—— (1968) 'Sociology and psychology', Pt 2, trans. I. N. Wohlfarth, *New Left Review*, 47: 79–97.
—— (1973) *Negative Dialectics*, trans. E. B. Ashton, London: Routledge & Kegan Paul.
Adorno, T. and Horkheimer, T. (1979) *Dialectic of Enlightenment*, trans. J. Cumming, London: Verso.
Agamben, G. (1993) *Infancy and History: essays on the destruction of experience*, trans. L. Heron, London: Verso.
Aglietta, M. (1987) *A Theory of Capitalist Regulation: the U.S. experience*, London: Verso.
—— (1998) 'Capitalism at the turn of the century: regulation theory and the challenge of social change', *New Left Review*, 232: 41–90.
Ahmed, K. and Mackie, R. (2001) 'Anger at cover up of BSE blunder', *Observer*, 21 October.
Albritton, R. (1991) *A Japanese approach to Stages of Capitalist Development*, London: Macmillan.
Alford, F. (1988) *Narcissism: Socrates, the Frankfurt School and psychoanalytic theory*, New Haven: Yale University Press.
Althusser, L. (1977) 'Lenin before Hegel', in *Lenin and Philosophy and Other Essays*, trans. B. Brewster, London: New Left Books.
—— (1984) *Essays on Ideology*, London: Verso.
—— (1984a) 'Ideology and the ideological state apparatuses', in 1984.
—— (1984b) 'Freud and Lacan', in 1984.
—— (1990) *For Marx*, trans. B. Brewster, London: Verso.
—— (1990a) 'Contradiction and overdetermination', in 1990.
—— (1990b) 'On the materialist dialectic', in 1990.
—— (1990c) 'Marxism and humanism', in 1990.
—— (1990d) 'Is it simple to be a Marxist in philosophy?', in *Philosophy and the Spontaneous Philosophy of the Scientists and Other Essays*, trans. G. Lock, London: Verso.
Althusser, L. and Balibar, E. (1970) *Reading Capital*, trans. B. Brewster, London: New Left Books.
Altman, D. (2001) 'Genetics and insurance', *Prospect*, April.
Amariglio, J. and Callari, A. (1993) 'Marxian value theory and the problem of the subject: the role of commodity fetishism', in Apter and Pietz.
Anderson, B. (1991) *The Imagined Community*, 2nd edn, London: Verso.
Appadurai, A. (1991) 'Global ethnoscapes: notes and queries for a transnational anthropology', in R. G. Fox (ed.) *Recapturing Anthropology: working in the present*, Santa Fe: School of American Research Press.

Appleby, J. O. (1978) *Economic Thought and Ideology in Seventeenth-Century England*, Princeton: Princeton University Press.
Apter, E. and Pietz, W. (eds) (1993) *Fetishism as Cultural Discourse*, London: Cornell University Press.
Archibugi, D. (1995) 'From the United Nations to cosmopolitan democracy', in D. Archibugi and D. Held (eds) *Cosmopolitan Democracy: an agenda for a New World Order*, Cambridge: Polity Press.
Arendt, H. (1958) *The Human Condition*, London: The University of Chicago Press.
—— (1964) *Eichmann in Jerusalem*, rev edn, New York: Viking Press.
—— (1968) *Men in Dark Times*, London: Harcourt Brace & Co.
—— (1968a) 'On humanity in dark times: thoughts about Lessing', in 1968.
—— (1968b) 'Karl Jaspers: citizen of the world?', in 1968.
—— (1971) 'Thinking and moral considerations: a lecture', *Social Research*, 38, 3: 417–46.
—— (1972) *Crises of the Republic*, New York: Harcourt Brace Jovanovich.
—— (1973a) *On Revolution*, Harmondsworth: Penguin Books.
—— (1973b) *The Origins of Totalitarianism*, rev edn, London: Harcourt Brace & Co.
—— (1977) *Between Past and Future*, London: Penguin Books.
—— (1977a) 'Truth and politics', in 1977.
—— (1977b) 'The conquest of space', in 1977.
—— (1977c) 'Crisis in culture', in 1977.
—— (1977d) 'Crisis in education', in 1977.
—— (1977e) 'The concept of history', in 1977.
—— (1978) *The Life of the Mind: vol. 1, Thinking*, London: Harcourt Brace Jovanovich.
—— (1979) 'Hannah Arendt on Hannah Arendt', in Hill.
—— (1989) *Lectures on Kant's Political Philosophy*, ed. R. Beiner, Brighton: The Harvester Press.
—— (1989a) 'Imagination', in 1989.
—— (1994) 'Understanding and politics', in J. Kohn (ed.) *Essays in Understanding: 1930–1954*, London: Harcourt Brace & Co.
Ariès, P. (1965) *Centuries of Childhood: a social history of family life*, trans. R. Baldick, New York: Vintage.
Armstrong, I. (2000) *The Radical Aesthetic*, Oxford: Blackwell Publishers.
Aronowitz, S. (1988) *Science as Power: discourse and ideology in modern society*, Basingstoke: Macmillan Press.
—— (1990) *The Crisis in Historical Materialism: class, politics and culture in Marxist theory*, 2nd edn, Basingstoke: Macmillan Press.
Arrighi, G. (1994) *The Long Twentieth Century: money, power and the origins of our times*, London: Verso.
Aston, T. H. and Philpin, C. H. E. (eds) (1985) *The Brenner Debate*, Cambridge: Cambridge University Press.
Atiyah, P. S. (1979) *The Rise and Fall of Freedom of Control*, Oxford: Oxford University Press.
Bakhurst, David (1991) *Consciousness and Revolution in Soviet Philosophy: from the Bolskeviks to Evald Ilyenkov*, Cambridge: Cambridge University Press.
Balbus, I. (1982) *Marxism and Domination: a neo-Hegelian feminist psychoanalytic theory of sexual, political and technological liberation*, London: Princeton.
Baldwin, P. (1990) *The Politics of Social Solidarity: class basis of the European welfare state 1875–1975*, Cambridge: Cambridge University Press.
Balibar, E. (1994) 'Subjection and subjectivation', in J. Copjec (ed.) *Supposing the Subject*, London: Verso.

—— (1995) *The Philosophy of Marx*, trans. C. Turner, London: Verso.
—— (1996) 'Structural causality, overdetermination, and antagonism', in Callari and Ruccio.
—— (2001) 'Outlines of a topography of cruelty: citizenship and civility in the era of global violence', *Constellations*, 8, 1: 15–29.
Ball, T. (1995) *Reappraising Political Theory: revisionist studies in the history of political thought*, Oxford: Clarendon Press.
Ball, T. and Farr, J. (eds) (1984) *After Marx*, Cambridge: Cambridge University Press.
Baran, P. and Sweezy, P. (1966) *Monopoly Capital*, New York: Monthly Review Press.
Barber, B. (1984) *Strong Democracy: participatory politics in a new age*, Berkeley: University of California Press.
—— (1997) 'The new telecommunications technology: endless frontiers or the end of democracy?' *Constellations*, 4, 2: 208–28.
Barnouw, D. (1990) *Visible Spaces: Hannah Arendt and the German-Jewish experience*, Baltimore: The Johns Hopkins University Press.
Barrett, M. and McIntosh, M. (1982) *The Anti-Social Family*, London: Verso.
Bartolovich, C. (2000) 'Inventing London', in Hill and Montag.
Baudrillard, J. (1975) *The Mirror of Production*, trans. M. Poster, St Louis: Telos Press.
—— (1981) *For a Critique of the Political Economy of the Sign*, trans. C. Levin, St Louis: Telos Press.
—— (1993) *Symbolic Exchange and Death*, trans. I. Hamilton Grant, London: Sage Publications.
—— (1996a) *The Perfect Crime*, trans. C. Turner, London: Verso.
—— (1996b) *The System of Objects*, trans. J. Benedict, London: Verso.
—— (1998) *The Consumption Society: myths and structures*, London: Sage Publications.
Bauman, Z. (1982) *Memories of Class: the pre-history and after-life of class*, London: Routledge & Kegan Paul.
—— (1999) *In Search of Politics*, Cambridge: Polity Press.
—— (2000) *Liquid Modernity*, Cambridge: Polity Press.
Beck, U. (1992) *Risk Society: towards a new modernity*, trans. M. Ritter, London: Sage Publications.
—— (2000) *What is Globalization?* trans. P. Camiller, Cambridge: Polity Press.
Beck, U., Giddens, A.. and Lash, S. (1994) *Reflexive Modernisation: politics, tradition, aesthetics and the modern social order*, Cambridge: Polity Press.
Beiner, R. (1989) 'Hannah Arendt on Judging', in Arendt 1989.
Bell, D. (1962) 'The end of ideology in the West', in *The End of Ideology: the exhaustion of political ideas in the fifties*, rev edn, New York: The Free Press.
Benhabib, S. (1992) *Situating the Self: gender, community and postmodernism in contemporary ethics*, Cambridge: Polity Press.
—— (1996) *The Reluctant Modernism of Hannah Arendt*, London: Sage Publications.
Beniger, J. R. (1986) *The Control Revolution: technological and economic origins of the information society*, Cambridge, Mass.: Harvard University Press.
Benjamin, J. (1977) 'The end of internalisation: Adorno's social psychology', *Telos*, 32: 42–63.
—— (1990) *The Bonds of Love*, London: Virago.
—— (1995) 'Sameness and difference: toward an "over-inclusive" theory of gender development', in Elliott and Frosh.
Benton, T. (1984) *The Rise and Fall of Structural Marxism*, London: Macmillan.
—— (2001) 'One more symptom: the foot and mouth crisis in Britain', *Radical Philosophy*, 110: 7–11.
Berlin, I. (1969) *Four Essays on Liberty*, Oxford: Oxford University Press.

Berman, M. (1982) *All That is Solid Melts into Air*, London: Verso.
Bernal, J. D. (1954) *Science in History*, London: Watts & Co.
Bernheimer, C. (1991) 'Castration as fetish', *Paragraph*, 14, 1: 1–10.
Bernstein, B. (1977) 'Class and pedagogies: visible and invisible', in J. Karabel and A. Halsey (eds) *Power and Ideology in Education*, Oxford: Oxford University Press.
Bernstein, J. (1995) *Recovering Ethical Life: Jürgen Habermas and the future of critical theory*, London: Routledge.
Best, S. (1995) *The Politics of Historical Vision: Marx, Foucault, Habermas*, London: The Guilford Press.
Bettelheim, B. (1982) *Freud and Man's Soul*, Harmondsworth: Penguin Books.
Bhaskar, R. (1989) *Reclaiming Reality: a critical introduction to contemporary philosophy*, London: Verso.
—— (1993) *Dialectic: The Pulse of Freedom*, London: Verso.
—— (1994) *Plato Etc.: the problems of philosophy and their resolution*, London: Verso.
—— (1997) *A Realist Theory of Science*, London: Verso.
Bickford, S. (1996) *The Dissonance of Democracy: listening, conflict and citizenship*, London: Cornell University Press.
Bion, W. R. (1962) 'A theory of thinking', *The International Journal of Psycho-Analysis*, XLIII: 306–10.
Blackburn, R. (1999) 'The new collectivism: Russian reform, grey capitalism and complex socialism', *New Left Review*, 233: 3–65.
—— (2002) 'The Enron debacle and the pensions crisis', *New Left Review*, 2nd series, 14: 26–41.
Blakely, E. and Snyder, M. (1997) *Fortress America*, Washington: The Brookings Institute.
Blaug, R. (1999) *Democracy Real and Ideal: discourse ethics and radical politics*, New York: State University of New York Press.
Blauner, R. (1964) *Alienation and Freedom: the factory worker and his industry*, Chicago: Chicago University Press.
Bohman, J. (1998) 'The globalization of the public sphere: cosmopolitan publicity and the problem of cultural pluralism', *Philosophy and Social Criticism*, 24, 2/3: 199–216.
Boothby, R. (1991) *Death and Desire: psychoanalytic theory in Lacan's return to Freud*, London: Routledge.
Borch-Jacobsen, M. (1988) *The Freudian Subject*, trans. C. Porter, London: Macmillan.
—— (1994) 'The Oedipus problem in Freud and Lacan', trans. D. Brick, *Critical Inquiry*, 20: 267–82.
Bourdieu, P. (1992) *The Logic of Practice*, trans. R. Nice, Cambridge: Polity Press.
—— (2000) *Pascalian Meditations*, trans. R. Nice, Cambridge: Polity Press.
Bowen-Moore, P. (1989) *Hannah Arendt's Philosophy of Natality*, Basingstoke: Macmillan.
Bowie, M. (1987) *Freud, Proust and Lacan: theory as fiction*, Cambridge: Cambridge University Press.
Bowles, S. and Gintis, H. (1986) *Democracy and Capitalism*, London: Routledge & Kegan Paul.
Boyte, H. C. (1990) 'The growth of citizen politics: stages in local community organizing', *Dissent*, Fall: 513–18.
—— (1992) 'The pragmatic ends of popular politics', in Calhoun.
Bradshaw, L. (1989) *Acting and Thinking: the political thought of Hannah Arendt*, London: The University of Toronto Press.
Braverman, H. (1974) *Labor and Monopoly Capital*, New York: Monthly Review Press.
Brennan, T. (1992) *The Interpretation of the Flesh: Freud and femininity*, London: Routledge.
—— (1993) *History after Lacan*, London: Routledge.

—— (2000) *Exhausting Modernity: grounds for a new economy*, New York: Routledge.
Brenner, J. (1999) 'Utopian families', in Panitch and Leys.
Brenner, R. (1998) *The Economics of Global Turbulence. A special report on the world economy 1958–98*, London: New Left Review.
Brewer, J. (1997) *The Pleasures of the Imagination: English culture in the eighteenth century*, London: HarperCollins Publishers.
Brewster, B. (1976) ' "Fetishism" in *Capital* and *Reading Capital*', *Economy and Society*, 5, 3: 344–51.
Bromley, S. (2001) 'The golden straitjacket: moving on from Seattle', *Radical Philosophy*, 107: 5–10.
Bruner, J. (1974) *Beyond the Information Given: studies in the psychology of knowing*, London: George Allen & Unwin Ltd.
Buchanan, J. M. (1991) 'Politics without romance: a sketch of positive public choice and its normative implications', in A. Hamlin and P. Pettit (eds) *Contemporary Political Theory*, New York: Macmillan.
Buchanan, R. A. (1992) *The Power of the Machine*, London: Penguin Books.
Buck-Morss, S. (2001) 'A global public sphere?', *Radical Philosophy*, 111: 2–10.
Burawoy, M. (1979) *Manufacturing Consent: changes in the labor process under monopoly capitalism*, Chicago: University of Chicago Press.
Butler, J. (1993) *Bodies that Matter: on the discursive limits of 'sex'*, London: Routledge.
Calhoun, C. (1982) *The Question of Class Struggle: social foundations of popular radicalism during the industrial revolution*, Oxford: Blackwell Publishers.
—— (ed.) (1992) *Habermas and the Public Sphere*, London: MIT Press.
Calhoun, C. and McGowan, J. (eds) (1997) *Hannah Arendt and the Meaning of Politics*, London: University of Minnesota Press.
Callari, A. and Ruccio, D. (eds) (1996) *Postmodern Materialism and the Future of Marxist Theory: essays in the Althusserian tradition*, London: Wesleyan University Press.
Callinicos, A. (1987) *Making History: agency, structure and change in social theory*, Cambridge: Polity Press.
—— (1989) *Against Postmodernism: a Marxist critique*, Cambridge: Polity Press.
—— (1993) 'What is living and what is dead in Althusser's Marxism?' in E. A. Kaplan and M. Sprinker (eds) *The Althusserian Legacy*, London: Verso.
Canovan, M. (1992) *Hannah Arendt: a reinterpretation of her political thought*, Cambridge: Cambridge University Press.
—— (2000) 'Arendt's theory of totalitarianism: a reassessment', in D. Villa (ed.) *The Cambridge Companion to Hannah Arendt*, Cambridge: Cambridge University Press.
Capra, F. (1983) *The Turning Point: science, society and the rising culture*, New York: Flamingo.
—— (2002) *Hidden Connections: a science for sustainable living*, London: HarperCollins.
Carchedi, G. (1983) *Problems in Class Analysis: production, knowledge and the function of capital*, London: Routledge & Kegan Paul.
Carey, J. W. (1989) *Communication as Culture; essays on media and society*, Boston: Unwin Hyman.
Carpignano, P. (1999) 'The shape of the sphere: the public sphere and the materiality of communication', *Constellations*, 6, 2: 177–89.
Carrithers, M. (1992) *Why Humans have Cultures: explaining anthropology and social diversity*, Oxford: Oxford University Press.
Carver, T. (1998) *The Postmodern Marx*, Manchester: Manchester University Press.
Cascardi, A. J. (1992) *The Subject of Modernity*, Cambridge: Cambridge University Press.

Castells, M. (1996) *The Information Age: economy, society and culture. The Rise of the Network Society*, Oxford: Blackwell Publishers.
—— (1997) *The Information Age: economy, society and culture. The Power of Identity*, Oxford: Blackwell Publishers.
—— (1998) *The Information Age: economy, society and culture. End of Millennium*, Oxford: Blackwell Publishers.
Castoriadis, C. (1995) 'Logic, imagination, reflection', in Elliott and Frosh.
—— (1997) *The Imaginary Institution of Society*, trans. K. Blamey, Cambridge: Polity Press.
Cavell, M. (1993) *The Psychoanalytic Mind: from Freud to philosophy*, London: Harvard University Press.
Chandler, A. (1962) *Strategy and Structure*, Cambridge, Mass: MIT Press.
Chasseguet-Smirgel, J. (1985) *The Ego Ideal: a psychoanalytic essay on the malady of the ideal*, trans. P. Barrows, London: Free Association Books.
Chasseguet-Smirgel, J. and Grunberger, B. (1986) *Freud or Reich? Psychoanalysis and illusion*, trans. C. Pajaczkowska, London: Free Association Books.
Chodorow, N. (1978) *The Reproduction of Mothering*, Berkeley, Calif.: University of California Press.
Clark, A. (1995) *The Struggle for the Breeches: gender and the making of the British working class*, London: Rivers Oram Press.
Clark, G. L. (2000) *Pension Fund Capitalism*, Oxford: Oxford University Press.
Cohen, G. A. (1978) *Karl Marx's Theory of History: a defence*, Oxford: Clarendon Press.
Colletti, L. (1976) *From Rousseau to Lenin: studies in ideology and society*, London: New Left Books.
Collier, A. (1981) 'Scientific realism and the human world: the case of psychoanalysis', *Radical Philosophy*, 29: 8–18.
Comninel, G. C. (1987) *Rethinking the French Revolution: Marxism and the revisionist challenge*, London: Verso.
Cooke, M. (1999) 'Habermas, feminism and the question of autonomy', in P. Dews (ed.) *Habermas: a critical reader*, Oxford: Blackwell Publishers.
Corrigan, P. and Sayer, D. (1985) *The Great Arch*, Oxford: Blackwell Publishers.
Coyle, D. (1997) *Weightless World: strategies for managing the digital economy*, Oxford: Capstone Publishing.
Cullenberg, S. (1996) 'Althusser and the decentering of the Marxist totality', in Callari and Ruccio.
Curtis, K. (1999) *Our Sense of the Real: aesthetic experience and Arendtian politics*, Ithaca, NY: Cornell University Press.
Dagger, R. (1997) *Civic Virtues: rights, citizenship, and republican liberalism*, Oxford: Oxford University Press.
Damasio, A. (1994) *Descartes' Error: emotion, reason and the human brain*, London: Papermack.
Davidoff, L. and Hall, C. (1987) *Family Fortunes; men and women of the English middle class, 1780–1850*, London: Hutchinson.
Dean, K. (2000) 'Capitalism, psychic immiseration, and decentered subjectivity', *Journal for the Psychoanalysis of Culture and Society*, 5, 1: 41–56.
Deane, P. (1973) 'Great Britain', in C. M. Cipolla (ed.) *The Fontana Economic History of Europe. The emergence of industrial societies. 1*, London: Fontana/Collins.
Debord, G. (1994) *The Society of the Spectacle*, New York: Zone Books.
Delanty, G. (2000) *Citizenship in a Global Age: society, culture, politics*, Buckingham: Open University Press.

—— (2001) *Challenging Knowledge: the university in the knowledge society*, Buckingham: The Society for Research into Higher Education and The Open University Press.

Deleuze, G. and Guattari, F. (1983) *Anti-Oedipus: capitalism and schizophrenia*, trans. R. Hurley, M. Seem and H. R. Lane, London: The Athlone Press.

Dews, P. (1987) *Logics of Disintegration: post-structuralist thought and the claims of critical theory*, London: Verso.

—— (1995) 'The crisis of oedipal identity: the early Lacan and the Frankfurt school', in *Limits of Disenchantment: essays on contemporary European philosophy*, London: Verso

Dickens, P. (2001) 'Changing nature, changing ourselves', *Journal of Critical Realism*, 4, 2: 9–19.

Dietz, M. G. (1985) 'Citizenship with a feminist face: the problem with maternal thinking', *Political Theory*, 13, 1: 19–37.

—— (1987) 'Context is all: feminism and theories of citizenship', *Daedalus*, Fall: 1–24.

—— (1995) 'Feminist receptions of Hannah Arendt', in B. Honig (ed.) *Feminist Interpretations of Hannah Arendt*, University Park: The Pennsylvania State University Press.

Dinnerstein, D. (1978) *The Rocking of the Cradle and the Ruling of the World*, London: Souvenir Press.

Disch, L. J. (1994) *Hannah Arendt and the Limits of Philosophy*, London: Cornell University Press.

—— (1997) '"Please sit down, but don't make yourself at home": Arendtian "visiting" and the prefigurative politics of consciousness-raising', in Calhoun and McGowan.

DiStephano, C. (1991) *Configurations of Masculinity: a feminist perspective on modern political theory*, Ithaca, NY: Cornell University Press.

Dodd, N. (1994) *The Sociology of Money: economics, reason and contemporary society*, New York: Continuum.

Donzelot, J. (1993) 'The promotion of the social', trans. G. Birchell, in M. Gane and T. Johnson (eds) *Foucault's New Domains*, London: Routledge.

Doray, B. (1988) *From Taylorism to Fordism: a rational madness*, trans. D. Macey, London: Free Association Books.

Doward, J. (2002) 'The day the WorldCom world was turned upside down', *Observer*, 30 June.

Dreyfus, H. and Rabinow, P. (1983) *Michel Foucault: beyond structuralism and hermeneutics*, Chicago: The University of Chicago Press.

Drucker, P. (1993) *Post-Capitalist Society*, Oxford: Butterworth-Heinemann.

Dryzek, J. S. (1996) *Democracy in Capitalist Times: ideals, limits, and struggles*, Oxford: Oxford University Press.

During, S. (ed.) (1999) *The Cultural Studies Reader*, 2nd edn, London: Routledge.

—— (1999a) 'Introduction', in During 1999.

Eagleton, T. (1990) *The Ideology of the Aesthetic*, Oxford: Basil Blackwell.

Eatwell, J. (2002) 'Basel II: the regulators strike back', *Observer*, 9 June.

Edwards, R. (1979) *The Contested Terrain: the transformation of the workplace in the twentieth century*, New York: Basic Books.

Eley, G. (1992) 'Nations, publics, and political cultures; placing Habermas in the nineteenth century', in Calhoun 1992.

Elger, T. and Smith, C. (1994) *Global Japanisation? The international transformation of the labour process*, London: Routledge.

Elias, N. (1994) *The Civilising Process: the history of manners and state formation and civilisation*, trans. E. Jephcott, Oxford: Blackwell Publishers.

Elliott, A. and Frosh, S. (eds) (1995) *Psychoanalysis in Contexts: paths between theory and modern culture*, London: Routledge.

Elshtain, J. B. (1981) *Public Man, Private Woman*, Princeton: Princeton University Press.
Engels, F. (1966) *Dialectics of Nature*, Moscow: Progress Publishers.
Esping-Anderson, G. (1990) *The Three Worlds of Welfare Capitalism*, Princeton: Princeton University Press.
Etzioni-Halevy, E. (1985) *The Knowledge Elite and the Failure of Prophecy*, London: George Allen & Unwin.
Falk, P. (1994) *The Consuming Body*, London: Sage Publications.
Farr, J. (1984) 'Marxism and positivism', in Ball and Farr.
Febvre, L. and Martin, H.-J. (1984) *The Coming of the Book: the impact of printing 1450–1800*, trans. D. Gerard, London: Verso.
Finlay, M. (1989) 'Post-modernizing psychoanalysis/psychoanalyzing post-modernity', *Free Associations*, 16: 43–80.
Flax, J. (1990) *Thinking Fragments: psychoanalysis, feminism, and postmodernism in the contemporary West*, Oxford: The University of California Press.
—— (1993) *Disputed Subjects: essays on psychoanalysis, politics, and philosophy*, London: Routledge.
Forbes, I. (1990) *Marx and the New Individual*, London: Unwin Hyman.
Forrester, J. (1981) 'Philology and the phallus', in C. McCabe (ed.) *The Talking Cure: Essays in Psychoanalysis and Language*, London: Macmillan.
Foucault, M. (1974) *The Order of Things: an archaeology of the human sciences*, London: Tavistock/Routledge.
—— (1975) *The Birth of the Clinic: an archaeology of medical perception*, trans. A. M. Sheridan Smith, New York: Vintage.
—— (1979) *Discipline and Punish: the birth of the prison*, trans. A. Sheridan, Harmondsworth: Penguin Books.
—— (1980) (ed. C Gordon) *Power/Knowledge: selected interviews and other writings, 1972–77*, London: Harvester Wheatsheaf.
—— (1983) 'Afterword. The subject and power' in Dreyfus and Rabinow.
Fraser, I. (1998) *Hegel and Marx: the concept of need*, Edinburgh: Edinburgh University Press.
Freud, S. (1957) *Leonardo da Vinci: a memory of his childhood*, London: Ark Paperbacks.
—— (1966) *Project for a Scientific Psychology*, in Pre-Psychoanalytic Publications and Unpublished Drafts. The standard edition of the complete psychological works of Sigmund Freud, vol. 1, trans. J. Strachey, London: The Hogarth Press.
—— (1973) *New Introductory Lectures on Psychoanalysis. The Pelican Freud library*, vol. 2, trans. J. Strachey, Harmondsworth: Penguin Books.
—— (1973a) 'The dissection of the psychical personality', in 1973.
—— (1973b) 'Anxiety and instinctual life', in 1973.
—— (1974) 'Miss Lucy R.', in J. Breuer and S. Freud, *Studies on Hysteria. Penguin Freud library*, vol. 3, trans. J. and A. Strachey, ed. A. Richards, Harmondsworth: Penguin Books.
—— (1976) *The Interpretation of Dreams. The Penguin Freud library*, vol. 4, trans. J. Strachey, ed. A. Richards, Harmondsworth: Penguin Books.
—— (1977) *On Sexuality. The Penguin Freud library*, vol. 7, trans. J. Strachey, ed. A. Richards, Harmondsworth: Penguin Books.
—— (1977a) *Three Essays on Sexuality*, in 1977.
—— (1977b) 'The dissolution of the Oedipus Complex', in 1977.
—— (1984) *On Metapsychology: the theory of psychoanalysis. The Penguin Freud library*, vol. 11, trans. J. Strachey, ed. A. Richards, Harmondsworth: Penguin Books.
—— (1984a) 'On narcissism', in 1984.
—— (1984b) 'Instincts and their vicissitudes', in 1984.

—— (1984c) 'Formulations on the two principles of mental functioning', in 1984.
—— (1984d) 'Negation', in 1984.
—— (1984e) *The Ego and the Id*, in 1984.
—— (1984f) 'Beyond the pleasure principle', in 1984.
—— (1984g) 'Repression', in 1984.
—— (1985) *Civilization, Society and Religion: The Pelican Freud library*, vol. 12, trans. J. Strachey, ed. A. Dickson, Harmondsworth: Penguin Books.
—— (1985a) *Civilization and its Discontents*, in 1985.
—— (1985b) *Group Psychology and the Analysis of the Ego*, in 1985.
—— (1985c) *The Future of an Illusion*, in 1985.
—— (1985d) '"Civilized" sexual morality and modern nervous illness', in 1985.
—— (1985e) *Totem and Taboo*, in A. Dickson (ed.) *The Origins of Religion. The Pelican Freud library*, vol. 13, trans. J. Strachey, Harmondsworth: Penguin Books.
—— (1986) 'An outline of psychoanalysis', in *Historical and Expository Works on Psychoanalysis. The Penguin Freud library*, vol. 15, trans. J. Strachey, ed. A. Dickson, Harmondsworth: Penguin Books.
Friese, H. and Wagner, P. (2001) 'Culture', in Wagner.
Frisby, D. (1985) *Fragments of Modernity. Theories of modernity in the work of Simmel, Kracauer and Benjamin*, Cambridge: Polity Press.
Frosh, S. (1991) *Identity Crisis: modernity, psychoanalysis and the self*, London: Macmillan.
Fukuyama, F. (1992) *The End of History and the Last Man*, New York: The Free Press.
Fuller, S. (2000) *The Governance of Science: ideology and the future of the open society*, Buckingham: The Open University Press.
Gagnier, R. (2000) *The Insatiability of Human Wants: economics and aesthetics in market society*, Chicago: The University of Chicago Press.
Gamble, A. (1994) *The Free Economy and the Strong State: the politics of Thatcherism*, 2nd edn, Basingstoke: Macmillan.
Gay, P. (1995) *The Cultivation of Hatred. The Bourgeois experience: Victoria to Freud*, vol. III, London: Fontana.
—— (1998) *The Naked Heart. The Bourgeois Experience: Victoria to Freud*, vol. IV, London: Fontana.
—— (1999a) *Education of the Senses. The Bourgeois Experience: Victoria to Freud*. vol. I, London: W. W. Norton.
—— (1999b) *The Tender Passion. The Bourgeois Experience: Victoria to Freud*, vol. II, London: W. W. Norton.
Gee, D. Wynn, B., Stirling, A. and Mac Garvin, M. (eds) (2002) *The Precautionary Principle in the 20th Century late lessons from early warnings*, London: Earthscan.
Geras, N. (1971) 'Essence and appearance: aspects of fetishism in Marx's *Capital*', *New Left Review*, 65: 69–86.
—— (2002) 'The ideal of multivious care (Utopia and inequality)', *Rethinking Marxism*, 14, 1: 1–7.
Giddens, A. (1984) *The Constitution of Society: outline of a theory of structuration*, Cambridge: Polity Press.
—— (1990) *The Consequences of Modernity*, Cambridge: Polity Press.
—— (1991) *Modernity and Self-Identity: self and society in the late modern age*, Cambridge: Polity Press.
—— (1994) *Beyond Left and Right: the future of radical politics*, Cambridge: Polity Press.
Gilbert, A. (1981) *Marx's Politics: communists and citizens*, Oxford: Martin Robertson.
Gilligan, C. (1982) *In a Different Voice*, Cambridge, MA: Harvard University Press.

—— (1986) 'Remapping the moral domain: new images of the self in relationship', in T. C. Heller *et al.* (eds) *Reconstructing Individualism: autonomy, individuality and the self in western thought*, Stanford: Stanford University Press.
Gilroy, P. (1993) *The Black Atlantic*, Cambridge, Mass.: Harvard University Press.
Ginsberg, P. (2002) 'Measuring the distance: the case of the family, 1968–2001', *Thesis 11*, 68: 46–63.
Glymour, C. (1991) 'Freud's androids', in Neu.
Godelier, M. (1988) 'Introduction', in Doray.
Goffman, E. (1971) *The Presentation of Self in Everyday Life*, Harmondsworth: Penguin Books.
Goldthorpe, J. H. (ed.) (1984) *Order and Conflict in Contemporary Capitalism*, Oxford: Clarendon Press.
Goldthorpe, J. H., Lockwood, D., Bechhofer, F. and Platt, J. (1968) *The Affluent Worker: political attitudes and behaviour*, Cambridge: Cambridge University Press.
Gorz, A. (1989) *Critique of Economic Reason*, trans. G. Hendyside and C. Turner, London: Verso.
Goux, J.-J. (1994), *The Coiners of Language*, trans. J. Curtiss Gage, Norman: The University of Oklahoma Press.
Graff, H. J. (1987) *The Labyrinths of Literacy: reflections on literacy past and present*, London: The Falmer Press.
Greenberg, J. R. and Mitchell, S. A. (1983) *Object Relations in Psychoanalytic Theory*, Harvard: Harvard University Press.
Griffith, B. (1999) 'Competition and containment in health care', *New Left Review*, 236: 24–52.
Gunn, J. A. W. (1969) *Politics and the Public Interest in the Seventeenth Century*, London: Routledge & Kegan Paul.
Habermas, J. (1970) 'A theory of communicative competence', in H. P. Dreitzel (ed.) *Recent Sociology*, no. 2, New York: Macmillan.
—— (1974) *Theory and Practice*, trans. J. Viertel, London: Heinemann.
—— (1979) *Communication and the Evolution of Society*, trans. T. McCarthy, London: Heinemann.
—— (1987) *Knowledge and Human Interests*, trans. J. J. Shapiro, Cambridge: Polity Press.
—— (1989) *The Theory of Communicative Action. vol. 2. Lifeworld and System: a critique of functionalist reason*, trans. T. McCarthy, Cambridge: Polity Press.
—— (1992a) *The Structural Transformation of the Public Sphere: an inquiry into a category of bourgeois society*, trans. T. Burger and F. Lawrence, Cambridge: Polity Press.
—— (1992b) 'Further reflections on the public sphere', in Calhoun 1992.
Hacking, I. (1990) *The Taming of Chance*, Cambridge: Cambridge University Press.
Hajnal, J. (1983) 'Two kinds of pre-industrial household formation system', in R. Wall (ed.) *Family Forms in Historic Europe*, Cambridge: Cambridge University Press.
Halevy, E. (1972) *The Growth of Philosophic Radicalism*, trans. M. Morris, London: Faber & Faber.
Hamilton, R. (1978) *The Liberation of Women: a study of patriarchy and capitalism*, London: George Allen & Unwin.
Hamilton, R. F. (1991) *The Bourgeois Epoch: Marx and Engels on Britain, France, and Germany*, London: The University of North Carolina Press.
Hamilton, V. (1993) *Narcissus and Oedipus: the children of psychoanalysis*, 2nd edn, London: Karnac Books.
Hansen, P. (1993) *Hannah Arendt: politics, history and citizenship*, Cambridge: Polity Press.

Hanson, D. W. (1970) *From Kingdom to Commonwealth: the development of civil consciousness in English political thought*, Cambridge Mass.: Harvard University Press.

Haraway, D. (1991) *Simians, Cyborgs, and Women: the reinvention of nature*, London: Free Association Books.

Harding, S. (1997) 'Is modern science an ethnoscience? Rethinking epistemological assumptions', in E.C. Eze (ed.) *Postcolonial African Philosophy*, Oxford: Blackwell Publishers.

Hardt, M. and Negri, A. (2000) *Empire*, Cambridge, Mass.: Harvard University Press.

Harmes, A. (2001) 'Mass investment culture', *New Left Review*, 2nd series, 9: 103–24.

Harvey, D. (1982) *The Limits to Capital*, Oxford: Blackwell Publishers.

—— (1989) *The Condition of Postmodernity: an enquiry into the origins of cultural change*, Oxford: Blackwell Publishers.

—— (1996) *Justice, Nature and the Geography of Difference*, Oxford: Blackwell Publishers.

Haug, W. F. (1987) *Commodity Aesthetics, Ideology and Culture*, New York: International General.

Hayles, N. K. (1990) *Chaos Unbound: orderly disorder in contemporary literature and science*, London: Cornell University Press.

—— (1999) *How We Became Posthuman*, Chicago: The University of Chicago Press.

Heater, D. (1990) *Citizenship: the civic ideal in world history, politics and education*, London: Longman.

—— (1991) 'Citizenship: a remarkable case of sudden interest', *Parliamentary Affairs*, 44, 1: 140–56.

Heims, M. (1993) *The Metaphysics of Virtual Reality*, Oxford: Oxford University Press.

Held, D. (1989) 'Citizenship and autonomy', in D. Held (ed.) *Political Theory and the Modern State*, Stanford: Stanford University Press.

Heller, A. (1976) *The Theory of Need in Marx*, London: Allison & Busby.

Herzfeld, M. (1993) *The Social Production of Indifference: exploring the symbolic roots of western bureaucracy*, London: The University of Chicago Press.

Hesse, M. (1978) 'Theory and value in the social sciences', in C. Hookway and P. Pettit (eds) *Action and Interpretation: studies in the philosophy of the social sciences*, Cambridge: Cambridge University Press.

Heyer, P. (1988) *Communication and History: theories of media, knowledge and civilization*, New York: Greenwood Press.

Hilferding, R. (1981) *Finance Capital*, London: Routledge & Kegan Paul.

Hill, C. (1967) *Reformation to Industrial Revolution: a social and economic history of Britain 1530–1780*, London: Weidenfeld & Nicolson.

Hill, M. A. (ed.) (1979) *Hannah Arendt: the recovery of the public world*, New York: St Martin's Press.

Hill, M. and Montag, W. (eds) (2000) *Masses, Classes and the Public Sphere*, London: Verso.

Hillman, J. (1994) '"Man is by nature a political animal" or, patient as citizen', in S. Shamdasani and M. Münchow (eds) *Speculations after Freud: psychoanalysis, philosophy and culture*, London: Routledge.

Hirschman, A. O. (1977) *The Passions and the Interest: political arguments for capitalism before its triumph*, Princeton: Princeton University Press.

Hirst, P. and Thompson, G. (1999) *Globalisation in Question – the international economy and the possibilities of governance*, 2nd edn, Cambridge: Polity Press.

Hobsbawm, E. J. (1975) *The Age of Capital 1848–1875*, London: Abacus.

—— (1977) *The Age of Revolution. Europe 1789–1848*, London: Abacus.

—— (1987) *The Age of Empire 1875–1914*, London: W. W. Norton.

—— (1998) 'Introduction to *The Manifesto of the Communist Party*', in Marx and Engels 1998.

Hobson, J. A. (1938) *Imperialism: a study*, 3rd edn, London: George Allen & Unwin.
Hoggart, R. (1957) *The Uses of Literacy*, Harmondsworth: Penguin Books.
Honneth, A. (1995) *The Fragmented World of the Social: essays in social and political philosophy*, C. W. Wright (ed.) New York: State University of New York Press.
Honneth, A. and Joas, H. (1988) *Social Action and Human Nature*, Cambridge: Cambridge University Press.
Horkheimer, M. (1947) 'Rise and decline of the individual', in *Eclipse of Reason*, New York: The Seabury Press.
—— (1972) 'Traditional and critical theory', in *Critical Theory: selected essays*, trans. M. J. O'Connell *et al.*, New York: Herder & Herder.
Hutton, W. (2002a) *The World We're In*, London: Little, Brown.
—— (2002b) 'Protect us from smooth-talking crooks', *Observer*, 19 May.
Isaac, J. C. (1998) *Democracy in Dark Times*, Ithaca, NY: Cornell University Press.
Jacoby, R. (1980) 'Narcissism and the crisis of capitalism', *Symposium on Narcissism, Telos*, 44: 58–65.
James, O. (1998) *Britain on the Couch. Why we're unhappier compared with 1950 despite being richer: a treatment for the low-serotonin society*, London: Arrow.
Jameson, F. (1988) 'Imaginary and symbolic in Lacan', in *The Ideologies of Theory. Essays 1971–1986. vol. 1. Situations of Theory*, London: Routledge.
—— (1992) *Postmodernism or the Cultural Logic of Late Capitalism*, London: Verso.
—— (1994) *The Seeds of Time*, London: Verso Press.
Jameson, F. and Miyoshi, M. (eds) (1998) *The Cultures of Globalisation*, London: Duke University Press.
Jardine, L. (1999) *Ingenious Pursuits: building the scientific revolution*, London: Abacus.
Jay, M. (1984) *Marxism and Totality: the adventures of a concept from Lukács to Habermas*, Berkeley: University of California Press.
—— (1993) *Downcast Eyes: the denigration of vision in twentieth-century French thought*, London: The University of California Press.
Jefferys, S. (2000) 'Western European trade unionism at 2000', in Panitch and Leys 2000.
Jessop, B. (1999), 'Narrating the future of the national economy and the national state: remarks on remapping regulation and reinventing governance', in G. Steinmetz (ed.) *State/Culture. State formation after the cultural turn*, London: Cornell University Press.
—— (2002) 'Time and space in the globalization of capital and their implications for state power', *Rethinking Marxism*, 4, 1: 97–117.
Joyce, P. (1984) *Work, Society and Politics: the culture of the factory in later Victorian England*, New Brunswick: Rutgers University Press.
Judt, T. (2001) ' 'Twas a famous victory', *New York Review of Books*, XLVIII, 12, 19 July.
Kakar, S. (1981) *The Inner World: a psychoanalytic study of childhood and society in India*, New Delhi: Oxford University Press.
Kalberg, S. (1993) 'Cultural foundations of modern citizenship', in Turner.
Kamen, H. (1984) *European Society, 1500–1700*, London: Hutchinson.
Kane, F. (2002) 'A god that failed us all', *Observer*, 23 June.
Kanth, R. K. (1986) *Political Economy and Laissez Faire: economics and ideology in the Ricardian era*, Tolowa: Rowman & Littlefield Publications Inc.
Kaplan, J. M. (2000) *The Limits and Lies of Human Genetic Research: dangers for social policy*, London: Routledge.
Kargon, R. H. (1977) *Science in Victorian Manchester: enterprise and expertise*, London: The Johns Hopkins University Press.

Katznelson, I. (1988) 'The welfare state as a contested institutional idea', *Politics and Society*, 16, 4: 517–31.
Kauffman, S. (2001) *Investigations*, Oxford: Oxford University Press.
Keane, J. (1984) *Public Life and Late Capitalism: towards a socialist theory of democracy*, Cambridge: Cambridge University Press.
Kearney, R. (1998) *Poetics of Imagining: modern to post-modern*, Edinburgh: Edinburgh University Press.
Keenan, T. (1993) 'The point is to [ex]change it: reading *Capital* rhetorically', in Apter and Pietz.
Keller, E. (1983) *A Feeling for the Organism: the life and work of Barbara McClintock*, San Francisco: W. H. Freeman.
—— (1985) *Reflections on Gender and Science*, London: Yale University Press.
—— (2000) *The Century of the Gene*, London: Harvard University Press.
—— (2002) *Making Sense of Life: explaining biological development with models, metaphors, and machines*, London: Harvard University Press.
Kennedy, N. (1989) *The Industrialization of Intelligence. Mind and machine in the modern world*, London: Unwin Hyman.
Kitcher, P. (2001) *Science, Truth, and Democracy*, Oxford: Oxford University Press.
Knights, D. and Willmott, H. (eds) (1990) *Labour Process Theory*, London: Macmillan.
Kosik, K. (1976) *Dialectics of the Concrete: a study on problems of man and world*, trans. K. Kovanda with J. Schmidt, Dordrecht: D. Reidel Publishing Co.
Kotter, J. (1995) *The New Rules*, New York: Dutton.
Kovel, J. (1988) *The Radical Spirit: essays on psychoanalysis and society*, London: Free Association Books.
—— (1988a) 'Marxism and psychoanalysis', in 1988.
—— (1988b) 'Narcissism', in 1988.
Kramnick, I. (1990) *Republicanism and Bourgeois Radicalism: political ideology in late eighteenth-century England and America*, London: Cornell University Press.
Kuhn, T. S. (1977) *The Essential Tension. Selected studies in scientific tradition and change*, London: The University of Chicago Press.
Lacan, J. (1979) *The Four Fundamental Concepts of Psycho-Analysis*, trans. A. Sheridan, ed. J.-A. Miller, Harmondsworth: Penguin Books.
—— (1980) *Ecrits: a selection*, trans. Alan Sheridan, London: Routledge.
—— (1980a) 'The mirror stage as formative of the function of the I', in Lacan 1980.
—— (1980b) 'The function and field of speech and language in psychoanalysis', in Lacan 1980.
Laclau, E. (1990) *New Reflections on the Revolution of Our Time*, London: Verso.
Laclau, E. and Mouffe, C. (2001) *Hegemony and Socialist Strategy: towards a radical democratic politics*, 2nd edn, London: Verso.
Landes, D. S. (1969) *The Unbound Prometheus: technological change and industrial development in Western Europe from 1750 to the present*, Cambridge: Cambridge University Press.
Landes, J. B. (1988) *Women and the Public Sphere in the Age of the French Revolution*, London: Cornell University Press.
Landow, G. P (1997) *Hypertext: the convergence of contemporary critical theory and technology*, 2nd edn, London: The Johns Hopkins University Press.
Langan, T. (2000) *Surviving the Age of Virtual Reality*, London: University of Missouri Press.
Laplanche, J. and Pontalis, J.-B. (1973) *The Language of Psychoanalysis*, trans. D. Nicholson-Smith, London: Karnac Books.
Lasch, C. (1977) *Haven in a Heartless World: the family besieged*, New York: Basic Books.

—— (1978) *The Culture of Narcissism: American life in an age of diminishing expectations*, New York: W. W. Norton.
Lash, S. and Urry, J. (1987) *The End of Organised Capitalism*, Cambridge: Polity Press.
—— (1994) *Economies of Signs and Space*, London: Sage Publications.
Lash, S. and Wynne, B. (1992) 'Introduction', in Beck 1992.
Lear, J. (1998) *Open Minded: working out the logic of the soul*, London: Harvard University Press.
Lee, B. (1992) 'Textuality, mediation, and public discourse', in Calhoun 1992.
Lefort, C. (1978) 'Marx: from one vision of history to another', *Social Research*, 45: 615–66.
Leiss, W. (1978) *The Limits of Satisfaction: on needs and commodities*, rev edn, London: Boyars.
Lenin, V. I. (1982) *Imperialism. The highest stage of capitalism*, Moscow: Progress Publishers.
Leroi-Gurhan, A. (1993) *Gesture and Speech*, trans. A. B. Berger, Cambridge, Mass.: MIT Press.
Levins, R. (1996) 'When science falls ill', *Soundings*, 4: 83–101.
Levins, R. and Lewontin, R. (1985) *The Dialectical Biologist*, Cambridge, Mass.: Harvard University Press.
Lewontin, R. (2002) 'The politics of science', *New York Review of Books*, XLIX, 8, 9 May.
Lichtman, R. (1982) *The Production of Desire: the integration of psychoanalysis into Marxist theory*, New York: The Free Press.
Linklater, A. (1998) *The Transformation of Political Community: ethical foundations of the post-Westphalian era*, Cambridge: Polity Press.
Loades, D. M. (1974) *Politics and the Nation 1450–1660: obedience, resistance and public order*, Brighton: The Harvester Press.
Lobkowicz, N. (1967) *Theory and Practice: history of a concept from Aristotle to Marx*, London: University of Notre Dame Press.
Lockwood, D. (1964) 'Social integration and system integration', in G. K. Zollschan and W. Hirsch (eds) *Explanations in Social Change*, Boston: Houghton Mifflin.
Love, N. S. (1995) 'What's left of Marx?', in White.
Luhmann, N. (1982) *The Differentiation of Society*, trans. S. Holmes and C. Larmore, New York: Columbia University Press.
Lukács, G. (1971) 'Reification and the consciousness of the proletariat', in *History and Class Consciousness: studies in Marxist dialectics*, trans. R. Livingstone, London: Merlin Press.
Luxemburg, R. (1963) *The Accumulation of Capital*, trans. A Schwarzschild, London: Routledge & Kegan Paul.
Lyotard, J.-F. (1984) *The Postmodern Condition: a report on knowledge*, trans. G. Bennington and B. Massumi, Manchester: Manchester University Press.
MacCannell, J. F. (1986) *Figuring Lacan: criticism and the cultural unconscious*, London: Croom Helm.
—— (1991) 'After the patriarchy: the regime of the brother', *Paragraph*, 14: 68–94.
McCarthy, T. (1991) 'Complexity and democracy: or the seducements of systems theory', in A. Honneth and H. Joas (eds) *Communicative Action. Essays on Jürgen Habermas's "The Theory of Communicative Action"*, trans. J. Gaines and D. L. Jones, Cambridge: Polity Press.
Macedo, S. (2000) *Diversity and Distrust: civic education in a multicultural democracy*, Cambridge, Mass.: Harvard University Press.
McGibben, B. (2001) 'Some like it hot', *New York Review of Books*, XLVIII, 11, 5 July.
McKie, R. (2002) 'Gene research labs at risk of being overrun by millions of mutant mice', *Observer*, 23 June.
Maffesoli, M. (1996) *The Time of the Tribes: the decline of individualism in mass society*, London: Sage Publications.
Maguire, J. M. (1978) *Marx's Theory of Politics*, Cambridge: Cambridge University Press.

Malinowski, B. (1922) *Argonauts of the South Pacific*, New York: Dutton.
Mandel, E. (1978) *Late Capitalism*, trans. J. De Bres, London: Verso.
Manicas, P. T. (1988) *A History and Philosophy of the Social Sciences*, Oxford: Basil Blackwell.
Marcuse, H. (1970) 'The obsolescence of the Freudian concept of man', in *Five Lectures: psychoanalysis, politics and utopia*, trans. J. J. Shapiro and S. M. Weber, Harmondsworth: Penguin Books.
—— (1982) 'Some social implications of modern technology', in A. Arato and E. Gebhardt (eds) *The Essential Frankfurt School Reader*, New York: Continuum.
—— (1986) *One-Dimensional Man: studies in the ideology of advanced industrial society*, London: Ark Paperbacks.
—— (1987) *Eros and Civilisation: a philosophical inquiry into Freud*, London: Ark Paperbacks.
Marshall, T. H. (1973) *Class, Citizenship and Social Development*, Westport: Greenwood Press.
Marx, K. (1951) *Theories of Surplus Value*, trans. G. A. Bonner and E. Burns, London: Lawrence & Wishart.
—— (1973) *Grundrisse: foundations of the critique of political economy*, trans. M. Nicolaus, Harmondsworth: Penguin Books.
—— (1974) *The First International and After: political writings*, vol. 3, ed. D. Fernbach, Harmondsworth: Penguin Books.
—— (1974a) 'The civil war in France. Address to the General Council', in 1974.
—— (1974b) 'Critique of the Gotha Programme', in 1974.
—— (1976a) *Capital: a critique of political economy*, vol. 1, trans. B. Fowkes, Harmondsworth: Penguin Books.
—— (1976b) 'Theses on Feuerbach', in Marx and Engels 1976.
—— (1977) *The Economic and Philosophic Manuscripts of 1844*, 5th edn, London: Lawrence & Wishart.
—— (1978) *The Poverty of Philosophy: answer to the 'Philosophy of Poverty' by M. Proudhon*, Peking: Foreign Languages Press.
—— (1994) *On the Jewish Question*, in *Early Political Writings*, ed. and trans. J. O'Malley with R. A. Davis, Cambridge: Cambridge University Press.
Marx, K. and Engels, F. (1976) *The German Ideology*, in *Collected Works*, vol. 5, London: Lawrence & Wishart.
—— (1998) *The Communist Manifesto*, London: Verso.
Massing, M. (1999) 'The End of Welfare?', *New York Review of Books*, XLVI, 15, 7 October.
Mayer, A. (1981) *The Persistence of the Old Regime: Europe to the Great War*, New York: Pantheon.
Mayhew, L. H. (1997) *The New Public: professional communication and the means of social influence*, Cambridge: Cambridge University Press.
Mazlish, B. (1993) *The Fourth Discontinuity; the co-evolution of humans and machines*, New Haven: Yale University Press.
Meek, J. (2002) 'Everyone has a voice', *London Review of Books*, 24, 13, 11 July.
Megill, A. (1991) 'Four senses of objectivity', *Annals of Scholarship. Rethinking objectivity. I*, 8, 3/4: 301–30.
Melucci, A. (1989) *Nomads of the Present: social movements and individual needs in contemporary society*, ed. J. Keane and P. Mier, Philadelphia: Temple University Press.
—— (1996a) *Challenging Codes: collective action in the information age*, Cambridge: Cambridge University Press.
—— (1996b) *The Playing Self: person and meaning in the planetary society*, Cambridge: Cambridge University Press.

Merchant, C. (1989) *The Death of Nature: women, ecology, and the scientific revolution*, San Francisco: Harper.
Merton, R. K. (1967) *Science, Technology and Society in Seventeenth Century England*, New York: Fertig.
Mészáros, I. (1975) *Marx's Theory of Alienation*, 4th edn, London: Merlin Press.
Meyrowitz, J. (1985) *No Sense of Place: the impact of electronic media on social behavior*, Oxford: Oxford University Press.
Mitchell, J. (1975) *Psychoanalysis and Feminism: a radical reassessment of Freudian psychoanalysis*, Harmondsworth: Penguin Books.
Miyoshi, M. (1993) 'A borderless world? from colonialism to transnationalism and the decline of the nation-state', *Critical Inquiry*, 19: 726–51.
Montag, W. (2000) 'The pressure of the street: Habermas's fear of the masses', in Hill and Montag.
Mooers, C. (1991) *The Making of Bourgeois Europe: absolutism, revolution, and the rise of capitalism in England, France and Germany*, London: Verso.
Moore, B. (1984) *Privacy: studies in social and cultural history*, New York: M. E. Sharpe, Inc.
Moore, P. B. (1987) 'Natality, *amor mundi* and nuclearism in the thought of Hannah Arendt', in J. Bernauer (ed.) *Amor Mundi: explorations in the faith and thought of Hannah Arendt*, Dordrecht: Martinus Nijhoff Publishers.
Moruzzi, N. C. (2000) *Speaking Through the Mask: Hannah Arendt and the politics of social identity*, Ithaca, NY: Cornell University Press.
Mouffe, C. (1992) 'Democratic Citizenship and the Political Community', in *Dimensions of Radical Democracy*, London: Verso.
Mullan, J. (1988) *Sentiment and Sociability: the language of feeling in the eighteenth century*, Oxford: Clarendon Press.
Nagel, T. (1989) *The View from Nowhere*, Oxford: Oxford University Press.
Neary, M. and Taylor, G. (1998) *Money and the Human Condition*, London: Macmillan Ltd.
Needham, J. (1969) *The Great Titration: science and society in East and West*, London: George Allen & Unwin.
Negri, A. and Hardt, M. (2001) *Empire*, London: Verso.
Neu, J. (ed.) (1991) *The Cambridge Companion to Freud*, Cambridge: Cambridge University Press.
Nicholson, L. J. (1986) *Gender and History: the limits of social theory in the age of the family*, New York: Columbia University Press.
Nimni, E. (1991) *Marxism and Nationalism: theoretical origins of a political crisis*, London: Pluto Press.
Noble, D. (1977) *America by Design: science, technology and the rise of corporate capitalism*, New York: Oxford University Press.
Nye, M. J. (1999) *Before Big Science: the pursuit of modern chemistry and physics 1880–1940*, Harvard: Harvard University Press.
Obeyesekere, G. (1990) *The Work of Culture: symbolic transformation in psychoanalysis and anthropology*, Chicago: The University of Chicago Press.
Offe, C. (1984) *Contradictions of the Welfare State*, London: Hutchinson.
Offe, C. and Wiesenthal, H. (1985) 'Two Logics of Collective Action', in C. Offe, *Disorganized Capitalism*, Cambridge: Polity Press.
O'Hagan, A. (2001) 'The end of British farming', *London Review of Books*, 23, 6, 22 March.
Oliver, D. (1991) 'Active citizenship in the 1990s', *Parliamentary Affairs*, 44, 2: 157–71.

Ollman, B. (1976) *Alienation: Marx's conception of man in capitalist society*, 2nd edn, Cambridge: Cambridge University Press.
—— (1993) *Dialectical Investigations*, London: Routledge.
O'Malley, P. (2000) 'Uncertain subjects: risks, liberalism and contract', *Economy and Society*, 29, 4: 460–84.
Ong, A. (1999) *Flexible Citizenship: the cultural logics of transnationality*, London: Duke University Press.
Ong, W. (1982) *Orality and Literacy: the technologizing of the word*, London: Methuen.
O'Shaughnessy, B. (1974) 'The id and the thinking process', in R. Wollheim (ed.) *Freud: a collection of critical essays*, New York: Anchor Books.
Owen, D. (1994) *Maturity and Modernity: Nietzsche, Weber, Foucault and the ambivalence of reason*, London: Routledge.
Panitch, L. (1994) 'Globalisation and the State', in R. Miliband and L. Panitch (eds) *Socialist Register*, London: Merlin Press.
Panitch, L. and Leys, C. (eds) (1999) *Socialist Register 2000: Necessary and Unnecessary Utopias*, London: Merlin Press.
—— (eds) (2000) *Socialist Register 2001: Working Classes, Global Realities*, London: Merlin Press.
Parekh, B. (1979) 'Hannah Arendt's critique of Marx', in Hill 1979.
Pecora, V. P. (1988) 'Simulacral economics', *Telos*, 75: 125–40.
Perkin, H. (1985) *Origins of Modern English Society*, London: Ark Paperbacks.
Perrot, M. (1979) 'The three ages of industrial discipline', in J. M. Merriman (ed.) *Consciousness and Class Experience in Nineteenth-Century Europe*, London: Holmes & Meier Publishers, Inc.
Piccone, P. (1980) 'Narcissism after the Fall: what's on the bottom of the pool?' *Symposium on Narcissism, Telos*, 44: 112–21.
Pietz, W. (1988) 'The problem of the fetish IIIa: Bosman's Guinea and the Enlightenment theory of fetishism', *Res*, 16: 105–23.
Pijl, K. van der (1998) *Transnational Classes and International Relations*, London: Routledge.
Piore, M. J. and Sabel, C. (1984) *The Second Industrial Divide: possibilities for prosperity*, New York: Basic Books.
Pirro, R. C. (2001) *Hannah Arendt and the Politics of Tragedy*, DeKalb: Northern Illinois University Press.
Pitkin, H. F. (1998) *The Attack of the Blob: Hannah Arendt's concept of the social*, London: The University of Chicago Press.
Polanyi, K. (1957) *The Great Transformation: the political and economic origins of our time*, Boston: Beacon Press.
Pollard, S. (1963) 'Factory discipline in the Industrial Revolution', *Economic History Review*, 16, 2: 254–71.
Porter, R. (2000) *Enlightenment: Britain and the creation of the modern world*, London: Penguin Press.
Porter, T. M. (1992) 'Objectivity as standardization: the rhetoric of impersonality in measurement, statistics, and cost–benefit analysis', *Annals of Scholarship. Rethinking objectivity. II*, 9, 1/2: 19–57,
Poster, M. (1978) *Critical Theory of the Family*, London: Pluto Press.
—— (1995) *The Second Media Age*, Cambridge: Polity Press.
Postone, M. (1992) 'Political theory and historical analysis', in Calhoun 1992.
—— (1993) *Time, Labor and Social Domination: a reinterpretation of Marx's critical theory*, Cambridge: Cambridge University Press.

Poulantzas, N. (1978) *Political Power and Social Classes*, London: New Left Books.
Prigogine, I. and Stengers, I. (1984) *Order out of Chaos: man's new dialogue with nature*, New York: Bantam.
Radice, H. (1999) 'Taking globalisation seriously', in L. Panitch and C. Leys (eds) *Global Capitalism Versus Democracy, Socialist Register*, London: Merlin Press.
Rattansi, A. (1982) *Marx and the Division of Labour*, London: Macmillan.
Reddy, J. (1996) 'Claims to expert knowledge and the subversion of democracy: the triumph of risk over uncertainty', *Economy and Society*, 25: 222–54.
Reich, A. (1953) 'Narcissistic object choice in women', *Journal of American Psychoanalytic Association*, 1, 1: 22–44.
Reich, R. B. (1991) *The Work of Nations: preparing ourselves for 21st-century capitalism*, New York: Simon & Schuster.
Reinhardt, M. (1997) *The Art of Being Free: taking liberties with Tocqueville, Marx, and Arendt*, London: Cornell Univesity Press.
Relph, E. (1976) *Place and Placelessness*, London: Pion.
Resch, R. P. (1992) *Althusser and the Renewal of Marxist Social Theory*, Oxford: The University of California Press.
Resnick, S. A. and Wolff, R. D. (1987) *Knowledge and Class: a Marxian critique of political economy*, Chicago: The University of Chicago Press.
Revill, J. (2002) 'Parents pay to choose baby's sex', *Observer*, 8 September.
Rheingold, H. (1993) *The Virtual Community: homesteading on the electric frontier*, Reading, Mass.: Addison-Wesley Publishers.
Rich, A. (1977) *Of Woman Born: motherhood as experience and institution*, London: Virago.
Ricoeur, P. (1970) *Freud and Philosophy: an essay on interpretation*, trans. D. Savage, London: Yale University Press.
—— (1990) 'Action, story and history: on re-reading *The Human Condition*', in R. Garner (ed.) *The Realm of Humanitas: responses to the writings of Hannah Arendt*, New York: Peter Lang.
Rifkin, J. (1998) *The Biotech Century: how genetic commerce will change the world*, London: Phoenix.
Ring, J. (1989) 'On needing both Marx and Arendt: alienation and the flight from inwardness', *Political Theory*, 17, 3: 432–48.
Ritzer, G. (1996) *The McDonaldization of Society*, Thousand Oaks: Pine Forge Press.
Robbins, J. (2001) *The Food Revolution*, Berkeley: Conari Press.
Rodowick, D. N. (2001) *Reading the Figural, or, Philosophy after the New Media*, London: Duke University Press.
Rorty, R. (1980) *Philosophy and the Mirror of Nature*, Oxford: Blackwell Publishers.
Rosdolsky, R. (1977) *The Making of Marx's 'Capital'*, London: Pluto Press.
Rose, H. (1994) *Love, Power and Knowledge: towards a feminist transformation of the sciences*, Cambridge: Polity Press.
Rose, N. (1985) *The Psychological Complex: psychology, politics and society in England 1869–1939*, London: Routledge & Kegan Paul.
Rose, S. (1997) *Lifelines: biology, freedom, determinism*, Harmondsworth: Penguin Books.
Rosenau, P. (1992) *Post-modernism and the Social Sciences: insights, inroads, and intrusions*, Princeton: Princeton University Press.
Ross, A. (1999) 'The challenge of science', in During 1999.
Roszak, T. (1988) *The Cult of Information: the folklore of computers and the true art of thinking*, London: Paladin Grafton Books.

Rothschild, E. (2000) *Economic Sentiments. Adam Smith, Condorcet and the Enlightenment*, Harvard: Harvard University Press.

Rowley, J. and Grosz, E. (1990) 'Psychoanalysis and feminism', in S. Gunew (ed.) *Feminist Knowledge: critique and construct*, London: Routledge.

Rustin, M. (1995) 'Lacan, Klein and politics: the positive and negative in psychoanalytic thought', in Elliott and Frosh.

Sahlins, M. (1976) *Culture and Practical Reason*, London: The University of Chicago Press.

Said, E. W. (1993) *Culture and Imperialism*, London: Vintage.

Sampson, A. (1995) *Corporate Man: the rise and fall of corporate life*, London: HarperCollins.

Sayer, A. (1992) *Method in Social Science: a realist approach*, London: Hutchinson.

—— (1995) *Radical Political Economy: a critique*, Oxford: Blackwell Publishers.

Sayer, D. (1987) *The Violence of Abstraction: the analytic foundations of historical materialism*, Oxford: Blackwell Publishers.

—— (1991) *Capitalism and Modernity: an excursus on Marx and Weber*, London: Routledge.

Schachtel, E. (1963) *Metamorphosis: on the development of affect, perception, attention and memory*, London: Routledge & Kegan Paul.

Schafer, R. (1968) *Aspects of Internalisation*, New York: International Universities Press.

Schneider, M. (1975) *Neurosis and Civilization: a Marxist/Freudian synthesis*, trans. M. Roloff, New York: The Seabury Press.

Schorske, C. E. (1980) *Fin-de-Siècle Vienna: politics and culture*, London: Weidenfeld & Nicolson.

Schrödinger, E. (1996) *Science and Humanism*, in *Nature and the Greeks and Science and Humanism*, Cambridge: Cambridge University Press.

Scott, J. (1988) 'Gender: a useful category of historical analysis', in *Gender and the Politics of History*, New York: Columbia University Press.

Scott, M. (2002) 'Hope to die before you get old', *Observer*, 23 June.

Seccombe, W. (1995) *A Millennium of Family Change: feudalism to capitalism in northwestern Europe*, London: Verso.

Sennett, R. (1977) 'Destructive Gemeinschaft', in N. Birnbaum (ed.) *Beyond the Crisis*, Oxford: Oxford University Press.

—— (1993a) *The Fall of Public Man*, London: Faber & Faber.

—— (1993b) *Authority*, London: W. W. Norton.

—— (1998) *The Corrosion of Character*, London: W. W. Norton.

Sennett, R. and Cobb, J. (1993) *The Hidden Injuries of Class*, London: W. W. Norton.

Sève, L. (1978) *Man in Marxist Theory and the Psychology of Personality*, trans. J. McGreal, Sussex: The Harvester Press.

Seymour, B. (2001) 'Nationalize this! What next for anti-globalization protests?', *Radical Philosophy*, 107: 2–5.

Shorter, E. (1975) *The Making of the Modern Family*, New York: Basic Books.

Simmel, G. (1990) *The Philosophy of Money*, 2nd edn, D. Frisby (ed.), trans. T. Bottomore and D. Frisby, London: Routledge.

Simon, B. and Blass, R. B. (1991) 'The development and vicissitudes of Freud's ideas on the Oedipus complex', in Neu.

Slater, D. (1997) *Consumer Culture and Modernity*, London: Polity Press.

Slaughter, S. and Leslie, L. (1997) *Academic Capitalism: politics, policies, and the entrepreneurial university*, London: The Johns Hopkins University Press.

Smith, A. (1982) *The Theory of Moral Sentiments*, Indianapolis: Liberty Classics.

Sohn-Rethel, A. (1978) *Intellectual and Manual Labour: a critique of epistemology*, London: Macmillan.

Solow, R. M. (2000) 'Welfare: the cheapest country', *New York Review of Books*, XLVII, 5, 23 March.
Soper, K. (1999) 'Other pleasures: the attractions of post-consumerism', in Panitch and Leys 1999.
Soysal, Y. N. (1994) *Limits of Citizenship: migrants and postnational membership in Europe*, Chicago: The University of Chicago Press.
Spence, D. P. (1982) *Narrative Truth and Historical Truth: meaning and interpretation in psychoanalysis*, London: W. W. Norton.
Stavrakakis, Y. (1999) *Lacan and the Political*, London: Routledge.
Stearns, P. H. (2001) *Consumerism in World History. The global transformation of desire*, London: Routledge.
Stein, T. (1997) 'Does the constitutional and democratic system work? The ecological crisis as a challenge to the political order of constitutional democracy', *Constellations*, 4, 3: 420–49.
Stevenson, J. (1985) 'The "moral economy" of the English crowd', in A. Fletcher and J. Stevenson (eds) *Order and Disorder in Early Modern England*, Cambridge: Cambridge University Press.
Stone, L. (1979) *The Family, Sex and Marriage in England 1500–1800*, Harmondsworth: Penguin Books.
Strange, S. (1986) *Casino Capitalism*, Oxford: Blackwell Publishers.
Strauss, C. and Quinn, N. (1997) *A Cognitive Theory of Cultural Meaning*, Cambridge: Cambridge University Press.
Strinati, D. (1990) 'A Ghost in the Machine? The state and the labour process in theory and practice', in Knights and Willmott.
Tapscott, D. (1995) *The Digital Economy. Promise and peril in the age of networked intelligence*, New York: McGraw Hill.
Taylor, C. (1992) *Sources of the Self*, Cambridge: Cambridge University Press.
Thomas, P. (1984) 'Alien politics: a Marxian perspective on citizenship and democracy', in Ball and Farr.
Thompson, E. P. (1967) 'Time, work-discipline and industrial capitalism', *Past and Present*, 38: 56–97.
—— (1968) *The Making of the English Working Class*, Harmondsworth: Penguin Books.
—— (1978) 'Eighteenth-century English society: class struggle without class?', *Social History*, 3, 2: 133–65.
Touraine, A. (1995) *Critique of Modernity*, trans. D. Macey, Oxford: Basil Blackwell.
Turkle, S. (1995) *Life on the Screen: identity in the age of the internet*, New York: Simon & Schuster.
Turner, B. S. (1986) 'Personhood and citizenship', *Theory, Culture and Society*, 3, 1: 1–16.
—— (ed.) (1993) *Citizenship and Social Theory*, London: Sage Publications.
—— (1993a) 'Outline of a theory of human rights', in Turner.
Uglow, J. (2002) *The Lunar Men: the friends who made the future*, London: Faber.
Urry, John (1995), *Consuming Places*, London: Routledge.
Venn, C. (2000) *Occidentalism: modernity and subjectivity*, London: Sage Publications.
Villa, D. (1996) *Arendt and Heidegger: the fate of the political*, Cambridge: Cambridge University Press.
Vygotsky, L. (1986) *Thought and Language*, trans. and ed. A. Kozulin, London: MIT Press.
Wagner, P. (2001) *A History and Theory of the Social Sciences: not all that is solid melts into air*, London: Sage Publications.
Wahrman, D. (1995) *Imagining the Middle Class. The political representation of class in Britain*, Cambridge: Cambridge University Press.

Wallerstein, I. (1979) *The Capitalist World-Economy: essays by Immanuel Wallerstein*, Cambridge: Cambridge University Press.
Warren, M. E. (1995) 'The self in discursive democracy', in White.
Weber, S. (1991) *Return to Freud: Jacques Lacan's dislocation of psychoanalysis*, trans. M. Levine, Cambridge: Cambridge University Press.
Weinberg, S. (2001) 'The future of science and the universe', *New York Review of Books*, XLVIII, 18, 15 November.
Weir, S. (2001) 'The quangos just grow and grow', *New Statesman*, 9 April.
Weiss, L. (1999) 'Managed openness: beyond neoliberal globalism', *New Left Review*, 238: 126–40.
Wellmer, A. (1997) 'Hannah Arendt on judgment: the unwritten doctrine of reason', in L. May and J. Kohn (eds) *Hannah Arendt: twenty years later*, Cambridge, Mass.: MIT Press.
Western, B. (1995) 'Union decline in eighteen advanced capitalist countries', *American Sociological Review*, 60, 2: 179–201.
Westphal, S. P. (2002) 'Your money or your life', *New Scientist*, 175, 2351.
White, S. K. (ed.) (1995) *The Cambridge Companion to Habermas*, Cambridge: Cambridge University Press.
Whitebook, J. (1985) 'Reason and happiness: some psychoanalytic themes in critical theory', in J. Bernstein (ed.) *Habermas and Modernity*, Cambridge: Polity Press.
—— (1995) *Perversion and Utopia: a study in psychoanalysis and critical theory*, Cambridge, Mass.: MIT Press.
Wiener, N. (1989) *The Human Use of Human Beings*, 2nd edn, New York: Free Association Books.
Wilbert, C. (2001) 'No to Kyoto', *Radical Philosophy*, 110: 2–7.
Wilde, L. (1989) 'The early development of Marx's concept of contradiction', in M. Cowling and L. Wilde (eds) *Approaches to Marx*, Milton Keynes: Open University Press.
Williams, R. (1961) *The Long Revolution*, London: Chatto & Windus.
—— (1983) *Towards 2000*, London: Chatto & Windus.
Willis, P. (1979) *Learning to Labour: how working class kids get working class jobs*, Farnborough: Saxon House.
Winnicott, D. W. (1971) 'Mirror-role of mother and family in child development', in *Playing and Reality*, London: Tavistock Publications.
Winston, M. (2002) *Travels in the Genetically Modified Zone*, Harvard: Harvard University Press.
Wolfenstein, E. V. (1993) *Psychoanalytic-Marxism: groundwork*, London: Free Association Books.
Wollheim, R. (1973) *Freud*, London: Fontana.
Wood, E. M. (1981) 'The separation of the economic and the political in capitalism', *New Left Review*, 127: 66–95.
Woolfson, C. (1982) *The Labour Theory of Culture: a re-examination of Engels's theory of human origins*, London: Routledge & Kegan Paul.
Wrong, D. (1961) 'The oversocialized conception of man in modern sociology', *American Sociological Review*, 26, 2: 189–93.
Wuthnow, R. (1989) *Communities of Discourse: ideology and social structure in the Reformation, the Enlightenment, and European socialism*, London: Harvard University Press.
Young, I. M. (1996) 'Communication and the Other: beyond deliberative democracy', in S. Benhabib (ed.) *Democracy and Difference: contesting the boundaries of the political*, Princeton: Princeton University Press.

Young, M. and Willmott, P. (1962) *Family and Kinship in East London*, rev edn, Harmondsworth: Penguin Books.

Zaretsky, E. (1976) *Capitalism, the Family, and Personal Life*, London, Pluto Press.

—— (1997) 'Hannah Arendt and the meaning of the public/private distinction', in Calhoun and McGowan.

Zilsel, E. (1945) 'The genesis of the concept of scientific progress', *Journal of the History of Ideas*, 6: 325–49.

Zizek, S. (1989) *The Sublime Object of Ideology*, London: Verso.

—— (1996) 'The seven veils of paranoia, or, why does the paranoiac need two fathers?', *Constellations*, 3, 2: 139–56.

—— (1997a) *The Plague of Fantasies*, London: Verso.

—— (1997b) 'Multiculturalism or, the cultural logic of multinational capitalism', *New Left Review*, 225: 28–51.

Index

absent causes 39–40, 146–7
absolute autonomy *see* autonomy
absolutism 52; and courtly life 52–3, 56
abstract consumption 7, 32, 43, 121, 122–41
abstract knowledge 32, 43, 142–61 *passim*
abstract labour 7, 32–3, 43, 84, 87, 90–2, 94, 100, 103–21, 139; and object loss 33
abstract universalism 175
abstraction 30, 48, 50, 87–95; and impersonal mediations 31, 32; as mode of domination 31, 32; and quantification 32
action 34, 35, 174
activity drive *see* drives
Adorno, T. 41, 48, 143, 144, 148
affect 52, 65, 76, 100, 101
Aglietta, M. 26, 107, 113
Albritton, R. 27, 34
Althusser, L. 6, 14, 16, 26, 27, 29, 30, 33, 89, 92, 103, 104, 151
Altman, D. 159
Amariglio, J. 89, 158
anaclisis 3, 20, 36, 79, 86
anaclitic rationality *see* rationality
Anderson, B. 17
Appadurai, A. 130
appearances 89, 90, 108, 114, 139, 146, 147, 148, 149, 150, 155, 157, 166
Appleby, J. O. 15, 146
Arendt, H. 3, 5, 11, 14, 16–18, 22, 23, 25, 31, 33–6, 39, 40, 48, 50, 54, 57, 61, 85, 99, 100, 111–12, 115, 132, 138, 144, 145–50, 154, 164, 166, 167, 169–70, 172–5, 179
Ariès, P. 54, 55, 77
aristocracy 52, 56, 57
aristocracy of labour 116, 119, 159, 162, 165, 176
Armstrong, I. 173
Aronowitz, S. 142, 154, 155, 160

Arrighi, G. 26, 26, 28, 30, 112
artisans 38, 41, 47, 51, 53, 57, 86, 100, 103, 132
atomism 4, 20, 24, 36, 57, 58, 65, 71, 77, 100, 107, 110, 157, 162, 163, 168, 171
atomization 95, 103, 107, 110, 191 n7
attachment 62, 64, 65, 93, 123, 126, 127, 171; serial 118, 138, 162
attention 37, 50, 72, 73, 75, 79, 110, 124, 125, 131, 137, 138, 172, 181
autonomy 11, 13, 22–3, 48, 64, 99, 109, 118, 127, 129, 130, 131, 133, 134, 139, 141, 161, 162,169; absolute 41, 57, 102, 104, 126, 128, 176; and atomism 162; as gift of culture 169; and heteronomy 104, 124,130, 141, 161, 164–5; as ideology 89; illusory 42, 127; means of 169; relative 20, 37, 42, 47, 53, 54, 57, 59, 62, 71, 75, 76, 88, 95, 96, 103, 104, 109, 126, 163, 171, 177, 180

Bacon, F. 143
bad objects 37, 85, 123, 124, 130, 139 *see also* good objects; virtual objects
Baldwin, P. 108
Balibar, E. 2, 4, 15, 28, 29, 151
Bartolovich, C. 38
Baudrillard, J. 36, 109, 130, 138, 139
Bauman, Z. 36, 41, 86, 113, 118, 119
bearers of structures 103, 105, 109, 110
Beck, U. 5, 8, 119, 144, 154, 155, 166
Beiner, R. 173
Benhabib, S. 11, 22
Benjamin, J. 11, 21, 37, 41, 60, 65, 76, 85, 86, 95, 96, 98, 99, 125–6, 136, 137
Benton, T. 89
Berlin, I. 170
Berman, M. 33, 119
Bernal, J. D. 39, 40, 147, 149

Bernstein, B. 106
Bernstein, J. 2
Best, S. 11
Bhaskar, R. 12, 13, 25, 147, 151, 159
Bickford, S. 17, 22, 174
Bion, W. R. 73
Blackburn, R. 142, 158, 159, 176
Blakely, E. 119
Bourdieu, P. 16, 51, 169
bourgeois public sphere 6, 43, 48, 56–8, 106
Bowie, M. 132
Braverman, H. 105, 106
breast-feeding 77, 135–6
Brennan, T. 19, 20, 36, 37, 69, 73, 75, 96, 98, 124, 131, 137, 138, 172
Brenner, J. 127
Brewer, J. 53
Buchanan, J. M. 2
Buchanan, R. A. 84
Buck-Morss, S. 5
bureaucracy 39, 40, 47, 84, 133
Butler, J.

calculation 51, 157–8
Calhoun, C. 41, 86
Callari, A. 89, 158
Callinicos, A. 29
capital/capitalism 14, 25–44, 141, 142, 163, 166, 167, 169, 173, 174, 179, 181, 184 n8; as abstract mode of domination 27, 92, 132–3; as closed system 28; formal/real subsumption of labour 6, 7, 26, 33, 41, 47, 53, 85, 86–7, 124, 171,186 n33; and law of value 25–7, 28; as mode of labour, consumption and truth 27; monopoly 41; periodization 41; as permanent revolution 35; and science 38–40, 142–61; and surplus value 30; as totality 26, 27–31 *see also* disorganized capitalism, hybrid bourgeois capitalism; liberal industrial capitalism, organized capitalism
capitalists 41, 47, 86, 103, 127, 157, 167, 177, 178
Capra, E. 152, 153, 154
Carey, J. W. 84, 122
Carrithers, M. 18, 182 n4
Carver, T. 30
Cascardi, A. H. 11, 134
casino capitalism 155
Castells, M. 105, 112–20, 155, 163, 164, 167, 176, 177
Castoriadis, C. 94, 135

cathexis 19–20, 59, 72–6, 84, 98, 123, 130, 135
causal powers 12–13, of capitalism 25–43; of humans 14–23
Cavell, M 18, 72
Chasseguet-Smirgel, J. 18, 37, 131
citizens 1, 4, 12, 18, 71, 107, 109, 157, 172, 173, 175, 177, 178; flexible 119, 195 n23; public-spirited 119, 166, 169, 171, 180
citizenship 22–3, 41–2, 74–6, 85, 141, 167, 169–70, 174, 175, 176, 177, 179; bourgeois 56–8; global 175; as clientelism 177–8; and consumerism 178; and democracy 176–8; and lack 176–8; public-spirited 1, 162–81; and victimhood 178
civic cosmopolitanism 4; and civic virtue 22; and global public-spiritedness 22
civic virtue 22, 68
civilization 49, 51, 58, 68, 88, 125, 132, 133
civilizing process 6, 49–53, 94, 103, 145, 163
classical political economy 28, 86
cognitive contradiction 8, 141, 142, 144, 145, 160, 164–5
cognitive crisis 143, 144, 151
cognitive mapping 116, 159
Cohen, G. A. 89
collective action 3, 4, 28 86, 107, 110, 164
Colletti, L. 91
commodification 32, 84, 87, 88, 94, 99, 109, 122, 130, 153, 156
commodity 88–90, 122, 139, 149
commodity aesthetic 123, 173 *see also* desire, fantasy
commodity fetishism 7, 8, 31–6, 43, 57, 77, 80, 83–102, 103, 104, 108, 112, 115, 117, 118, 129, 132, 134, 141, 156, 157, 160, 179; and abstraction 31; and dereification 31, 33–6; and reification 31, 32–3 *see also* worldlessness
common sense 16–17, 40, 41, 47, 50, 54, 61, 85, 101, 115, 137, 140, 144, 147, 149, 150, 157, 166, 169
communication 17, 83; electronic 17, 139–40, 179; speech 16, 56–8, 179; print 179
communicative rationality *see* rationality
*Communist Manifesto*163, 164, 166–9
community 175, 180
companionate marriage 77–9
consumerism 109,121, 131, 138, 152, 176

consumption 109, 115, 130, 142; and destruction 111, 138
consumption power 123, 146
contemplation 172, 175
contradiction 42, 57; and capitalism 26; and crisis 29, 43; experienced 8; intra-psychic 71; and overdetermination 29 *see also* cognitive contradiction
Cooke, M. 11, 172
cost-benefit analysis 104, 109, 157, 158
cosmopolitanism 175
Coyle, D. 113
critical realism 12 *see also* dialectical critical realism
critical theory 11, 143 *see also*Frankfurt School
Cullenberg, S. 29
cultural parenting *see* parenting
culture 18–21, 43,105, 130, 182 n4; and biology 18–19; and cathexis 19–20; as lawfulness 13, 18–19, 128, 130; as reality principle 19, 20; representatives 19, 23, 37, 85, 114, 124, 143; as social formation 27
Curtis, K. 16, 34, 119, 174
cybernetics 152

Dagger, R. 22
Damasio, A.
Davidoff, L. 54, 77
daydreaming 124, 136–8 *see also* fantasizing
dead labour 85, 93, 94, 101, 114 *see also* living labour
Debord, G. 110
decommodification 108
dedifferentiation 120, 165; and redifferentiation 159; *see also* dereification, network, process
Delanty, G. 4, 5, 113, 118, 156
delayed gratification 58, 61, 67, 79, 126
Deleuze, G. 139
dematerialization 113
democracy 2, 176–7
dependence 3, 20, 75, 99, 102, 125, 126, 171, 180; maternal 66, 78, 171; *see also* autonomy, independence, interdependence
dereification 7, 31, 33–6, 48, 84, 92, 105,106, 111–20, 142, 143, 144, 148, 149, 162; *see also* dedifferentiation, network, process
desire 92, 121, 123, 128, 131, 140 *see also* commodity aesthetic, fantasy, lack
desirousness 130–2, 134, 136, 140–1, 158
destructive *Gemeinschaft* 87, 192 n9

detachment 37, 62, 65, 93, 98, 118, 127
determinacy24, 36, 75, 83, 105, 113, 125, 153, 160, 170; *see also* indeterminacy, relative determinacy
determinant judgement 8, 39, 144, 145–6, 157, 166, 169, 171, 172, 179
determinism 12, 13, 152
Dews, P. 128
dialectic 14, 28–30; of human and cultural 15; materialist 29, and overdetermination 29; of subject and object 25, 143; of transformation and reconstitution (of capitalism) 88; of use and exchange 26, 42, 104, 106, 113, 115, 123, 130, 150, 151, 155, 178, 180 *see also*law of value; obsolescence
dialectical critical realism 3, 6, 25
dichotomies 92, 99, 104, 191 n2; lived 92; masculine/feminine 95–100; mind/body 173
Dickens, P . 14
differentiation 6, 41, 43, 49, 57, 58, 66, 83, 87, 92, 94, 96, 100, 101, 103, 105, 106, 119, 120, 134, 144, 145, 157, 158, 170, 172; as abstraction 84, 85; as civilization 50; of masculinity/femininity 95–100; of rationality and affect 74; and subjectivity 49–53 *see also*mediations, money
Disch, L. 174
disorganized capitalism 7, 8, 41, 42, 104, 111–20, 124, 129, 130, 133, 134, 140, 142, 150
DiStephano, C. 75
division of labour 27, 39, 43, 50, 55, 65, 76–101 *passim,*106, 120, 167
domestication of men 127
domestication of women 37, 76, 77, 78, 86, 95–100, 101
Doray, B. 91, 107, 112
Dreyfus, H. 106, 132
drives 20, 43, 66, 67–76, 95, 100, 130, 134, 135, 171; activity drive 15, 37, 38, 60, 65, 66, 67, 70, 78, 84, 85, 98, 100, 104, 109, 110, 129, 131, 134; contradiction between ego and sex drive 48; ego drive 48, 66, 70, 77, 84, 100, 104, 136, 174; involution of 37, 38, 124, 126, 137; muting of 51–2, 58, 66, 70, 75, 136; and representatives 19–20, 25, 66, 83; sex drive 48, 66, 70, 77, 136; and surplus repression 21; *see also* ego interests, sex interests

Drucker, P. 176
Dryzek, J. 2, 4, 39, 161

Eagleton, T. 173
Eatwell, J. 151
education 113; and life-long learning 118; as self-transformation 117, 118, 163; and transferrable skills 118; worldly 169; ego 20, 59–61, 59, 67, 70, 86, 103, 128, 189 n1 *see also* id, superego
ego interests 20, 65, 110 *see also* drives, sex interests
'egoistic universalism' 169
electoral politics 107
electronics 112, 115, 122, 139–40, 150
Elias, N. 6, 47, 49–53, 58, 59, 76, 77, 84, 163; and psychoanalysis 187n12
energy *see* psychic energy
Engels, F. 14, 33, 49, 111, 119, 166, 168
enlarged mentality 172, 179; as mental visiting 174
Enlightenment 11, 12
Enronitis 158
Eros *see* social love
essence/appearance 145, 146; closure of the gap 166, 167
Etzioni-Halevy, E. 144
eudaimonism 171
Euro-America 1, 2, 5, 11, 91, 105, 165, 176
everyday world 50, 53, 54, 77, 145, 170
exchangeability 86–95
expertise 42, 142, 147, 158, 161; artisanal 53; and laity 95, 147, 164, 167; scientific 5, 40, 43, 53, 95, 127, 132, 142, 157
exploitation 164–5

factory 17, 33, 58, 87, 90, 106–7, 110, 112, 114, 120; as principle of organization 7, 105 *see also* reification
family 95, 128, 131; disorganized 127–34 *passim*; hybrid bourgeois 6, 54–80, 96, 124–6, liberal capitalist 20, 74, 75, 76, 86, 95–100, 124, 126–7; nuclear 127; oedipal 125–7; organized 127–34 *passim*
fantasizing 121, 123, 129, 130–2, 134, 135–41, 161, 196 n18
fantasy 14, 72, 123, 131, 134, 137, 173 *see also* commodity aesthetic, desire
femininity/masculinity 65, 95, 127
fetish 89, 93, 139
fetishism *see* commodity fetishism
fetishized co-operation 93–5

figurational change 52
finance capital 112, 115, 150–1
financialization 112, and deregulation of capital 113, 150
Flax, 18, 37, 171
flexibility 113, 118, 119
Forbes, I. 48
foresight 52, 53
formal subsumption of labour under capital *see* capital/capitalism
Forrester, J. 128
Foucault, M. 11, 106, 132, 145
Frankfurt School 3 *see also* critical theory
Fraser, I. 15
freedom 170
Freud, S. 3, 14, 18–21, 23, 25, 36–8, 49, 58–61, 64–80, 84, 85, 95–100, 111, 123, 125, 130, 133, 136–137, 175
Frosh, S. 131, 139
frustration 73, 125, 137, 140
Fuller, S. 154, 156
functional rationality *see* rationality
functionary 41, 105, 106, 127

Gagnier, R. 93
Gamble, A. 109, 110
gated communities 119, 120
Gay, P. 55, 95, 96, 97
generic labourers 117, 162, 168
genetic engineering 157, 160
geneticists 153
genetics 144, 152–4, 156
Geras, N. 89
Giddens, A. 145, 147, 157, 158, 163, 169
Gilbert, A. 48
Gilligan, C. 3
Gilroy, P. 38
global public-spiritedness 126, 166, 174, 180; citizenship 5; public sphere 172
globalization 113
Godelier, M. 107
Goffman, E. 114
Goldthorpe, J. 108, 109
good objects 37, 75, 85, 111, 123, 124, 125, 129, 131, 134, 137, 139, 140, 180 *see also* bad objects, virtual objects
Gorz, A. 16, 35, 103, 107
Goux, J.-J. 133
Grunberger, B. 18
Guattari, F. 139

Habermas, J. 2, 3, 6, 11, 18, 22, 47, 49, 54–8, 59, 67, 103, 106, 175, 177, 179

habituation 58; and drilling 106; and Panopticon 132
Halevy, E.
Hall, C. 54, 77
hallucinations 72, 135–6 *see also* bad objects, virtual objects
Hamilton, R. 77
Hamilton, V. 73
Hansen, P. 34, 172, 173, 174
Haraway, D. 146, 151, 152, 153, 159
Hardt, M. 113
Harmes, A. 142, 159, 176
Harvey, D. 26, 27, 28, 30, 88, 113, 115, 151, 173
Haug, W. F. 92, 109, 123, 139
having 93, 139, as mode of attachment 138 *see also* mediations, money
Hayles, K. 122, 145, 149, 153
Heater, D. 179
hedonism 11, 171
Heims, M. 122
Held, D. 11
Heller, A. 15
Herzfeld, M. 108
Hesse, M. 151, 159
heteronomy *see* autonomy
Heyer, P. 55
Hilferding, R. 104
Hill, C. 38, 53
Hillman, J. 123
historical materialism 14
Hobbes, T. 51
Hobsbawm, E. 96, 97, 147
homo oeconomicus 31, 38, 41, 42, 101, 103, 104, 157, 158
Honneth, A. 130
Horkheimer, M. 41, 48, 143, 144
hubris 179, 181
human nature 11–24; activity drive 15; and capitalism 26, 27; indeterminable development 16, 40; indeterminacy 6, 14, 85, 130; intentionality 12; interdependence 3; as open system 13; prematurity 16, 18–21; and reality principle 18–19
humanity 5, 57, 89, 91, 134, 143, 146, 150, 163, 166, 168, 174, 175, 176; as abstract category 26; the active animal 14–16; the cultural animal 13–14; as lived category 26; the worldly animal 15, 16–18; as *zoon politikon* 15
Hutton, W. 159

hybrid bourgeois capitalism 52, 53–80, 79, 94, 109, 129, 187 n7, 188,n28
hybridity 6, 7, 47, 48

id 59–61, 69, 103, 131 *see also* ego, superego
ideal ego 37, 97, 128, 131, 139
identification 60, 75, 80, 131, 139–40, 174
idness 67, 72, 74, 190 n11
imaginary 7, 123, 124, 128, 129, 130–2, 134, 139, 141
imagination 53, 55, 56, 90, 91, 136, 137, 163, 166, 173, 174, 175, 179; and commodification 98, 130; and rationality 22; and science 13 *see also* daydreaming, fantasy, natality, praxis
immiseration 168
independence 99, 126, 128 *see also* autonomy, interdependence
indeterminacy 20, 22–3, 24, 25, 31, 35, 36, 40, 68, 75, 83, 104, 105, 115, 124, 125, 129, 133, 134, 135, 139, 141, 153, 156, 158, 160, 170, 180 *see also* determinacy, relative determinacy
individuality 24, 62, 83, 101, 107, 125, 171 *see also* atomism, autonomy
indifference 90–1, 95, 99, 100, 102, 108, 110, 118, 119, 120, 122, 139
industrialization 7, 35, 41, 49, 57, 80, 90, 94, 101, 103, 150
infants 14, 58–80. 95, 126, 128, 131–2, 136, 141
information 115, 153–4, 160
'informational capitalism' 155, 159, 168
instincts 18 *see also* drives
insurance 157, 159, 161
intangibility 113
intelligibility 32, 49, 73, 87, 100, 130, 141, 149, 165, 167, 177
intentionality 12, 35, 47, 72, 89, 154
interdependence 3, 20, 64, 75, 80, 84, 86, 87, 92, 93, 99, 101, 108, 126, 169, 180 *see also* autonomy, individuality
internalization 60, 69, 75, 125, 126, 140, 141, 180, 195 n2
intimacy 54–5, 64, 67, 80, 87, 125, 140; and breast-feeding 77, 78
introspectivity 49, 55, 64
involution of drives *see* drives
irrationality 168, 179
Isaac, J. C. 1

Jacoby, R. 94
Jameson, F. 27, 28, 116, 128, 158, 159

Jefferys, S. 108
Jessop, B. 30
Judgement *see* determinant judgement, reflective judgement
Judt, T. 117
justice 5, 176, 180

Kane, F. 142
Kanth, R. K. 28, 86
Kaplan, J. M. 154
Kargon, R. H. 40, 147
Katznelson, J. 179
Keane, J. 107, 167
Keenan, T. 31, 32
Keller, E. F, 151, 152
Keynesianism 113
kinship 4, 22, 106
Kitcher, P. 156, 159
Knights, D. 113
knowledge *see* abstract knowledge, common sense, science, *sensus communis*
Kosik, K. 16, 35
Kotter, J. 118
Kovel, J. 36, 90
Kuhn, T. 147

laboratory 143, 154, 155
labour 144, 167, 177, 178 *see also* abstract labour; aristocracy of labour; generic labourers; self-programmable workers
labour power 91–2, 94, 113, 120, 123, 146
labouring 34–6, 111–12
Lacan, J. 11, 18, 37, 123–4, 128–34, 141
Lacanian categories 124, 125–34
lack 7, 123, 124, 128, 130–2, 134, 139, 140, 141, 158, 168, 171; politicization 176–8
Laclau, E. 143, 163, 169, 177
Landes, D. 40, 77
Landow, G. P. 122
Langan, T. 122
Laplanche, J. 37
Lasch, C. 36, 127, 132
Law of the Father 128, 130
Lash, S. 41, 104, 105, 108, 113
law of insurance 145, 157
law of the lottery 145, 157
law of value 6, 25–7, 39, 40, 43, 47, 86–95, 111, 113, 118, 119, 121, 129, 132, 144, 146, 147, 148, 149, 155, 156, 158, 160, 162; and abstraction 30–1; actualization in England 28; and classical political economy 28; and commodity fetishism 31; and contradiction 29; and indeterminacy 31; and innovation 27; and non-linearity 29; and power/knowledge complexes 28; and subject-constitution 89; and totality 26
lawfulness 25; and capitalism 25–7; and intentional human action 25; and Panopticon 132 *see also* law of value
Lefort, C. 49
Leiss, W. 139
Leslie, L. 118, 144, 150, 153, 156
Levins, R. 144, 151
Lewontin, R. 151
liberal industrial capitalism 41, 83–102, 105, 124, 126
libidinal energy 68
libido 68, 74; desexualization 68; *see also* social love
Lichtman, R. 59
life sciences *see* genetics
Linklater, A. 4, 175, 177
literacy 49, 72
living labour 94, 101, 114 *see also* dead labour
Lockwood, D. 58
loss of reality *see* narcissism, object loss, worldlessness
Love, N. 163
Luhmann, N. 89
Lukács, G. 14, 15, 31–3, 36, 39, 40, 84, 88
Lyotard, F. 143, 144, 156

MacCannell, J. F. 18, 23, 124, 133
McGibben, B. 5
McJobs 117, 118
Maguire, J. M. 48
making 18, 34–6, 111–12, 143, 144, 178
Manicas, P. T. 147
Marcuse, H. 21, 41, 48, 69, 70, 104, 105, 110, 120, 127, 129, 139, 143, 146, 173
Marshall, T. H. 177
Marx, K. 3, 14–16, 18, 22, 23, 25, 27–33, 38, 41, 47, 48, 53, 61, 83–95, 105, 107, 111, 112, 157, 163–4, 166–9
masculinity *see* femininity/masculinity
mass production 106, 107, 110, 113
Massing, M. 114
mastery 159
mathematics 148; as language of science 148
Mayhew, L. H. 161
means of production 47, 57
mechanization 47, 57, 93
mediations 54, 57, 84, 94–5, 103, 124; impersonal 6, 32, 39, 43, 49, 79, 170;

importance of balance 6; personal 6, 43, 49, 79, 83, 170; and totality 28–36 *see also* commodity fetishism, money, virtuality
Melucci, A. 177
mental functioning *see* attention, primary process functioning, secondary process functioning
Merchant, C. 39, 149, 151
Meyrowitz, J. 121, 140, 179
Mitchell, J. 98
Miyoshi, M. 27
mode of production 52
modes of communication 163
modes of materiality 113, 115, 122
money 47, 84, 87, 88, 112, 122, 139; as abstract compulsion 87; as capital 32, 112; capitalization 57; monetization 57, 84, 87, 92–3, 94, 105, 109, and wage contract 87
money/capital 84, 87, 100
Moore, P. B. 17
mortgages 159, 161
Mouffe, C. 143, 176, 177
muting of drives *see* drives

narcissism 31, 36–8, 85, 86, 94, 95–100, 133, 169, 175, 181; and atomism 38; and communalism 38, 43; of capitalists 97–8; of capitalists' wives 97–100; contradictory 119, 168; primary 131
natality 14,17–18, 21, 22–3, 34, 40, 51, 56, 85, 164, 166, 169–75 *see also* the enlarged mentality, reflective judgement
nation 4, 174, 177
naturalization 89
nature 15, 159, 164
Neary, M. 145, 157, 158
necessity 12, 13; as 'leaning on' 182 n. 5
need/needs 92, 93,109, 111, 123,130, 135, 137,138, 139, 140, 141, 150, 164, 175, 179
neediness 123
Negri, A. 113
neoliberalism 113, 150, 157, 158, 163,165, 167
network 121, 142, 155; and abstract labour 116–18; and dereification 7, 118–20; and disorganized capitalism 7, 120; as principle of organization 105, 112–16, 130
new political economy 156, 169
Newtonian physics 151–2

nihilism 11
Nimni, E. 168
nomads 177
non-sensuous presencing 47, 139, 140

object loss 33, 36, 129, 135–6, 139–40
objective/subjective 94, 107
objectivism 94, 120 *see also* subjectivism
objectivity 88, 94, 143, 144, 151, 160, 162
objects 129, 135–6, 139–40, 155, 170; and exchange 26, 32–3; and subjectivation 19; unexperienced 145 *see also* bad objects, good objects, virtual objects
obsolescence 34, 36, 88, 111, 130, 140, 141, 151, 155, 156, 167 *see also* dialectic of use and exchange, law of value
occupational sphere 116–20, 123, 139, 140
Oedipal complex 21, 60, 65, 66, 68, 69, 99
Oedipal family 80; hybrid bourgeois 6, 7, 76–7; liberal capitalist 7, 95–100; pre-oedipal phase 65, 66, 76–9, 125, 126, 130–2, 141 *see also* family, parenting
'Oedipal riddle' 65, 76
Offe, C. 108
office 105, 106, 109
O'Hagan, A. 155
Oliver, D. 179
Ollman, B. 15
O'Malley, P. 113
Ong, A. 119
Ong, W.
opinion *see* public opinion
organized capitalism 7, 41, 42, 104, 106–10, 115, 117, 124, 127, 129, 133, 134,140, 177
O'Shaughnessy, B. 72
overdetermination 29–30
oversocialization 4
Owen, D. 132

Panopticon 106, 132
parenting 43, 124, 129, 141, 158; cultural 6, 7,13, 22, 62, 85, 104, 127, 133, 163,176, 180; personally authoritative127, 129; and public-spiritedness 22, 64–80 *see also* family
particular/particulars 146 *see also* universal/particular
paternalism 106, 107
peasants 38, 53, 57, 100
pensions 142, 157, 159, 161; politicization 176; and 'post-capitalism' 176, 180

performance principle 7, 104, 120, 127, 129, 130, 140, 143
Perkin, H. 97
Piccone, P. 36, 94
Pietz, W. 89
Pijl, K. van der 113, 116
Pitkin, H. 139
place 49, 54, 83, 112, 114–15, 118, 120, 122, 172, 175, 179 *see also* space
pleasure principle 59, 73
plurality 119, 166, 168, 172, 174, 175, 176, 179, 180, 181
Polanyi, K. 28, 86
political aesthetic 173–5
Pontalis, J.-B. 37
Porter, R. 55
Porter, T. M. 145
Poster, M. 20, 96, 98, 140
Postone, M. 6, 12, 15, 26, 26, 31, 32, 84, 87, 88, 91, 94, 168
poststructuralism 11, 143, 170
Poulantzas, N. 30, 104
praxis 14, 15, 221, 22–3, 34, 40, 51, 85, 173 *see also* imagination, making
predictability 13, 51, 75, 115 *see also* determinacy, determinism, indeterminacy Prigogine, I. 152
primary process functioning 59, 71, 72–3, 75, 119, 123, 130, 133, 136, 163; *see also* secondary process functioning
privacy 57, 123, 172; non-privative 54–5, 122; privative 86, 95–100, 122–41
private sphere 54–5, 86, 109, 110, 140
privatization 65, 87, 110, 157
process 7, 105, 111–12, 113, 122, 123, 130, 138, 142, 143, 148 *see also* dedifferentiation, dereification, network
production 36, 113
production process 100, 107, 120
proletarian 41, 47, 86, 100, 103, 106, 127, 157, 167, 168
property 112, 150, 172
psychic differentiation 52–3, 58–61, 66, 80
psychic energy 58, 59, 67, 72–6, 75, 123, 135 *see also* cathexis, drives
psychic nourishment 77–9
psychic strength 47–80 *passim* 99, 125, 129, 132, 142
psychic vacant possession 118, 123
psychoanalysis 18, 96, 123, 127, 129; as energetic-hermeneutics 18, 66
psychologization 49–61, 103, 120
public choice theory 2

public opinion 56, 174, 175, 180
public relations 161
public sphere 6, 86, 99, 110, 126, 140 *see also* bourgeois public sphere
public-spiritedness 3, 5, 22–3, 36, 42, 43, 48, 53, 54, 61, 67, 70–5, 78, 84, 86, 123, 137, 141, 157, 158, 161, 163, 166, 177; as human potential 5; political necessity 5 *see also* bourgeois public sphere, global public-spiritedness

quantification 145
Quinn, N. 50

Rabinow, P. 106, 132
Radice, H. 113
rational choice 94, 158, 165
rationality 3, 22, 66, 76, 91, 98, 101, 104, 157, 173, 179, 181; abstract 38–40, 43, 50, 148; anaclitic 3, 7, 16, 22, 36, 39, 41, 43, 47, 48, 50, 56, 61, 71, 78, 79, 84, 132, 148, 161, 172, 173, 179; artisanal 41; atomized 51, 86, 157; cold 39, 62, 79, 86; communicative 2, 22; divorce of rationality and affect 74, 76, 77, 79, 87, 95, 192 n8; divorce of rationality and sociability 85, 86, 103, 132; economic 2, 4, 8, 22, 39, 42, 84, 94, 100, 102, 110, 121, 127, 158, 161, 165–6, 170, 171, 179; functional 48, 86, 101, 103, 107, 109; instrumental 35, 178; kinesthetic 16, 39, 43, 47, 50, 51, 132, 145; multi-dimensional 22, 51, 64, 126; one-dimensional 110, 126; post-capitalist 161, 199 n21; and sociability 3, 7, 85; systemic 41, 43 *see also* common sense, science, *sensus communis*
Rattansi, A. 15, 33
reading 54–5, 56, 64, 83
real 7, 123, 124, 128, 129, 133–4, 139, 141; non-human 143
real objects *see* good objects
real subsumption of labour under capital *see* capital/capitalism
reality 17, 36, 131, 136, 141, 165, 181
reality principle 6, 7, 37, 43, 73, 85, 103, 104, 105, 108, 111, 120, 125, 127, 128, 130, 134, 137, 145, 163
reality-testing 37, 65, 73, 75, 79, 103, 104, 105, 107, 109, 118, 119, 127, 131, 136, 140, 143, 158, 165, 169, 170, 174, 178
Reddy, J. 154
redistribution 164

230 *Index*

reflective judgement 8, 164, 169–75, 179, 180; and *sensus communis* 8, 148
reflexivity 68, 163, 164, 169; public-spirited 164 *see also* secondary process functioning
regime of truth 8, 40, 143, 160
Reich, A. 139
Reich, R. 117
reification 7, 8, 31, 32–3, 48, 84, 92, 100, 105, 105, 112, 120, 149, 162 *see also* commodity fetishism
relational combination 123
relations 100, 105, 109, 139, 153; at-a-distance 146; bureaucratic 76; commodified 86, 142; contractual 56, 100, 114; face-to-face 54, 56, 108; impersonal 85, 129, 171; monetized 76, 92–3; personally authoritative 125; sensuously-present 175; unauthoritative personal 171; virtual 129, 139–40, 171, 179 *see also* social relations
relative autonomy *see* autonomy
relative determinacy 24, 40, 52, 75, 85, 129, 130, 140, 170, 178, 180 *see also* determinacy, indeterminacy
repression 21, 59, 66, 68–70, 75, 97
Resnick, S. A. 30
responsibility 3, 5, 11, 42, 120, 121, 142, 177, 179, 180; collective 176; global 175, 176; means of 169
retirement pension *see* pensions
Rheingold, H. 17
Rich, A. 78
Ricoeur, P. 18, 21, 34, 66, 70
Rifkin, J. 145, 153, 154, 155, 159
Ring, J. 34
risk 8, 158, 159, 163 *see also* uncertainty, volatility
Ritzer, G. 117
Rodowick, D. N. 139
Róheim, G. 70
role (social) 163
Rorty, R. 149
Rosdolsky, R. 92
Rose, S. 152
Roszak, T. 155
Rustin, M. 134

Sahlins, M. 50
Sampson, A. 108
Sayer, A. 167
Sayer, D. 2, 33, 87

Schachtel, E. 15, 20, 21, 37, 60, 61, 67, 68, 85, 131, 136
Schafer, R. 59, 140
Schneider, M. 69
Schrödinger, E. 152
science 47, 50, 86, 101, 142–61, 166, 167, 169, 171, 178–9, 181; as abstract knowledge 8, 32; Baconian 28, 132, 143, 144, 145; and capitalism 38–40, 142–61; and commodification 8; and constancy 149, 150, 160; design-fault 151; and imagination 13; and inconstancy 149–50; and language 148–9; mathematization 147; modern 145–50; politicization 157; postmodern 144, 145, 148, 149, 150–7, 159; professionalization 147; and two-worldness 146–7; as underlabourer of citizens 169
scientists 95, 149, 157, 160; as entrepreneurs 155, 167
Scott, M. 159
secondary process functioning 6, 49, 59, 60, 65, 66–8, 70, 73–4, 75, 79, 83, 103, 105, 106, 107, 109, 123, 125, 127, 133, 136, 143, 149, 160, 163, 170–2 *see also* primary process functioning
self-discipline 50, 52, 53, 55, 58, 64, 70, 73, 99, 125, 138 *see also* a autonomy, self-maintenance
self-interest 110, 173–5
self-maintenance 90–1, 114, 142, 162, 163 *see also* autonomy, self-discipline
self-programmable workers 117–20, 162, 168
Sennett, R. 36, 87, 98, 104, 106, 113, 114, 115, 118, 174
sensuous presencing 16, 23, 47, 65, 80, 125, 175 *see also* non-sensuous presencing, virtual presencing
sensus communis 6, 41, 47, 48, 52, 53–8, 64, 65, 66, 78, 79, 85, 95, 125, 132, 161, 164, 167, 169, 170, 172, 179 *see also* reflective judgement
sentimentality 87, 98
Sève, L. 15
sex interests 65 *see also* drives, ego interests
Shorter, E. 77
Simmel, G. 92, 93
Slater, D. 93
Slaughter, S. 118, 144, 150, 153, 156
Smith, A. 90, 187 n14
Snyder, M. 119

sociability 22, 36, 37, 40, 41, 47, 48, 49, 50, 56, 57, 61, 62, 64, 65, 71, 73, 74, 80, 84–102 *passim*, 105, 108, 109, 110, 114, 115, 126, 130, 131, 134, 136, 141, 157, 167, 169, 170, 177, 179, 181,188 n22, 192 n16; divorce of sociability and rationality 85, 86, 103, 132; as functional necessity 76–7; as teamwork 118
social formation 27, 29, 39, 40, 101, 142, 145, 146
social love 3, 47, 68, 74, 78, 84, 86, 100, 110, 23, 126, 130, 136, 137, 170
social relations 113, 114, 124, 142, 170, 177 *see also* relations
social strength 4
socialization of labour 107–8, 166
socialization of ownership (of capital) 176
society 91, 95, 99, 101, 162
Sohn-Rethel, A. 15
solidarity 175–6
solidarity principle 163, 166, 176, 179
Solow, R. M. 114
Soper, K. 1, 176
Soysal, Y. N. 1
space 114–16, 121, 122 *see also* place
speech 17, 134, 174; as deliberation 56, 170, 172, 173, 178–9; communicative 76; dialogical 132, 166, 172, 174; face-to-face 183 n14
stability 36,108, 120, 152, 155
state 8, 51, 52, 56, 58, 104, 109, 110, 113, 157, 162 *see also* welfare state
Stavrakakis, Y. 128
Stein, T. 157
Stengers, I. 152
stimulus/response *see* habituation
stock market 142
Stone, L. 61, 77
Strange, S. 155
Strauss, C. 50
structural irrelevance 166
structuralism 88
subjectivation 2, 129, 129, 139 *see also* family,parenting
subjectivism 56, 94, 171, 174 *see also* objectivism
subjectivity 11, 14, 41, 87, 88, 103, 119, 133, 142, 143, 162
subjects/objects 165
sublimation 6, 21, 59, 60, 66, 68, 69, 70–1, 75, 79, 80, 86, 110, 170, 171, 190 n10, 190 n11 *see also* secondary process functioning
sublimated secondary process functioning 66–80 *passim*, 83, 170, 179
substitutability 36, 88, 140, 151, 156
superego 59–61, 67, 68–70, 80, 86, 97, 103, *see also* ego, id
surplus value 30, 40, 90, 100, 104, 122, 167, 169
swaddling 77
symbolic 7, 123, 124, 127, 128, 129, 130,132–3, 134, 139, 141
symbolic analysts 117
systematicity 58, 93 *see also* totality
systems 12, 89, 151, 160; closed/open 12–13, 25–6; capitalism as system 28; culture as 13; human organism as 13

Tapscott, D. 113
taste 173–4
Taylor, C. 38, 171
Taylor, G. 145, 157, 158
technocracy 109, 166
technoscience 156
technology 154–7
theoretical understanding *see* science, *sensus communis*
thinking 166, 172–5; and cognition 178–9; dialogical 173 *see also* two-worlds thinking
Thomas, P. 108
Thompson, E. P. 38, 41
totalitarianism 36, 167
totality 16, 54, 72, 87, 89, 90, 101, 105, 127, 129, 143, 144, 145–7, 169, 170, 171, 180, 185 n19; and capitalism 28–31; and contradiction 28, 39, 43; and overdetermination 29; and two-worldness 146–7, 178; and unintelligibility 40
Touraine, A. 11
trade 50, 52, 146
transport 47, 57, 83
Turkle, S. 139
Turner, B. 176
two-worlds thinking 144, 145–7, 171; and two-worldness 166–9, 180

uncertainty 104, 154–7, 159 *see also* obsolescence,risk, volatility
unintelligibility 32, 35, 47, 109, 112, 120; and science 40, 92,

universal/ particular 146, 147–50
unpredictability 120, 144 *see also* indeterminacy, obsolescence, uncertainty, volatility
Urry, J. 41, 104, 105, 108, 113

value *see* law of value
value's law *see* law of value
Venn, C. 38, 174
Villa, D. 173
virtual objects 131, 139–40 *see also* bad objects
virtual presencing 74, 135–41 *passim see also* fantasizing
virtual reality principle 140, 142
virtuality 115–16, 121, 122, 136–40
volatility 88, 120, 131, 140, 142, 144, 158, 159 *see also* indeterminacy, obsolescence, uncertainty

wage contract 90–1, 169
Wahrman, D. 77
Wallerstein, I. 26
wealth 112, 150
welfare state 108, 109, 113, 124, 161, 177 *see also* state
Westphal, S.P. 156
Whitebook, J. 21, 38

Wiener, N. 65
Williams, R. 55
Willis, P. 127
Willmott, H. 113
Winston, M. 154
wishfulness 74, 138
Wolfenstein, E. V. 18
Wolff, R. D. 30
working-class atomism/collectivism 108
workshop 7, 33, 87, 89, 90
world care 11, 121, 126, 165, 173, 178
world-engagement 37, 48, 87, 93, 98, 177
worldlessness 7, 37, 43, 55, 59, 73, 84, 92, 104, 111, 115, 119, 121, 123, 138, 149, 159, 160, 172, 179 *see also* commodity fetishism
worldliness 6, 16–18, 38, 48, 51, 85, 97, 114, 129, 145, 151, 159, 166, 171, 172, 174, 175, 176, 180
Wrong, D. 4
Wynne, B. 154

Young, I.M. 5

Zaretsky, E. 96, 126
Zilsel, E. 149
Zizek, S. 124, 128, 137, 139